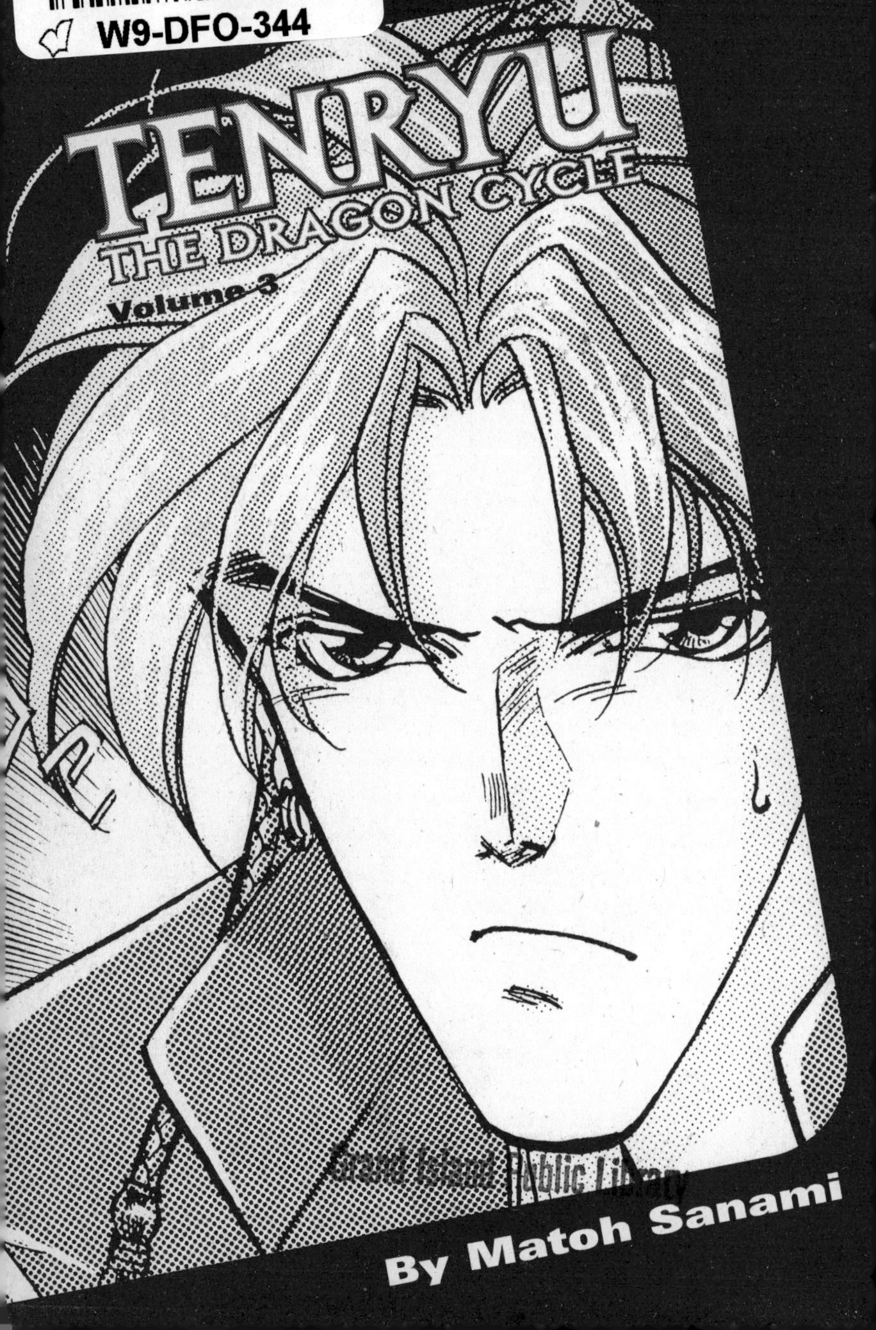
TENRYU
THE DRAGON CYCLE
Volume 3
By Matoh Sanami

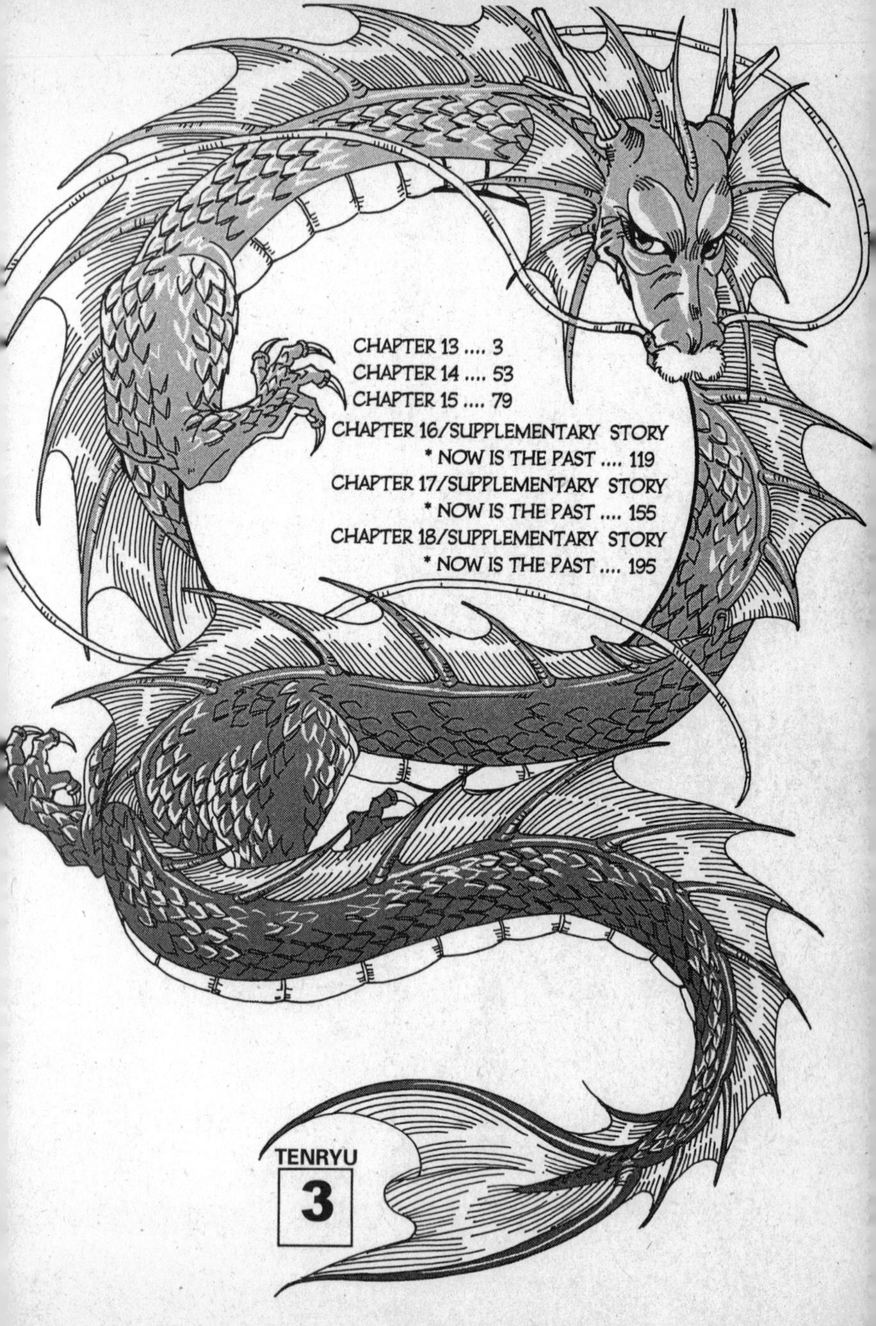

TENRYU

3

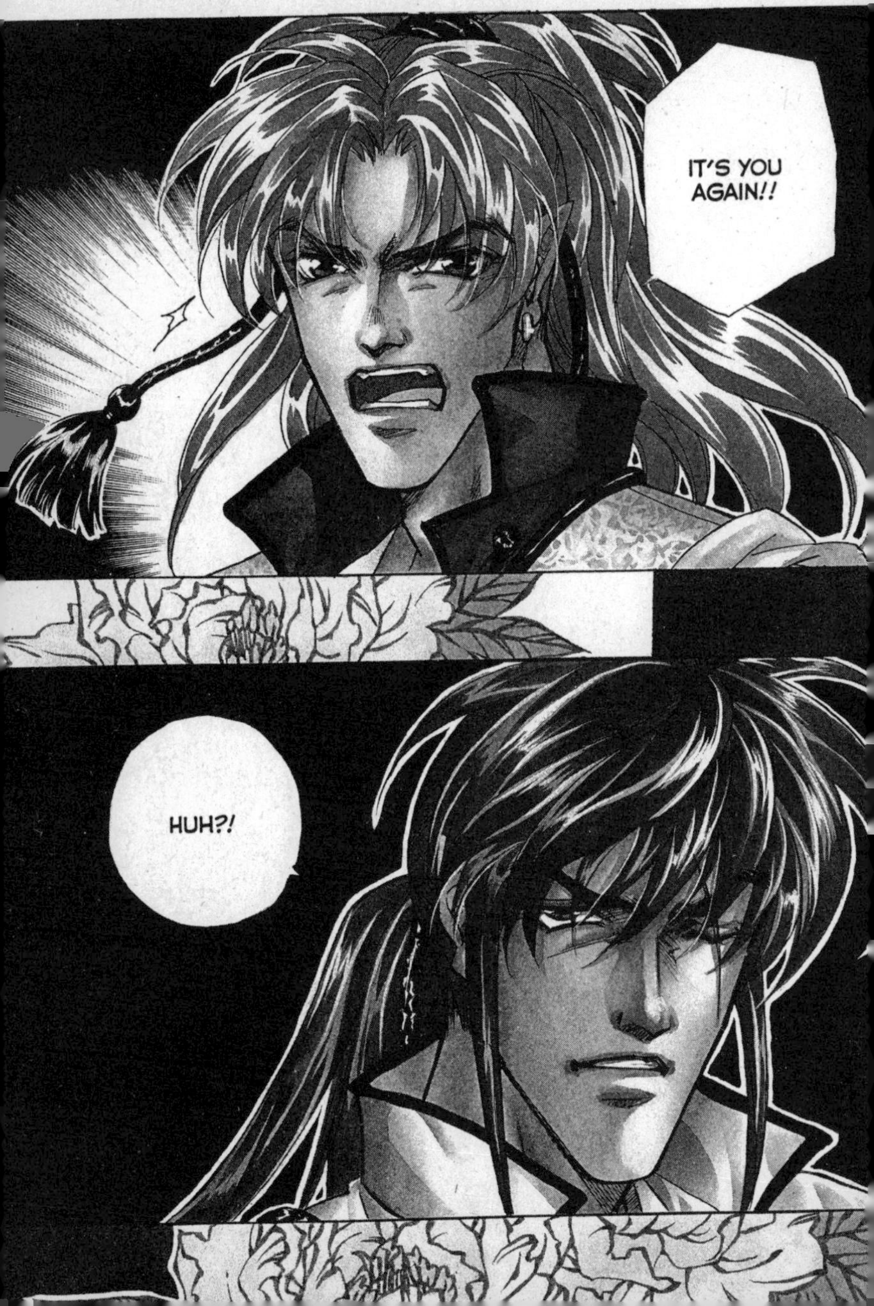
IT'S YOU AGAIN!!
HUH?!

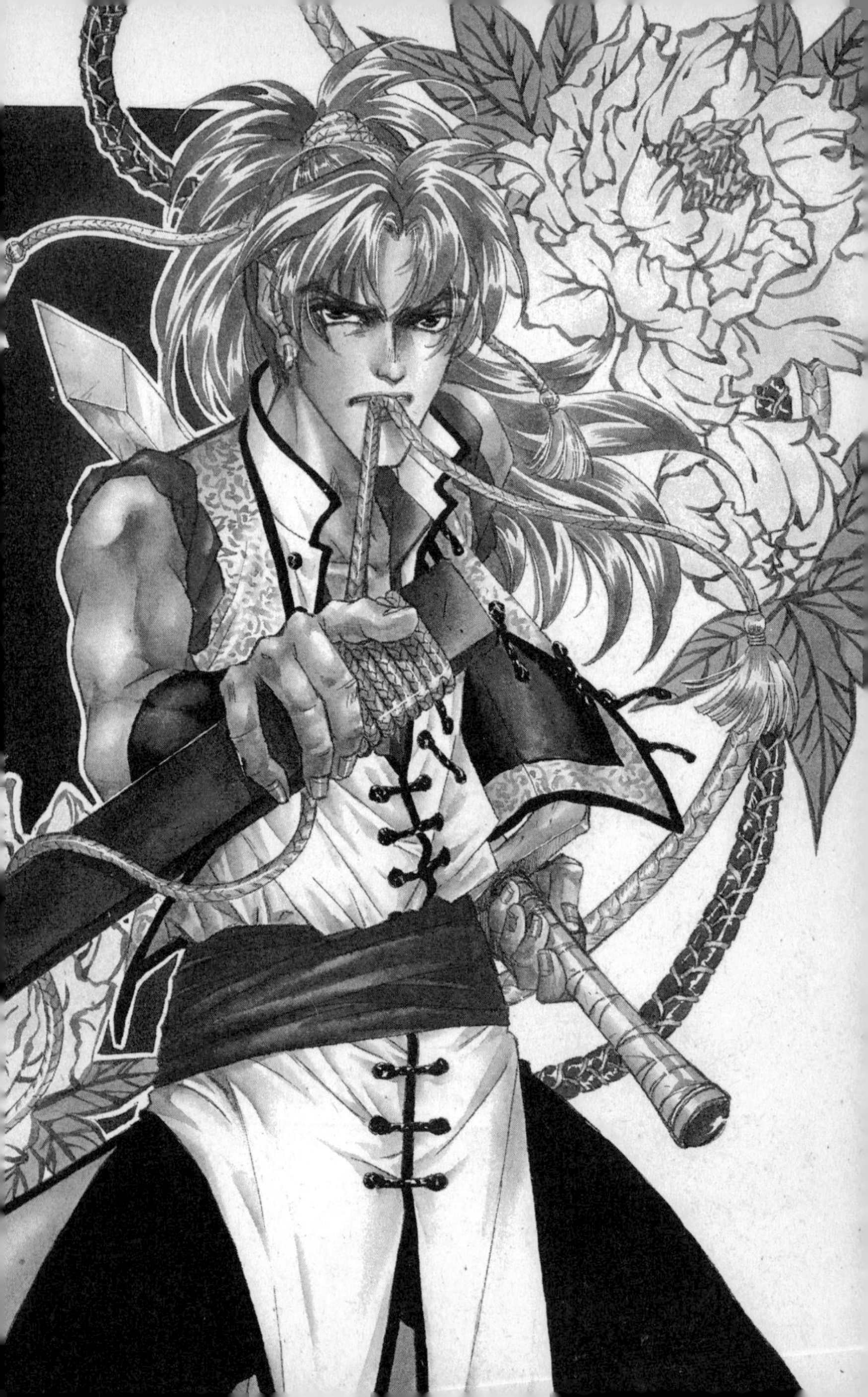

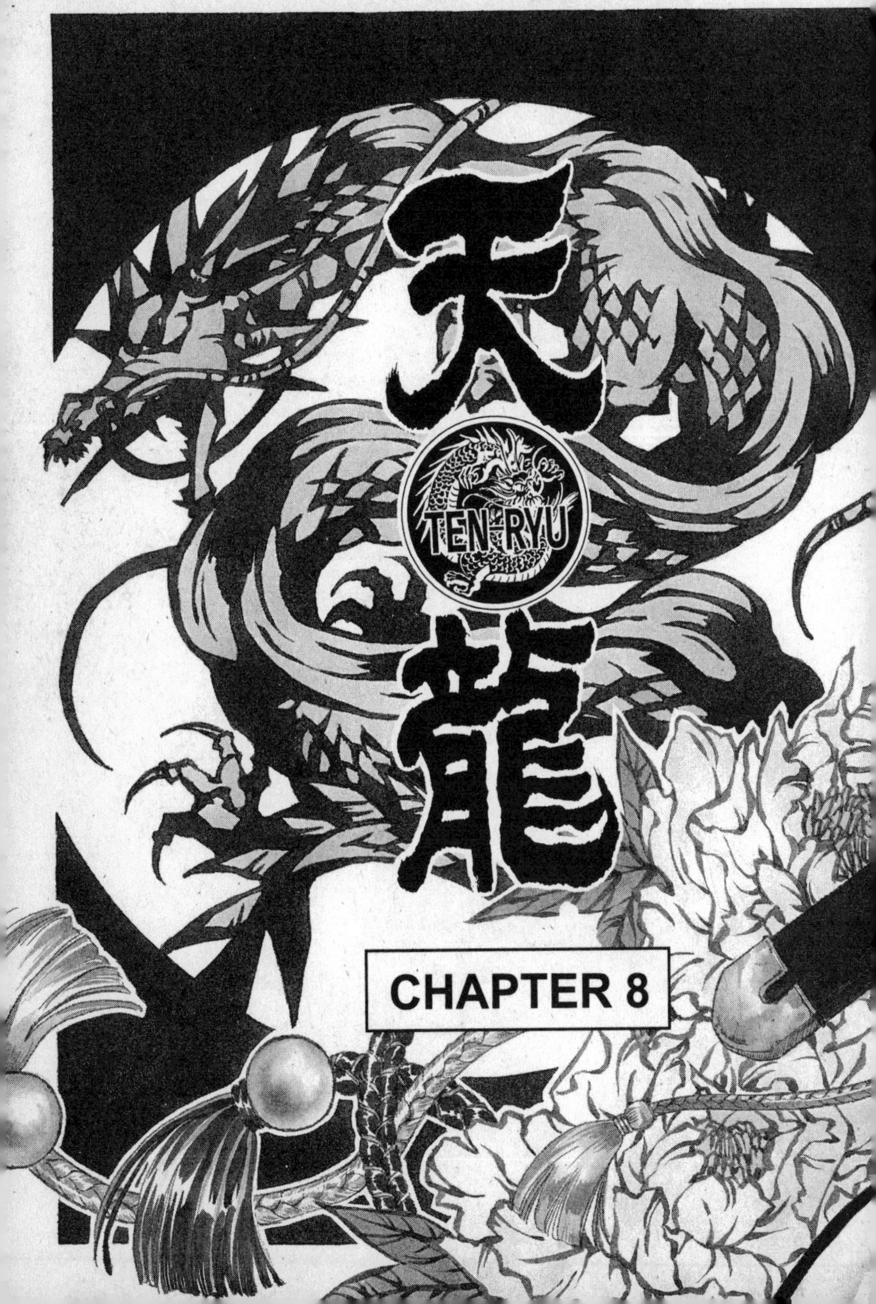
天龍
TEN-RYU
CHAPTER 8

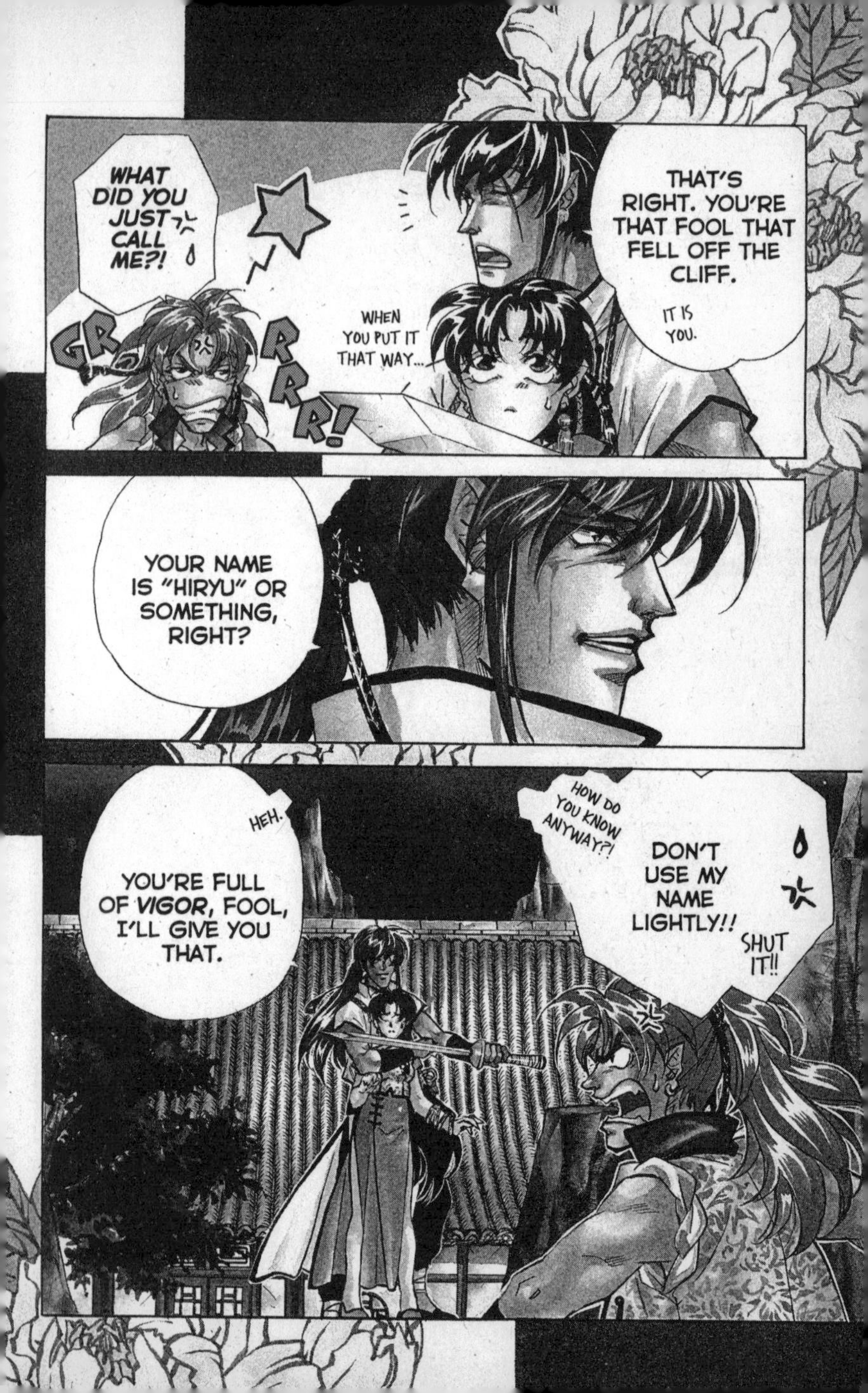
THAT'S RIGHT. YOU'RE THAT FOOL THAT FELL OFF THE CLIFF.
IT IS YOU.
WHEN YOU PUT IT THAT WAY...
WHAT DID YOU JUST CALL ME?!
GRRRR!
YOUR NAME IS "HIRYU" OR SOMETHING, RIGHT?
DON'T USE MY NAME LIGHTLY!!
SHUT IT!!
HOW DO YOU KNOW ANYWAY?!
HEH.
YOU'RE FULL OF VIGOR, FOOL, I'LL GIVE YOU THAT.

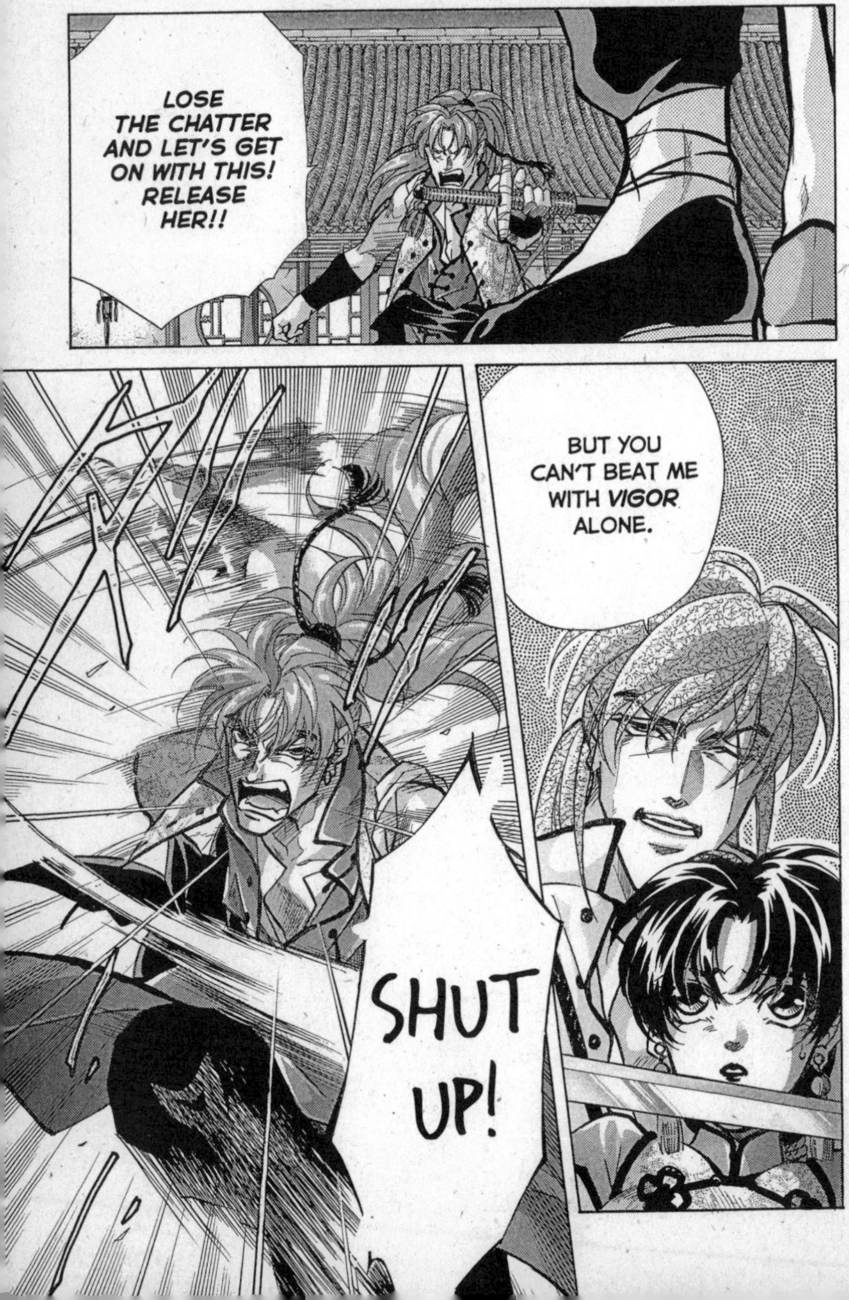
LOSE THE CHATTER AND LET'S GET ON WITH THIS! RELEASE HER!!
BUT YOU CAN'T BEAT ME WITH *VIGOR* ALONE.
SHUT UP!

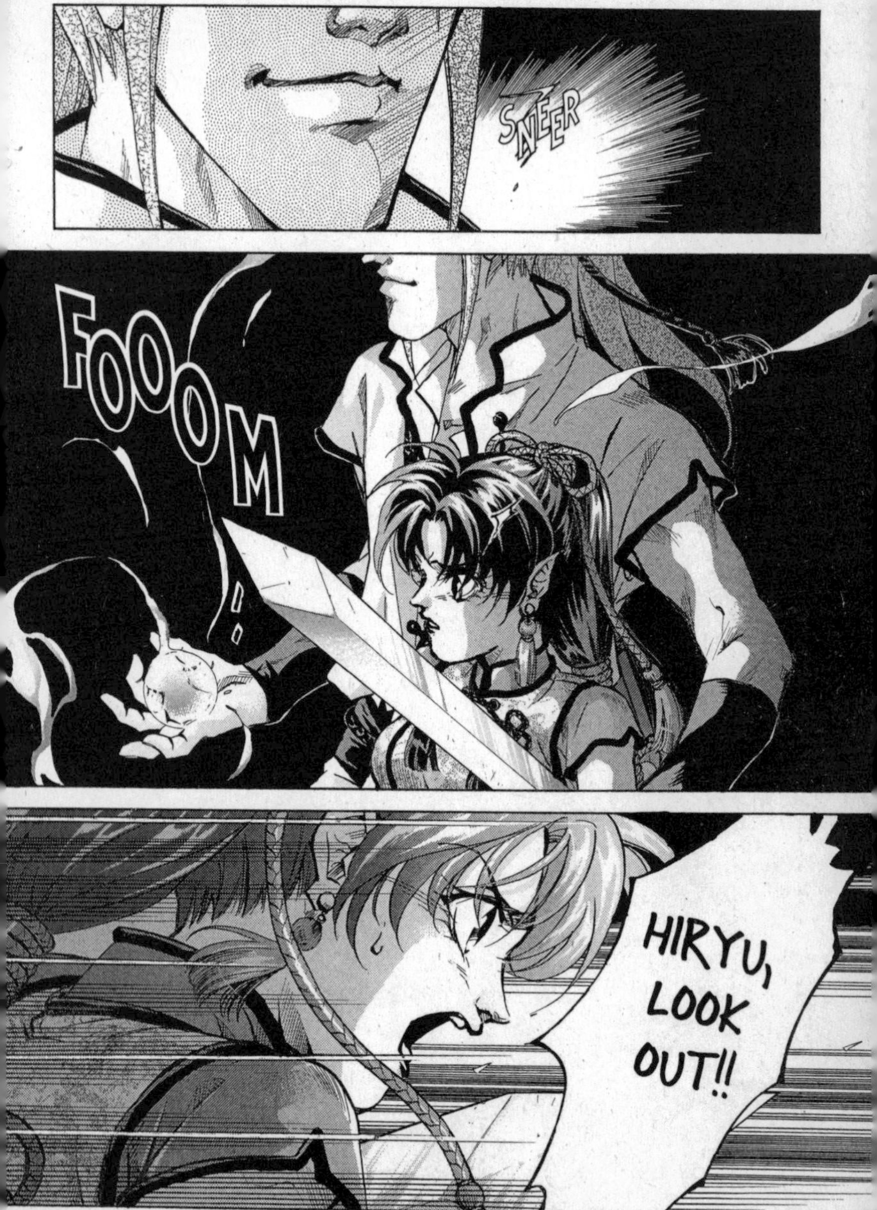
SNEER
FOOOM
HIRYU, LOOK OUT!!

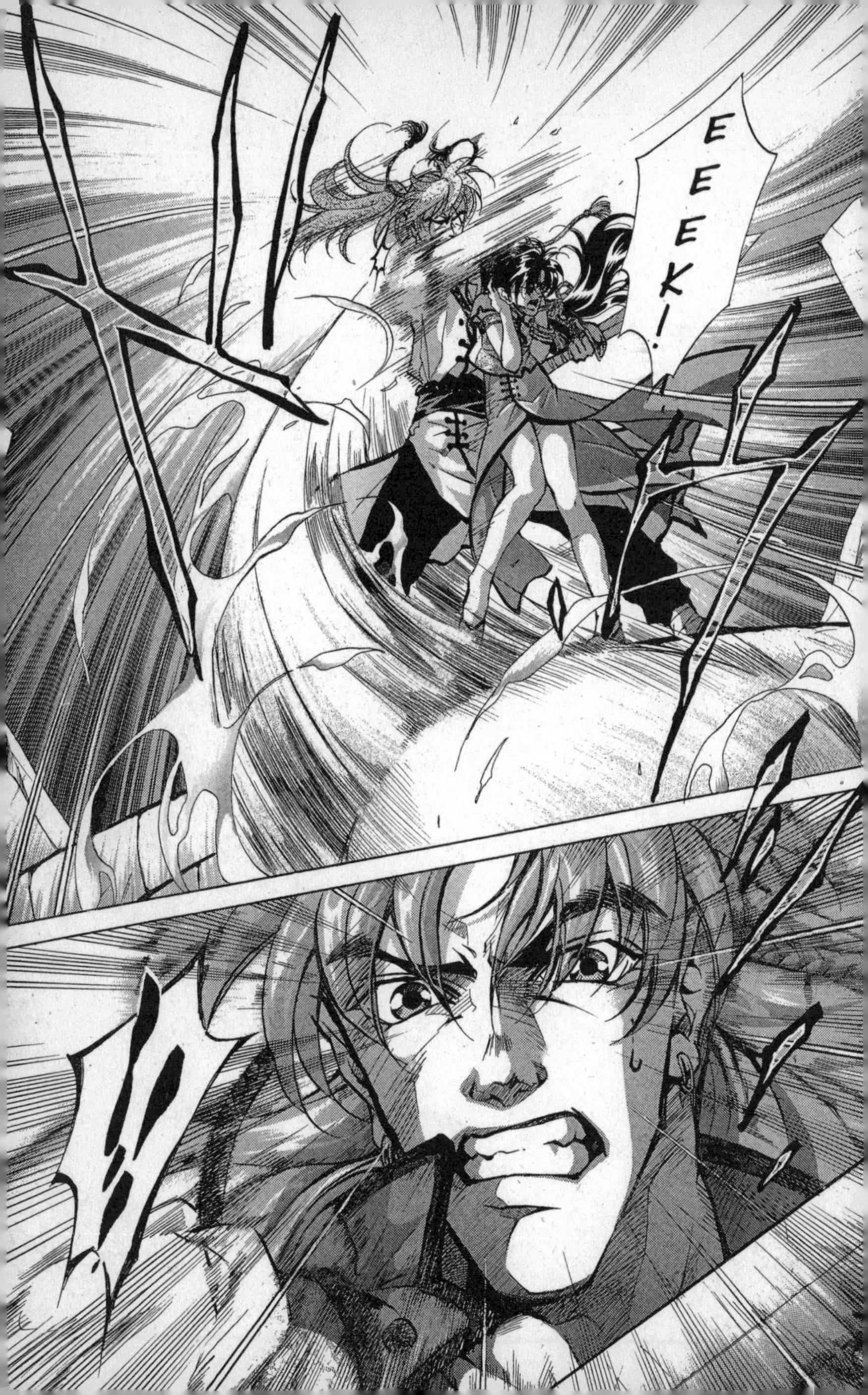
EEEEK!

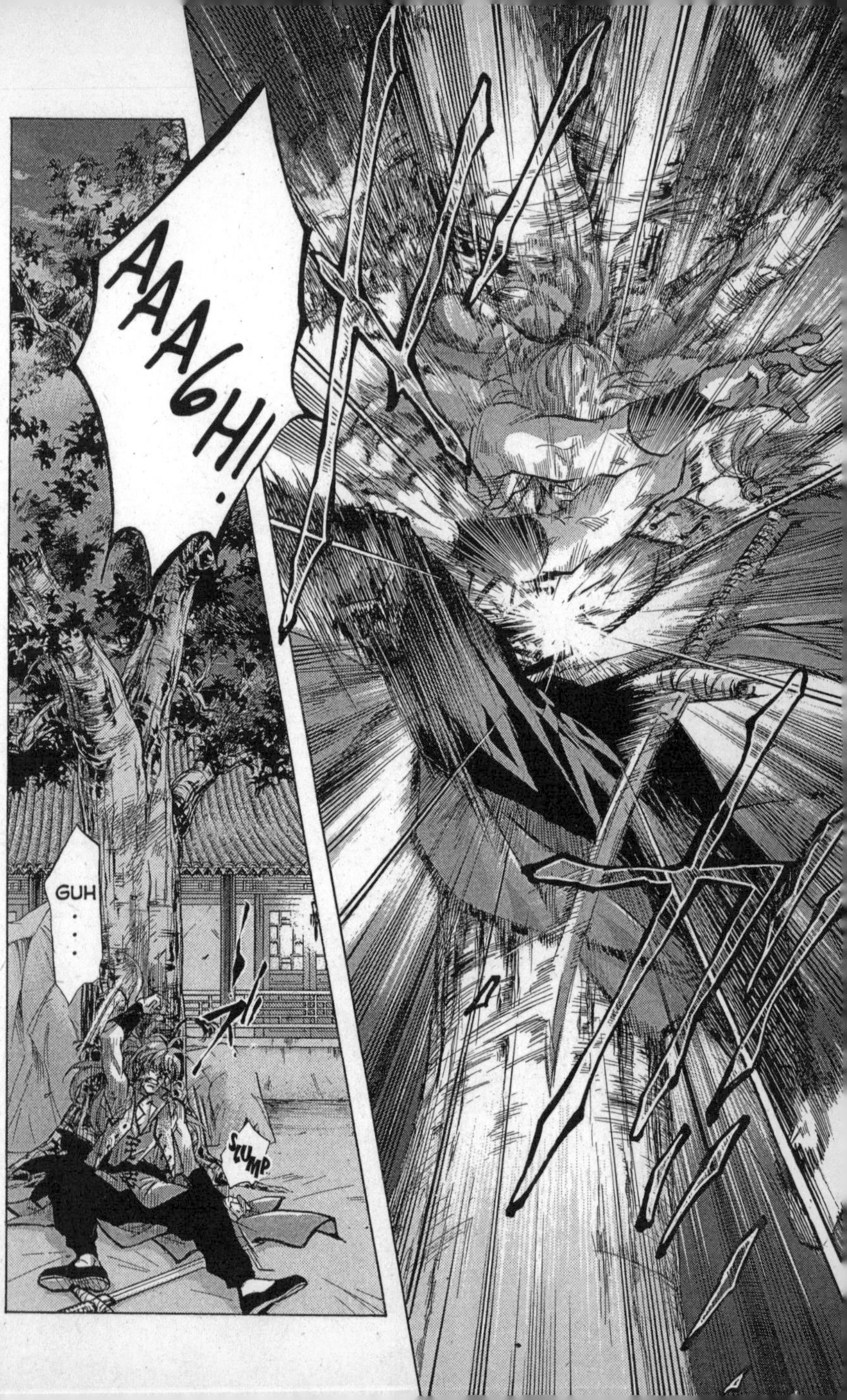
AAAGH!!
GUH . . .
SLUMP

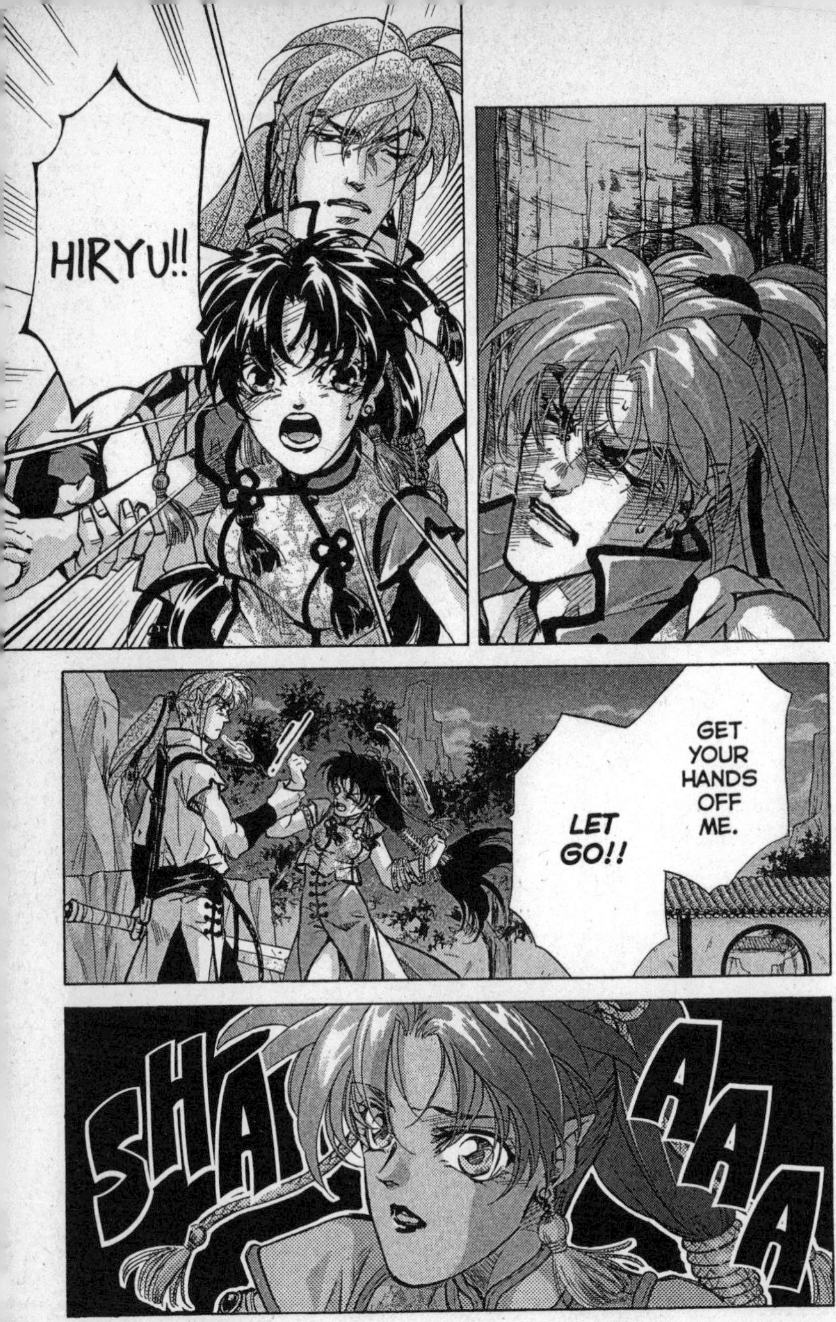
HIRYU!!
GET YOUR HANDS OFF ME.
LET GO!!
SHA
AAAA

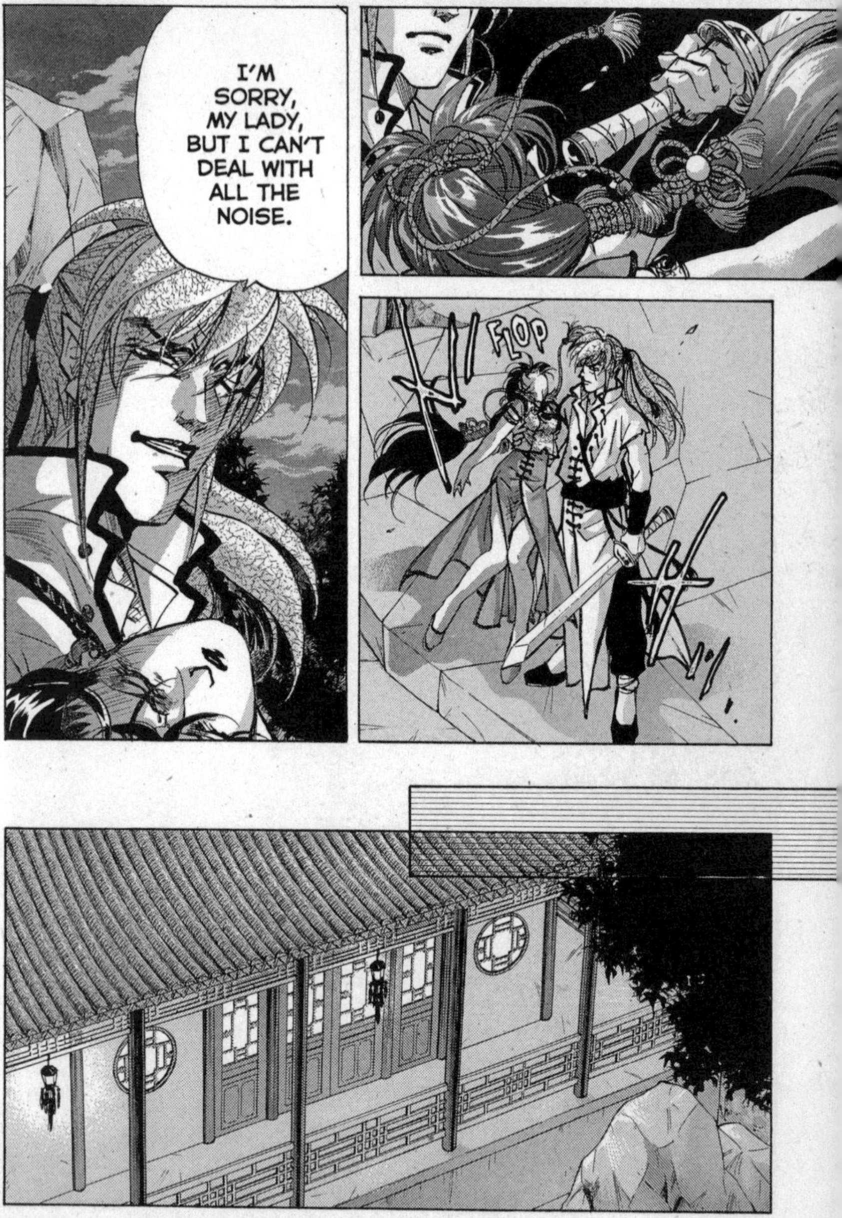
FLOP
I'M SORRY, MY LADY, BUT I CAN'T DEAL WITH ALL THE NOISE.

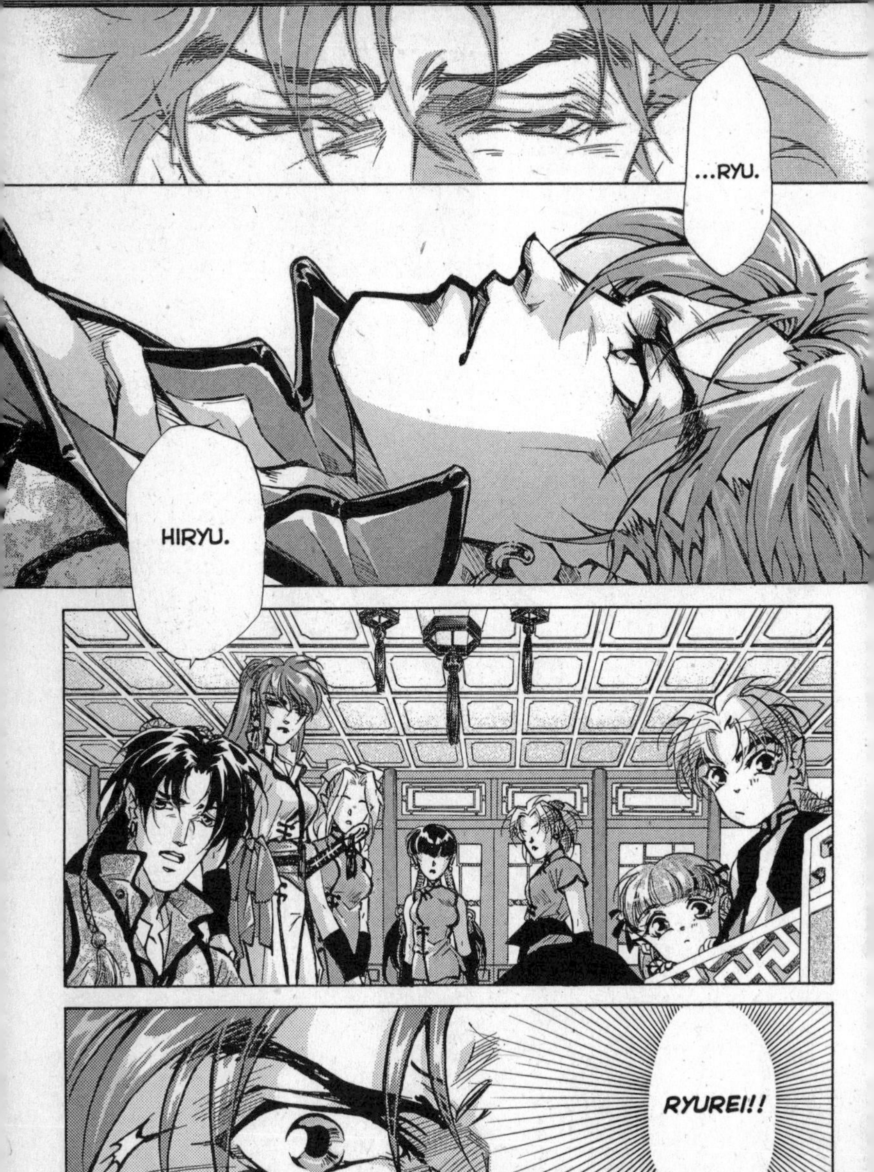
...RYU.
HIRYU.
RYUREI!!

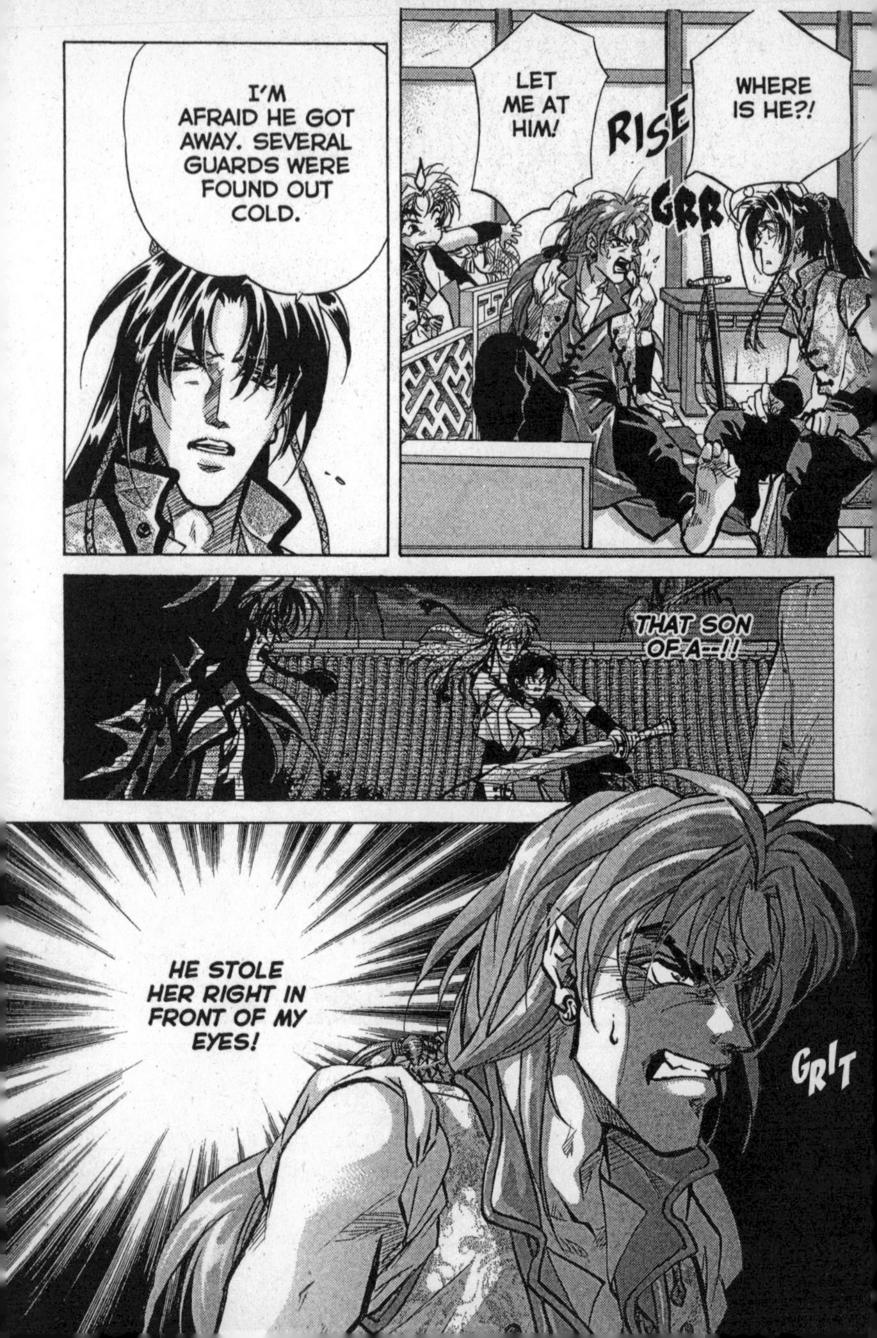
WHERE IS HE?!
LET ME AT HIM!
RISE
GRR
I'M AFRAID HE GOT AWAY. SEVERAL GUARDS WERE FOUND OUT COLD.
THAT SON OF A--!!
HE STOLE HER RIGHT IN FRONT OF MY EYES!
GRIT

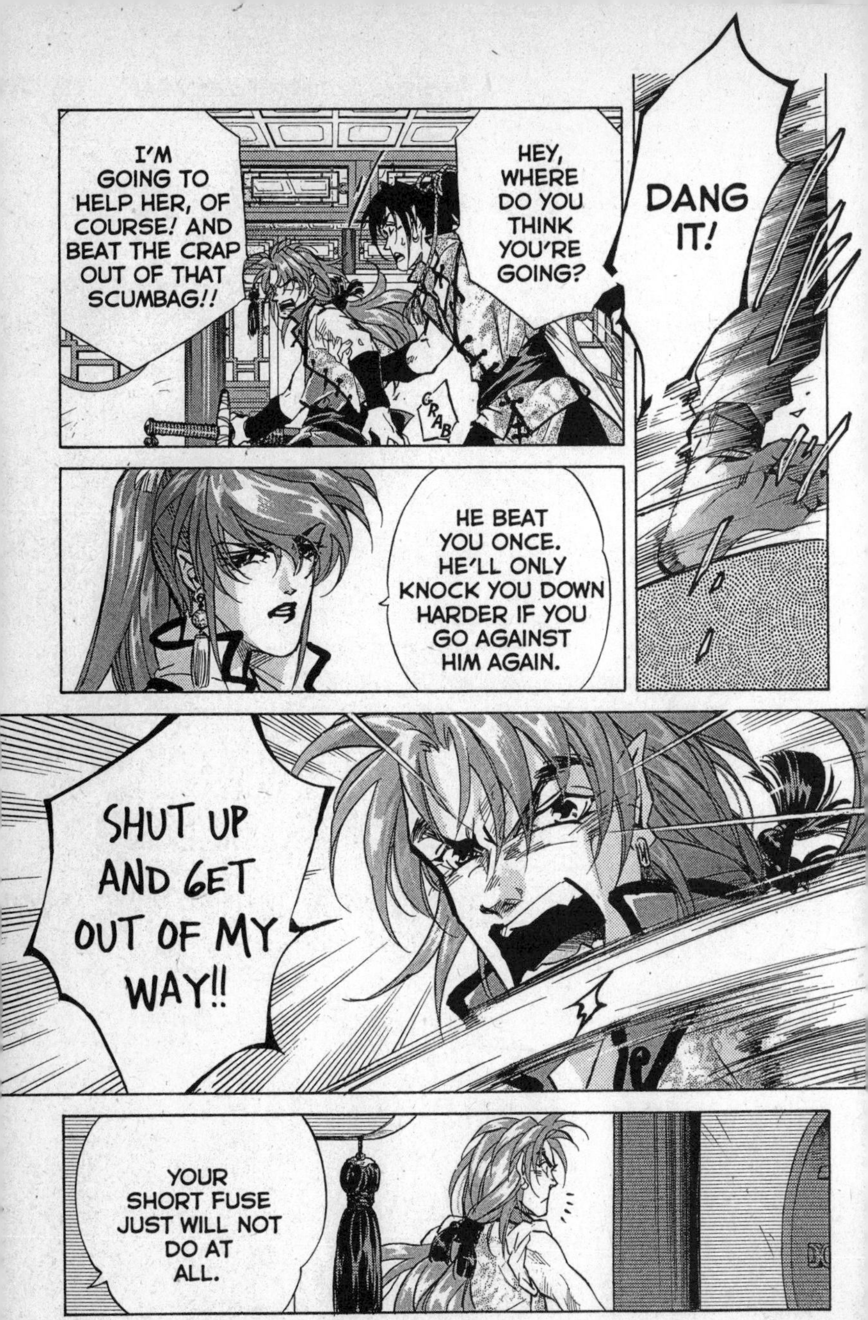
DANG IT!
HEY, WHERE DO YOU THINK YOU'RE GOING?
GRAB
I'M GOING TO HELP HER, OF COURSE! AND BEAT THE CRAP OUT OF THAT SCUMBAG!!
HE BEAT YOU ONCE. HE'LL ONLY KNOCK YOU DOWN HARDER IF YOU GO AGAINST HIM AGAIN.
SHUT UP AND GET OUT OF MY WAY!!
YOUR SHORT FUSE JUST WILL NOT DO AT ALL.

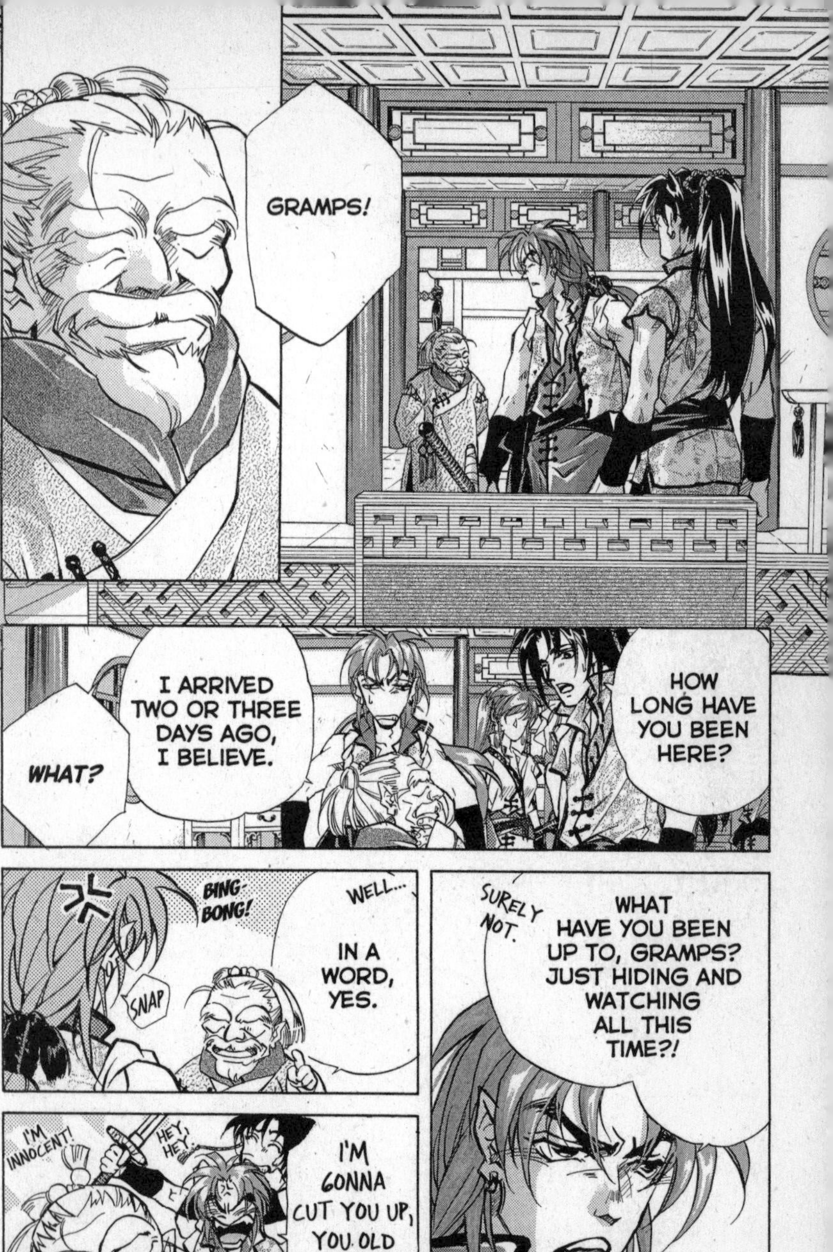
GRAMPS!
HOW LONG HAVE YOU BEEN HERE?
I ARRIVED TWO OR THREE DAYS AGO, I BELIEVE.
WHAT?
SURELY NOT.
WHAT HAVE YOU BEEN UP TO, GRAMPS? JUST HIDING AND WATCHING ALL THIS TIME?!
WELL...
IN A WORD, YES.
BING-BONG!
SNAP
I'M GONNA CUT YOU UP, YOU OLD COOT!!
HEY, HEY.
I'M INNOCENT!

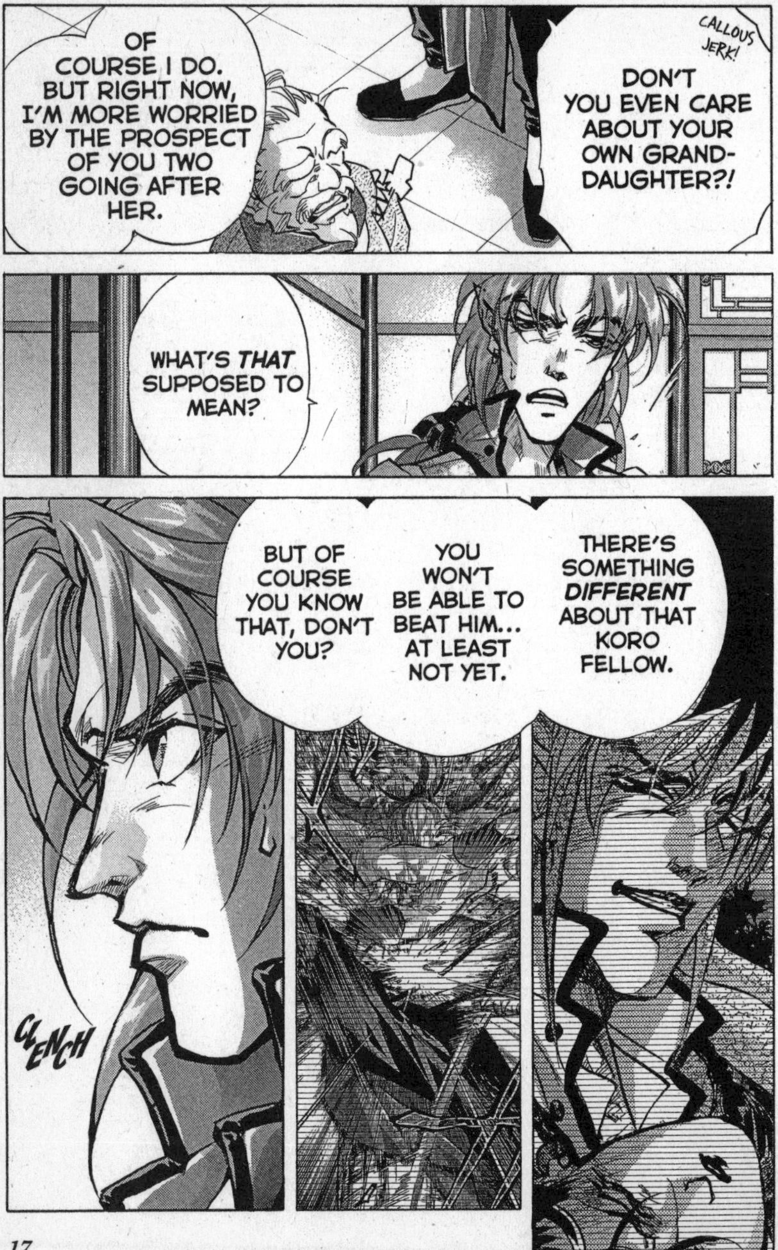
DON'T YOU EVEN CARE ABOUT YOUR OWN GRAND-DAUGHTER?!
CALLOUS JERK!
OF COURSE I DO. BUT RIGHT NOW, I'M MORE WORRIED BY THE PROSPECT OF YOU TWO GOING AFTER HER.
WHAT'S *THAT* SUPPOSED TO MEAN?
THERE'S SOMETHING *DIFFERENT* ABOUT THAT KORO FELLOW.
YOU WON'T BE ABLE TO BEAT HIM... AT LEAST NOT YET.
BUT OF COURSE YOU KNOW THAT, DON'T YOU?
CLENCH

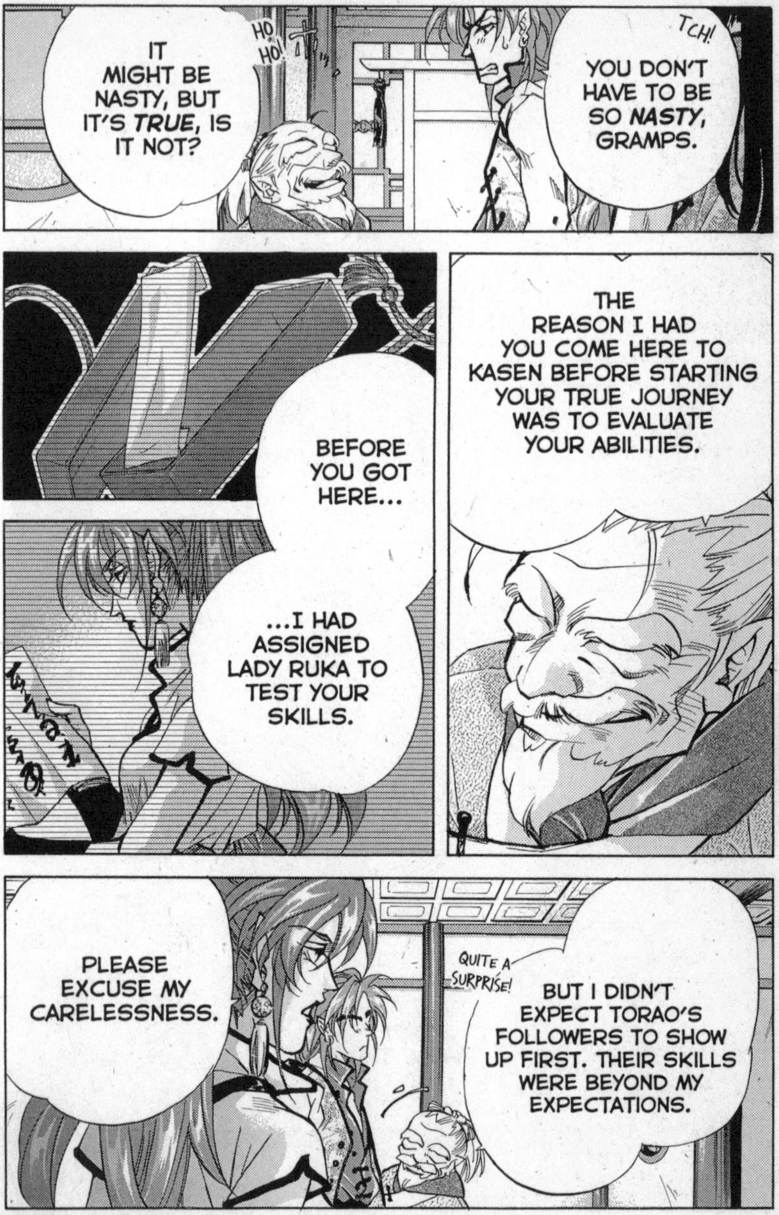
TCH!
YOU DON'T HAVE TO BE SO NASTY, GRAMPS.
HO HO!
IT MIGHT BE NASTY, BUT IT'S TRUE, IS IT NOT?
THE REASON I HAD YOU COME HERE TO KASEN BEFORE STARTING YOUR TRUE JOURNEY WAS TO EVALUATE YOUR ABILITIES.
BEFORE YOU GOT HERE...
...I HAD ASSIGNED LADY RUKA TO TEST YOUR SKILLS.
QUITE A SURPRISE!
BUT I DIDN'T EXPECT TORAO'S FOLLOWERS TO SHOW UP FIRST. THEIR SKILLS WERE BEYOND MY EXPECTATIONS.
PLEASE EXCUSE MY CARELESSNESS.

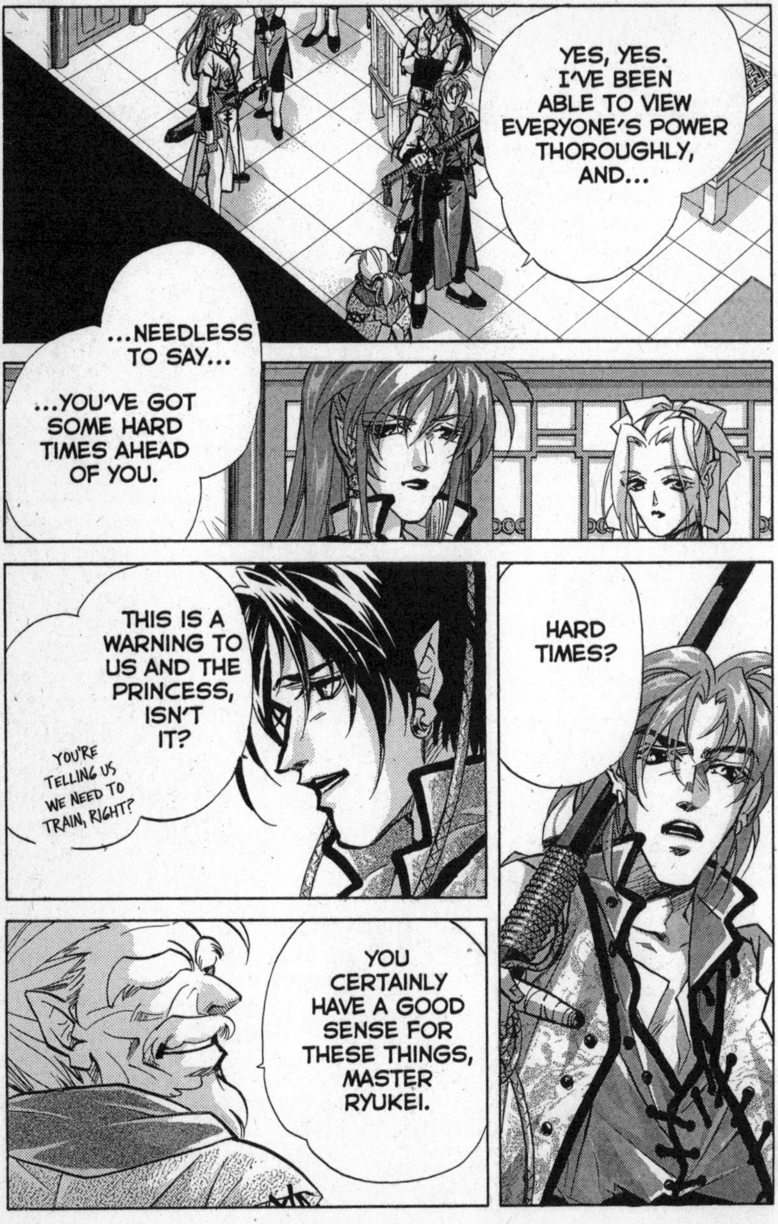
YES, YES. I'VE BEEN ABLE TO VIEW EVERYONE'S POWER THOROUGHLY, AND...
...NEEDLESS TO SAY...
...YOU'VE GOT SOME HARD TIMES AHEAD OF YOU.
HARD TIMES?
THIS IS A WARNING TO US AND THE PRINCESS, ISN'T IT?
YOU'RE TELLING US WE NEED TO TRAIN, RIGHT?
YOU CERTAINLY HAVE A GOOD SENSE FOR THESE THINGS, MASTER RYUKEI.

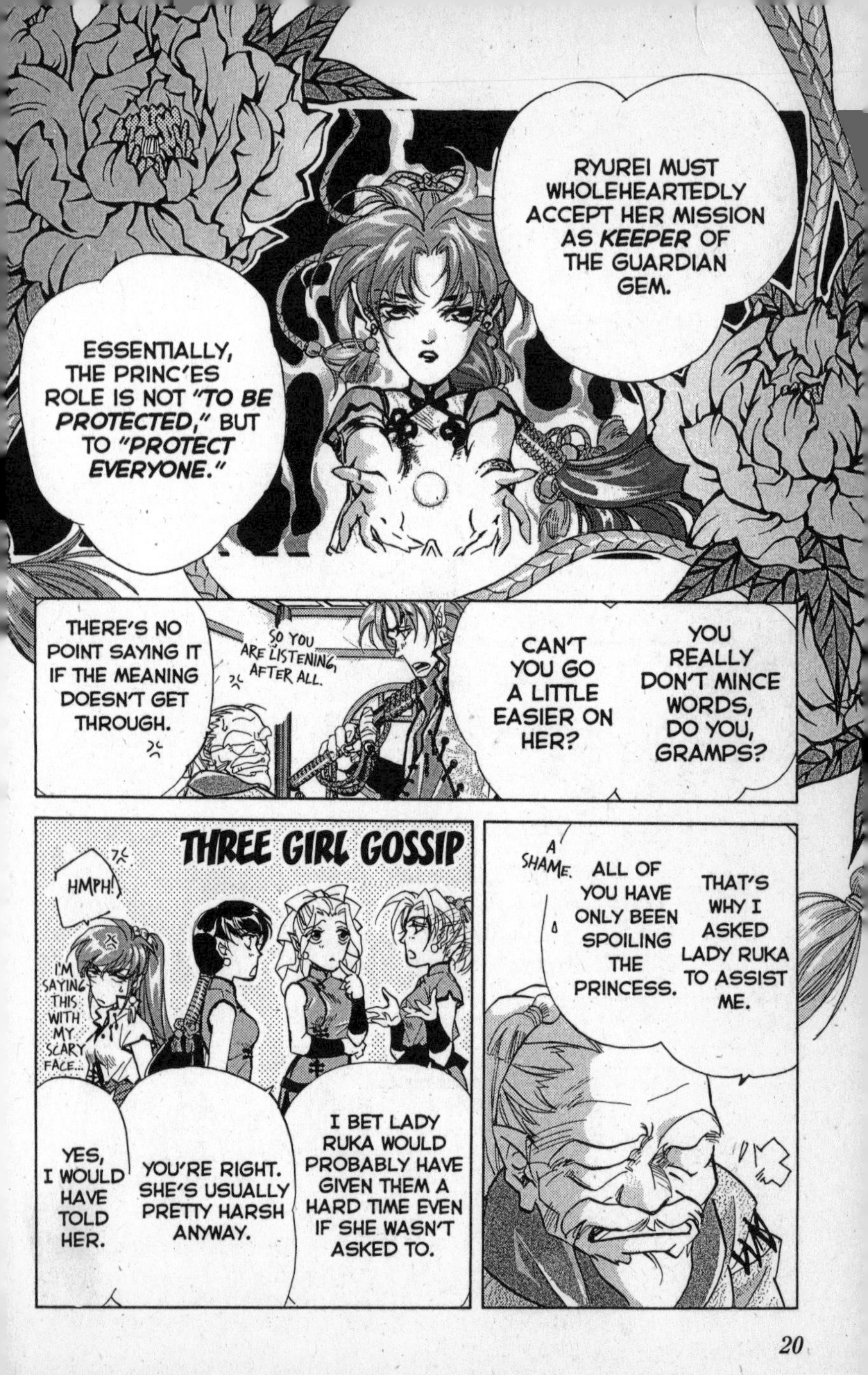

RYUREI MUST WHOLEHEARTEDLY ACCEPT HER MISSION AS *KEEPER* OF THE GUARDIAN GEM.
ESSENTIALLY, THE PRINC'ES ROLE IS NOT *"TO BE PROTECTED,"* BUT TO *"PROTECT EVERYONE."*
YOU REALLY DON'T MINCE WORDS, DO YOU, GRAMPS?
CAN'T YOU GO A LITTLE EASIER ON HER?
SO YOU ARE LISTENING, AFTER ALL.
THERE'S NO POINT SAYING IT IF THE MEANING DOESN'T GET THROUGH.
THAT'S WHY I ASKED LADY RUKA TO ASSIST ME.
ALL OF YOU HAVE ONLY BEEN SPOILING THE PRINCESS.
A SHAME.
THREE GIRL GOSSIP
HMPH!
I'M SAYING THIS WITH MY SCARY FACE...
I BET LADY RUKA WOULD PROBABLY HAVE GIVEN THEM A HARD TIME EVEN IF SHE WASN'T ASKED TO.
YOU'RE RIGHT. SHE'S USUALLY PRETTY HARSH ANYWAY.
YES, I WOULD HAVE TOLD HER.

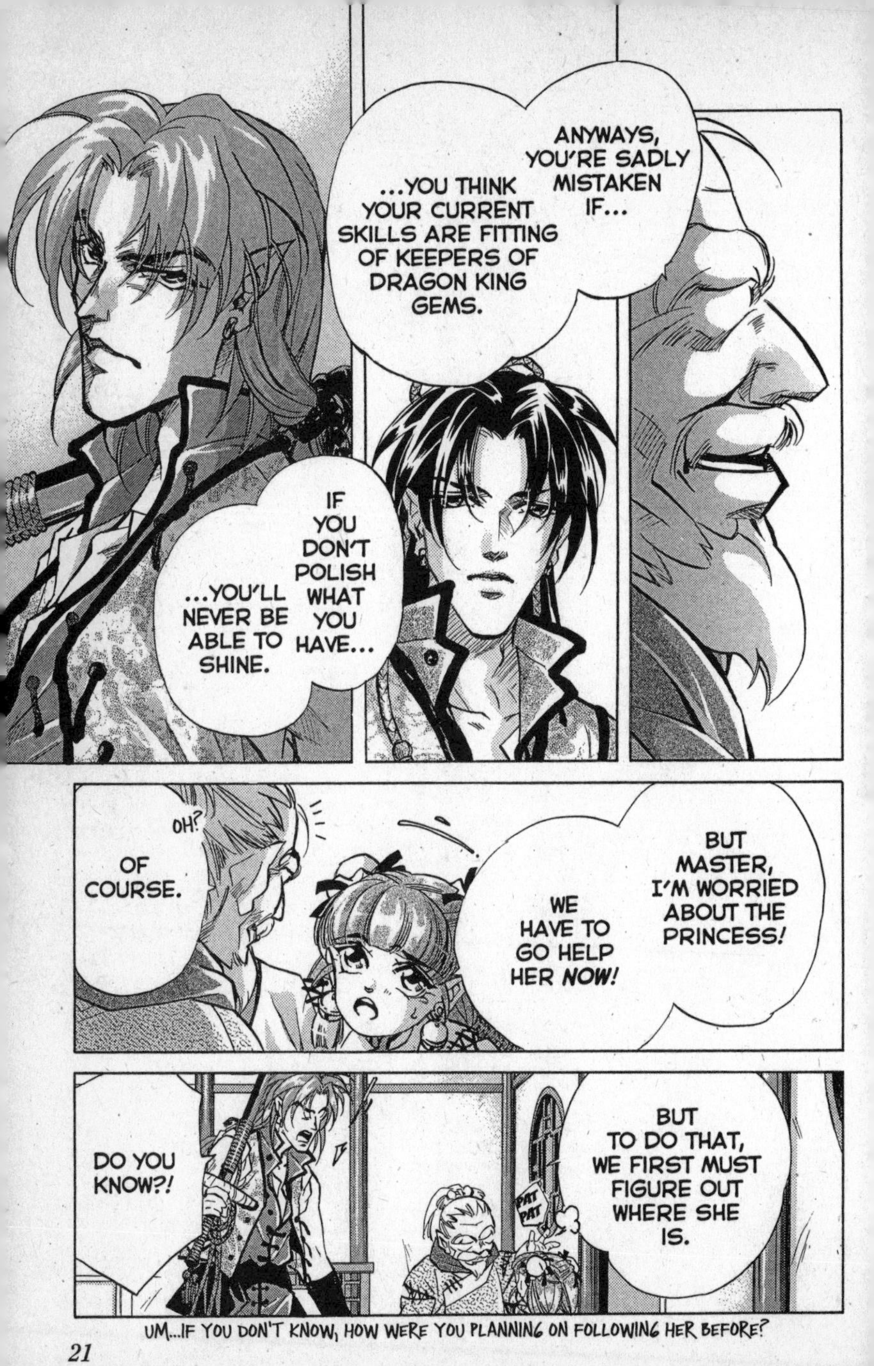
ANYWAYS, YOU'RE SADLY MISTAKEN IF...
...YOU THINK YOUR CURRENT SKILLS ARE FITTING OF KEEPERS OF DRAGON KING GEMS.
IF YOU DON'T POLISH WHAT YOU HAVE...
...YOU'LL NEVER BE ABLE TO SHINE.
BUT MASTER, I'M WORRIED ABOUT THE PRINCESS!
WE HAVE TO GO HELP HER *NOW!*
OH?
OF COURSE.
BUT TO DO THAT, WE FIRST MUST FIGURE OUT WHERE SHE IS.
PAT PAT
DO YOU KNOW?!

UM...IF YOU DON'T KNOW, HOW WERE YOU PLANNING ON FOLLOWING HER BEFORE?

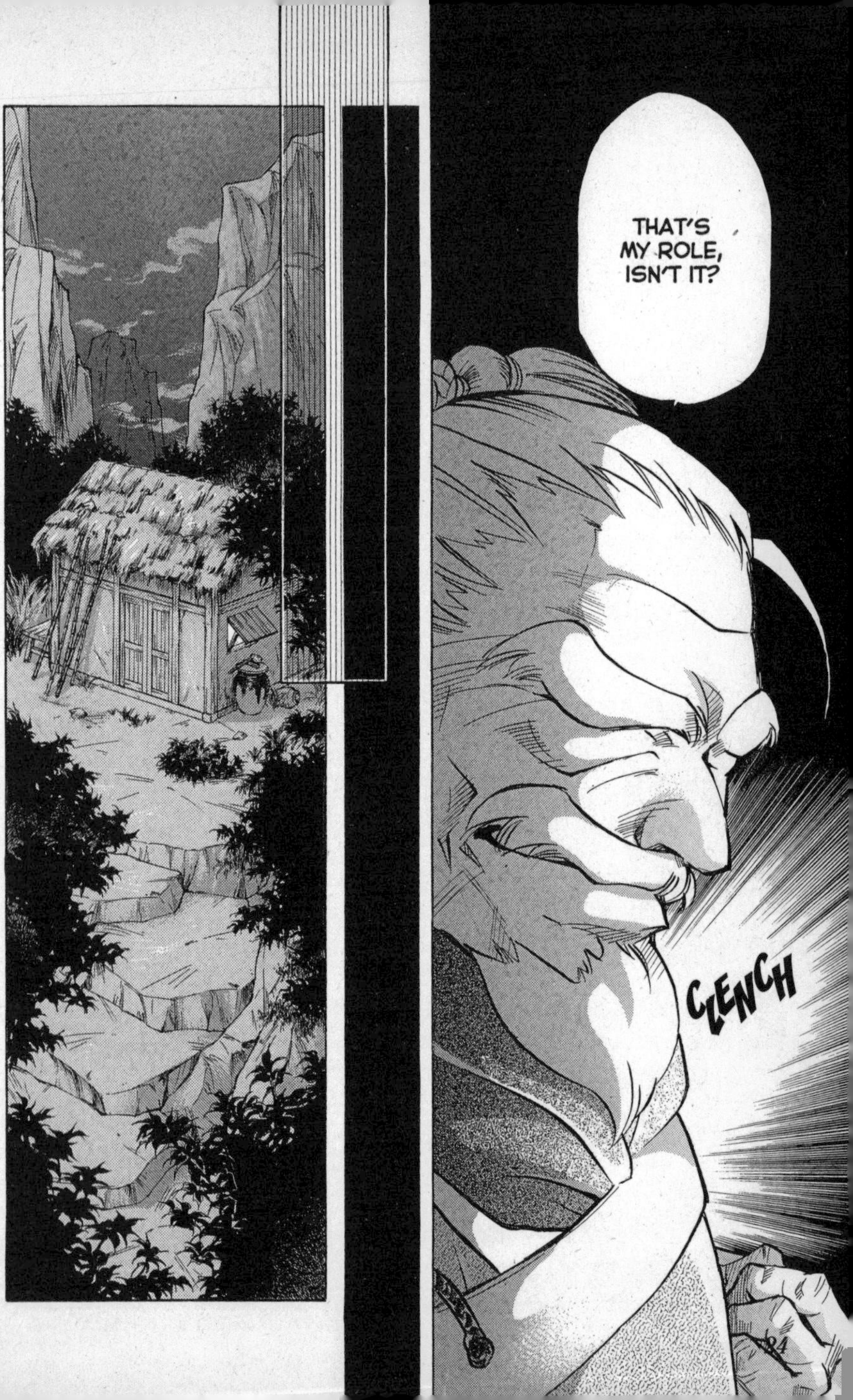
THAT'S MY ROLE, ISN'T IT?
CLENCH

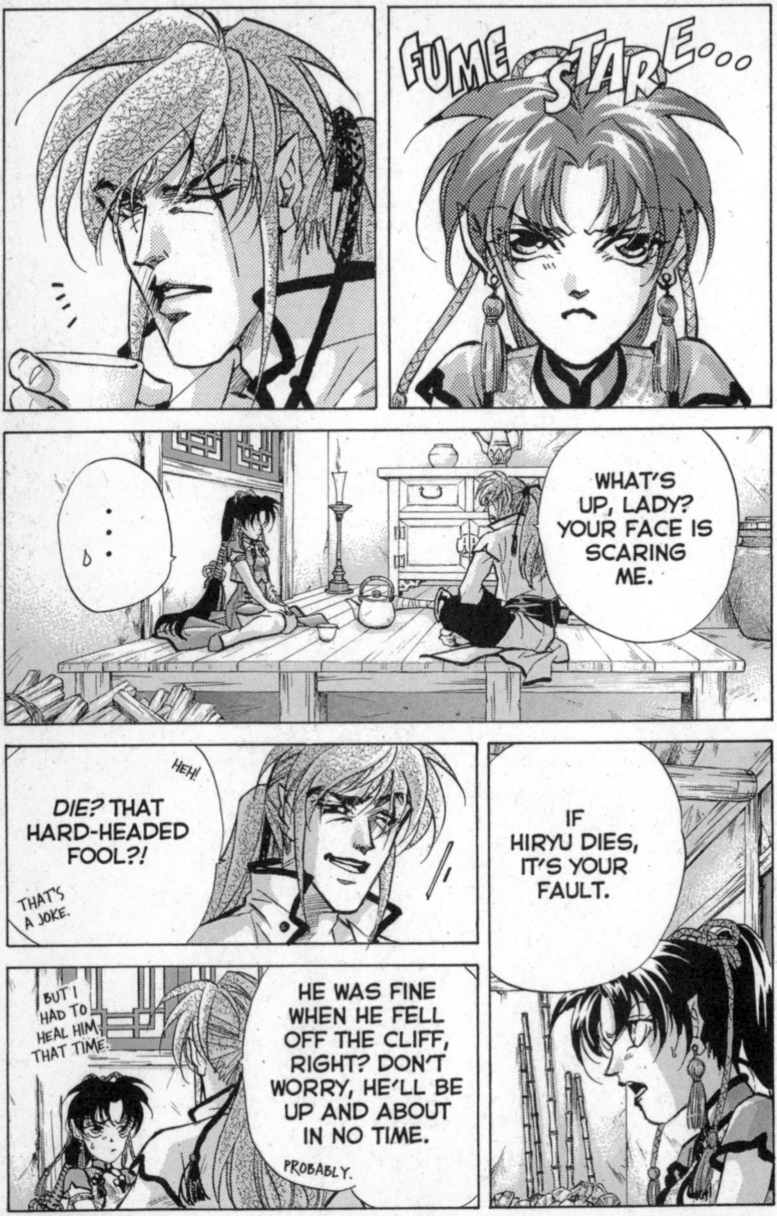
FUME STARE...
...
WHAT'S UP, LADY? YOUR FACE IS SCARING ME.
IF HIRYU DIES, IT'S YOUR FAULT.
HEH!
DIE? THAT HARD-HEADED FOOL?!
THAT'S A JOKE.
HE WAS FINE WHEN HE FELL OFF THE CLIFF, RIGHT? DON'T WORRY, HE'LL BE UP AND ABOUT IN NO TIME.
PROBABLY.
BUT I HAD TO HEAL HIM THAT TIME.

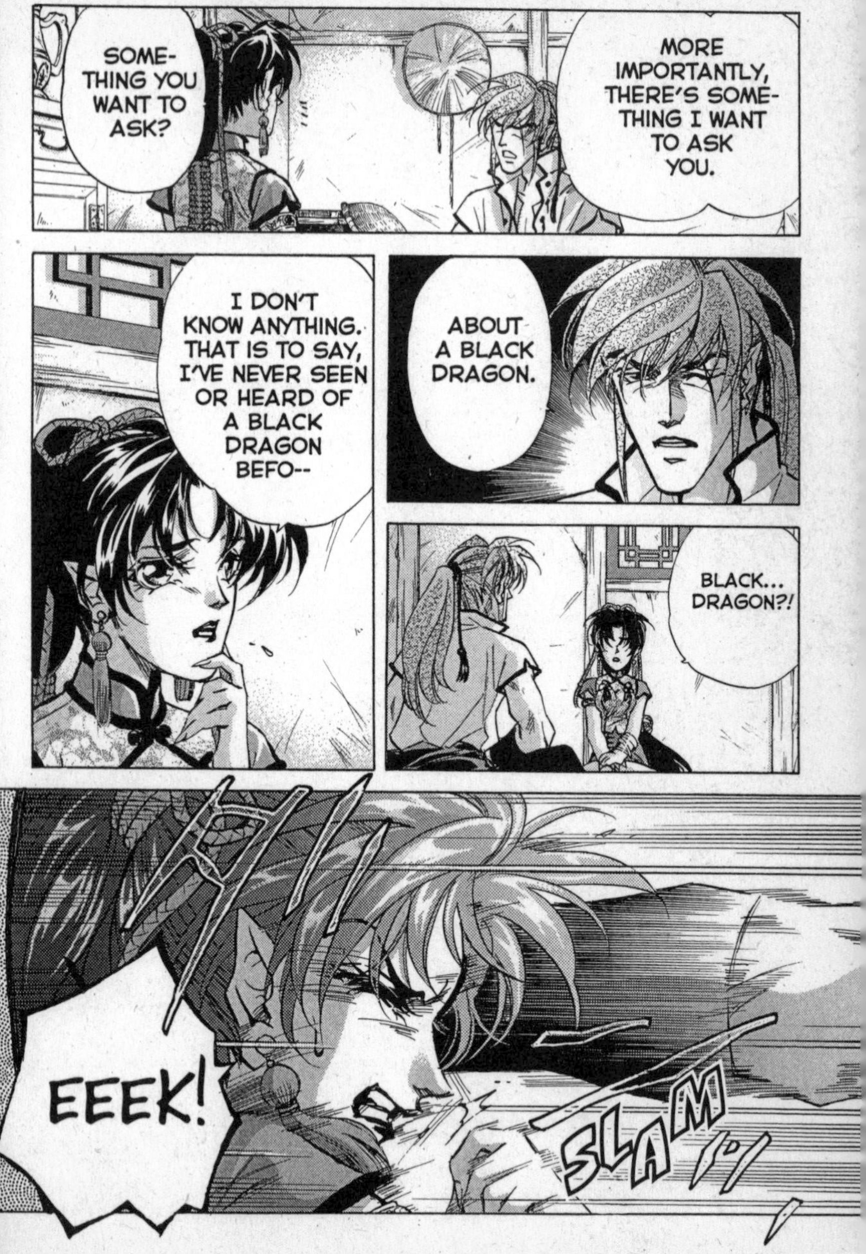
MORE IMPORTANTLY, THERE'S SOME-THING I WANT TO ASK YOU.
SOME-THING YOU WANT TO ASK?
ABOUT A BLACK DRAGON.
BLACK... DRAGON?!
I DON'T KNOW ANYTHING. THAT IS TO SAY, I'VE NEVER SEEN OR HEARD OF A BLACK DRAGON BEFO--
SLAM
EEEK!

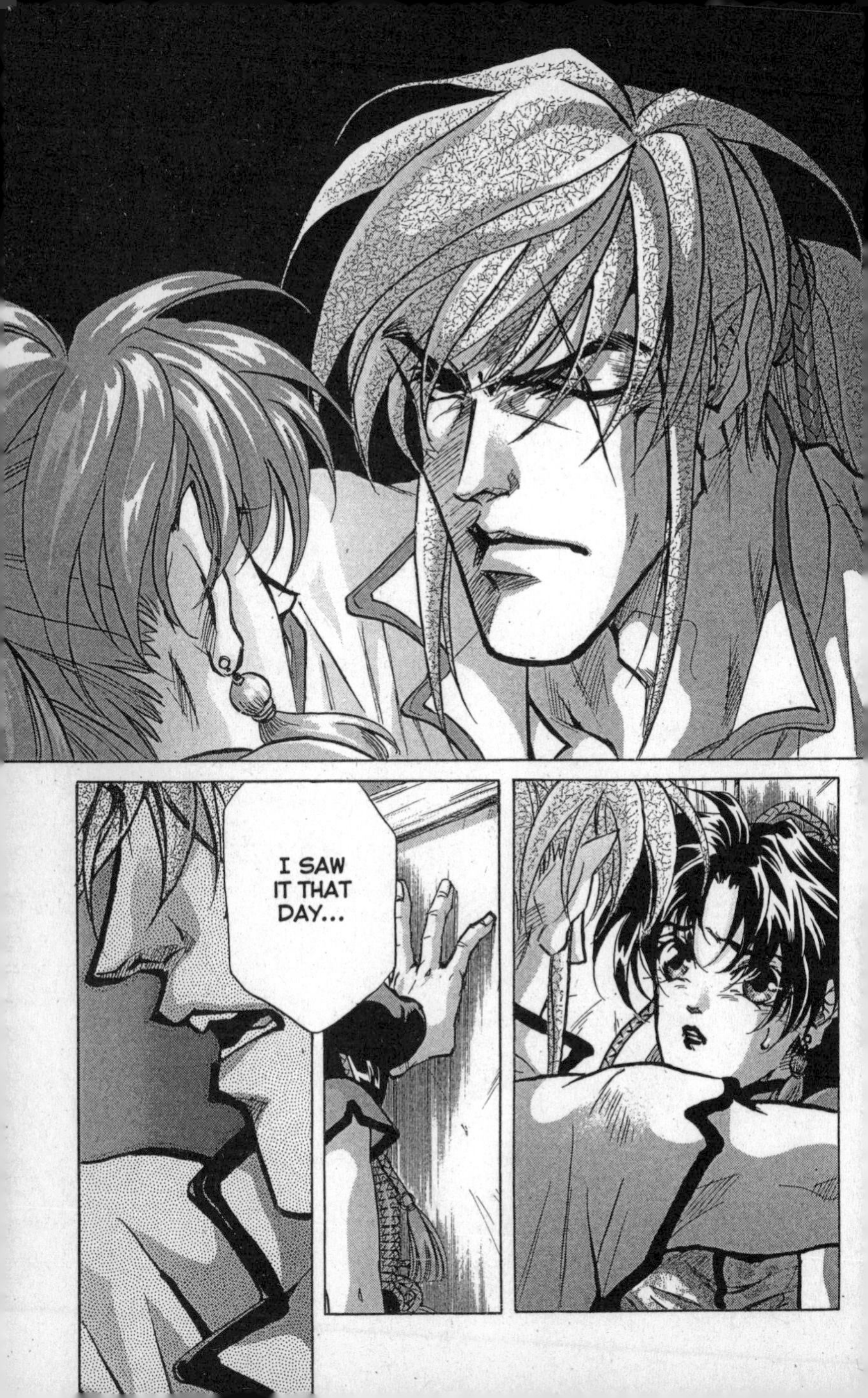
I SAW IT THAT DAY...

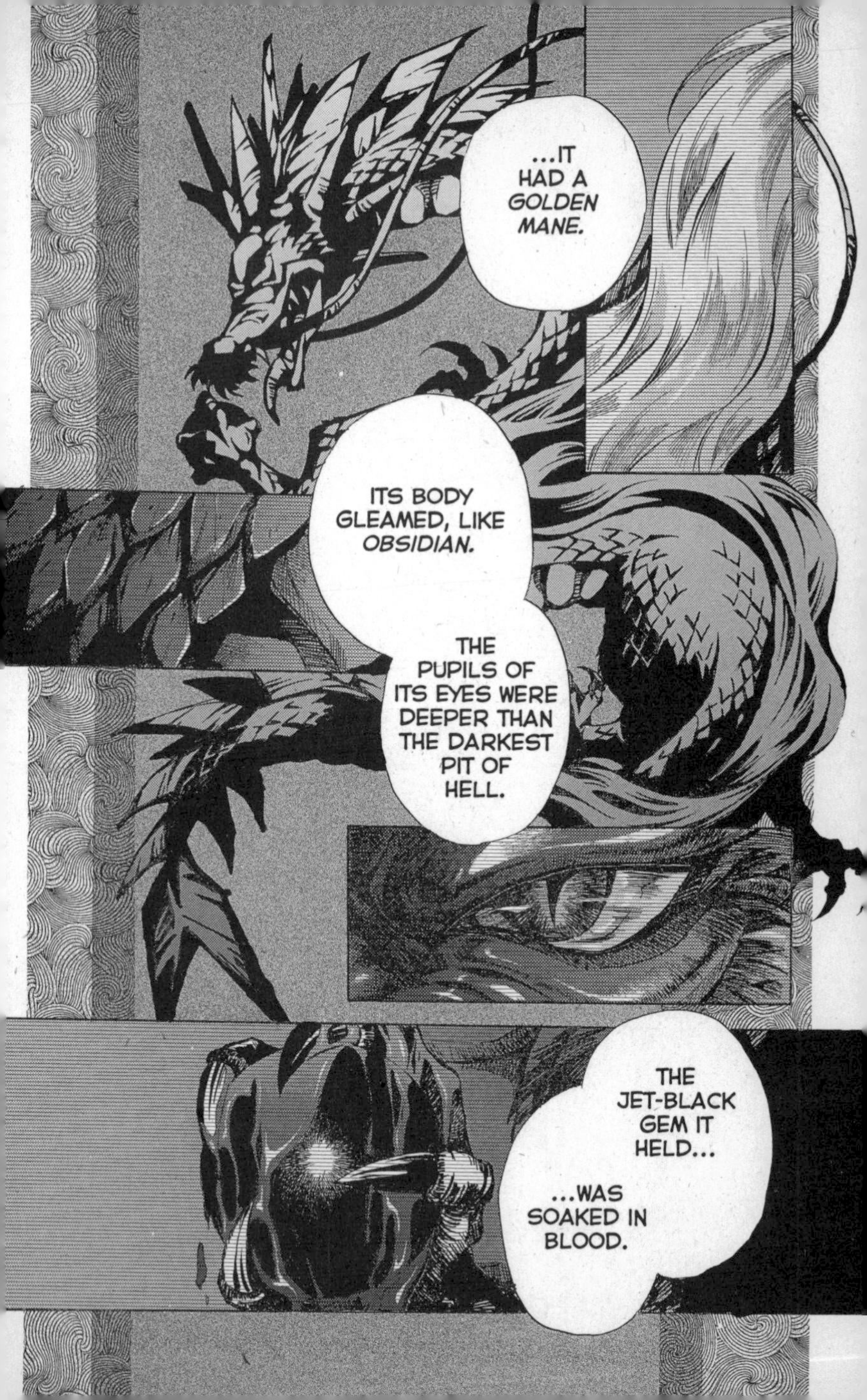
...IT HAD A GOLDEN MANE.
ITS BODY GLEAMED, LIKE OBSIDIAN.
THE PUPILS OF ITS EYES WERE DEEPER THAN THE DARKEST PIT OF HELL.
THE JET-BLACK GEM IT HELD...
...WAS SOAKED IN BLOOD.

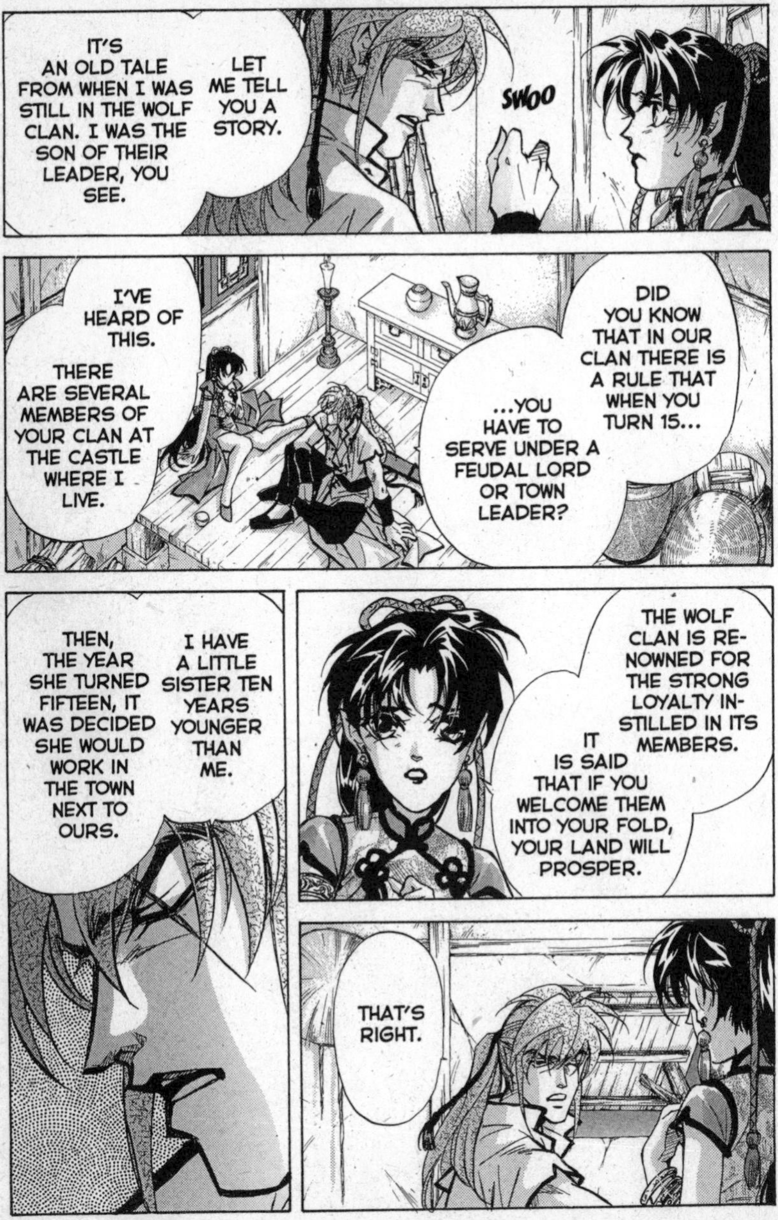
SWOO
LET ME TELL YOU A STORY.
IT'S AN OLD TALE FROM WHEN I WAS STILL IN THE WOLF CLAN. I WAS THE SON OF THEIR LEADER, YOU SEE.
DID YOU KNOW THAT IN OUR CLAN THERE IS A RULE THAT WHEN YOU TURN 15...
...YOU HAVE TO SERVE UNDER A FEUDAL LORD OR TOWN LEADER?
I'VE HEARD OF THIS.
THERE ARE SEVERAL MEMBERS OF YOUR CLAN AT THE CASTLE WHERE I LIVE.
THE WOLF CLAN IS RENOWNED FOR THE STRONG LOYALTY INSTILLED IN ITS MEMBERS.
IT IS SAID THAT IF YOU WELCOME THEM INTO YOUR FOLD, YOUR LAND WILL PROSPER.
THAT'S RIGHT.
I HAVE A LITTLE SISTER TEN YEARS YOUNGER THAN ME.
THEN, THE YEAR SHE TURNED FIFTEEN, IT WAS DECIDED SHE WOULD WORK IN THE TOWN NEXT TO OURS.

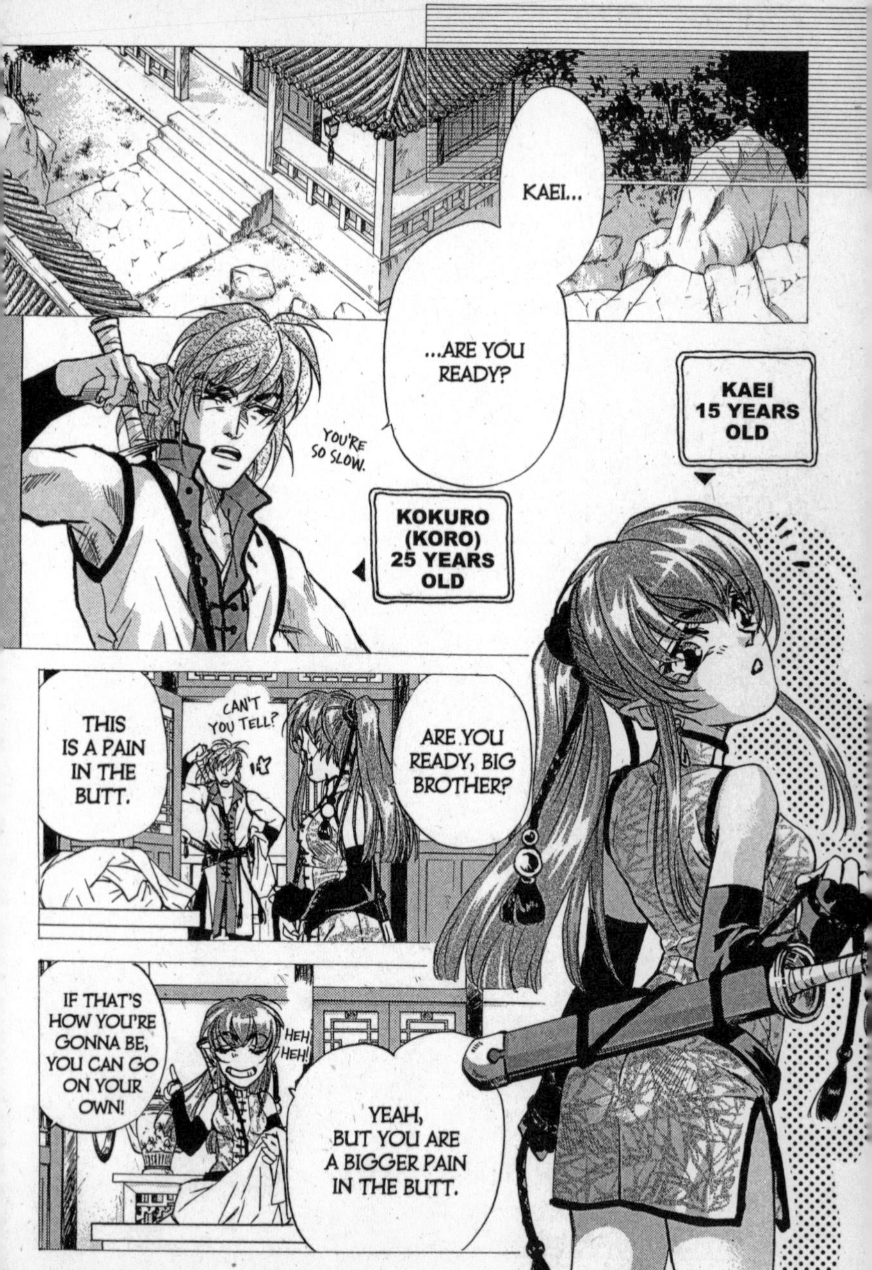
KAEI...
...ARE YOU READY?
YOU'RE SO SLOW.
KOKURO (KORO) 25 YEARS OLD
KAEI 15 YEARS OLD
ARE YOU READY, BIG BROTHER?
CAN'T YOU TELL?
THIS IS A PAIN IN THE BUTT.
YEAH, BUT YOU ARE A BIGGER PAIN IN THE BUTT.
HEH HEH!
IF THAT'S HOW YOU'RE GONNA BE, YOU CAN GO ON YOUR OWN!

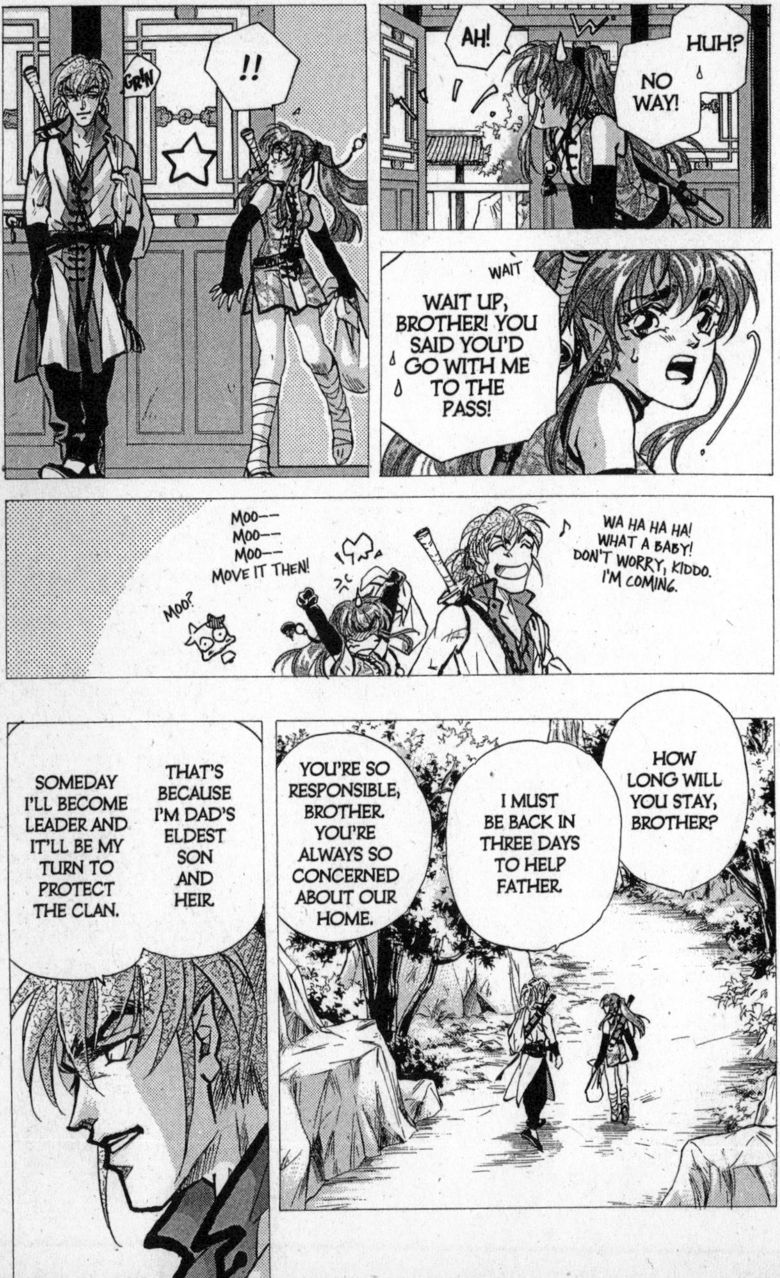
HUH?
NO WAY!
AH!
WAIT
WAIT UP, BROTHER! YOU SAID YOU'D GO WITH ME TO THE PASS!
!!
GRIN
WA HA HA HA! WHAT A BABY! DON'T WORRY, KIDDO. I'M COMING.
MOO-- MOO-- MOO-- MOVE IT THEN!
MOO?
HOW LONG WILL YOU STAY, BROTHER?
I MUST BE BACK IN THREE DAYS TO HELP FATHER.
YOU'RE SO RESPONSIBLE, BROTHER. YOU'RE ALWAYS SO CONCERNED ABOUT OUR HOME.
THAT'S BECAUSE I'M DAD'S ELDEST SON AND HEIR.
SOMEDAY I'LL BECOME LEADER AND IT'LL BE MY TURN TO PROTECT THE CLAN.

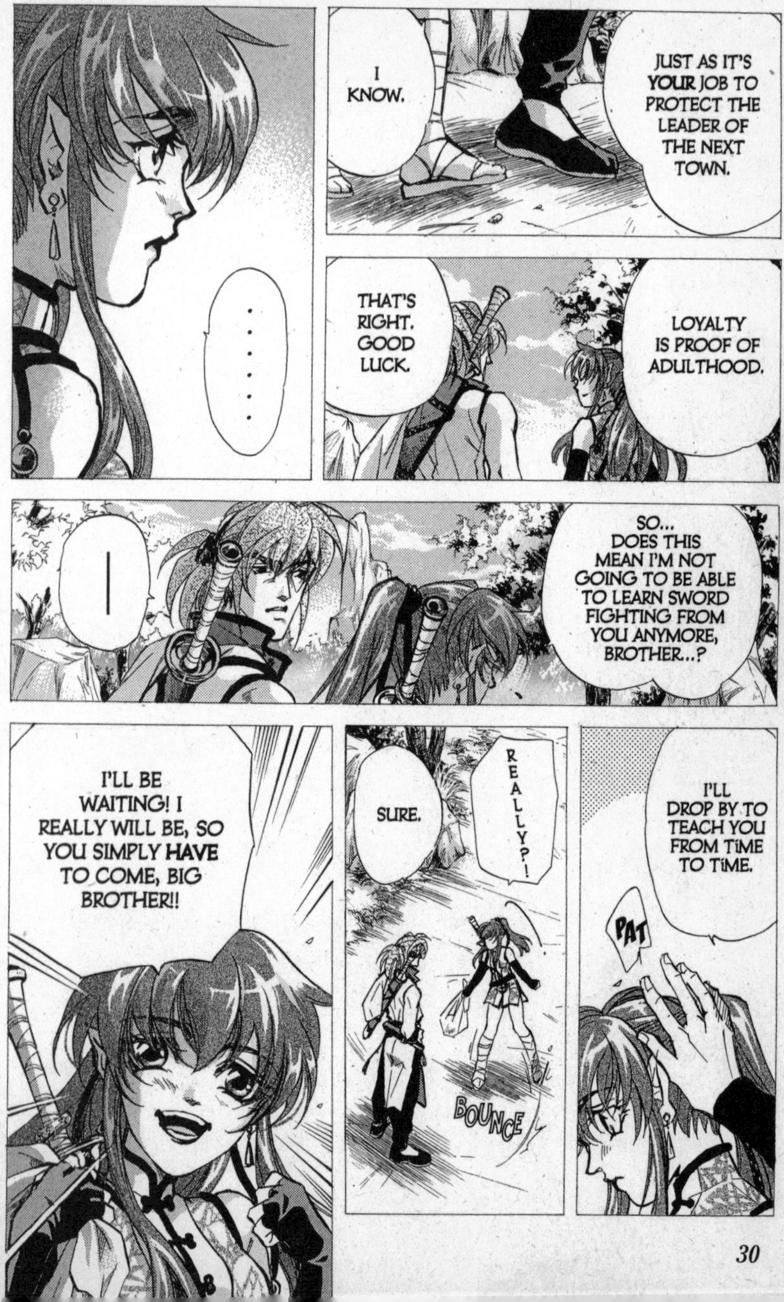

JUST AS IT'S YOUR JOB TO PROTECT THE LEADER OF THE NEXT TOWN.
I KNOW.
LOYALTY IS PROOF OF ADULTHOOD.
THAT'S RIGHT. GOOD LUCK.
......
SO... DOES THIS MEAN I'M NOT GOING TO BE ABLE TO LEARN SWORD FIGHTING FROM YOU ANYMORE, BROTHER...?
—
I'LL DROP BY TO TEACH YOU FROM TIME TO TIME.
PAT
REALLY?!
SURE.
BOUNCE
I'LL BE WAITING! I REALLY WILL BE, SO YOU SIMPLY HAVE TO COME, BIG BROTHER!!

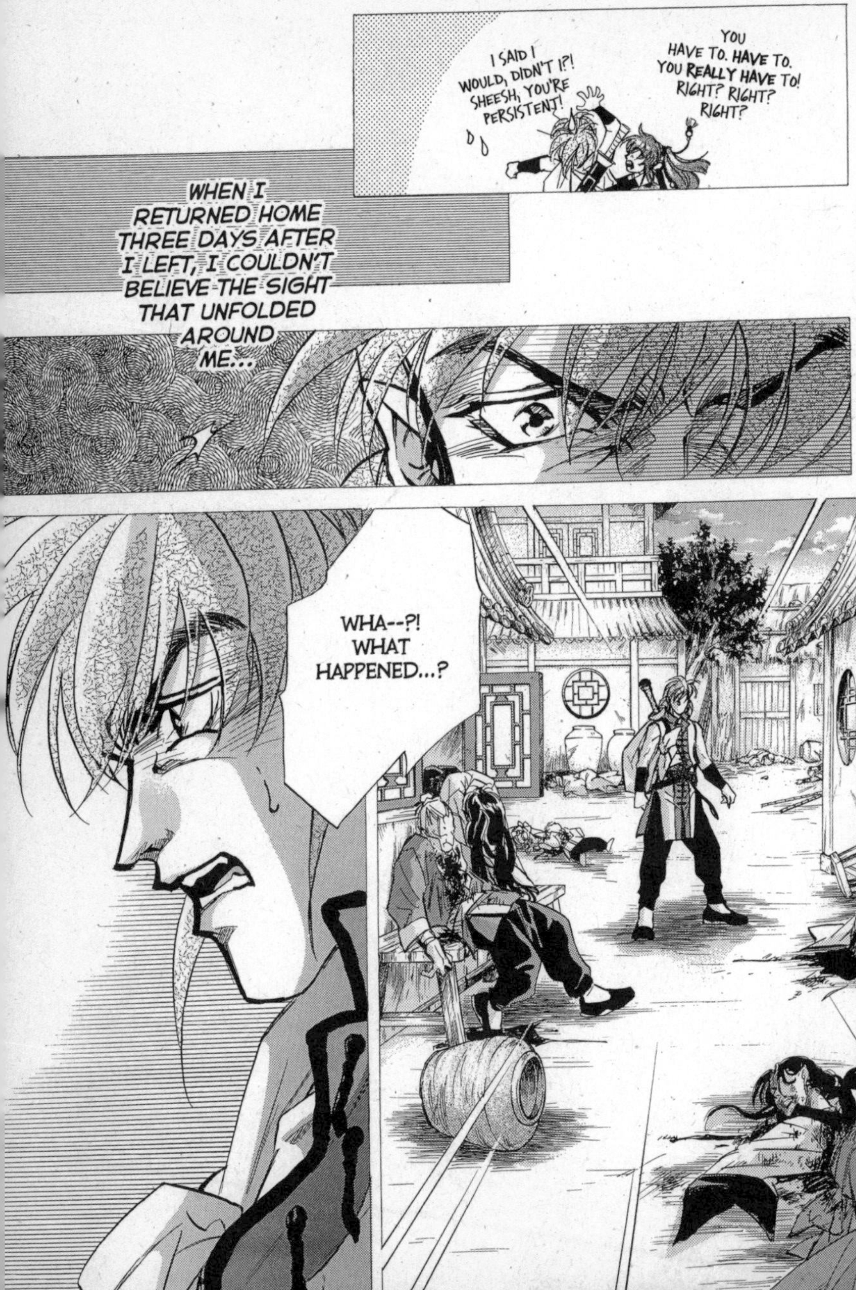
YOU HAVE TO. HAVE TO. YOU REALLY HAVE TO! RIGHT? RIGHT? RIGHT?
I SAID I WOULD, DIDN'T I?! SHEESH, YOU'RE PERSISTENT!
WHEN I RETURNED HOME THREE DAYS AFTER I LEFT, I COULDN'T BELIEVE THE SIGHT THAT UNFOLDED AROUND ME...
WHA--?! WHAT HAPPENED...?

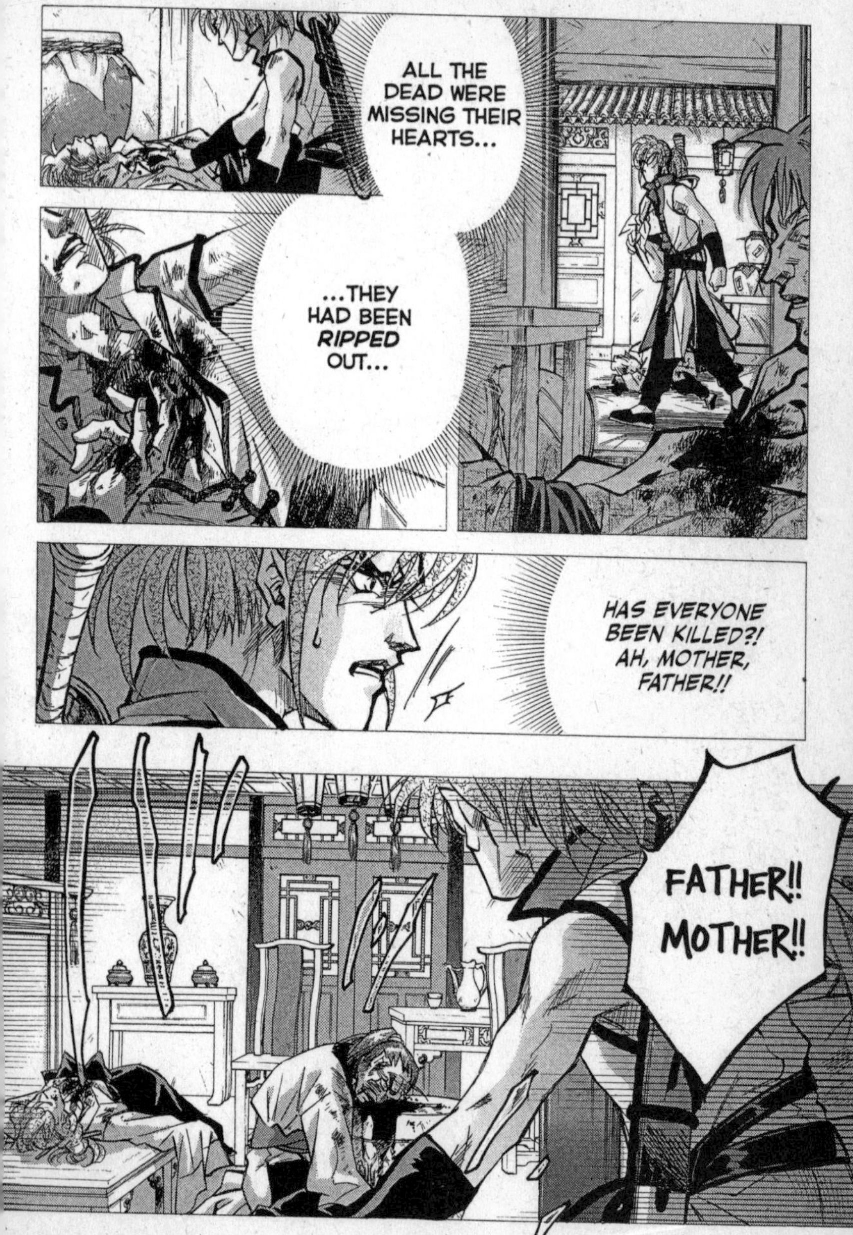
ALL THE DEAD WERE MISSING THEIR HEARTS...
...THEY HAD BEEN *RIPPED* OUT...
HAS EVERYONE BEEN KILLED?! AH, MOTHER, FATHER!!
FATHER!! MOTHER!!

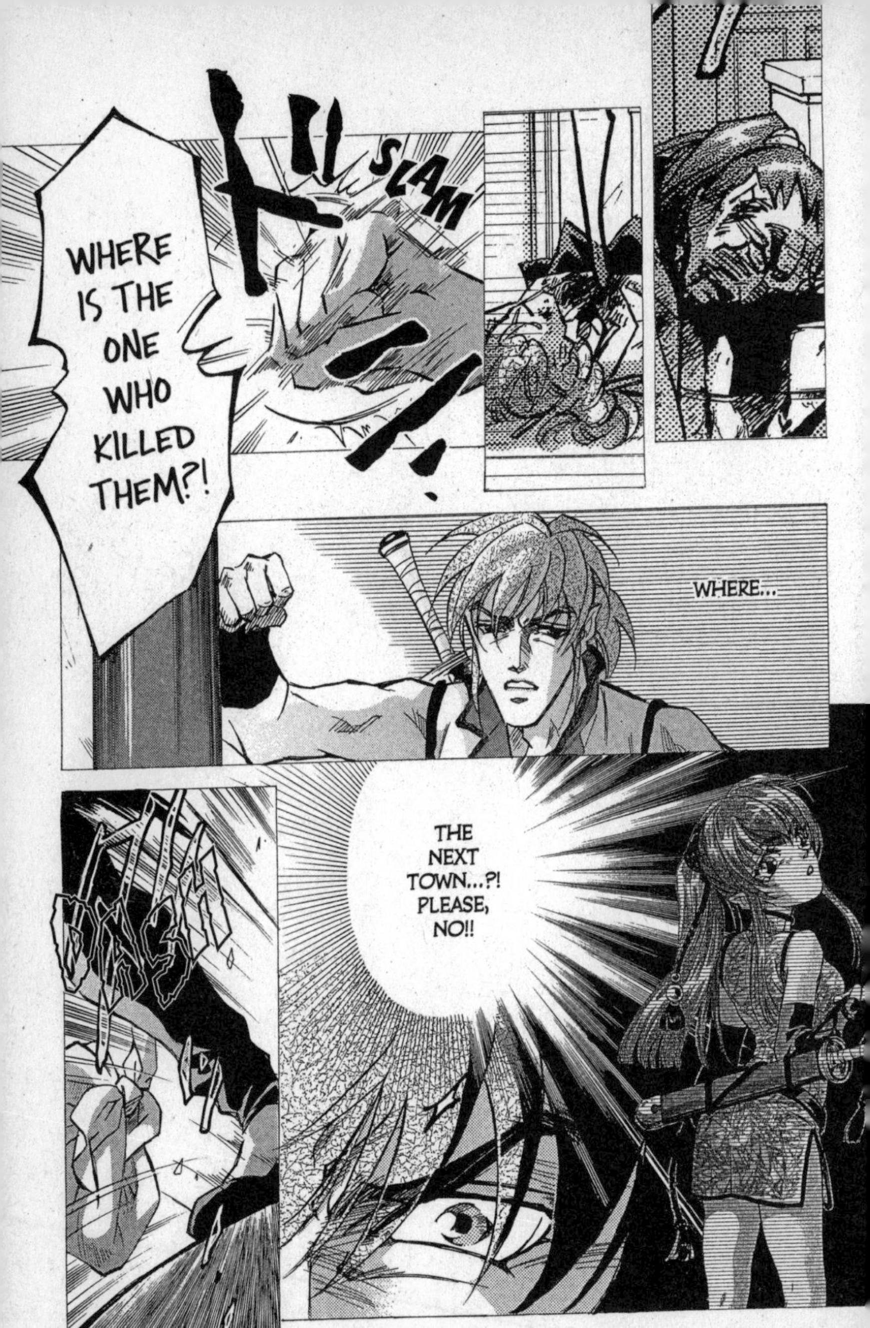
SLAM
WHERE IS THE ONE WHO KILLED THEM?!
WHERE...
THE NEXT TOWN...?! PLEASE, NO!!

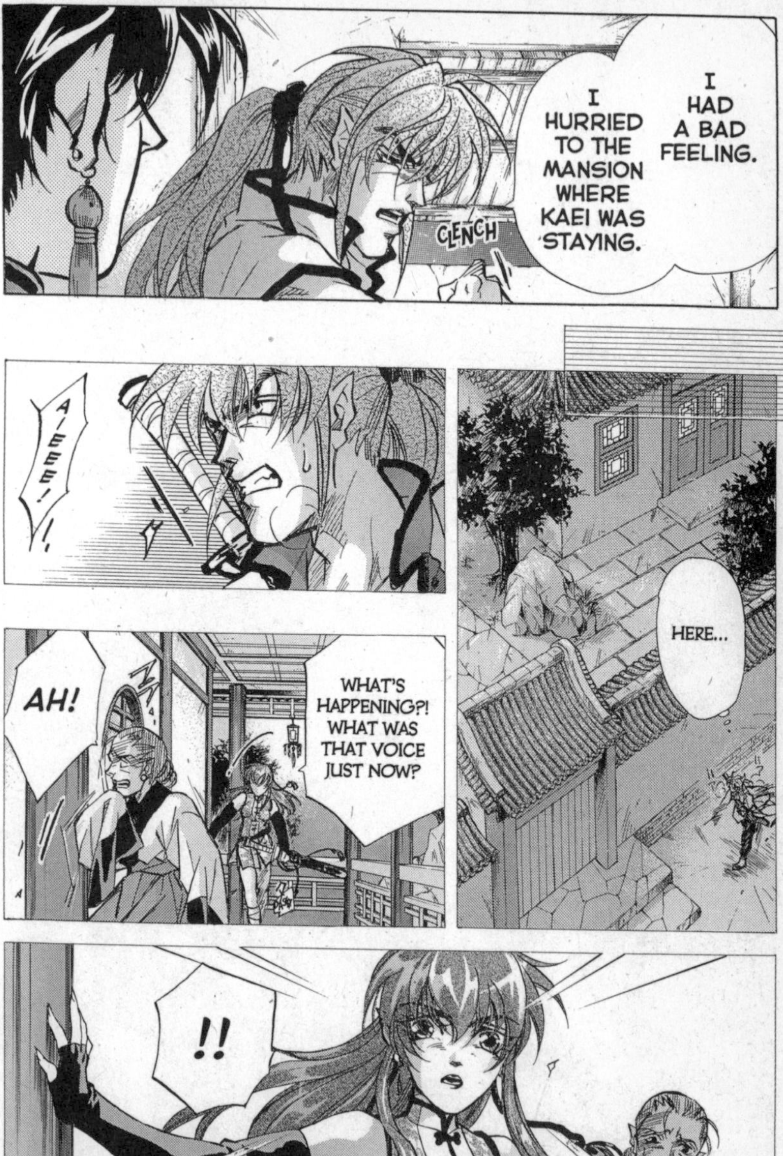
I HAD A BAD FEELING.
I HURRIED TO THE MANSION WHERE KAEI WAS STAYING.
CLENCH
HERE...
AIEEEE!
WHAT'S HAPPENING?! WHAT WAS THAT VOICE JUST NOW?
AH!
!!

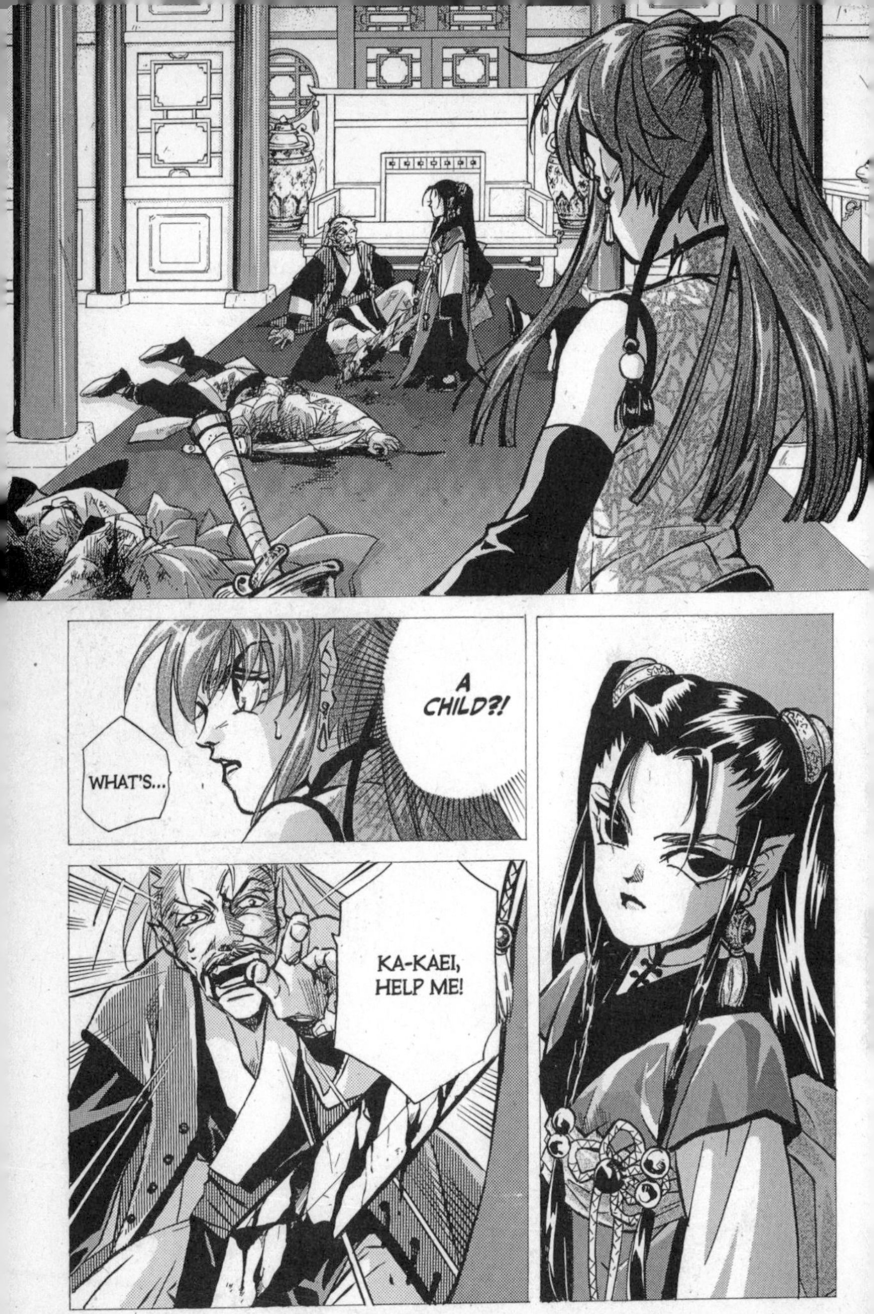
A CHILD?!
WHAT'S...
KA-KAEI, HELP ME!

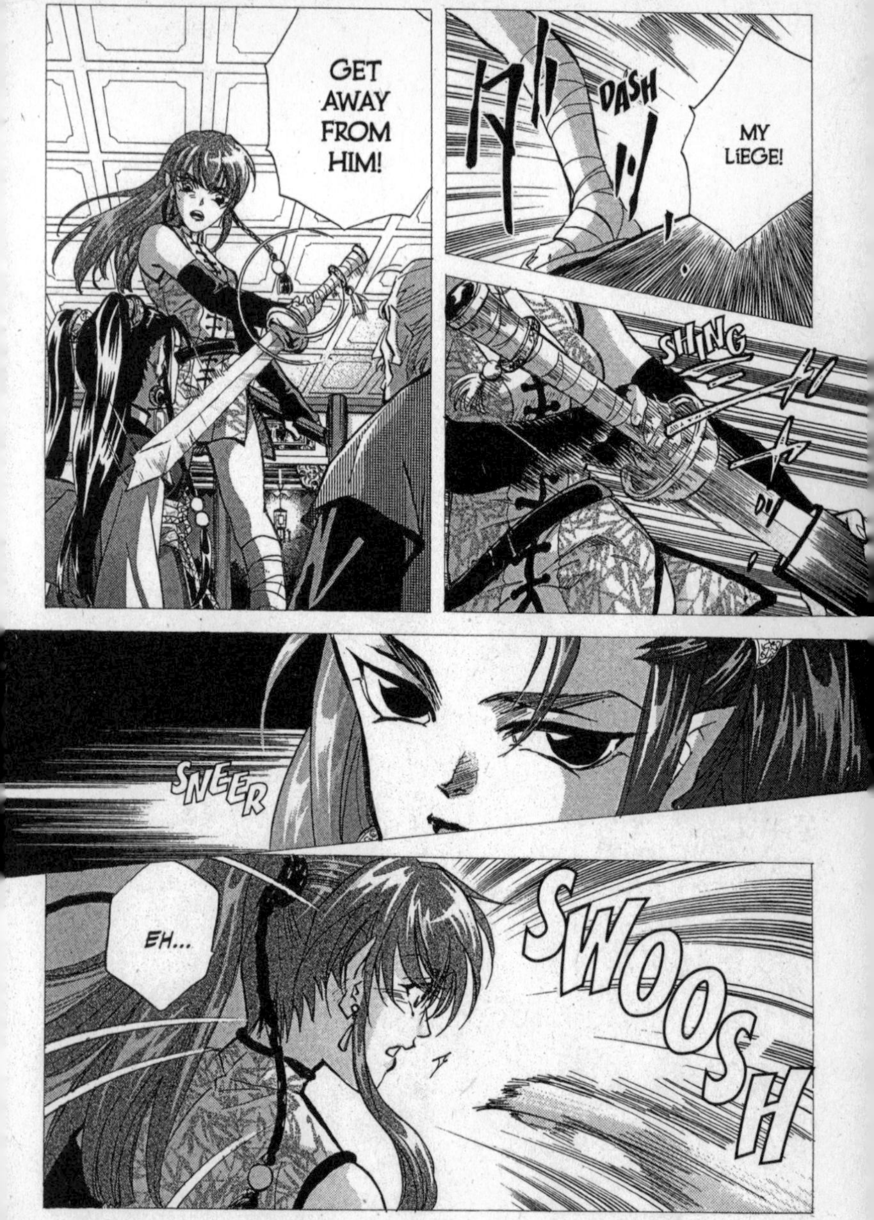
DASH
MY LIEGE!
SHING
GET AWAY FROM HIM!
SNEER
SWOOSH
EH...

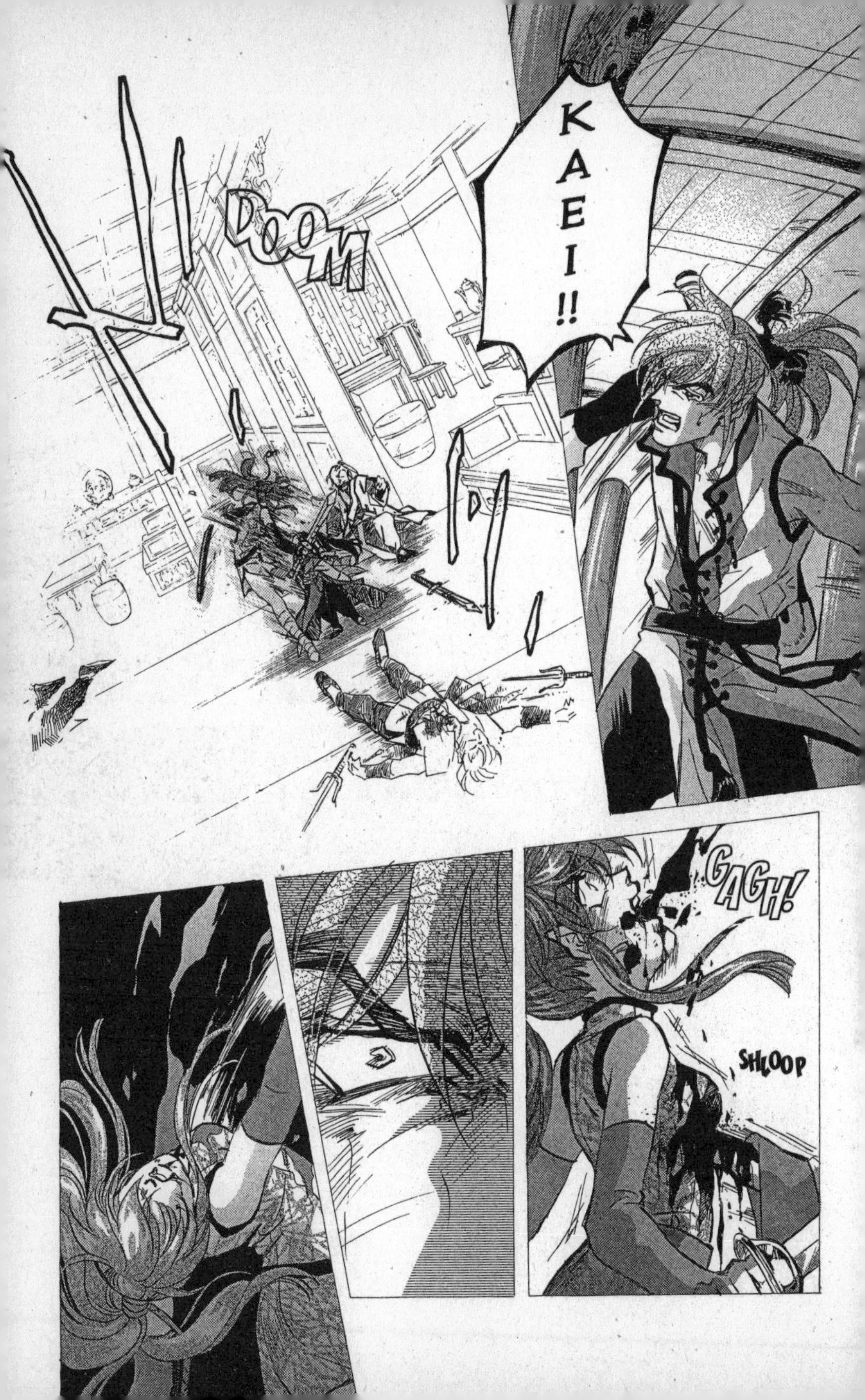
KAEI!!
DOOM
GAGH!
SHLOOP

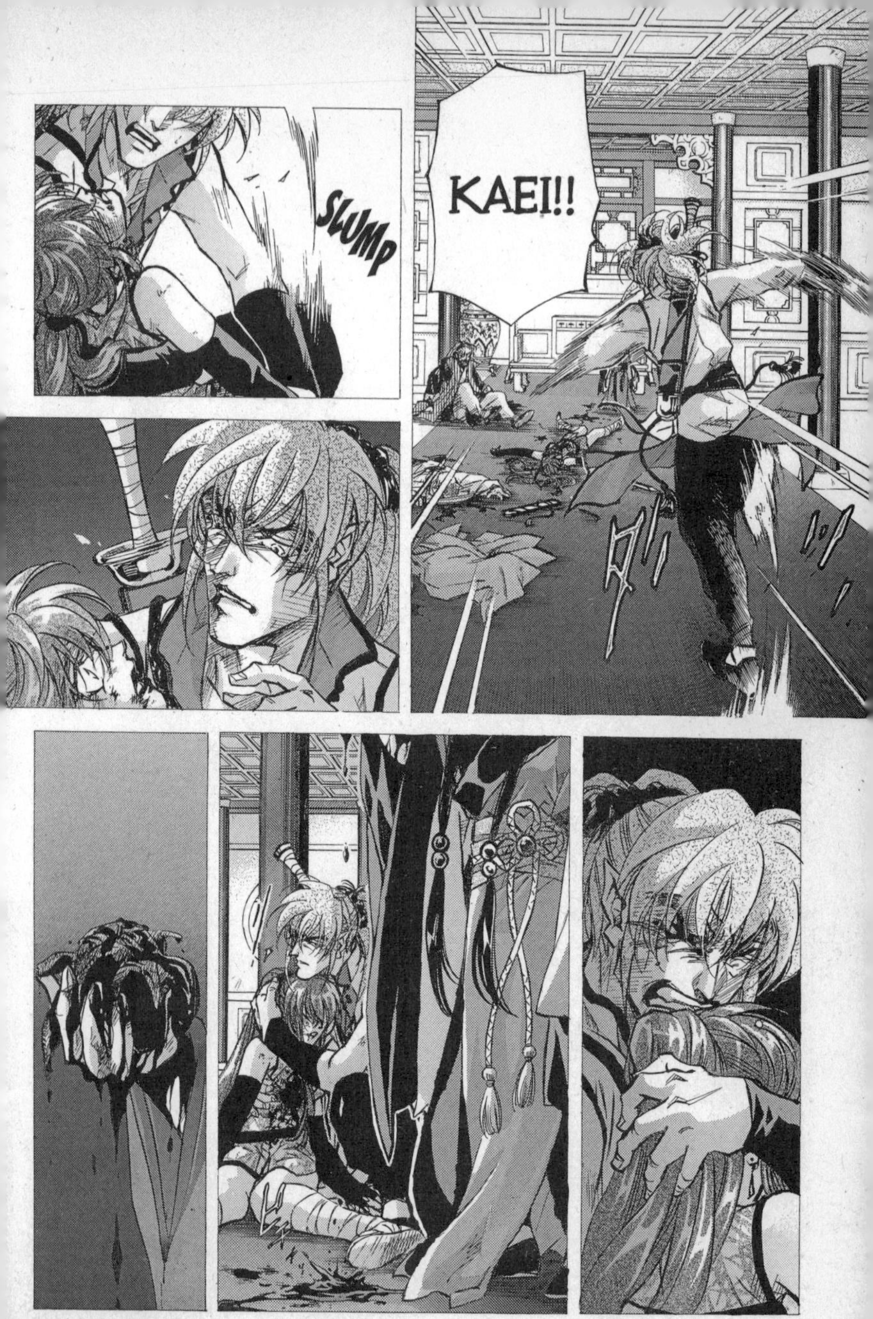
KAEI!!
SLUMP

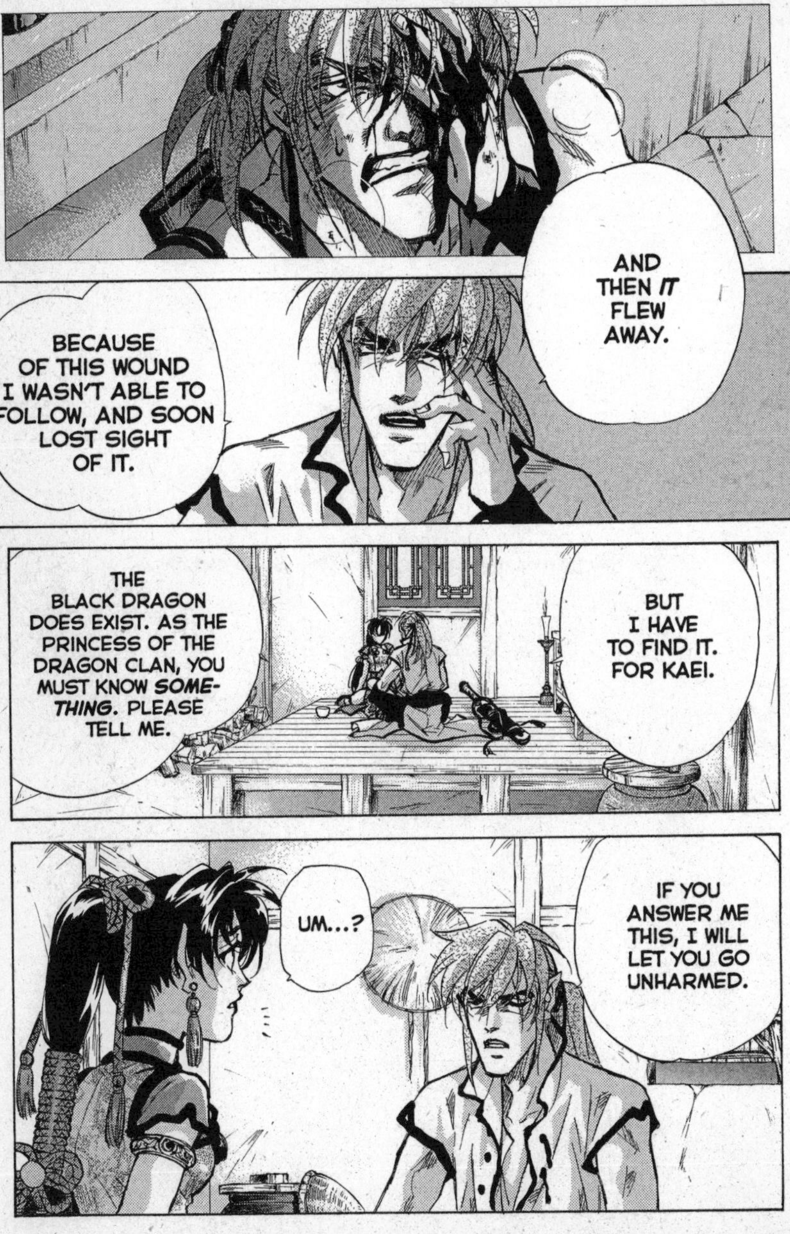
AND THEN *IT* FLEW AWAY.
BECAUSE OF THIS WOUND I WASN'T ABLE TO FOLLOW, AND SOON LOST SIGHT OF IT.
BUT I HAVE TO FIND IT. FOR KAEI.
THE BLACK DRAGON DOES EXIST. AS THE PRINCESS OF THE DRAGON CLAN, YOU MUST KNOW *SOMETHING*. PLEASE TELL ME.
IF YOU ANSWER ME THIS, I WILL LET YOU GO UNHARMED.
UM...?

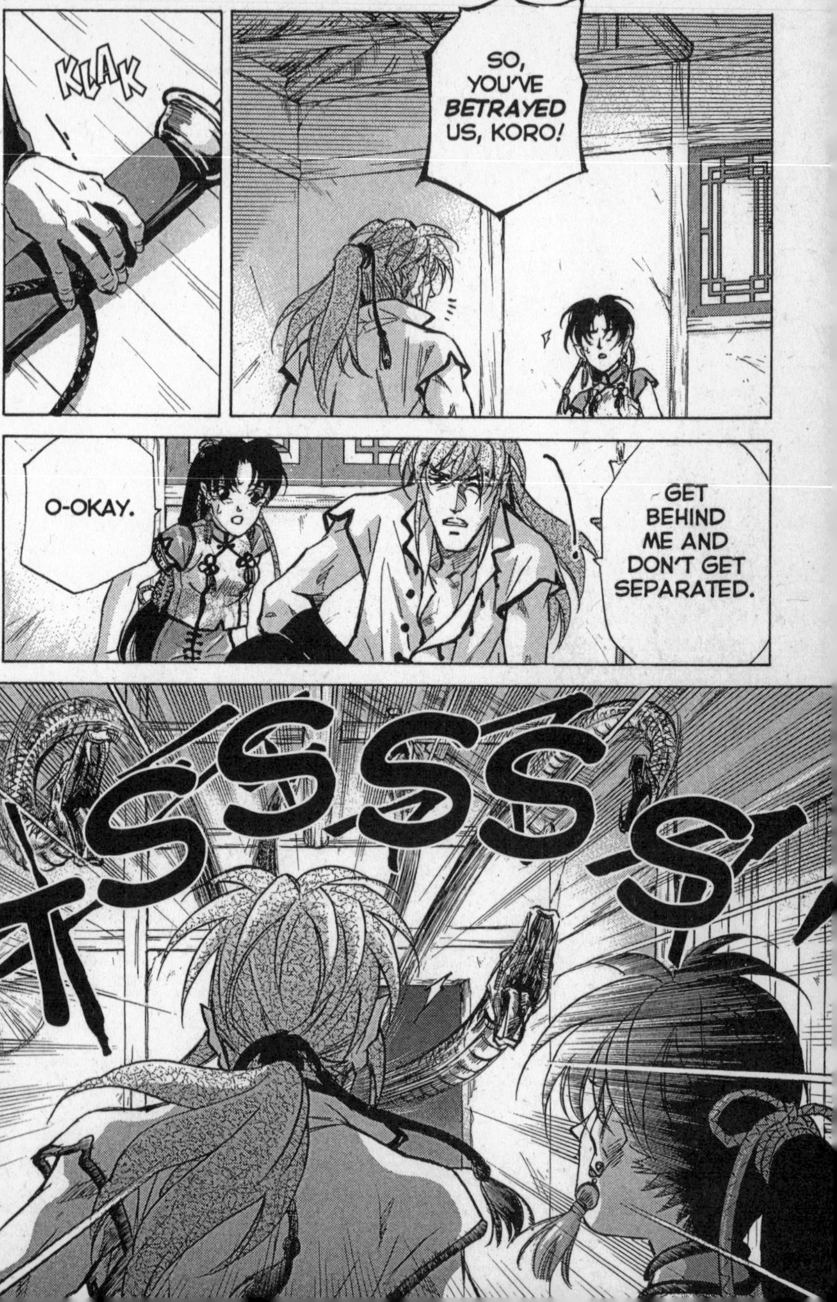
SO, YOU'VE BETRAYED US, KORO!
KLAK
GET BEHIND ME AND DON'T GET SEPARATED.
O-OKAY.
TSSSSS

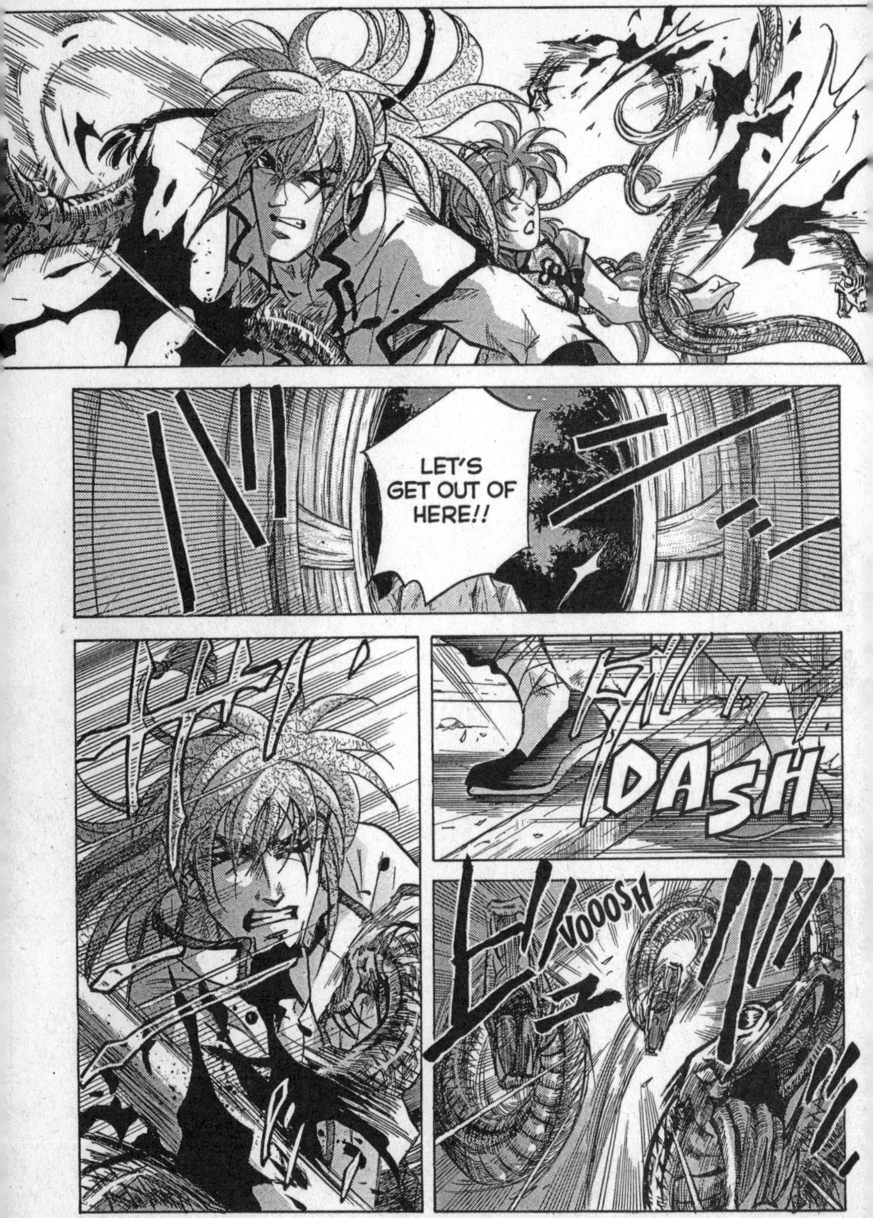
LET'S GET OUT OF HERE!!
DASH
VOOOSH

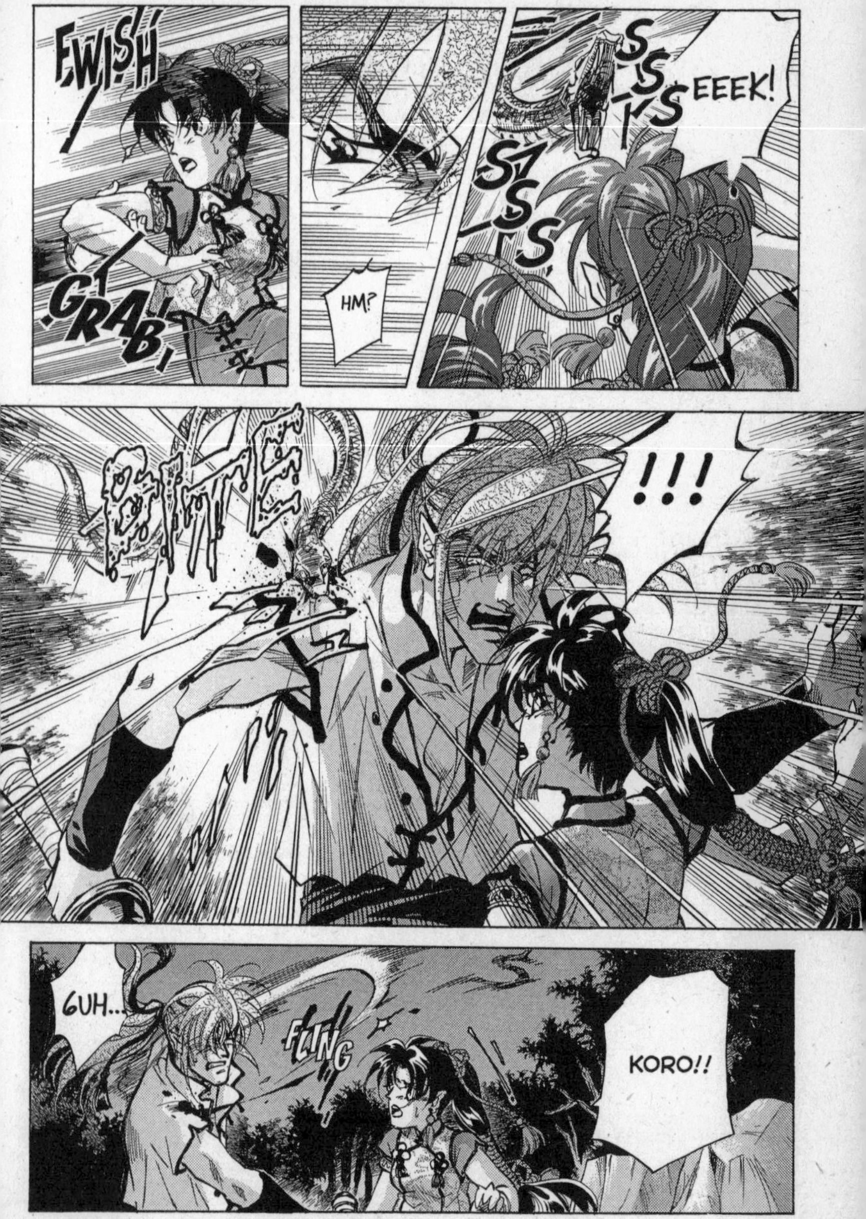
EEEK!
SSS
SSS
HM?
FWISH
GRAB
!!!
BITE
KORO!!
FLING
GUH...

WE MUST PUT TO DEATH THOSE WHO WOULD STAB US IN THE BACK. ISN'T THAT RIGHT, KORO?

HA! IT'S NOT LIKE WE WERE EVER FRIENDS, TORAJA!

I'LL DO YOU THE FAVOR OF DELIVERING THIS GIRL TO TORAO...

HM.

...YOU CAN STOP WORRYING AND DIE.

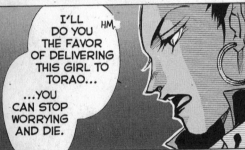

GLOW

DRAGONS OF THE FOUR ELEMENTS, HEAR MY CALL!

RISE

CLENCH

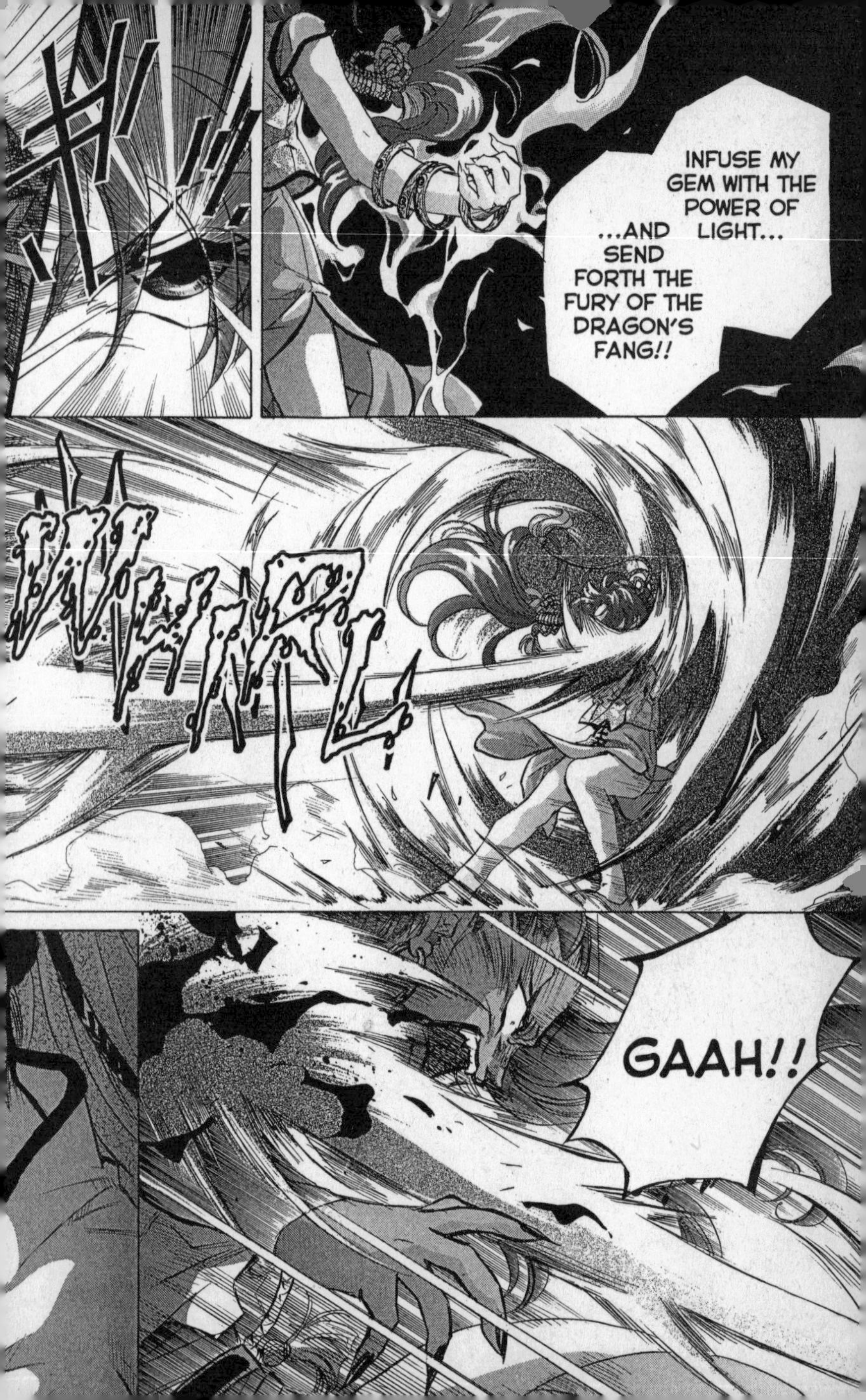
INFUSE MY GEM WITH THE POWER OF LIGHT...
...AND SEND FORTH THE FURY OF THE DRAGON'S FANG!!
WHIRL
GAAH!!

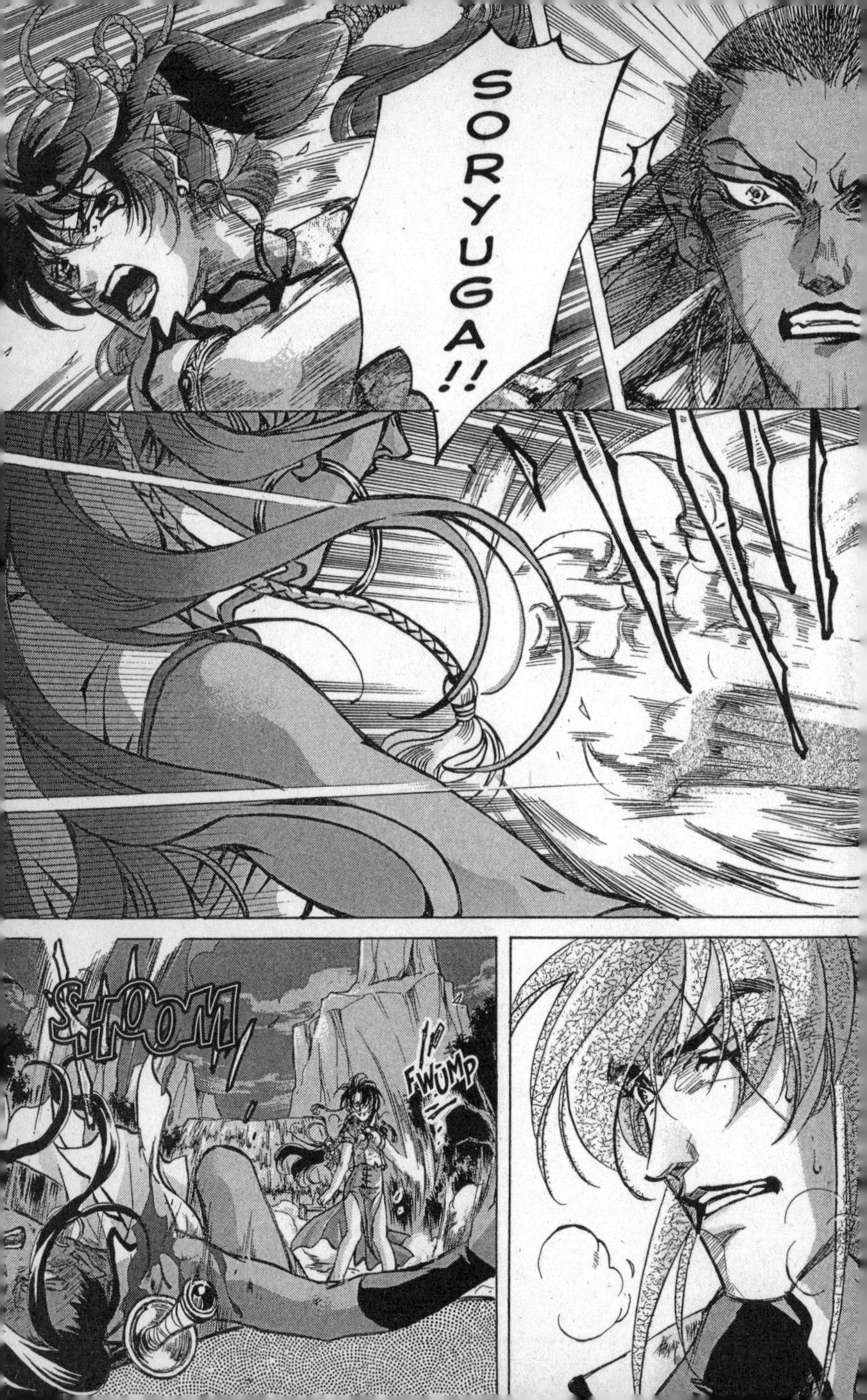
SORYUGA!!
FWUMP
SHOOM

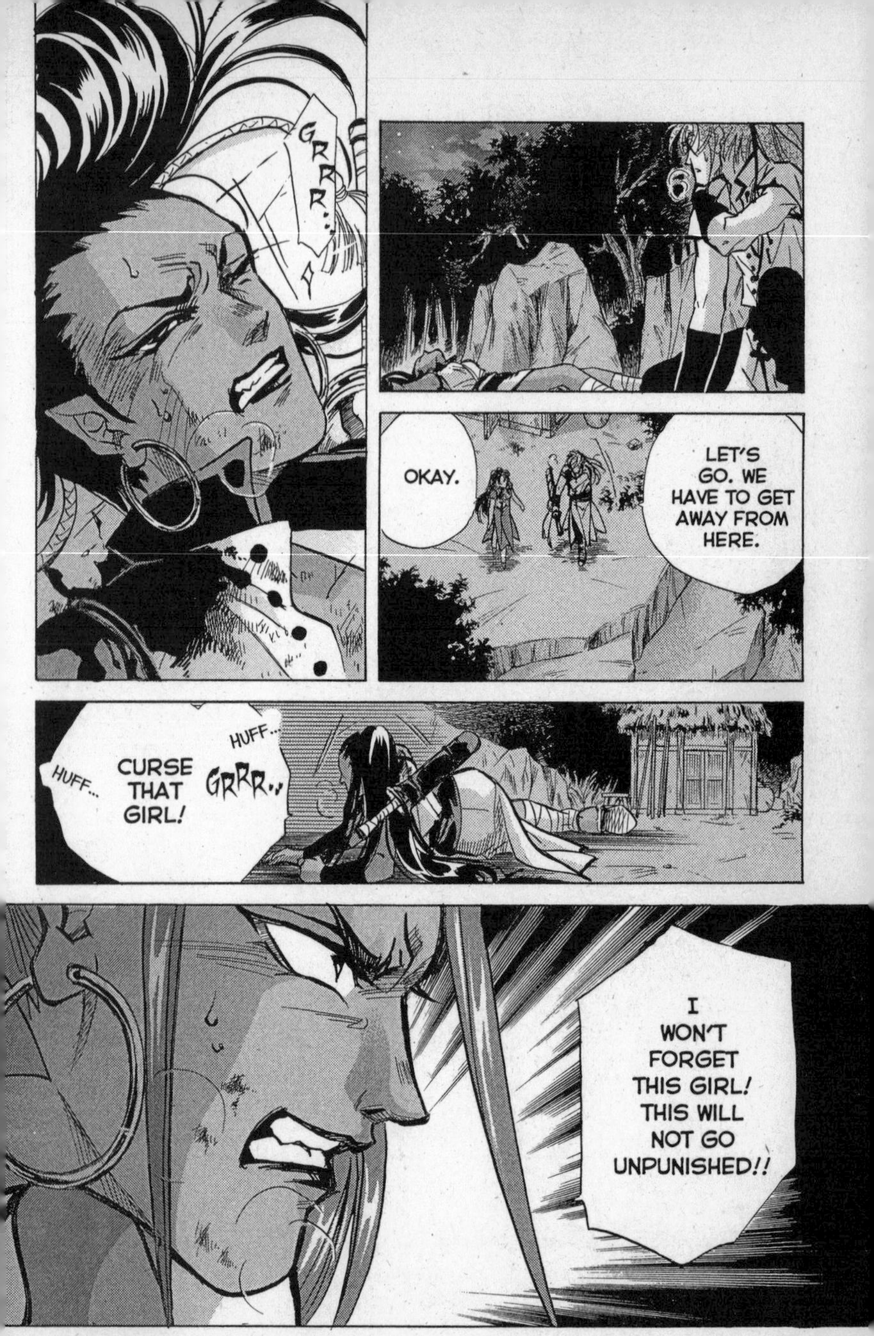

LET'S GO. WE HAVE TO GET AWAY FROM HERE.
OKAY.
GRRR...
HUFF...
GRRR..
CURSE THAT GIRL!
HUFF...
I WON'T FORGET THIS GIRL! THIS WILL NOT GO UNPUNISHED!!

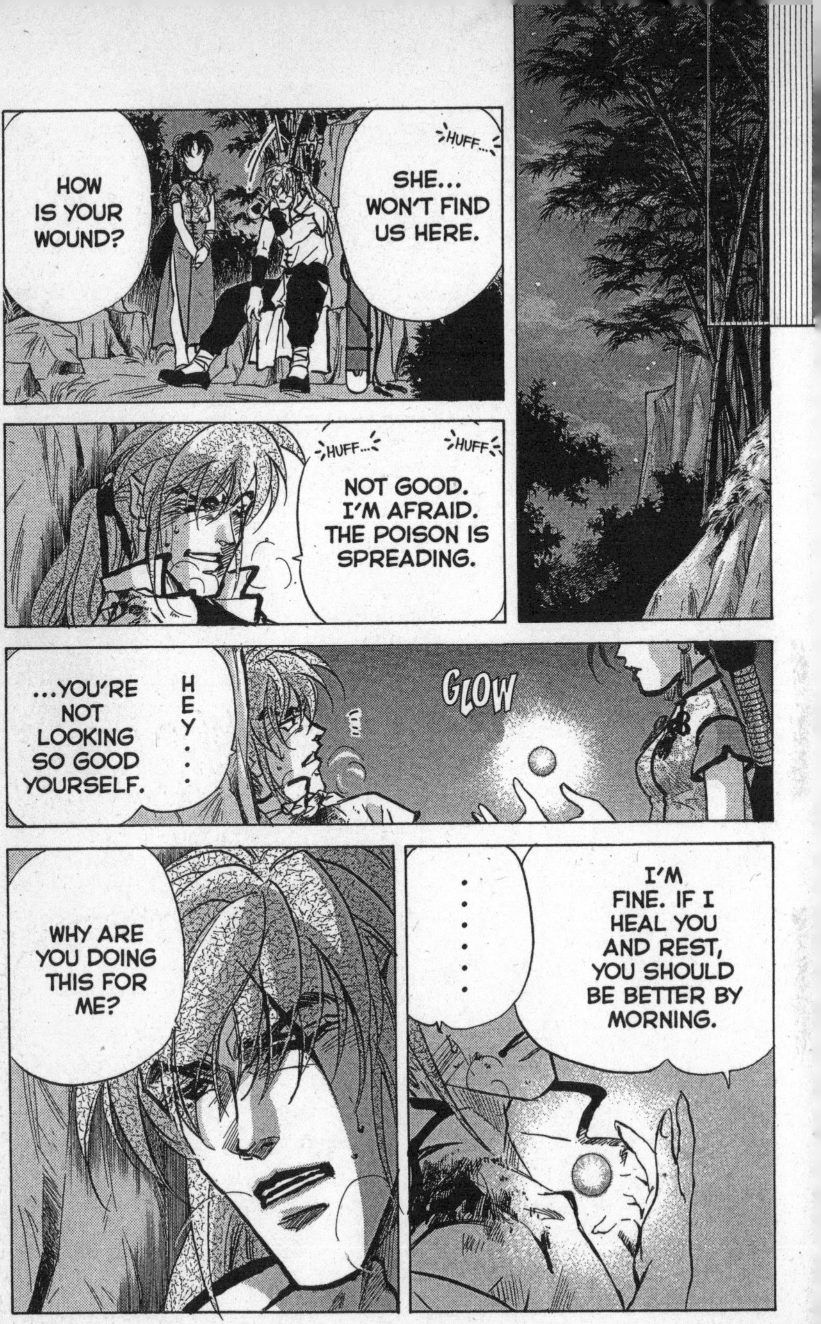
HUFF...
SHE... WON'T FIND US HERE.
HOW IS YOUR WOUND?
HUFF
HUFF...
NOT GOOD. I'M AFRAID. THE POISON IS SPREADING.
GLOW
HEY...
...YOU'RE NOT LOOKING SO GOOD YOURSELF.
I'M FINE. IF I HEAL YOU AND REST, YOU SHOULD BE BETTER BY MORNING.
......
WHY ARE YOU DOING THIS FOR ME?

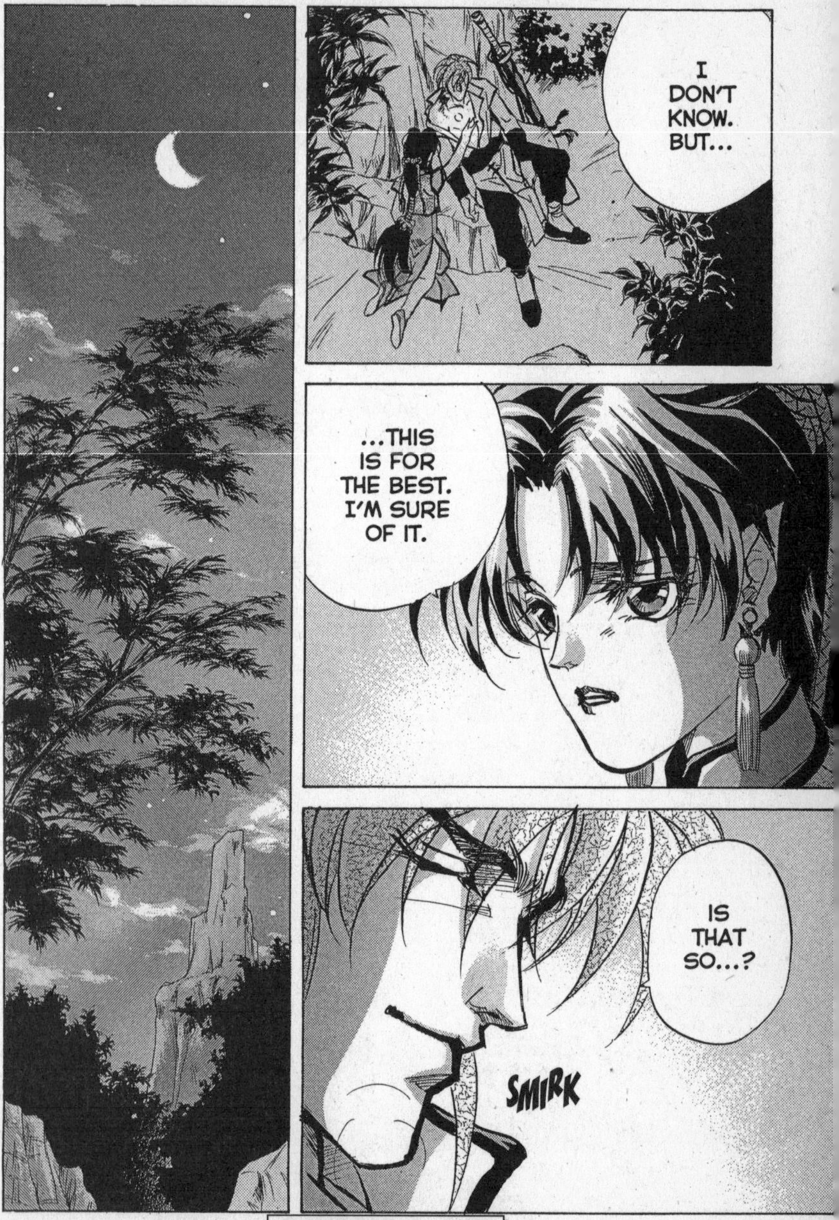
I DON'T KNOW. BUT...
...THIS IS FOR THE BEST. I'M SURE OF IT.
IS THAT SO...?
SMIRK

CHAPTER 8: END

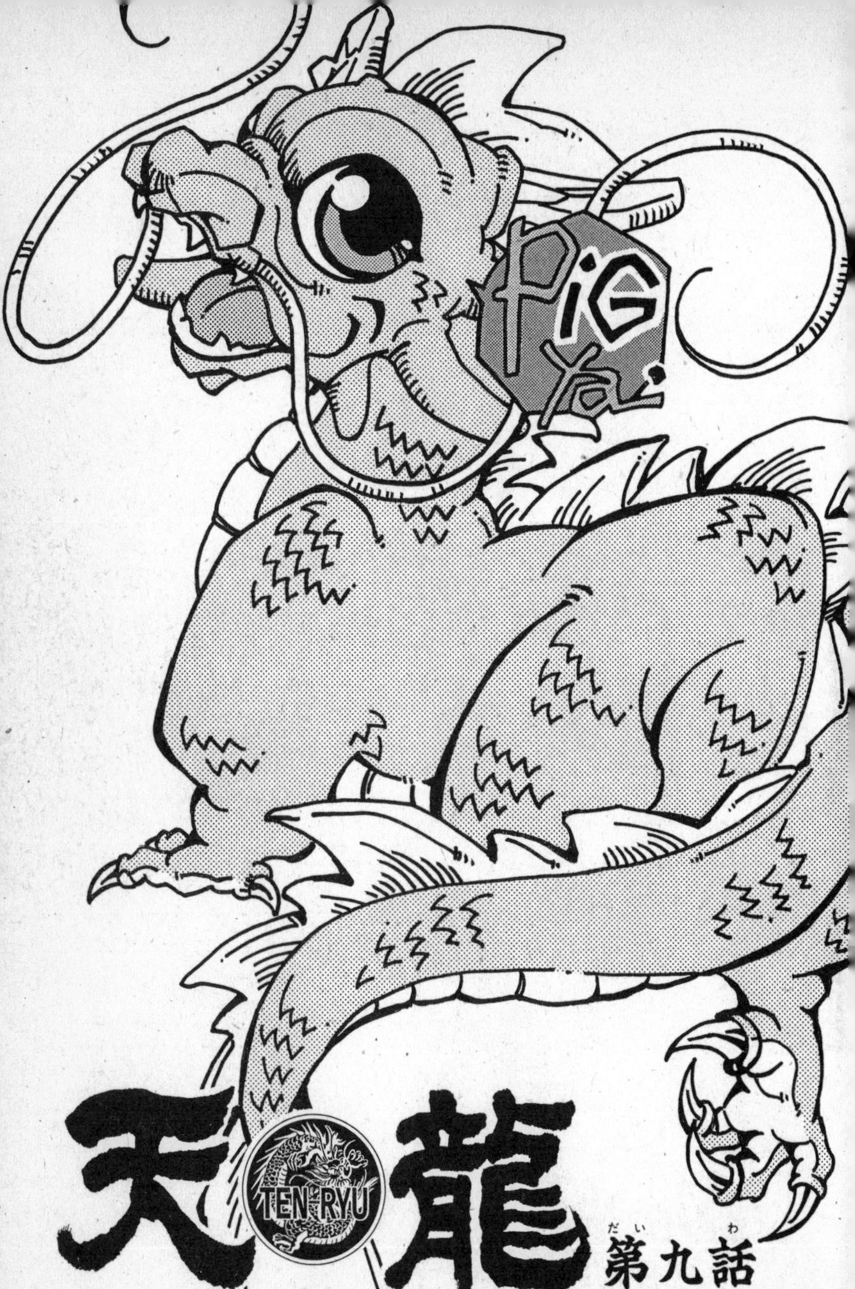
PiG
Ya.

天 TEN-RYU 龍

第九話

CHAPTER 9

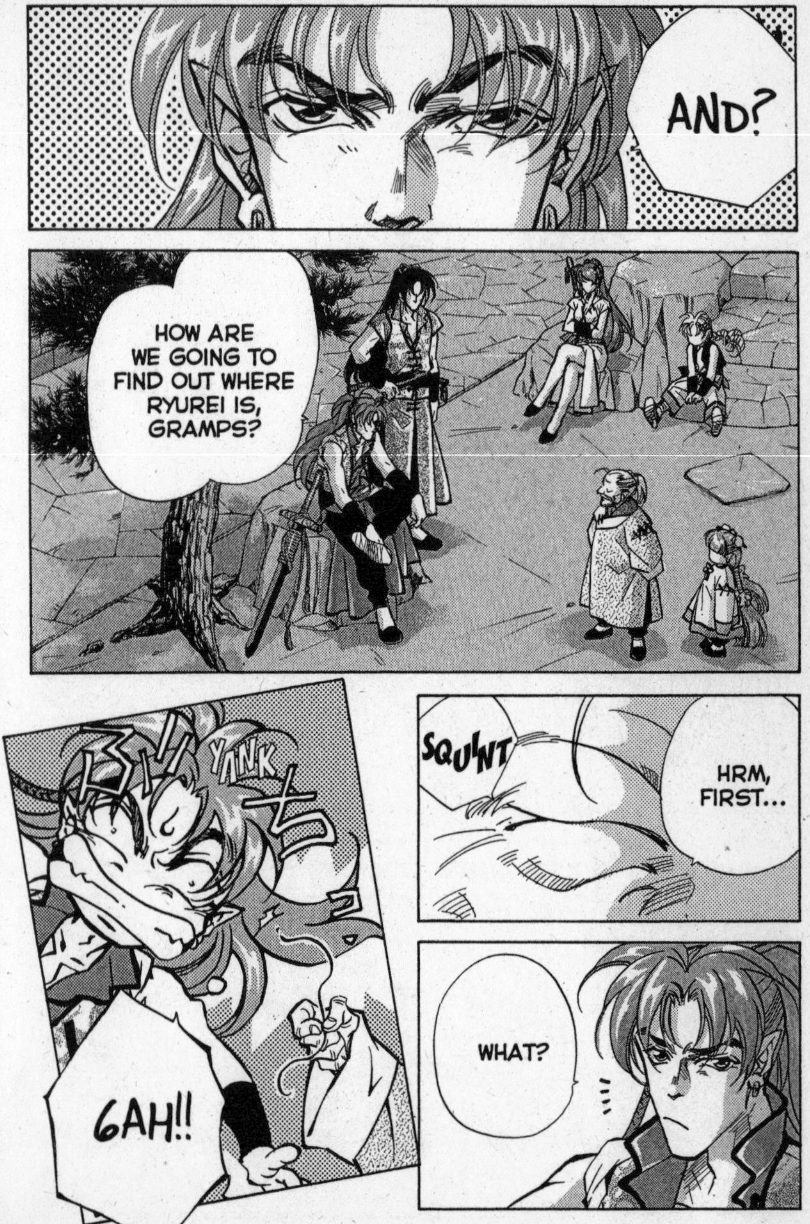
AND?
HOW ARE WE GOING TO FIND OUT WHERE RYUREI IS, GRAMPS?
SQUINT
HRM, FIRST...
WHAT?
YANK
GAH!!

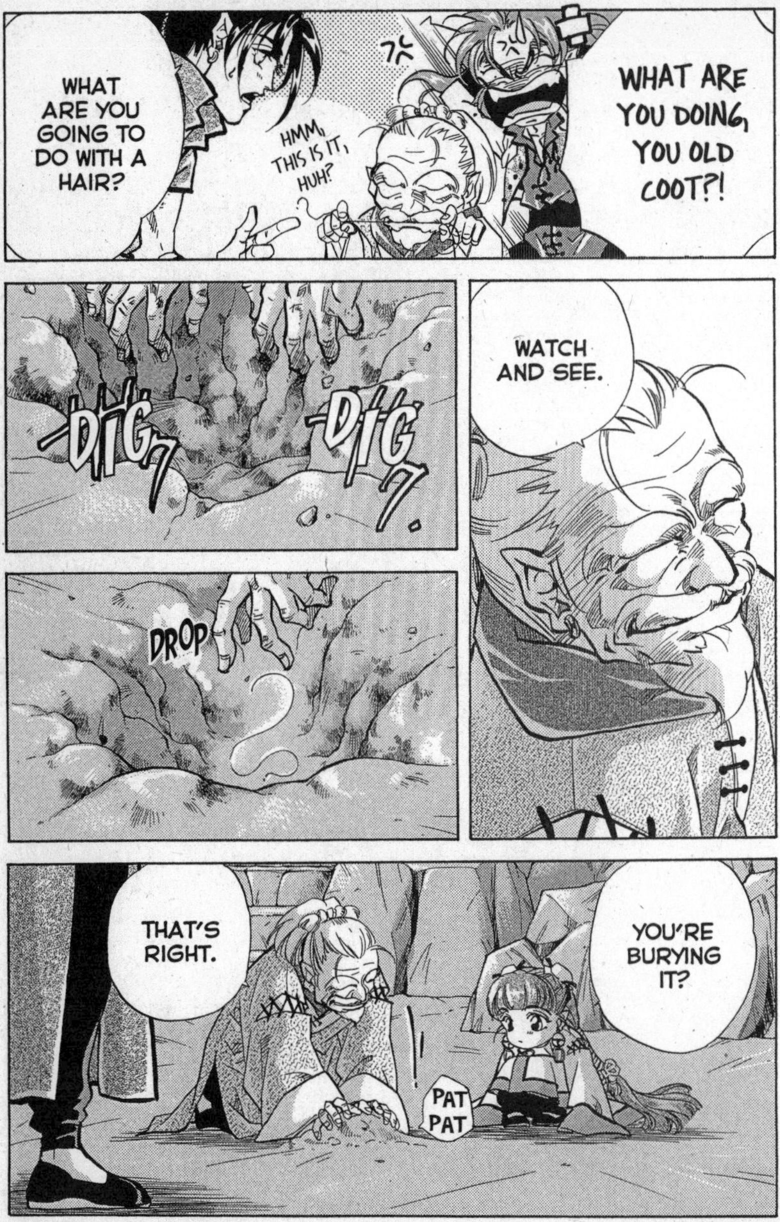
WHAT ARE YOU DOING, YOU OLD COOT?!
HMM, THIS IS IT, HUH?
WHAT ARE YOU GOING TO DO WITH A HAIR?
WATCH AND SEE.
DIG
DIG
DROP
YOU'RE BURYING IT?
PAT PAT
THAT'S RIGHT.

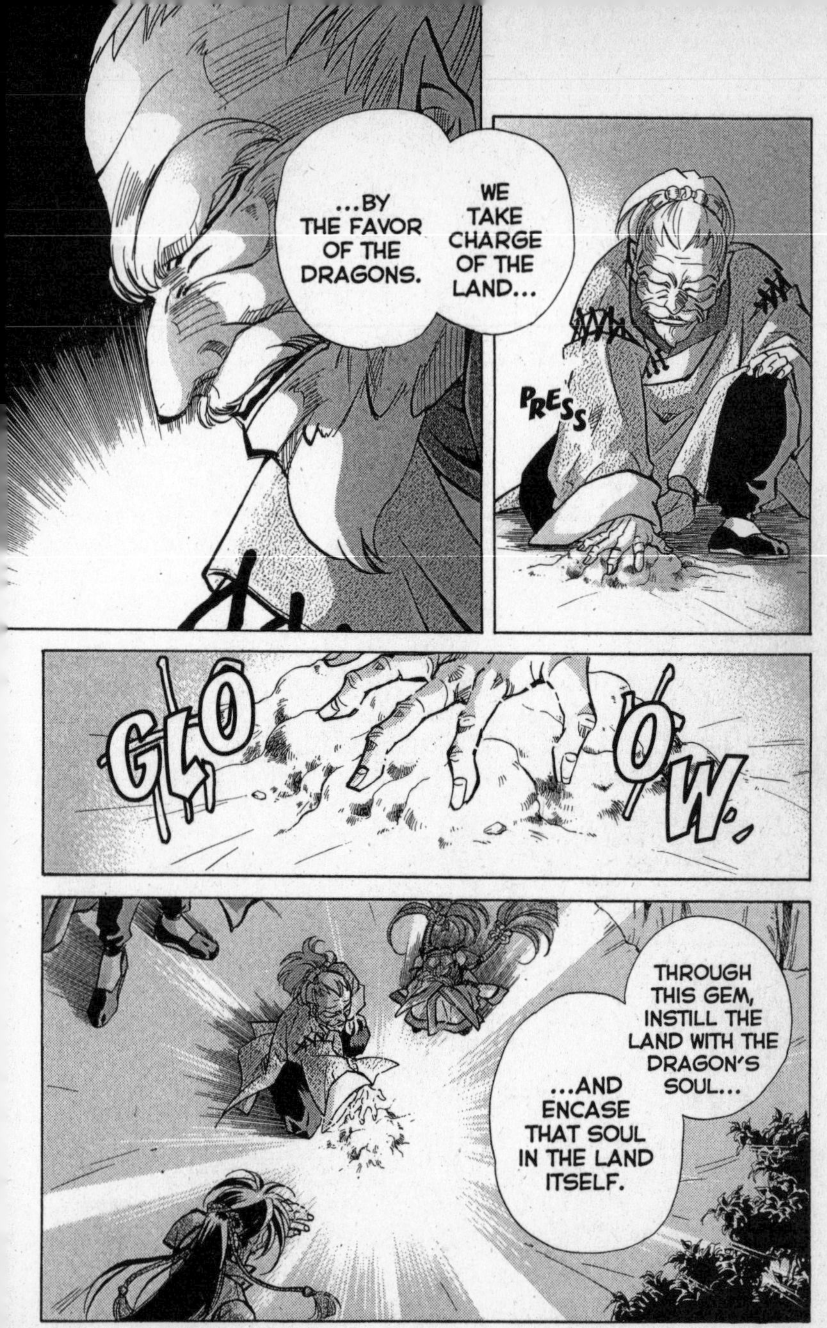
WE TAKE CHARGE OF THE LAND...
...BY THE FAVOR OF THE DRAGONS.
PRESS
GLOOW
THROUGH THIS GEM, INSTILL THE LAND WITH THE DRAGON'S SOUL...
...AND ENCASE THAT SOUL IN THE LAND ITSELF.

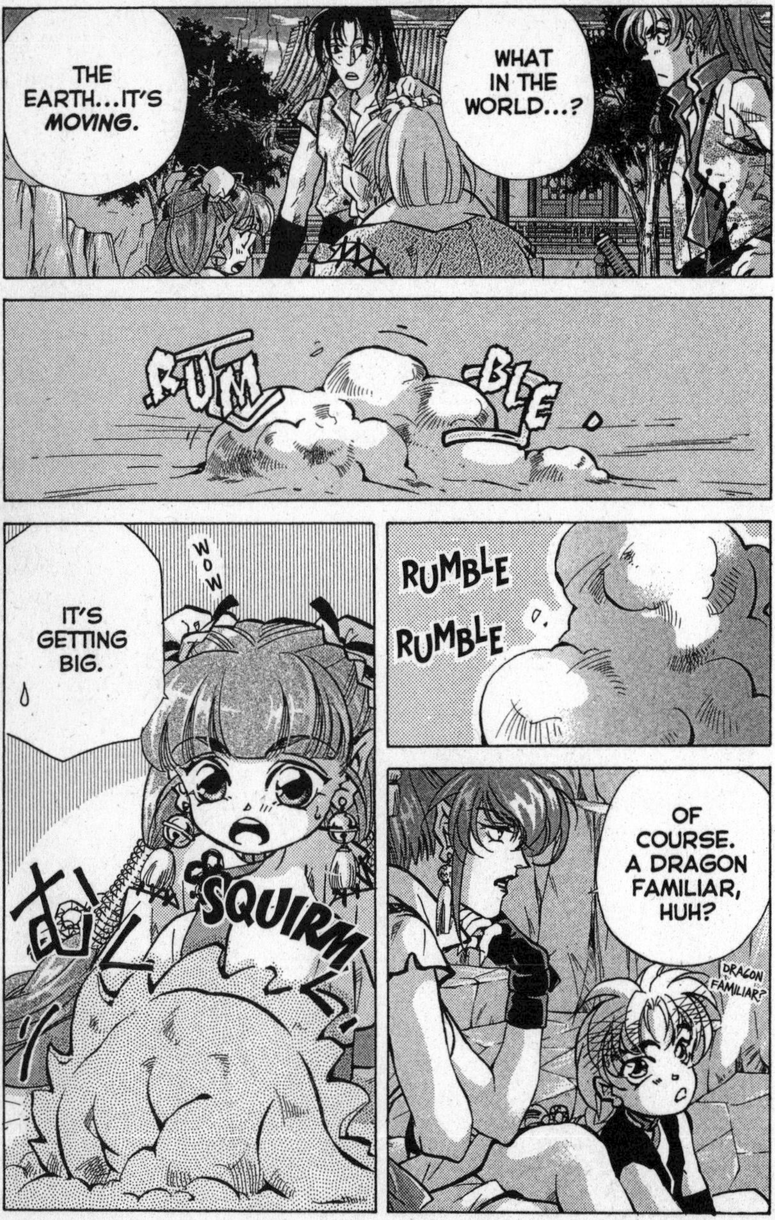
WHAT IN THE WORLD...?
THE EARTH...IT'S *MOVING.*
RUM-BLE
RUMBLE RUMBLE
OF COURSE. A DRAGON FAMILIAR, HUH?
DRAGON FAMILIAR?
WOW
IT'S GETTING BIG.
SQUIRM

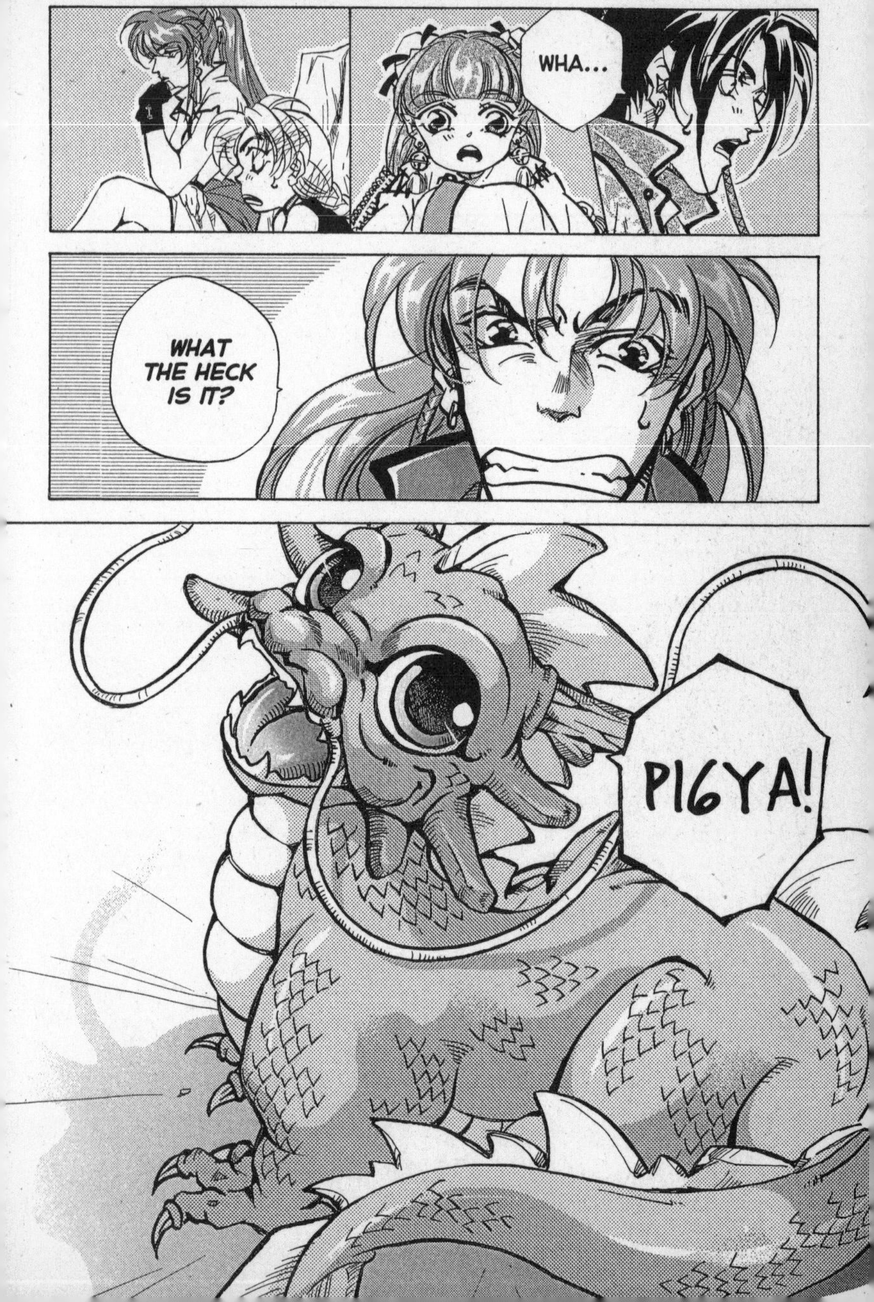
WHA...
WHAT THE HECK IS IT?
PIGYA!

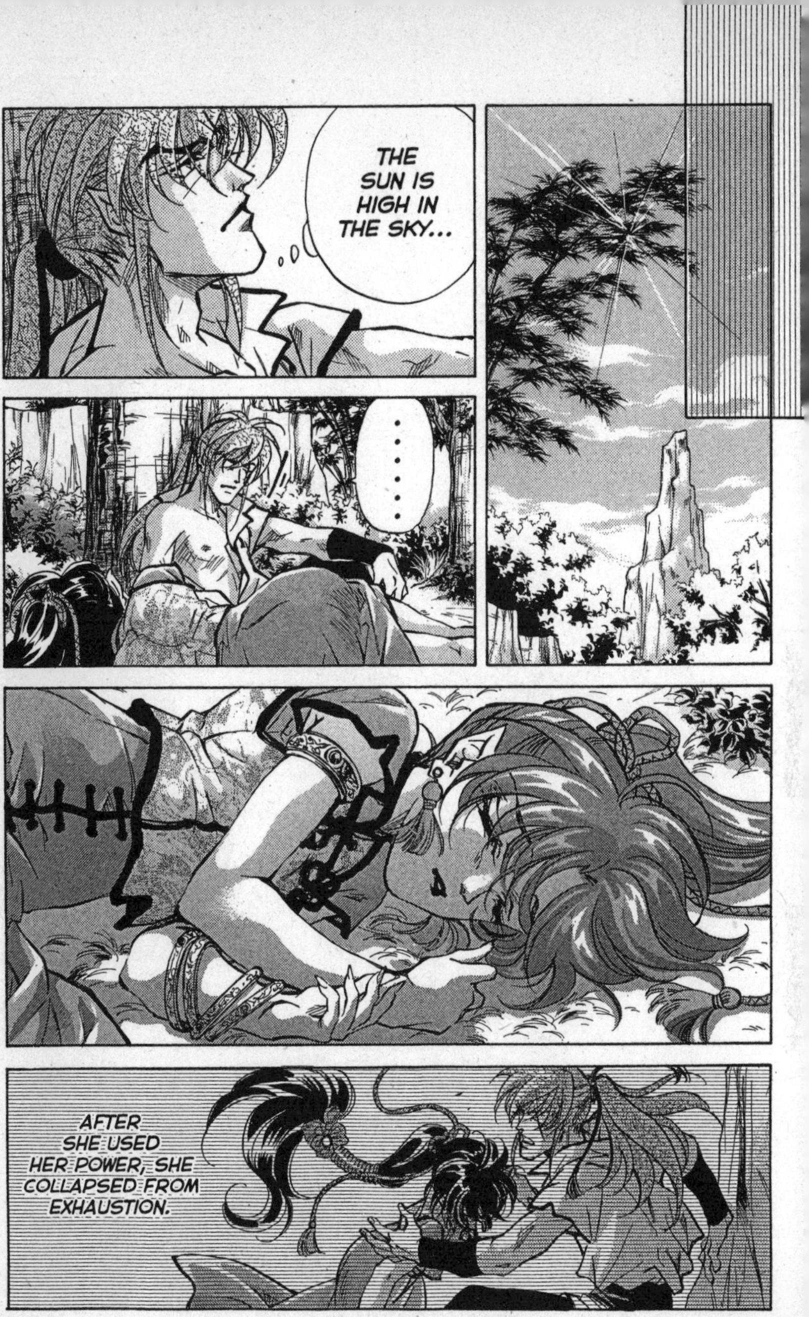
THE SUN IS HIGH IN THE SKY...
......
AFTER SHE USED HER POWER, SHE COLLAPSED FROM EXHAUSTION.

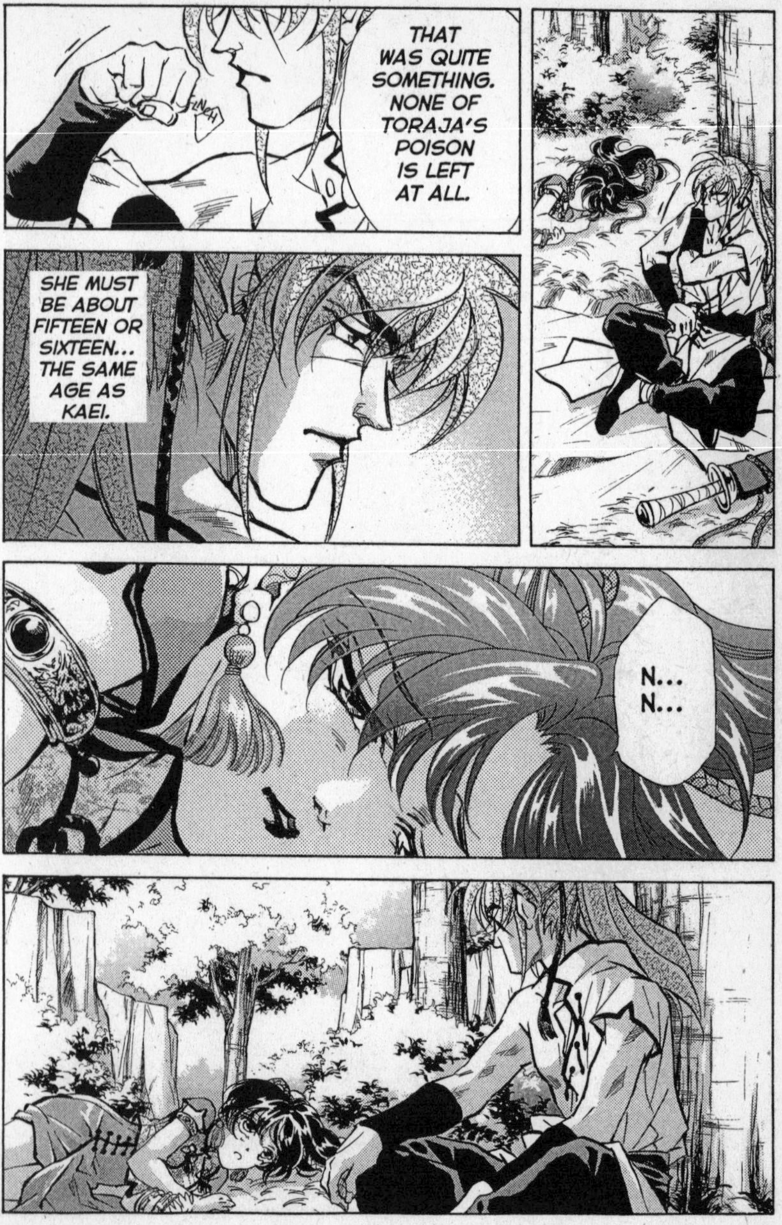
THAT WAS QUITE SOMETHING. NONE OF TORAJA'S POISON IS LEFT AT ALL.
SHE MUST BE ABOUT FIFTEEN OR SIXTEEN... THE SAME AGE AS KAEI.
N... N...

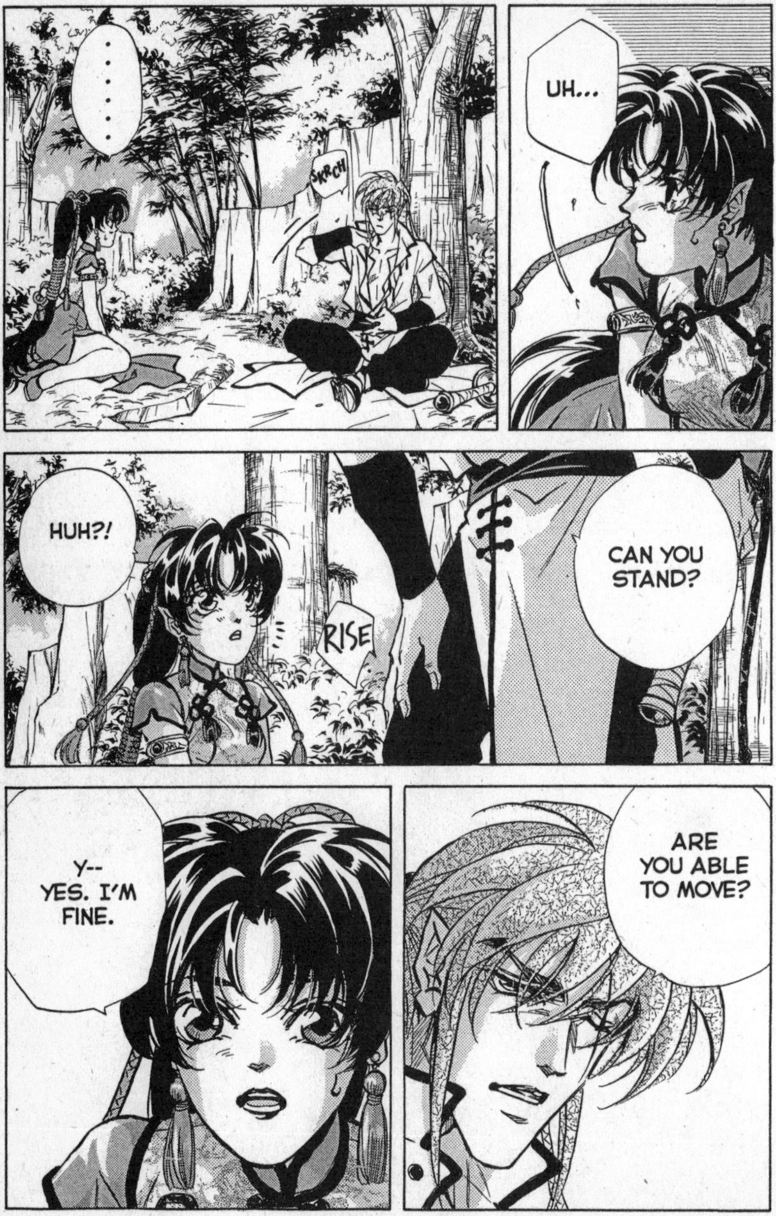
UH...
......
SKRCH
CAN YOU STAND?
RISE
HUH?!
ARE YOU ABLE TO MOVE?
Y-- YES. I'M FINE.

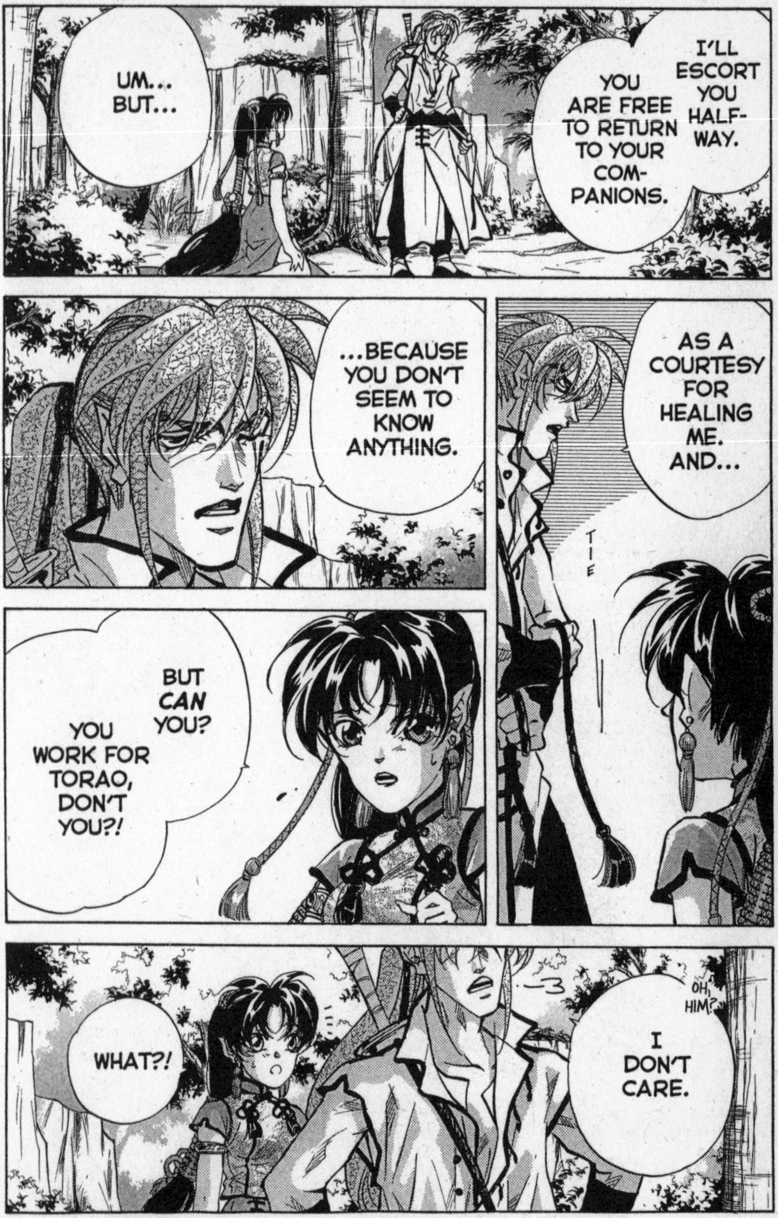
I'LL ESCORT YOU HALF-WAY.
YOU ARE FREE TO RETURN TO YOUR COM-PANIONS.
UM... BUT...
AS A COURTESY FOR HEALING ME. AND...
TIE
...BECAUSE YOU DON'T SEEM TO KNOW ANYTHING.
BUT *CAN* YOU?
YOU WORK FOR TORAO, DON'T YOU?!
OH, HIM?
I DON'T CARE.
WHAT?!

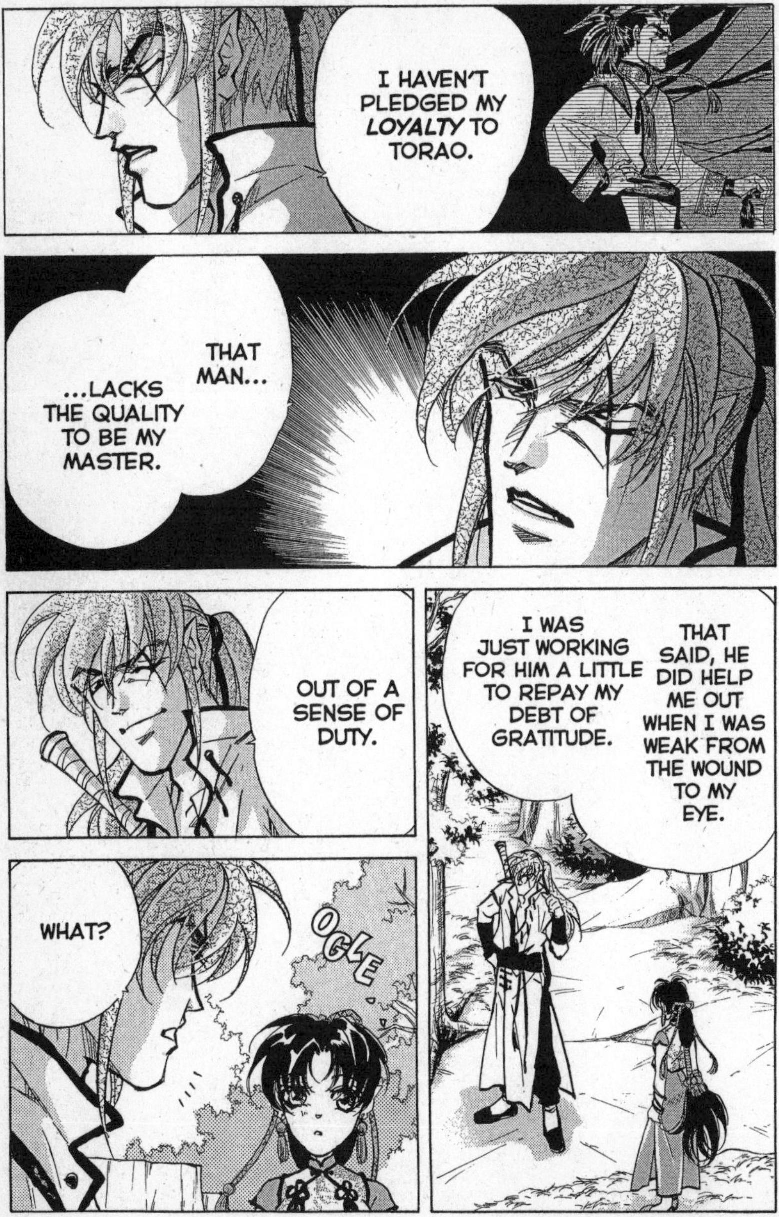
I HAVEN'T PLEDGED MY *LOYALTY* TO TORAO.
THAT MAN...
...LACKS THE QUALITY TO BE MY MASTER.
THAT SAID, HE DID HELP ME OUT WHEN I WAS WEAK FROM THE WOUND TO MY EYE.
I WAS JUST WORKING FOR HIM A LITTLE TO REPAY MY DEBT OF GRATITUDE.
OUT OF A SENSE OF DUTY.
WHAT?
OGLE

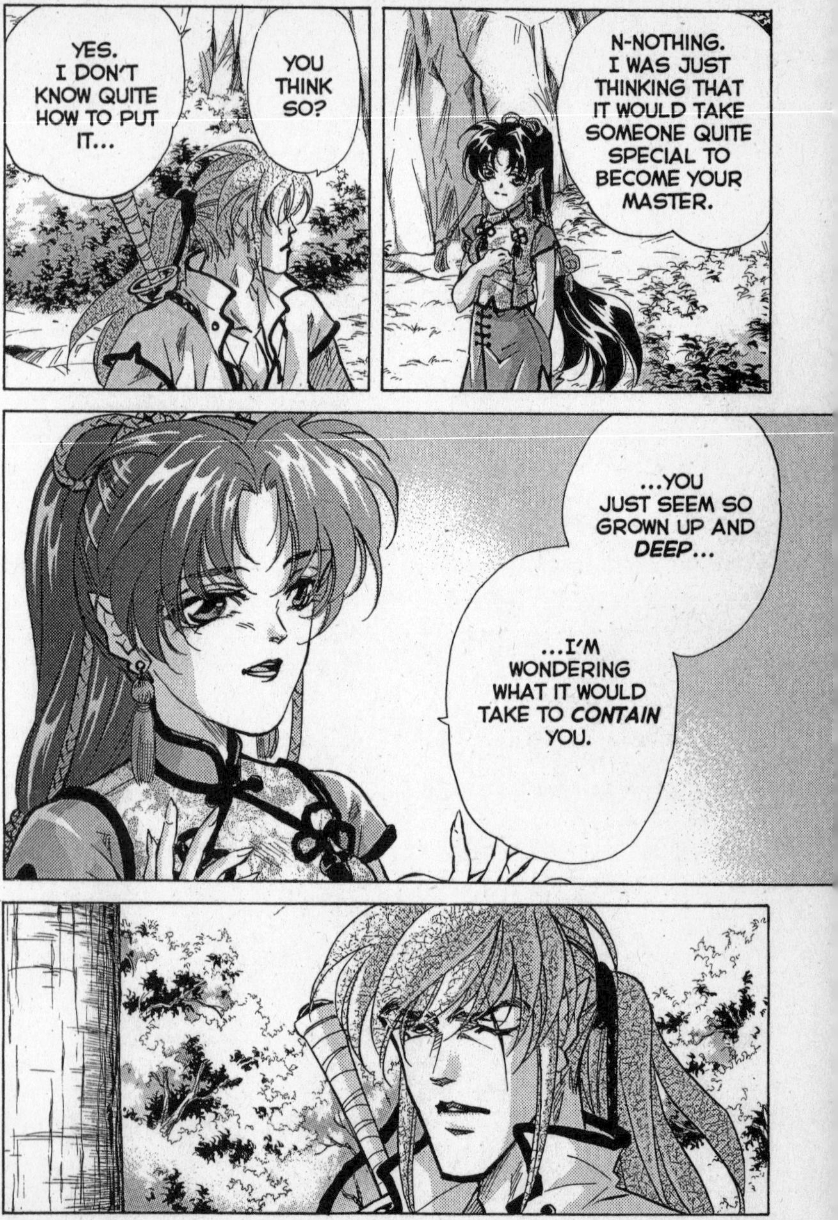
N-NOTHING. I WAS JUST THINKING THAT IT WOULD TAKE SOMEONE QUITE SPECIAL TO BECOME YOUR MASTER.
YOU THINK SO?
YES. I DON'T KNOW QUITE HOW TO PUT IT...
...YOU JUST SEEM SO GROWN UP AND *DEEP*...
...I'M WONDERING WHAT IT WOULD TAKE TO *CONTAIN* YOU.

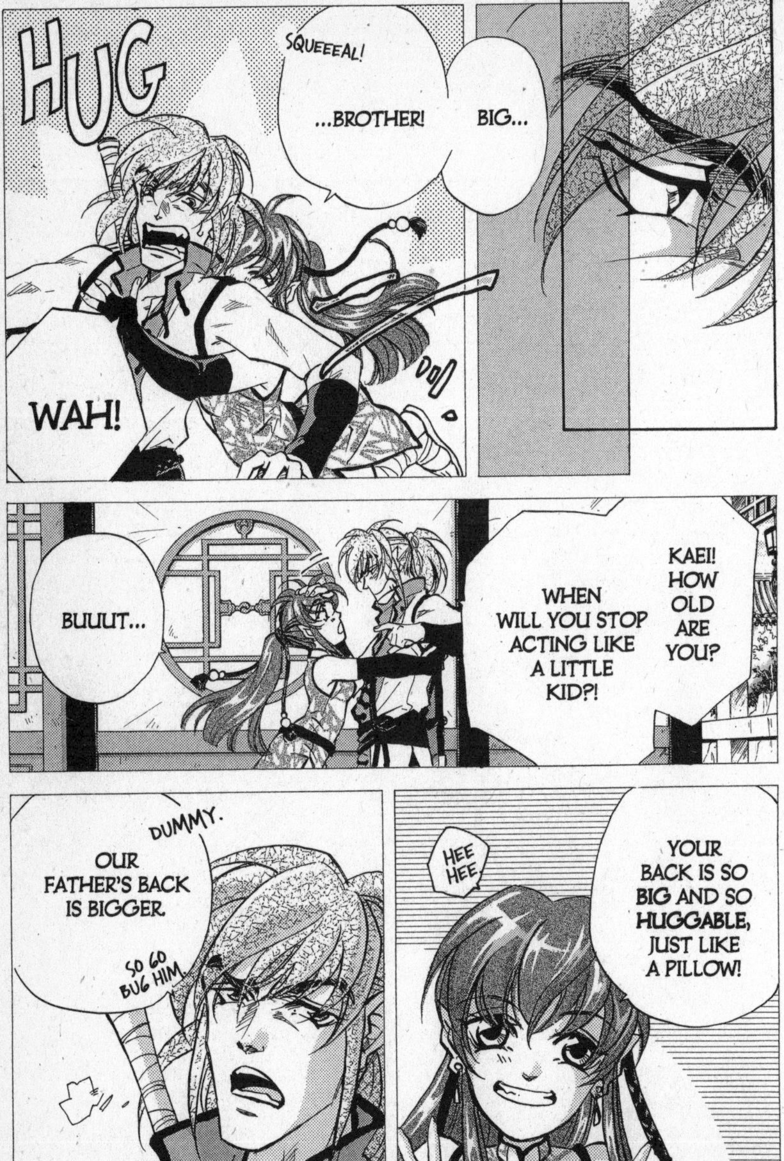
BIG...
...BROTHER!
SQUEEEAL!
HUG
WAH!
KAEI! HOW OLD ARE YOU?
WHEN WILL YOU STOP ACTING LIKE A LITTLE KID?!
BUUUT...
YOUR BACK IS SO BIG AND SO HUGGABLE, JUST LIKE A PILLOW!
HEE HEE
DUMMY.
OUR FATHER'S BACK IS BIGGER.
SO GO BUG HIM.

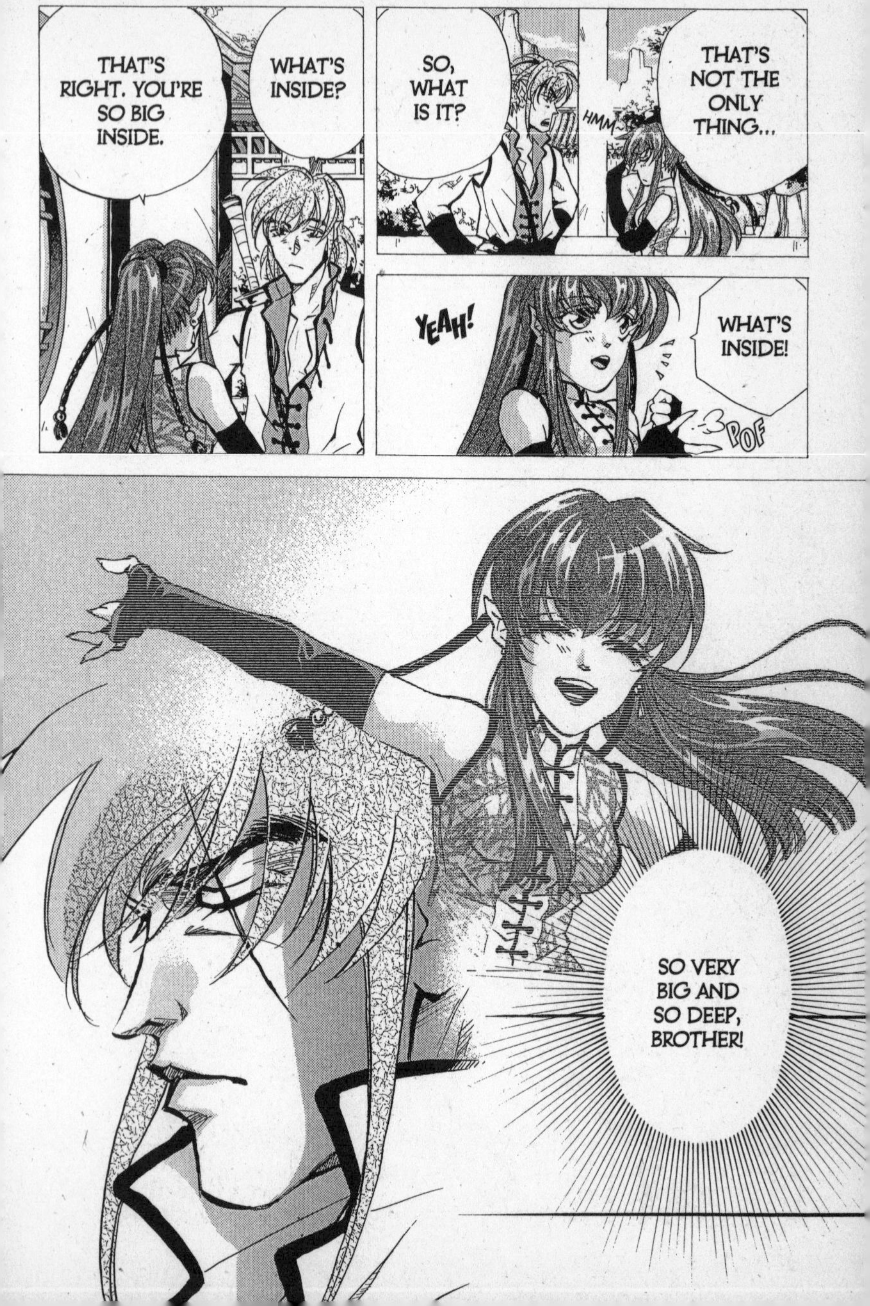
THAT'S RIGHT. YOU'RE SO BIG INSIDE.
WHAT'S INSIDE?
SO, WHAT IS IT?
HMM
THAT'S NOT THE ONLY THING...
YEAH!
WHAT'S INSIDE!
POF
SO VERY BIG AND SO DEEP, BROTHER!

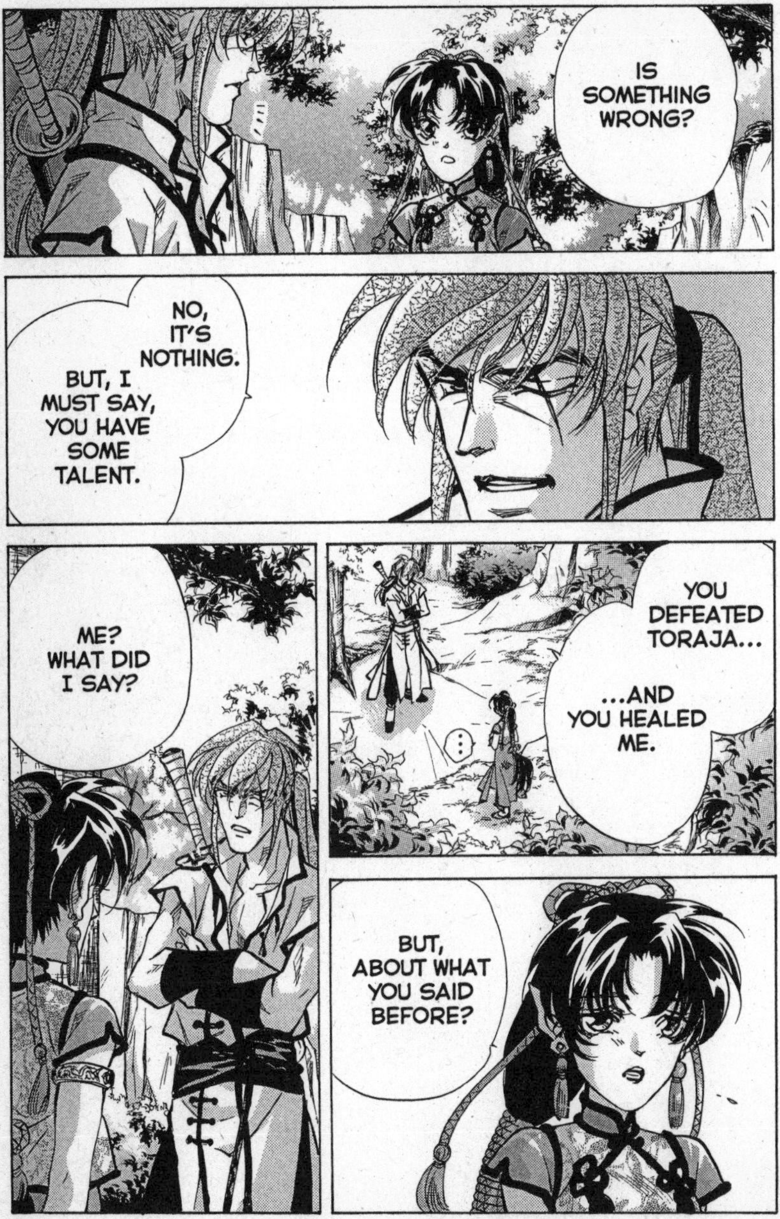

IS SOMETHING WRONG?
...
NO, IT'S NOTHING.
BUT, I MUST SAY, YOU HAVE SOME TALENT.
YOU DEFEATED TORAJA...
...AND YOU HEALED ME.
...
BUT, ABOUT WHAT YOU SAID BEFORE?
ME? WHAT DID I SAY?

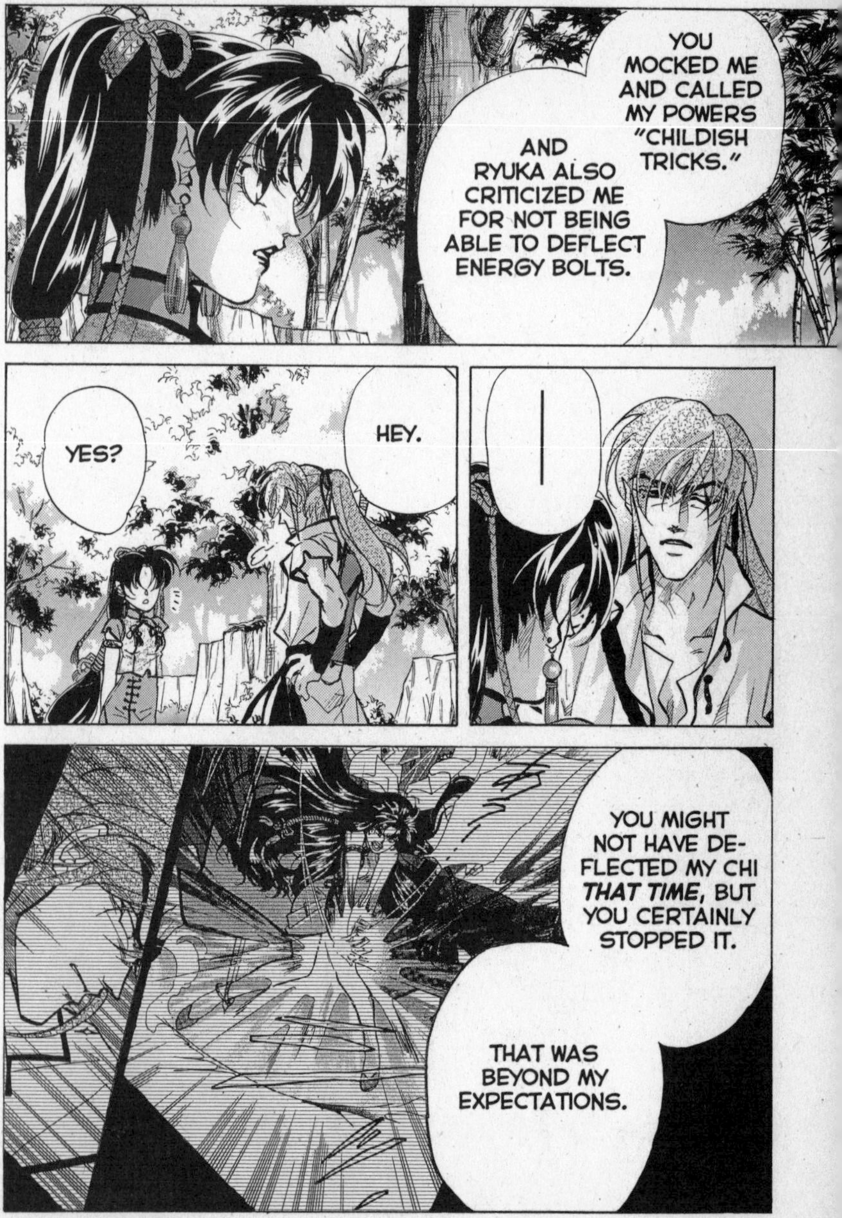
YOU MOCKED ME AND CALLED MY POWERS "CHILDISH TRICKS."
AND RYUKA ALSO CRITICIZED ME FOR NOT BEING ABLE TO DEFLECT ENERGY BOLTS.
—
HEY.
YES?
YOU MIGHT NOT HAVE DE-FLECTED MY CHI *THAT TIME*, BUT YOU CERTAINLY STOPPED IT.
THAT WAS BEYOND MY EXPECTATIONS.

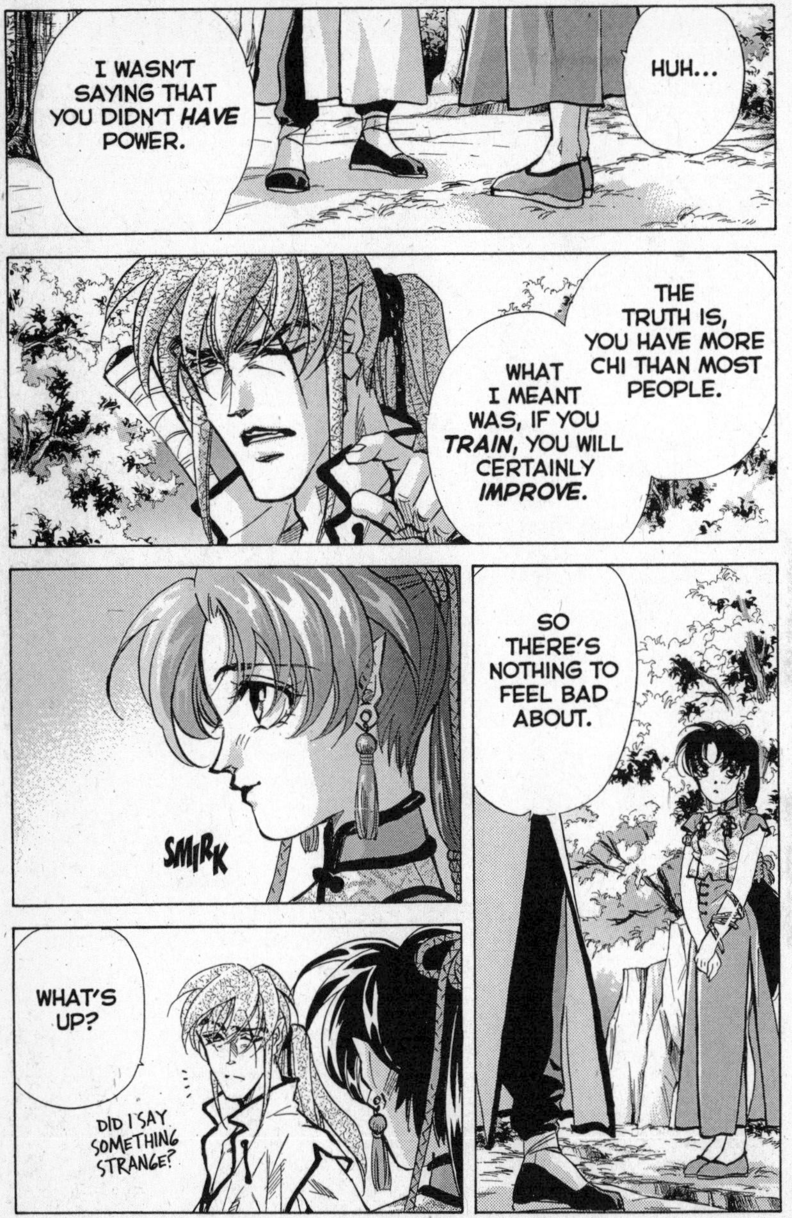
HUH...
I WASN'T SAYING THAT YOU DIDN'T *HAVE* POWER.
THE TRUTH IS, YOU HAVE MORE CHI THAN MOST PEOPLE.
WHAT I MEANT WAS, IF YOU *TRAIN*, YOU WILL CERTAINLY *IMPROVE*.
SO THERE'S NOTHING TO FEEL BAD ABOUT.
SMIRK
WHAT'S UP?
DID I SAY SOMETHING STRANGE?

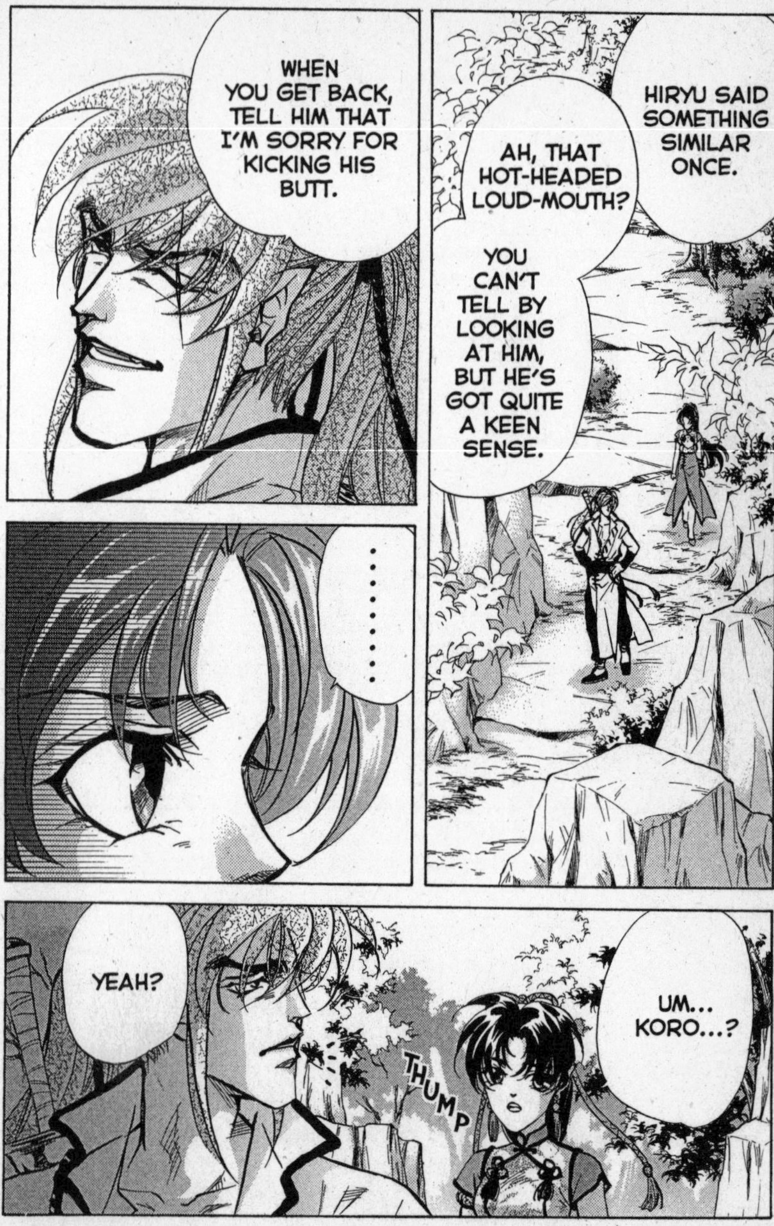
HIRYU SAID SOMETHING SIMILAR ONCE.
AH, THAT HOT-HEADED LOUD-MOUTH?
YOU CAN'T TELL BY LOOKING AT HIM, BUT HE'S GOT QUITE A KEEN SENSE.
WHEN YOU GET BACK, TELL HIM THAT I'M SORRY FOR KICKING HIS BUTT.
....
UM... KORO...?
THUMP
YEAH?

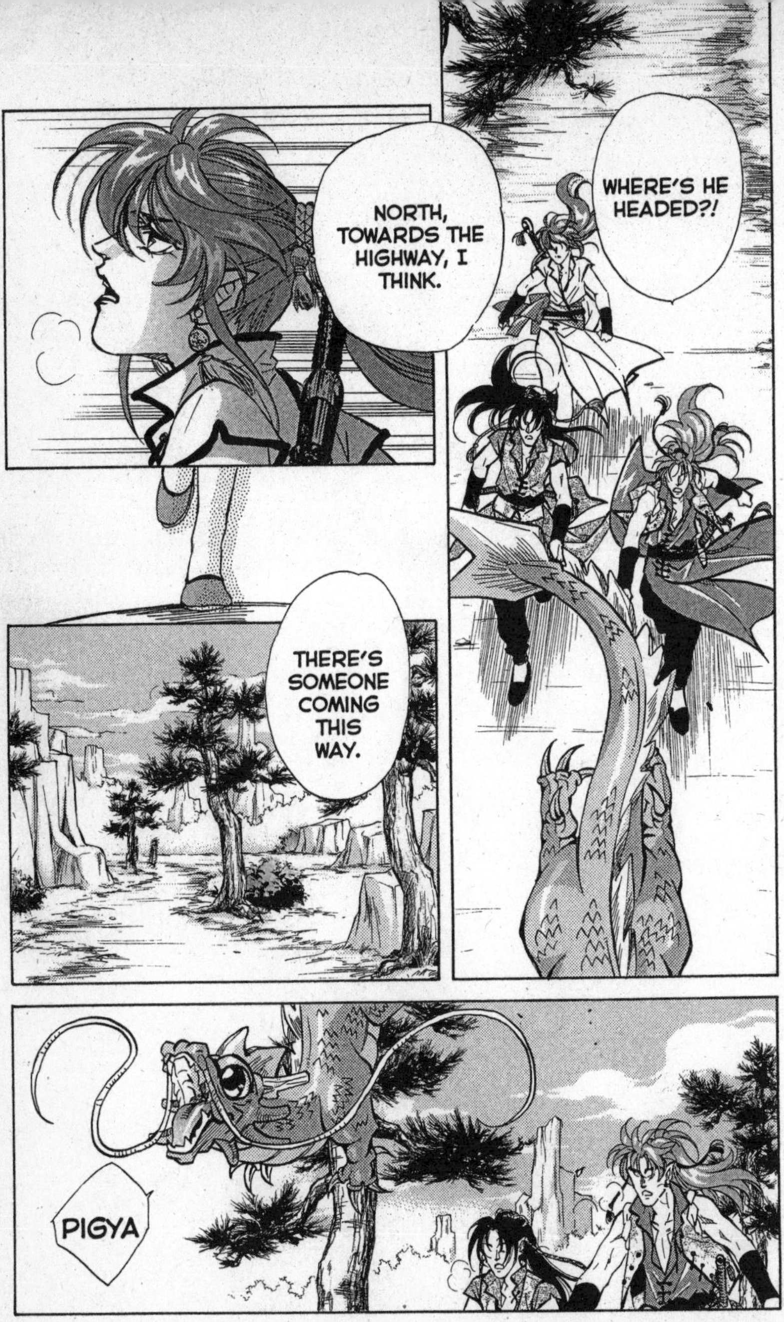
WHERE'S HE HEADED?!
NORTH, TOWARDS THE HIGHWAY, I THINK.
THERE'S SOMEONE COMING THIS WAY.
PIGYA

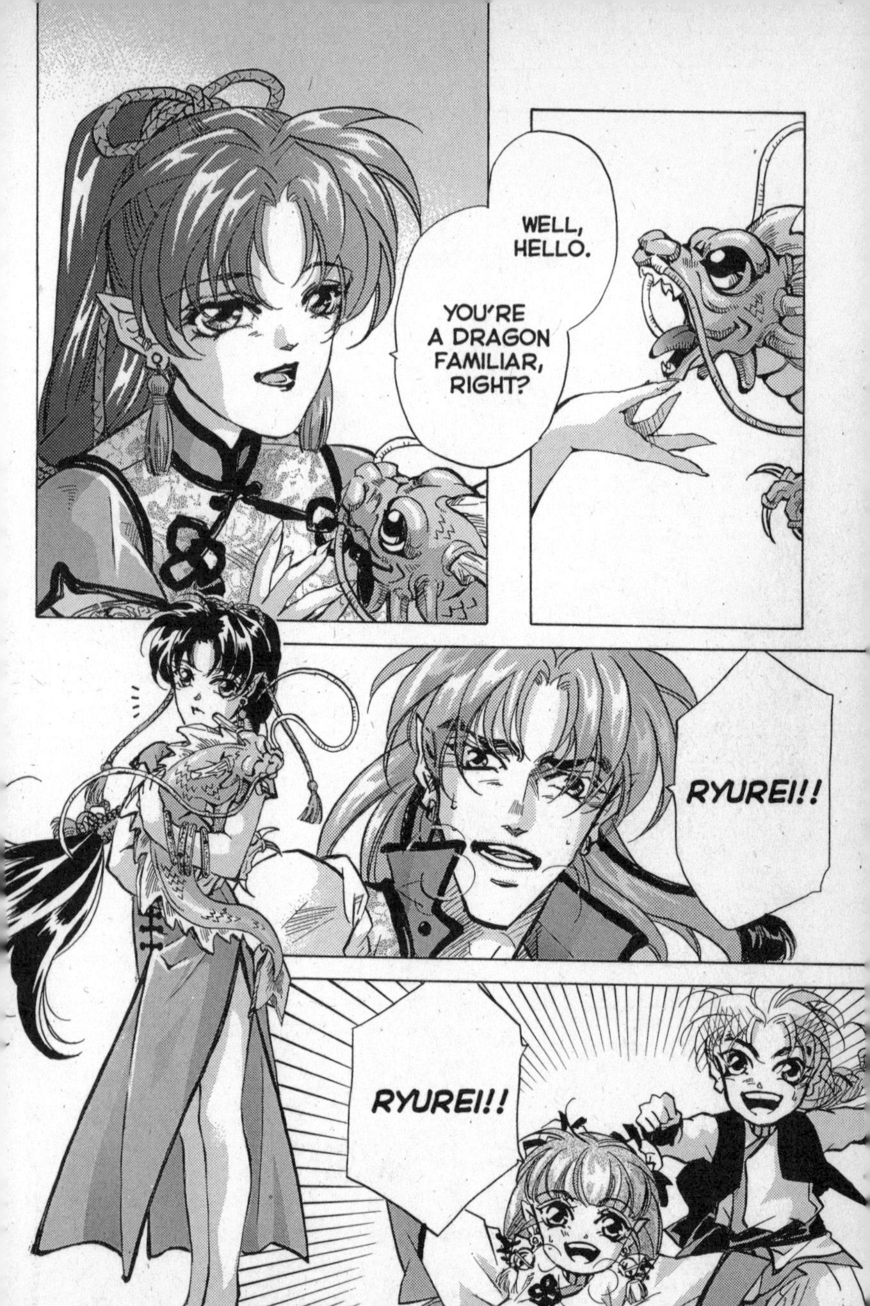
WELL, HELLO.
YOU'RE A DRAGON FAMILIAR, RIGHT?
RYUREI!!
RYUREI!!

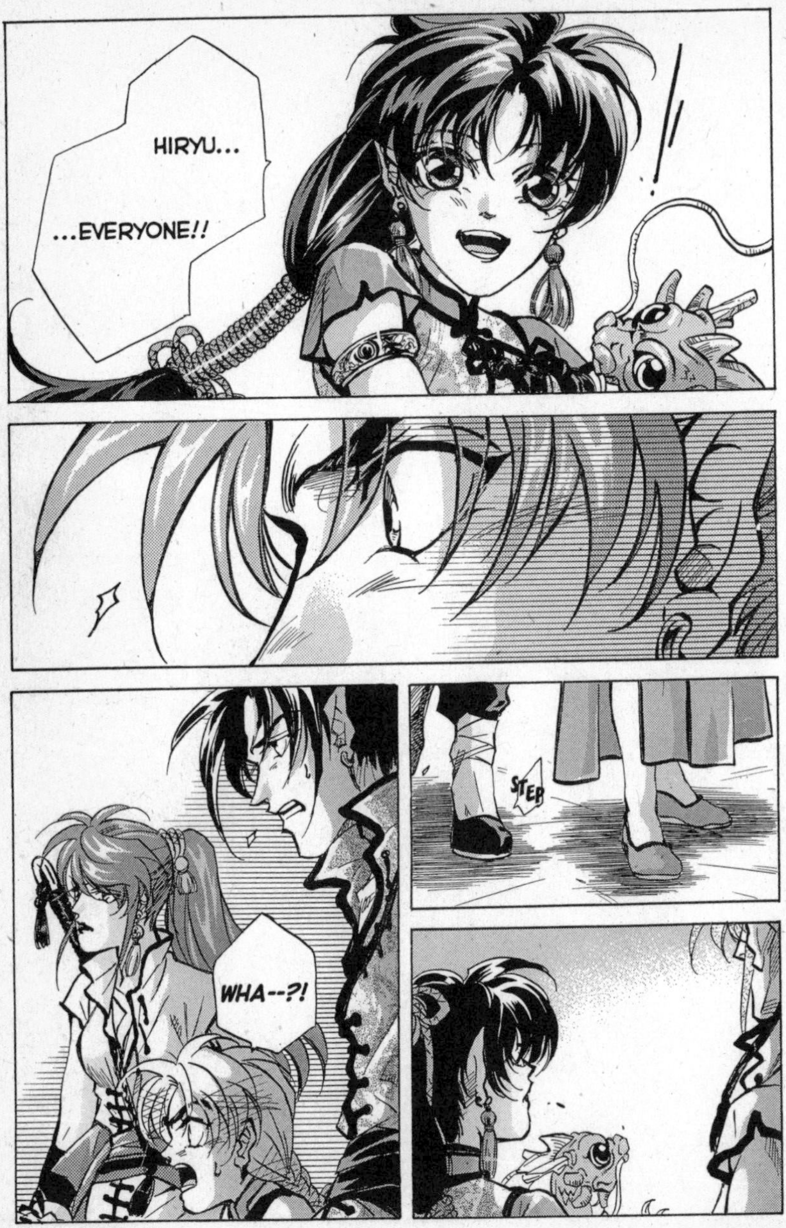
HIRYU...
...EVERYONE!!
STEP
WHA--?!

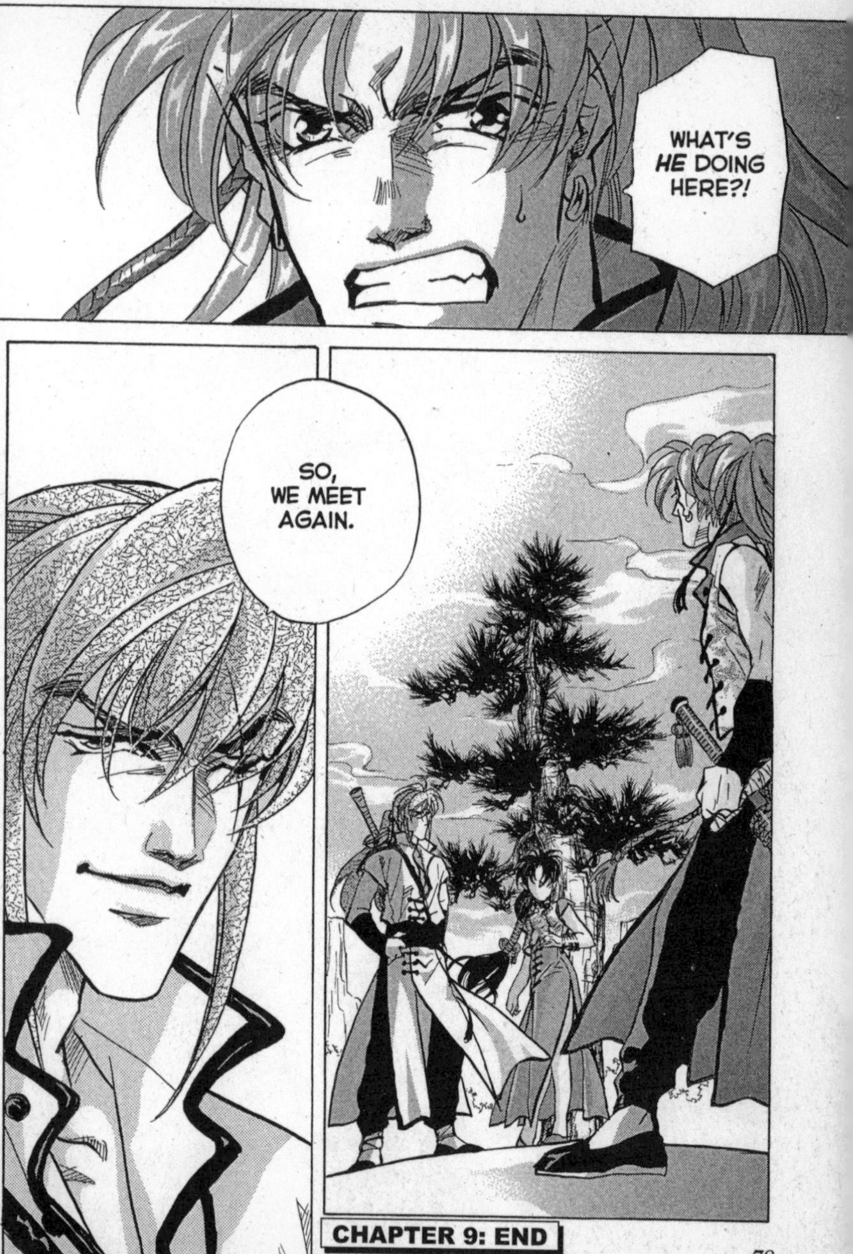
WHAT'S *HE* DOING HERE?!
SO, WE MEET AGAIN.
CHAPTER 9: END

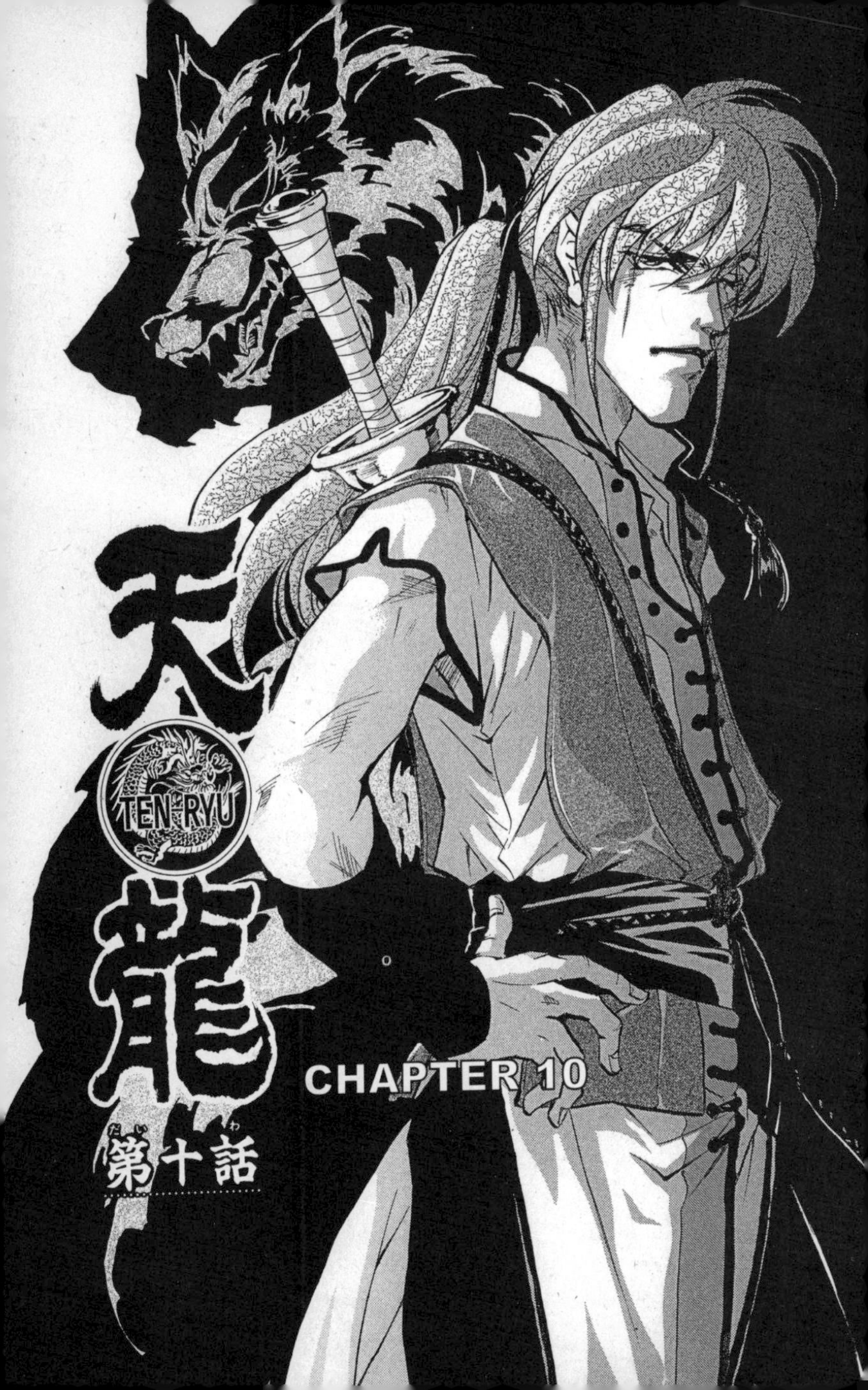
天龍
TEN-RYU
CHAPTER 10
第十話

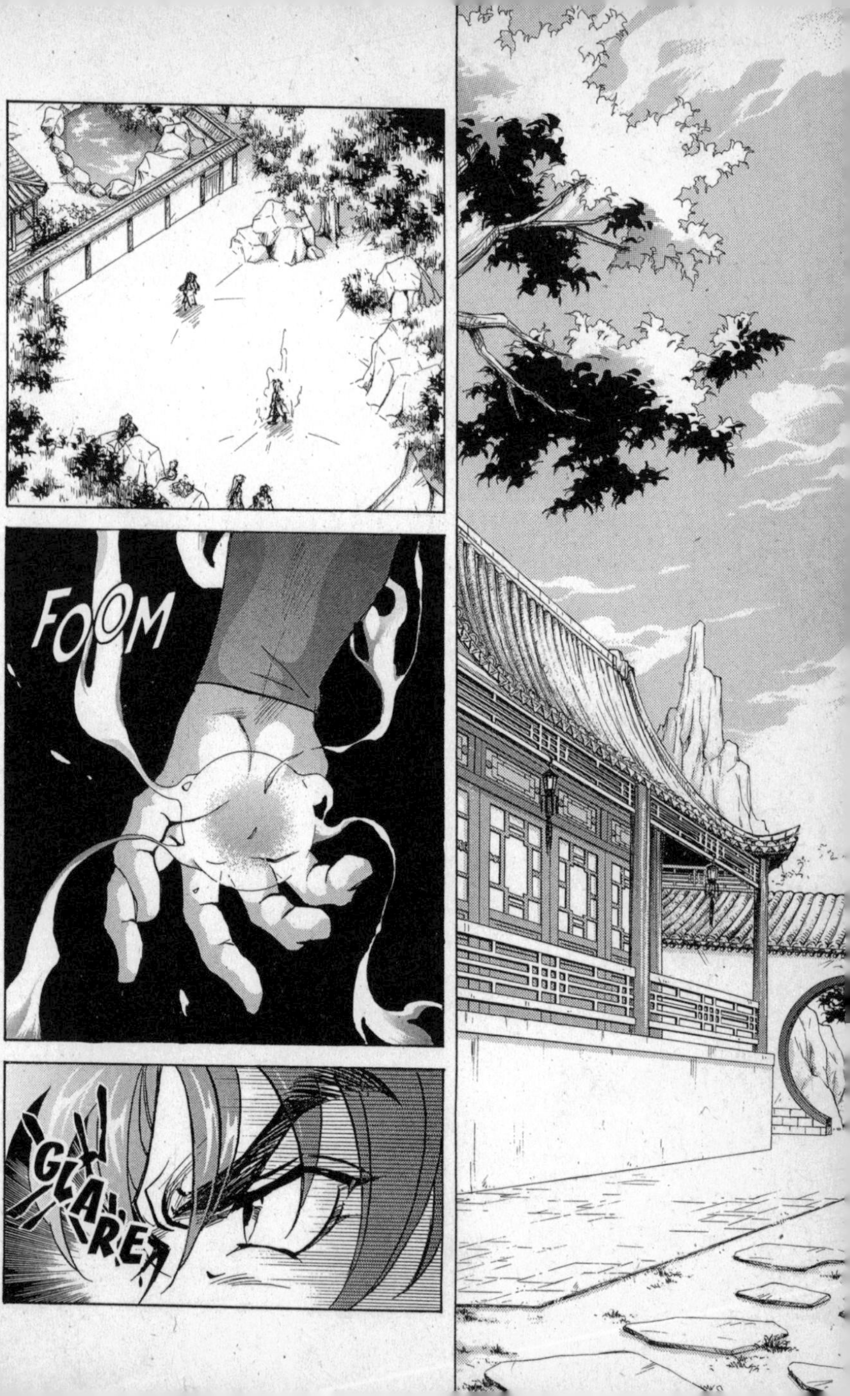
FOOM
GLARE

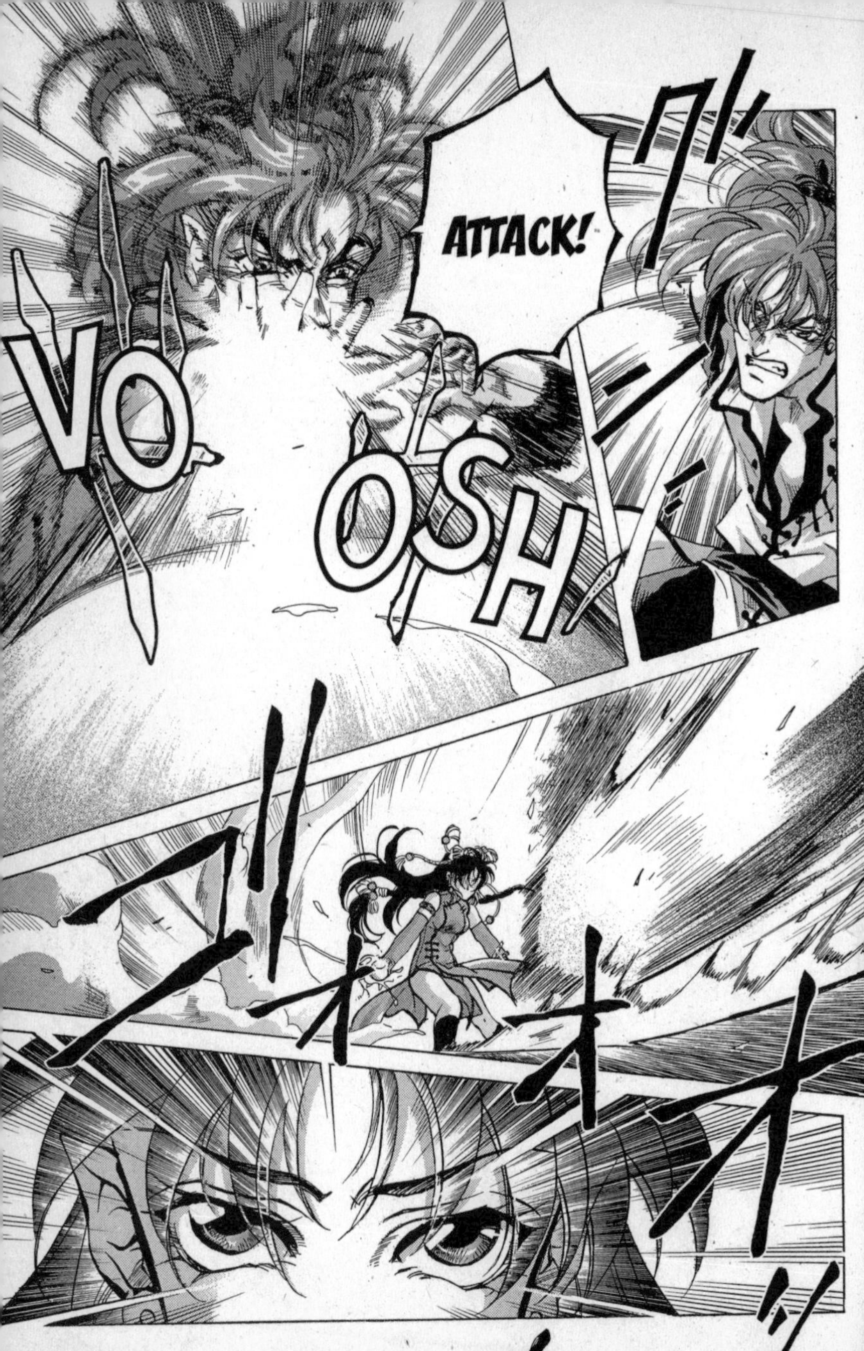
ATTACK!
VOOSH

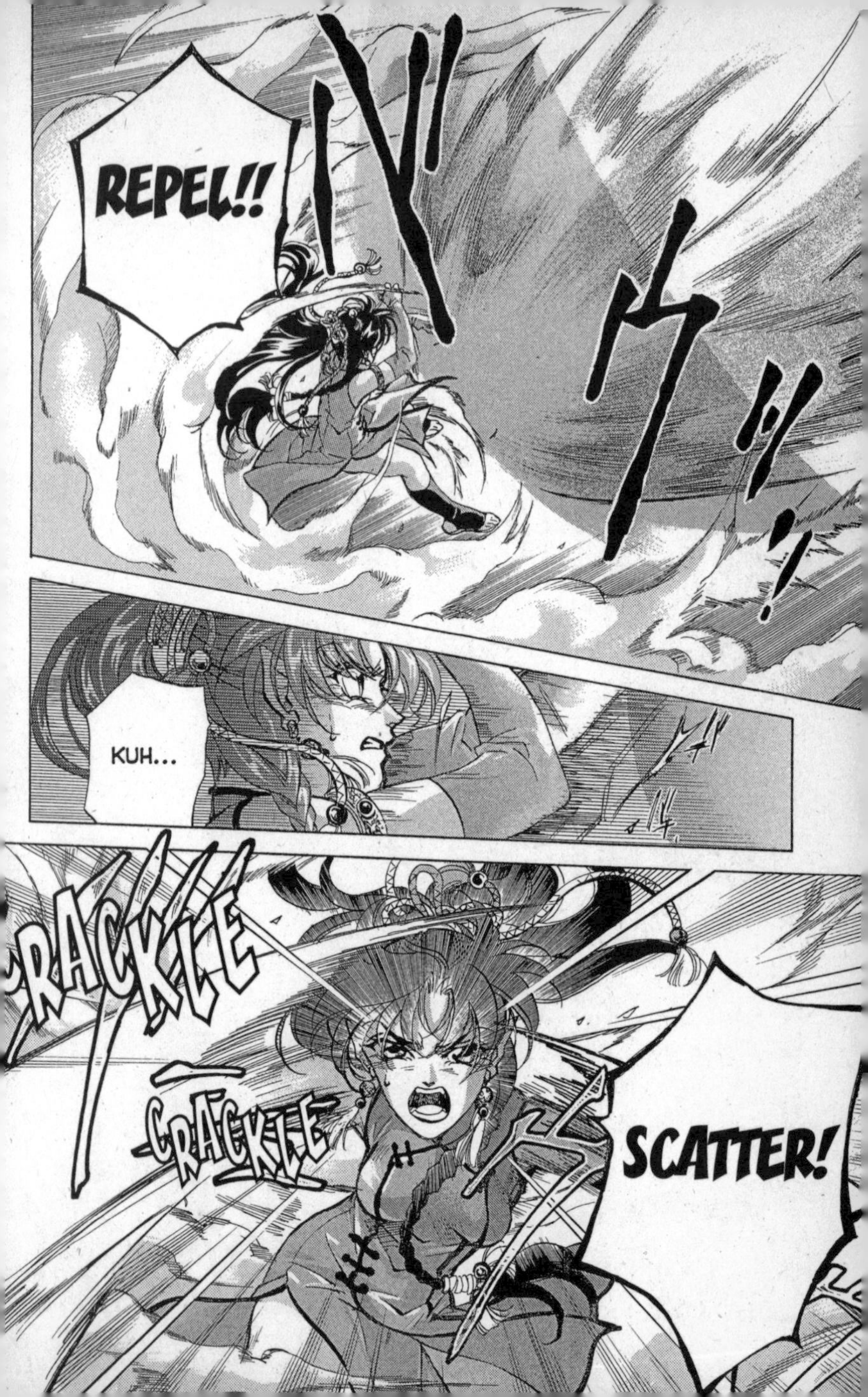

REPEL!!
KUH...
SCATTER!
CRACKLE
CRACKLE

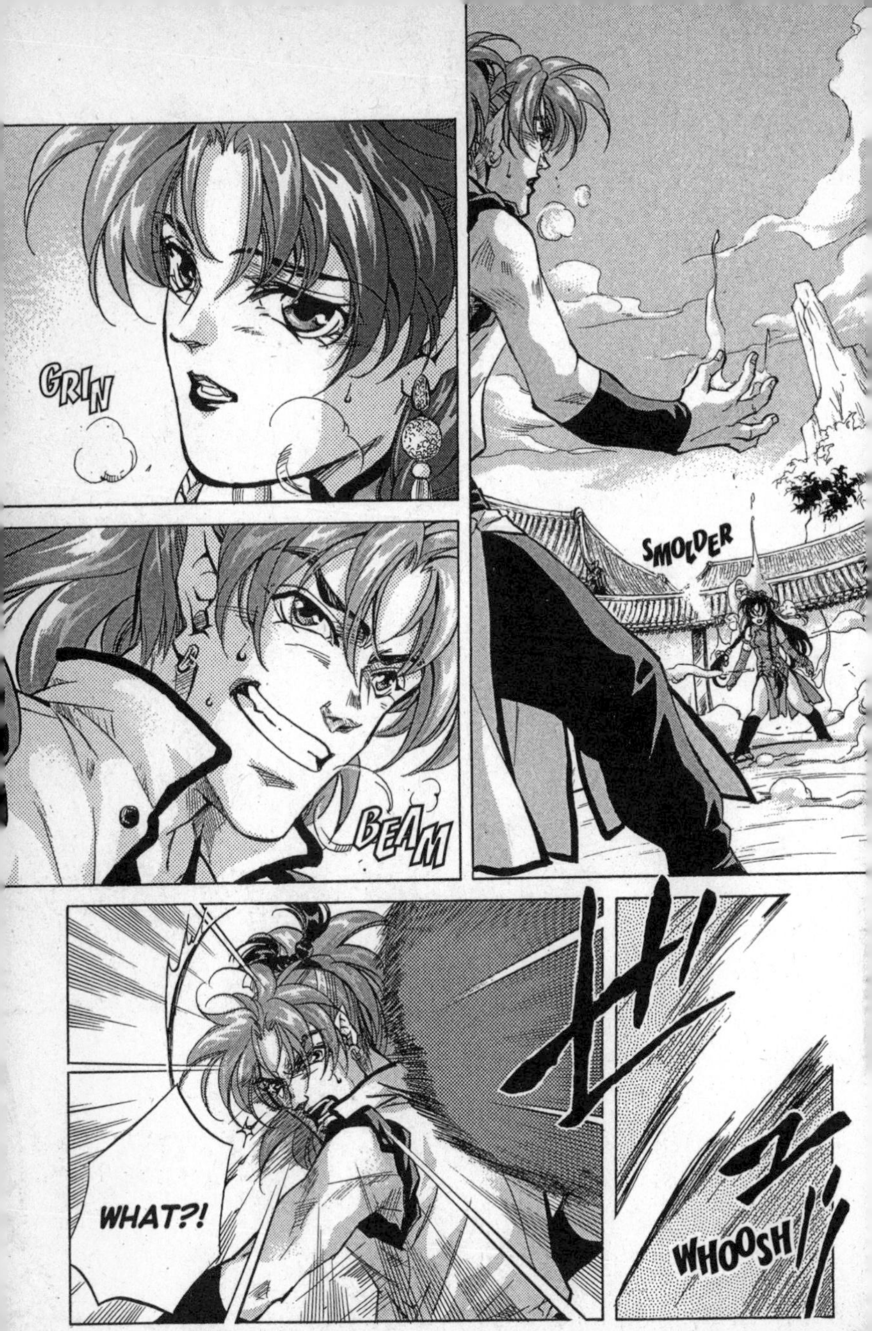
SMOLDER
GRIN
BEAM
WHOOSH
WHAT?!

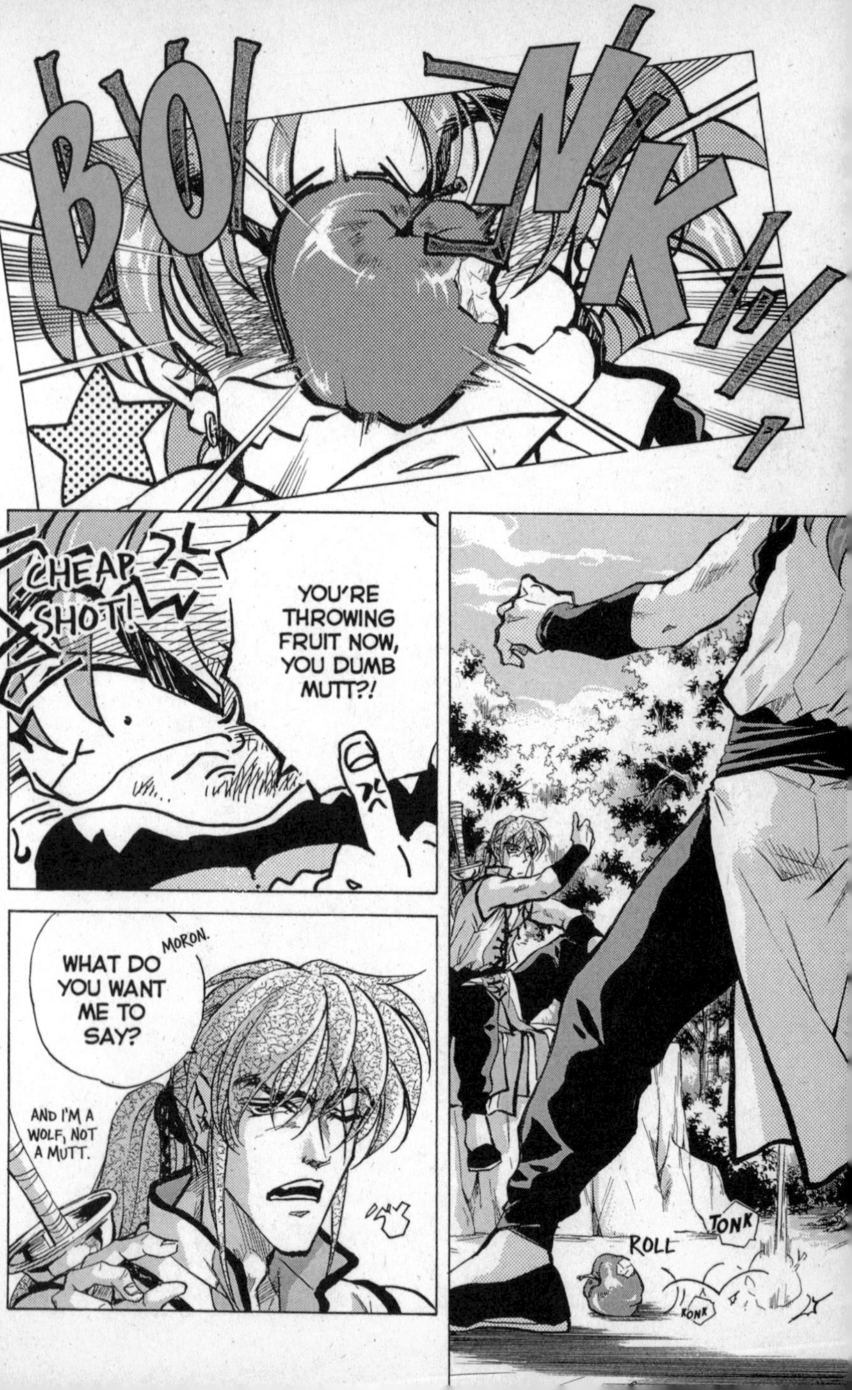
BOINK!!
TONK
ROLL
KONK
CHEAP SHOT!
YOU'RE THROWING FRUIT NOW, YOU DUMB MUTT?!
MORON.
WHAT DO YOU WANT ME TO SAY?
AND I'M A WOLF, NOT A MUTT.

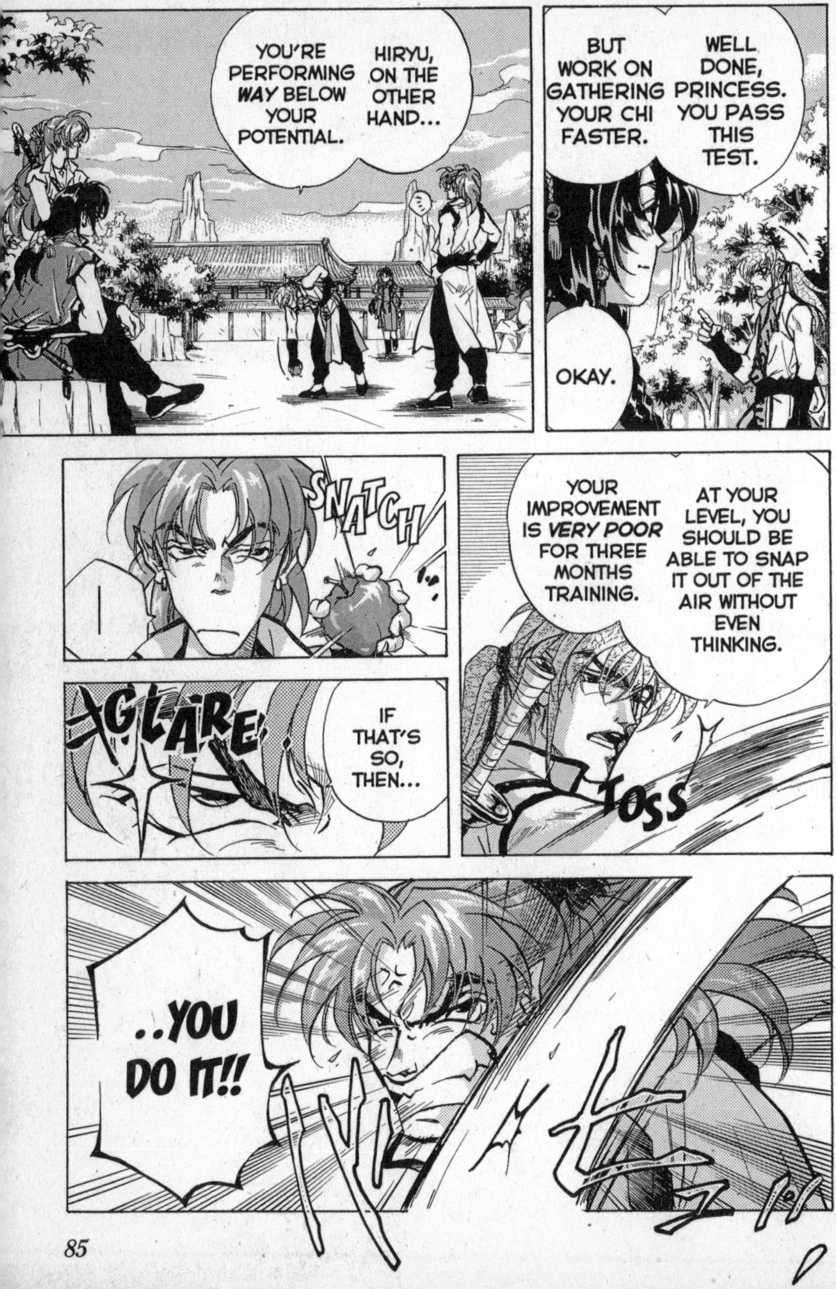

WELL DONE, PRINCESS. YOU PASS THIS TEST.
BUT WORK ON GATHERING YOUR CHI FASTER.
OKAY.
HIRYU, ON THE OTHER HAND...
YOU'RE PERFORMING *WAY* BELOW YOUR POTENTIAL.
AT YOUR LEVEL, YOU SHOULD BE ABLE TO SNAP IT OUT OF THE AIR WITHOUT EVEN THINKING.
YOUR IMPROVEMENT IS *VERY POOR* FOR THREE MONTHS TRAINING.
TOSS
SNATCH
GLARE
IF THAT'S SO, THEN...
..YOU DO IT!!

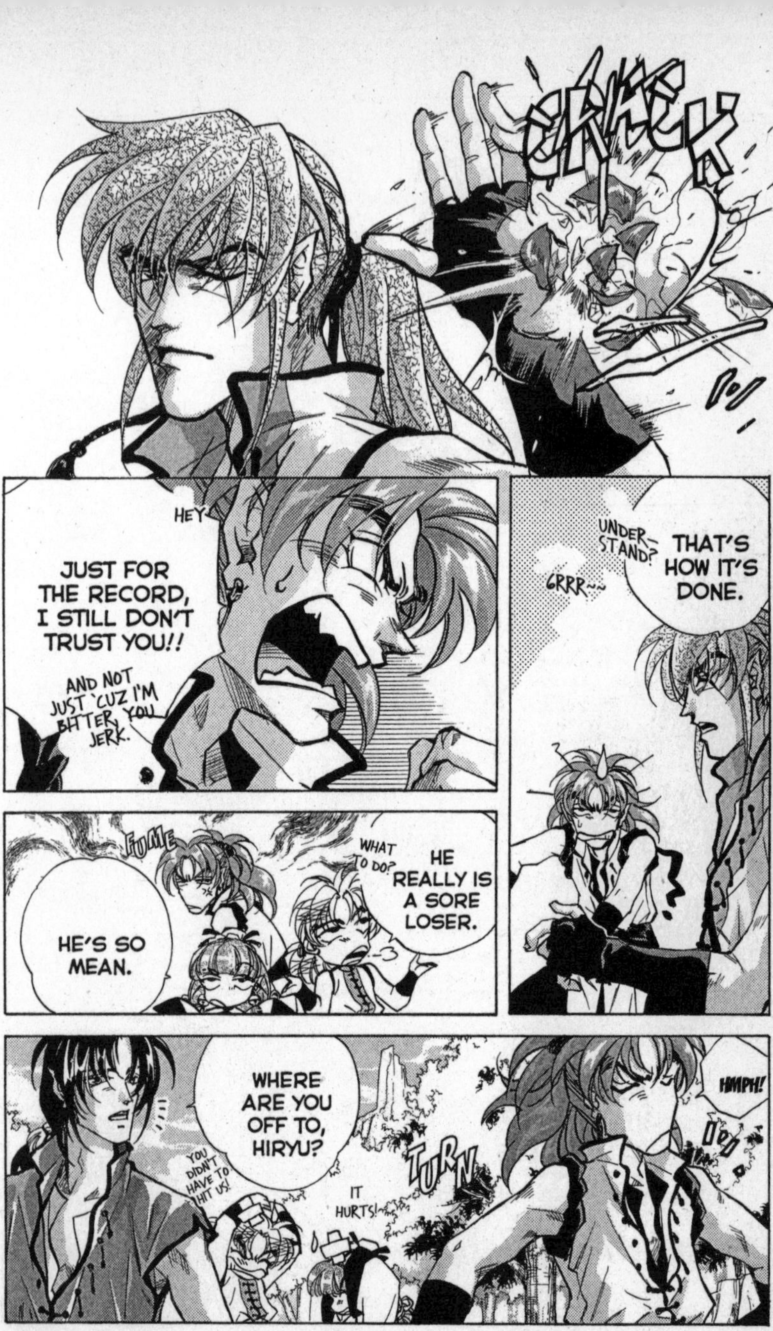
CRACK
THAT'S HOW IT'S DONE.
UNDER-STAND?
GRRR~~
HEY
JUST FOR THE RECORD, I STILL DON'T TRUST YOU!!
AND NOT JUST 'CUZ I'M BITTER, YOU JERK.
FUME
HE REALLY IS A SORE LOSER.
WHAT TO DO?
HE'S SO MEAN.
HMPH!
TURN
WHERE ARE YOU OFF TO, HIRYU?
IT HURTS!
YOU DIDN'T HAVE TO HIT US!

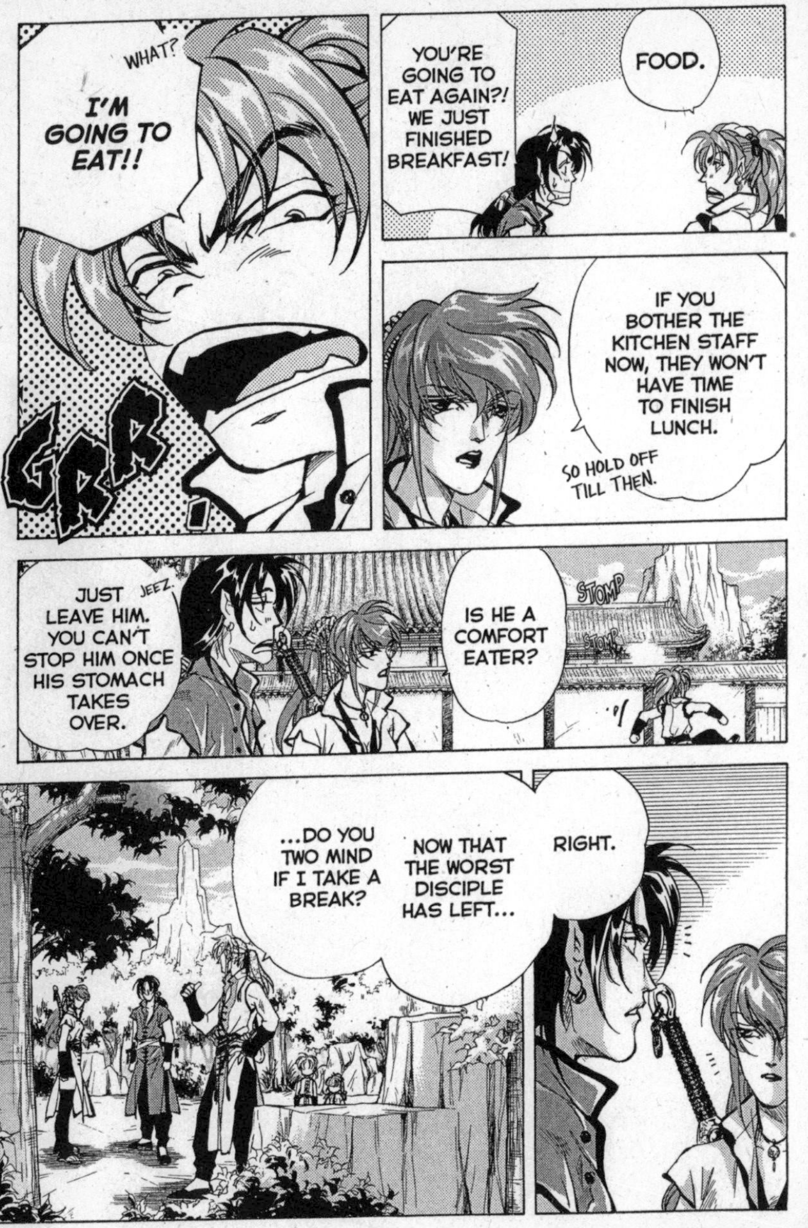
FOOD.
YOU'RE GOING TO EAT AGAIN?! WE JUST FINISHED BREAKFAST!
IF YOU BOTHER THE KITCHEN STAFF NOW, THEY WON'T HAVE TIME TO FINISH LUNCH.
SO HOLD OFF TILL THEN.
WHAT?
I'M GOING TO EAT!!
GRR
STOMP
STOMP
IS HE A COMFORT EATER?
JEEZ.
JUST LEAVE HIM. YOU CAN'T STOP HIM ONCE HIS STOMACH TAKES OVER.
RIGHT.
NOW THAT THE WORST DISCIPLE HAS LEFT...
...DO YOU TWO MIND IF I TAKE A BREAK?

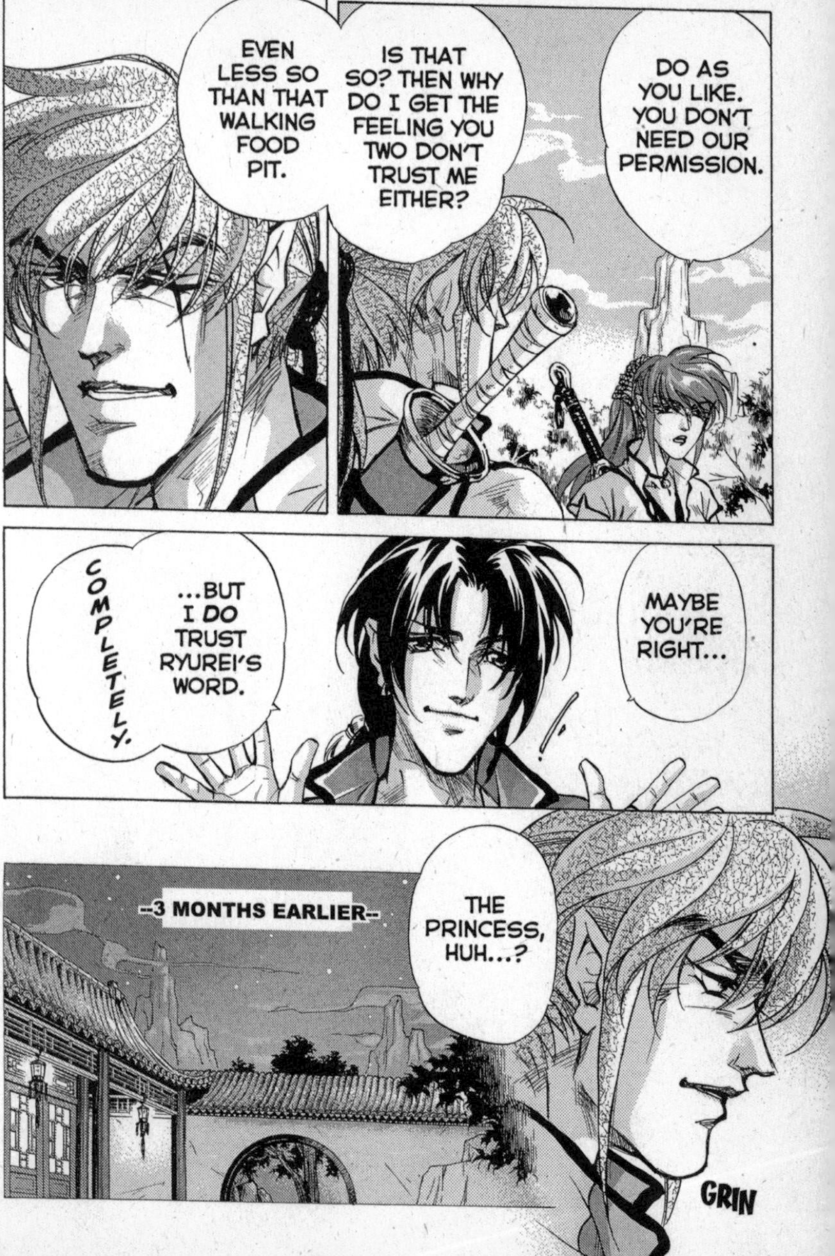
DO AS YOU LIKE. YOU DON'T NEED OUR PERMISSION.
IS THAT SO? THEN WHY DO I GET THE FEELING YOU TWO DON'T TRUST ME EITHER?
EVEN LESS SO THAN THAT WALKING FOOD PIT.
MAYBE YOU'RE RIGHT...
...BUT I DO TRUST RYUREI'S WORD.
COMPLETELY.
THE PRINCESS, HUH...?
GRIN
--3 MONTHS EARLIER--

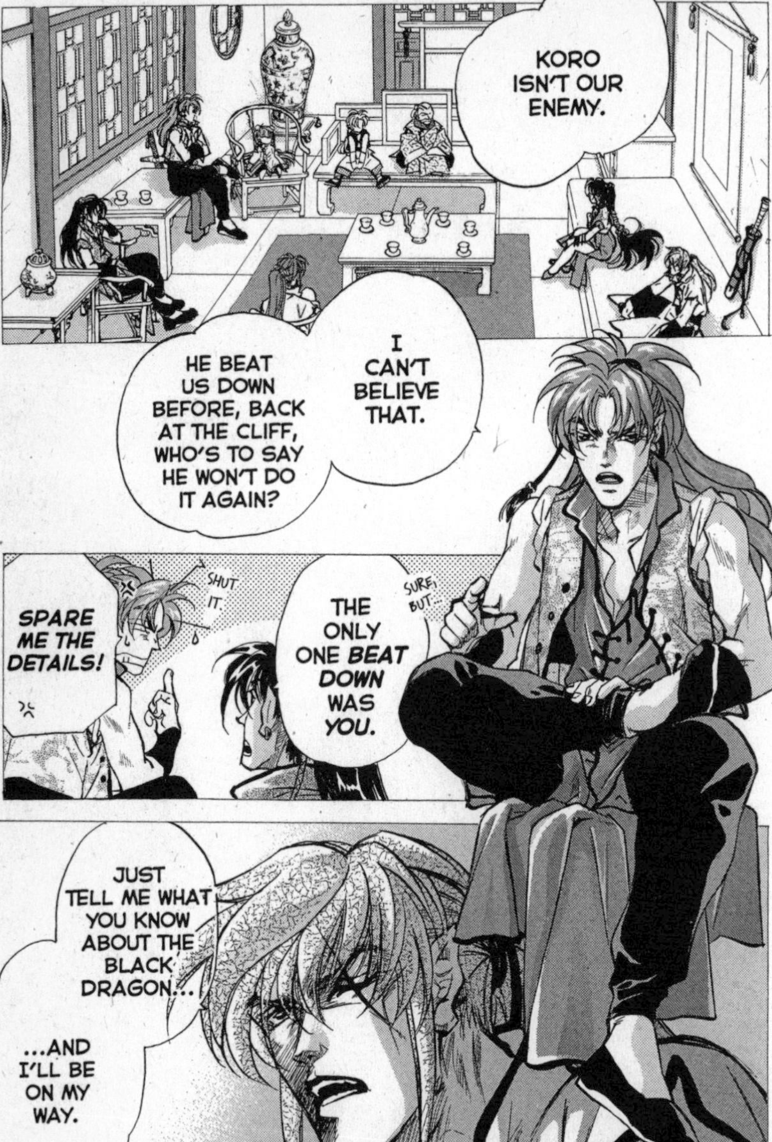
KORO ISN'T OUR ENEMY.
I CAN'T BELIEVE THAT.
HE BEAT US DOWN BEFORE, BACK AT THE CLIFF, WHO'S TO SAY HE WON'T DO IT AGAIN?
SURE, BUT...
THE ONLY ONE BEAT DOWN WAS YOU.
SHUT IT.
SPARE ME THE DETAILS!
JUST TELL ME WHAT YOU KNOW ABOUT THE BLACK DRAGON...
...AND I'LL BE ON MY WAY.

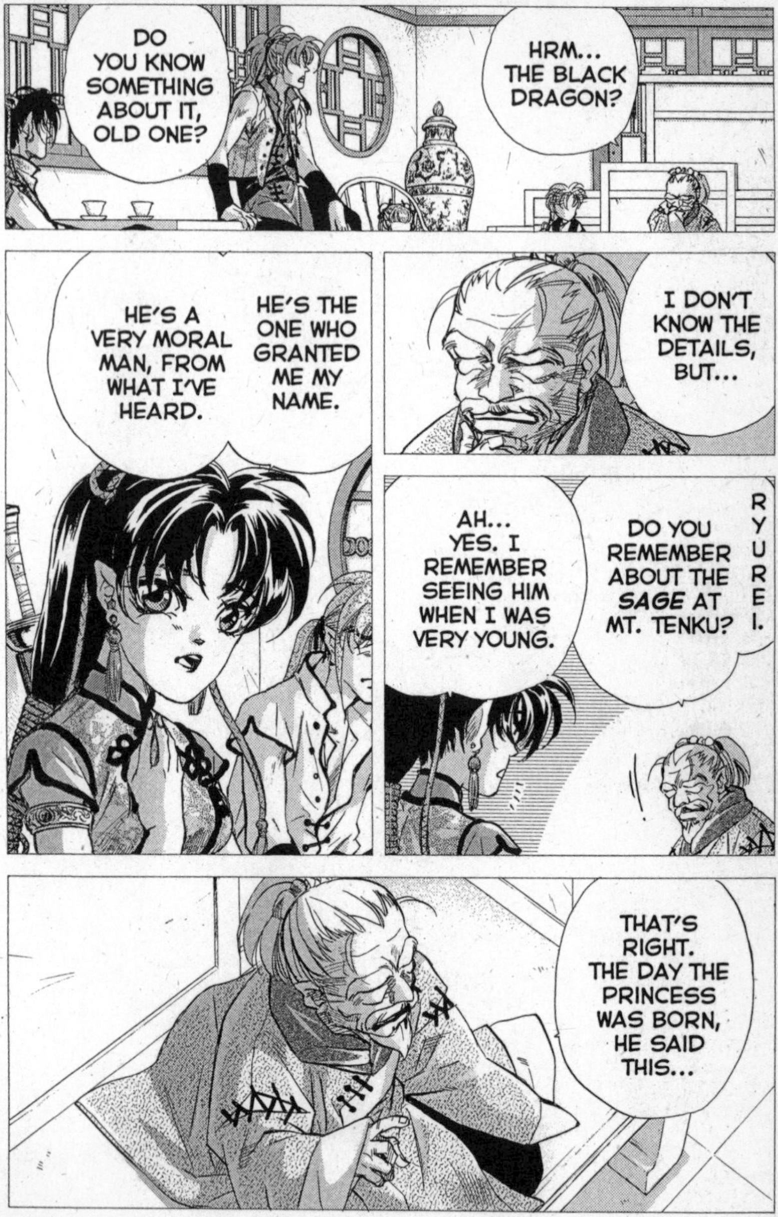
HRM... THE BLACK DRAGON?
DO YOU KNOW SOMETHING ABOUT IT, OLD ONE?
I DON'T KNOW THE DETAILS, BUT...
RYUREI.
DO YOU REMEMBER ABOUT THE *SAGE* AT MT. TENKU?
AH... YES. I REMEMBER SEEING HIM WHEN I WAS VERY YOUNG.
HE'S THE ONE WHO GRANTED ME MY NAME.
HE'S A VERY MORAL MAN, FROM WHAT I'VE HEARD.
THAT'S RIGHT. THE DAY THE PRINCESS WAS BORN, HE SAID THIS...

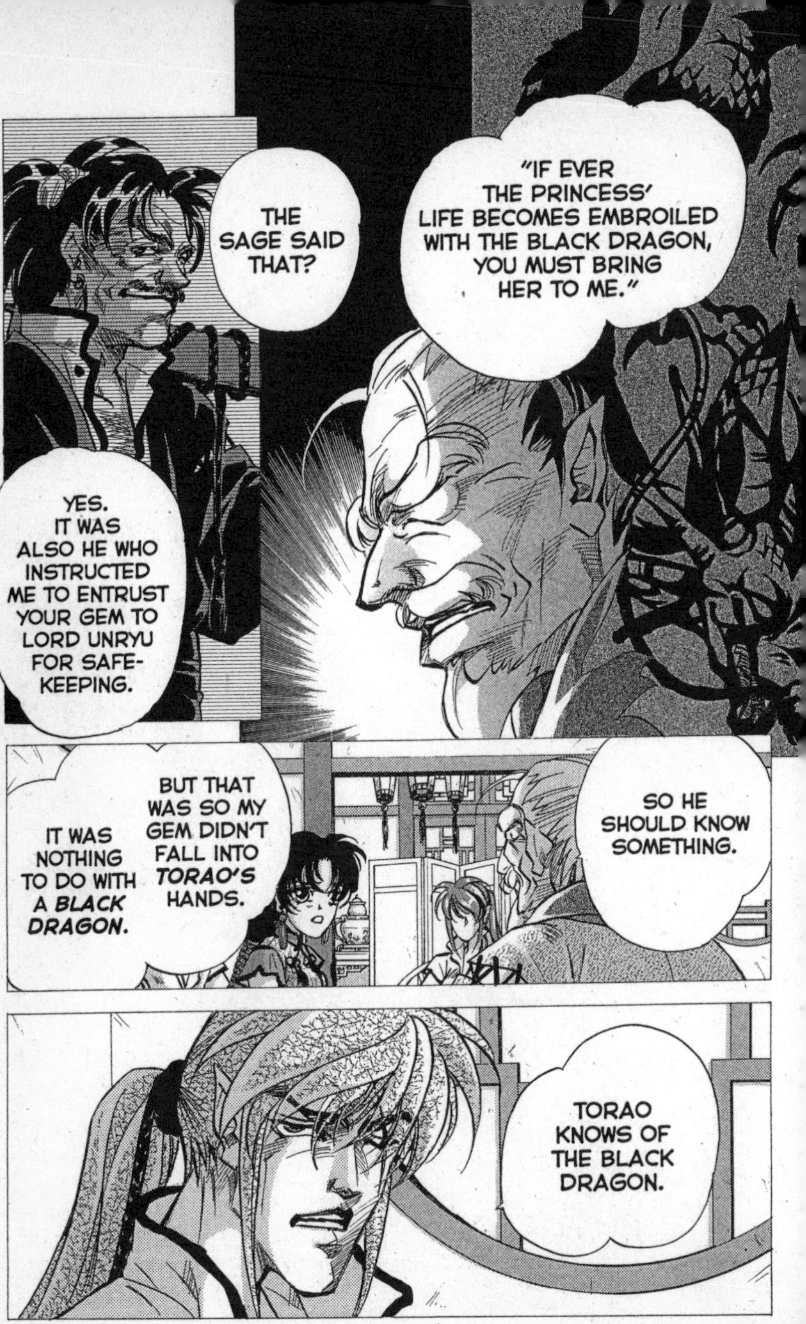
"IF EVER THE PRINCESS' LIFE BECOMES EMBROILED WITH THE BLACK DRAGON, YOU MUST BRING HER TO ME."
THE SAGE SAID THAT?
YES. IT WAS ALSO HE WHO INSTRUCTED ME TO ENTRUST YOUR GEM TO LORD UNRYU FOR SAFE-KEEPING.
SO HE SHOULD KNOW SOMETHING.
BUT THAT WAS SO MY GEM DIDN'T FALL INTO *TORAO'S* HANDS.
IT WAS NOTHING TO DO WITH A *BLACK DRAGON*.
TORAO KNOWS OF THE BLACK DRAGON.

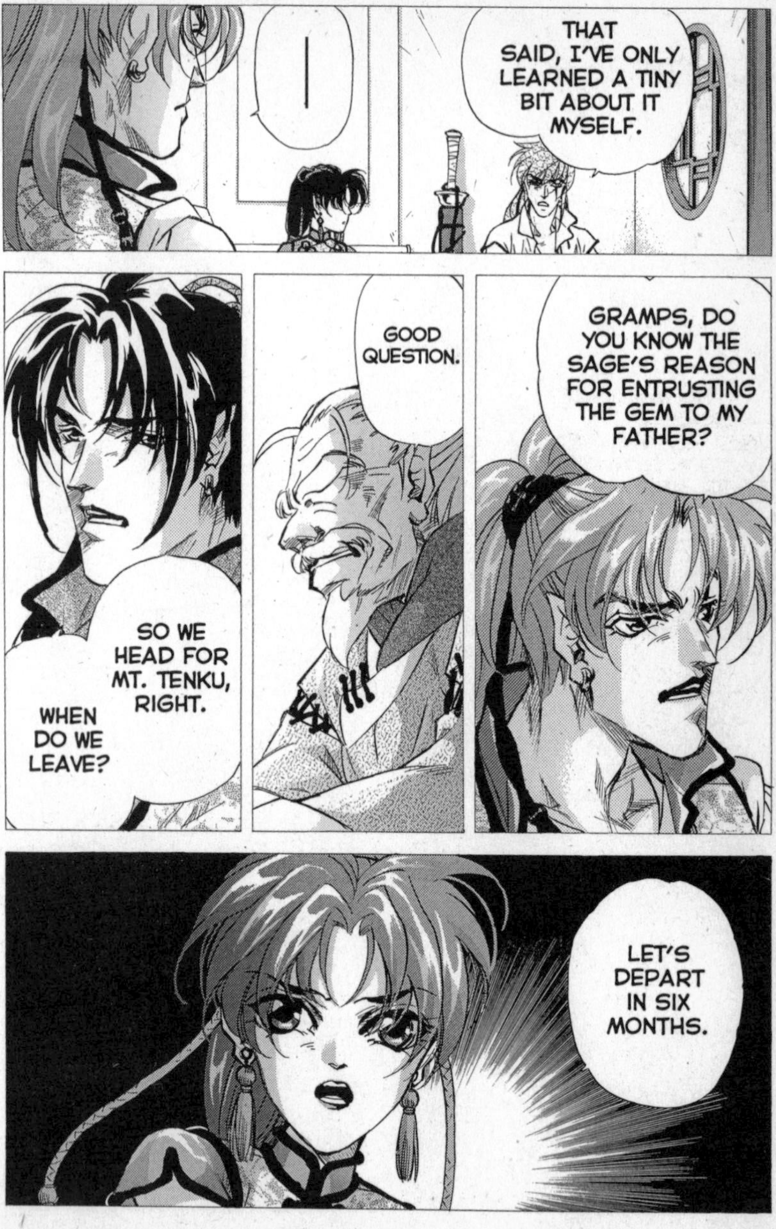
THAT SAID, I'VE ONLY LEARNED A TINY BIT ABOUT IT MYSELF.
—
GRAMPS, DO YOU KNOW THE SAGE'S REASON FOR ENTRUSTING THE GEM TO MY FATHER?
GOOD QUESTION.
SO WE HEAD FOR MT. TENKU, RIGHT.
WHEN DO WE LEAVE?
LET'S DEPART IN SIX MONTHS.

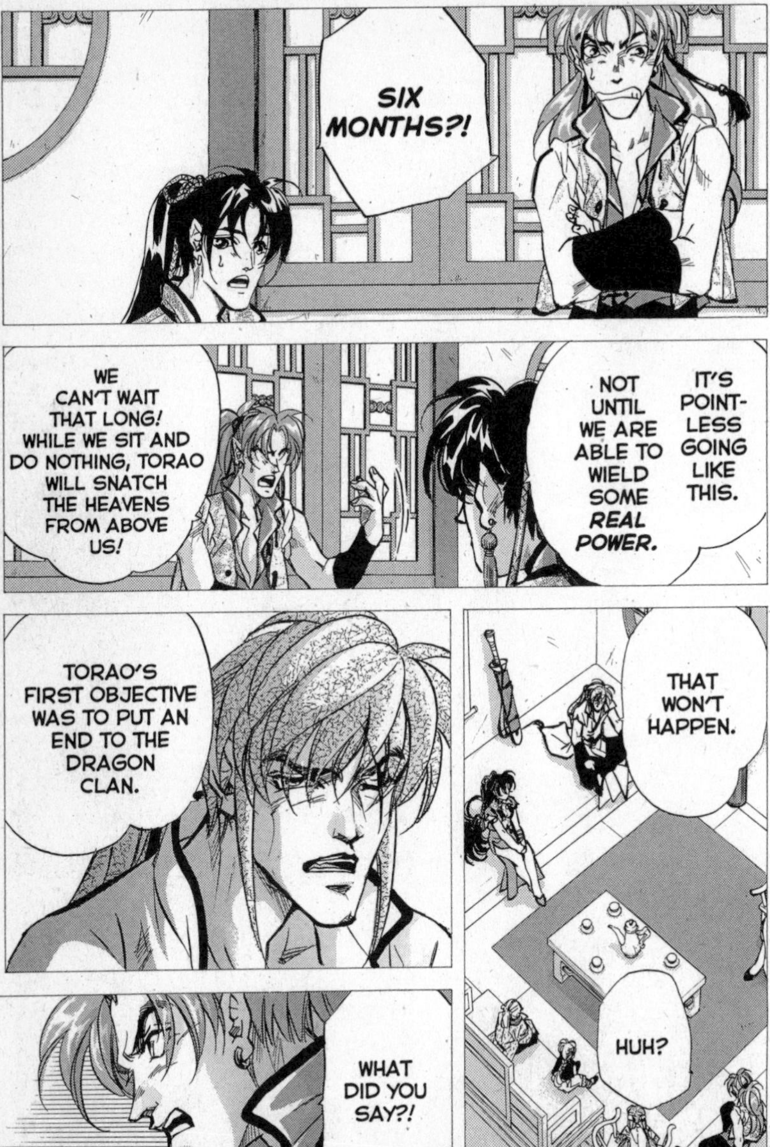
SIX MONTHS?!
IT'S POINTLESS GOING LIKE THIS.
NOT UNTIL WE ARE ABLE TO WIELD SOME *REAL POWER.*
WE CAN'T WAIT THAT LONG! WHILE WE SIT AND DO NOTHING, TORAO WILL SNATCH THE HEAVENS FROM ABOVE US!
THAT WON'T HAPPEN.
HUH?
TORAO'S FIRST OBJECTIVE WAS TO PUT AN END TO THE DRAGON CLAN.
WHAT DID YOU SAY?!

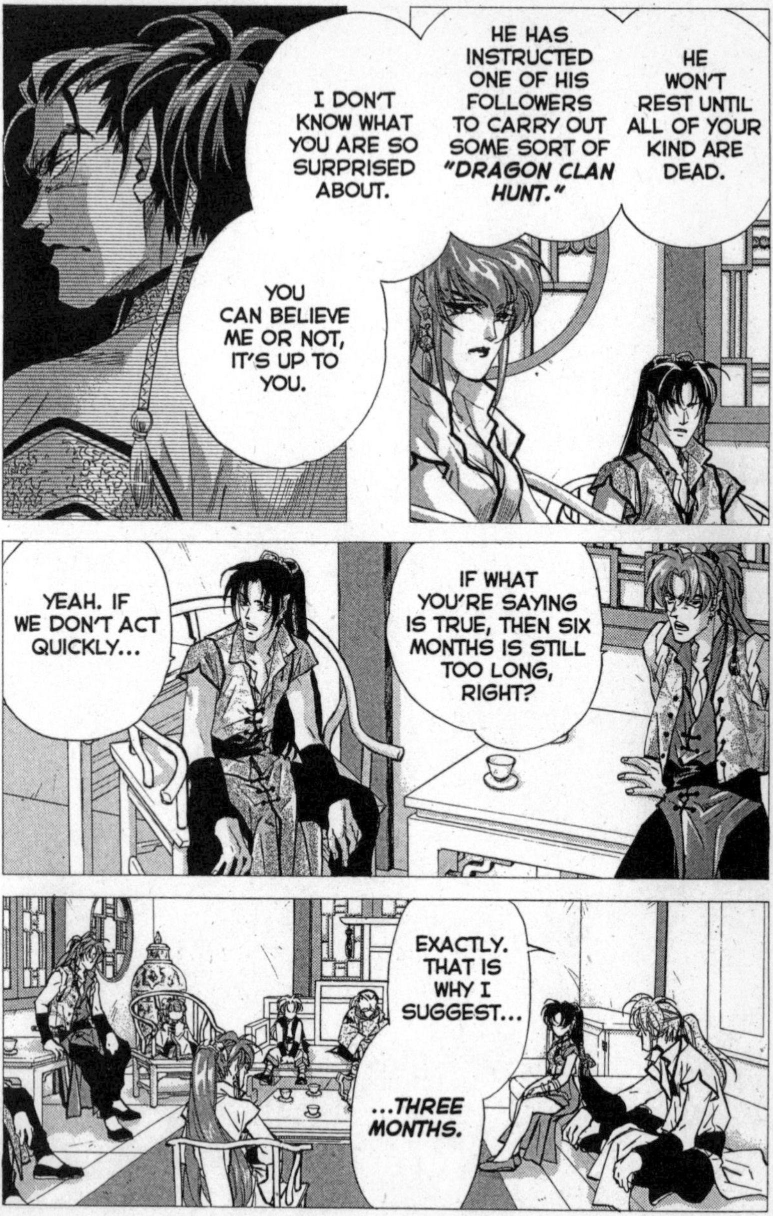
HE WON'T REST UNTIL ALL OF YOUR KIND ARE DEAD.
HE HAS INSTRUCTED ONE OF HIS FOLLOWERS TO CARRY OUT SOME SORT OF "DRAGON CLAN HUNT."
I DON'T KNOW WHAT YOU ARE SO SURPRISED ABOUT.
YOU CAN BELIEVE ME OR NOT, IT'S UP TO YOU.
IF WHAT YOU'RE SAYING IS TRUE, THEN SIX MONTHS IS STILL TOO LONG, RIGHT?
YEAH. IF WE DON'T ACT QUICKLY...
EXACTLY. THAT IS WHY I SUGGEST...
...THREE MONTHS.

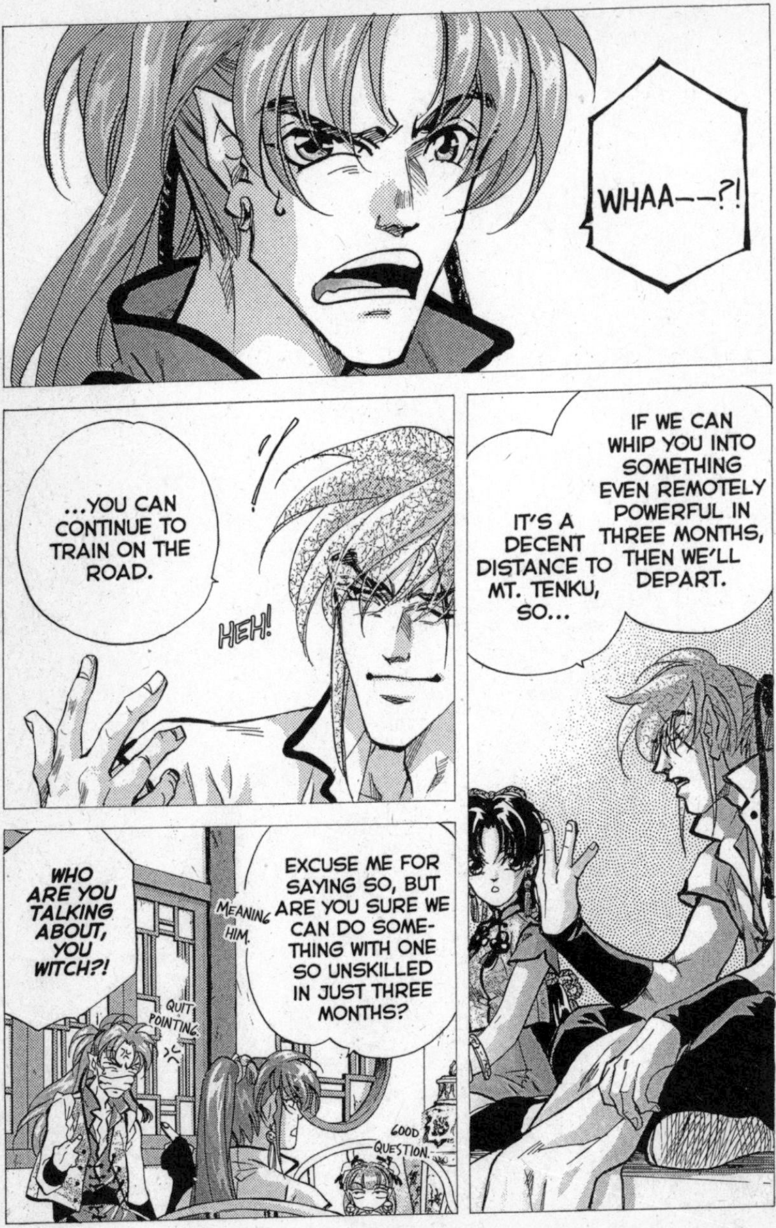
WHAA--?!
IF WE CAN WHIP YOU INTO SOMETHING EVEN REMOTELY POWERFUL IN THREE MONTHS, THEN WE'LL DEPART.
IT'S A DECENT DISTANCE TO MT. TENKU, SO...
...YOU CAN CONTINUE TO TRAIN ON THE ROAD.
HEH!
EXCUSE ME FOR SAYING SO, BUT ARE YOU SURE WE CAN DO SOME-THING WITH ONE SO UNSKILLED IN JUST THREE MONTHS?
MEANING HIM.
WHO ARE YOU TALKING ABOUT, YOU WITCH?!
QUIT POINTING.
GOOD QUESTION.

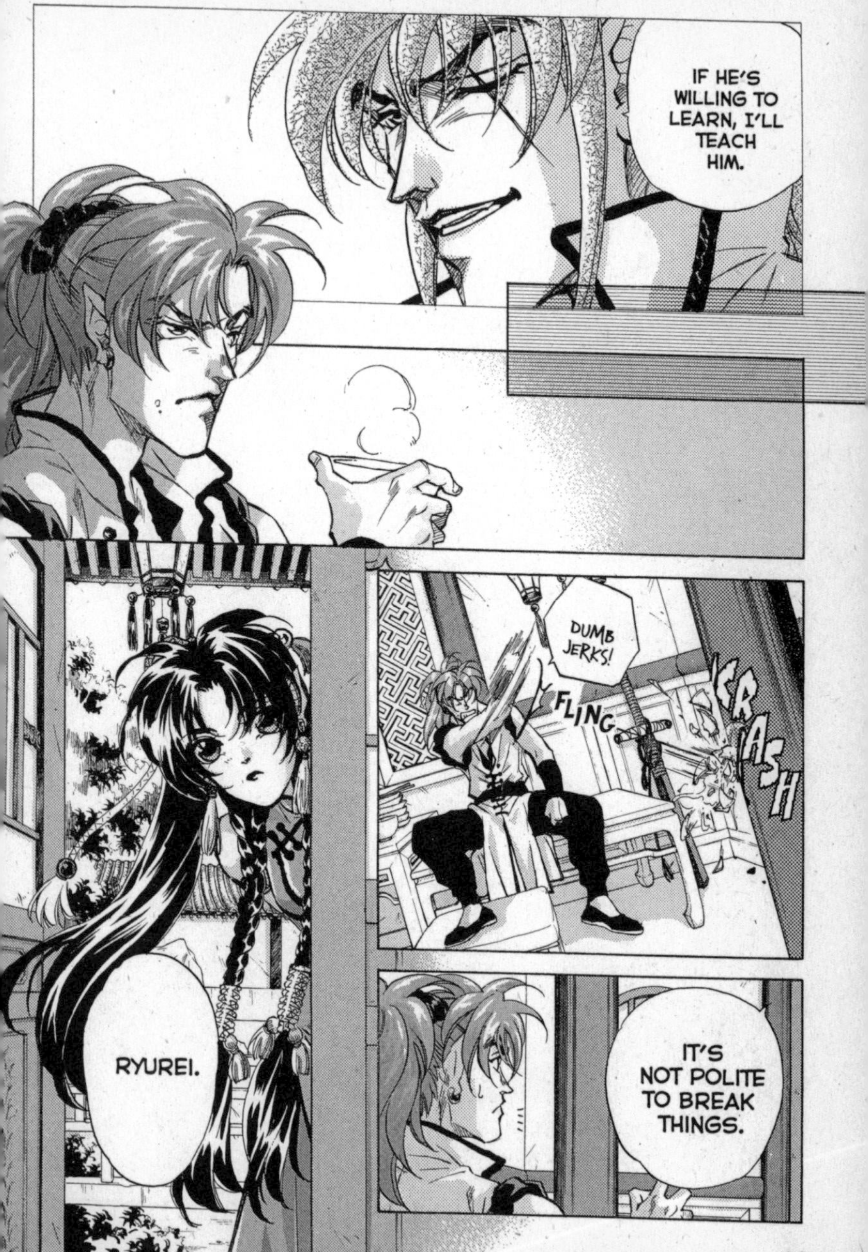
IF HE'S WILLING TO LEARN, I'LL TEACH HIM.
DUMB JERKS!
FLING
CRASH
IT'S NOT POLITE TO BREAK THINGS.
RYUREI.

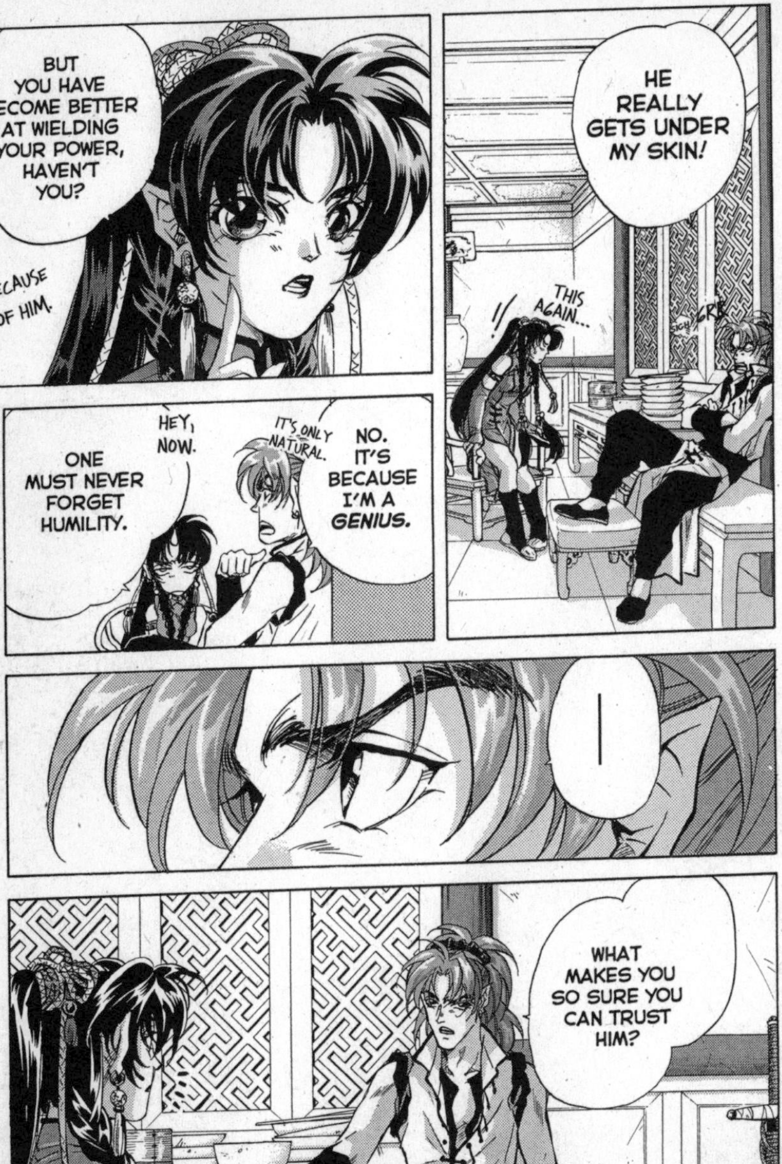
THIS AGAIN...
SIGH GRR
HE REALLY GETS UNDER MY SKIN!
BUT YOU HAVE BECOME BETTER AT WIELDING YOUR POWER, HAVEN'T YOU?
BECAUSE OF HIM.
NO. IT'S BECAUSE I'M A GENIUS.
IT'S ONLY NATURAL.
HEY, NOW.
ONE MUST NEVER FORGET HUMILITY.
WHAT MAKES YOU SO SURE YOU CAN TRUST HIM?

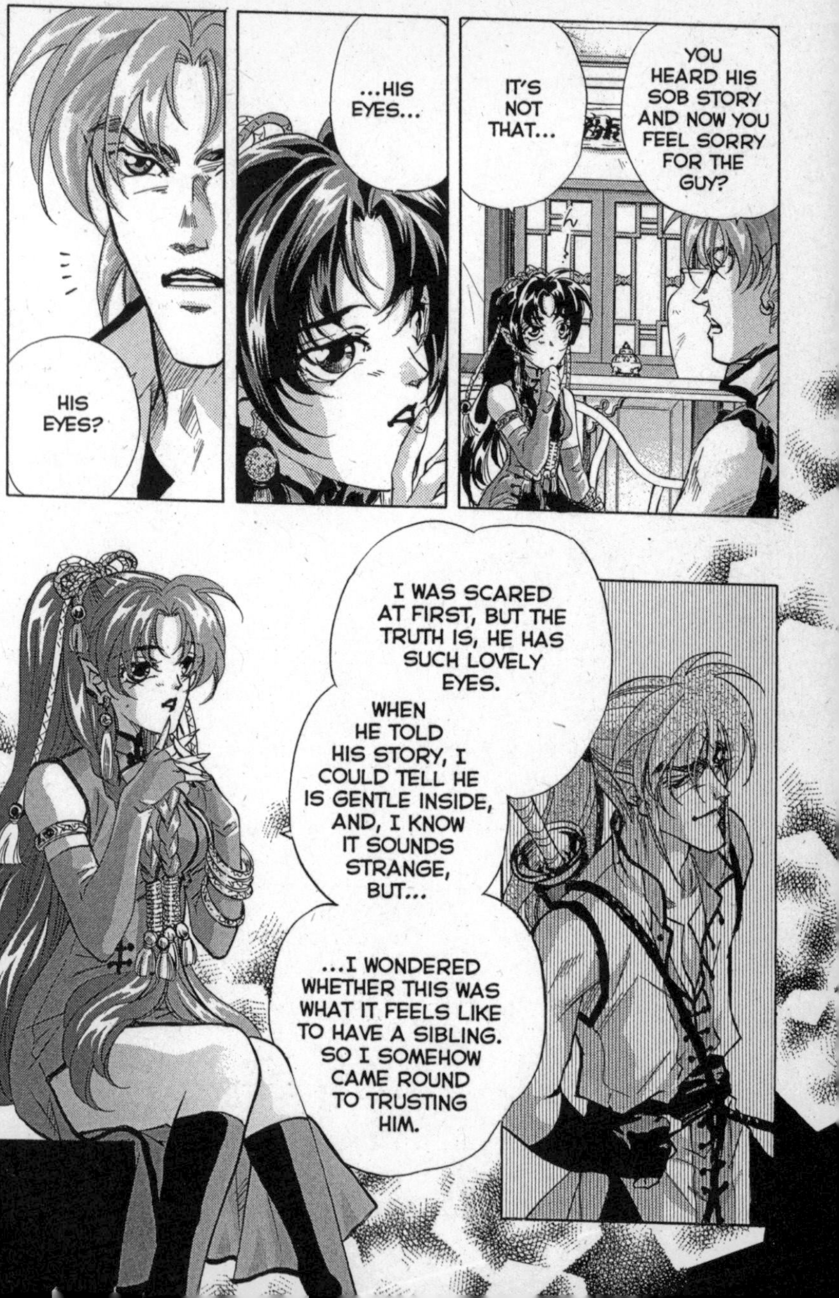
YOU HEARD HIS SOB STORY AND NOW YOU FEEL SORRY FOR THE GUY?
IT'S NOT THAT...
...HIS EYES...
HIS EYES?
I WAS SCARED AT FIRST, BUT THE TRUTH IS, HE HAS SUCH LOVELY EYES.
WHEN HE TOLD HIS STORY, I COULD TELL HE IS GENTLE INSIDE, AND, I KNOW IT SOUNDS STRANGE, BUT...
...I WONDERED WHETHER THIS WAS WHAT IT FEELS LIKE TO HAVE A SIBLING. SO I SOMEHOW CAME ROUND TO TRUSTING HIM.

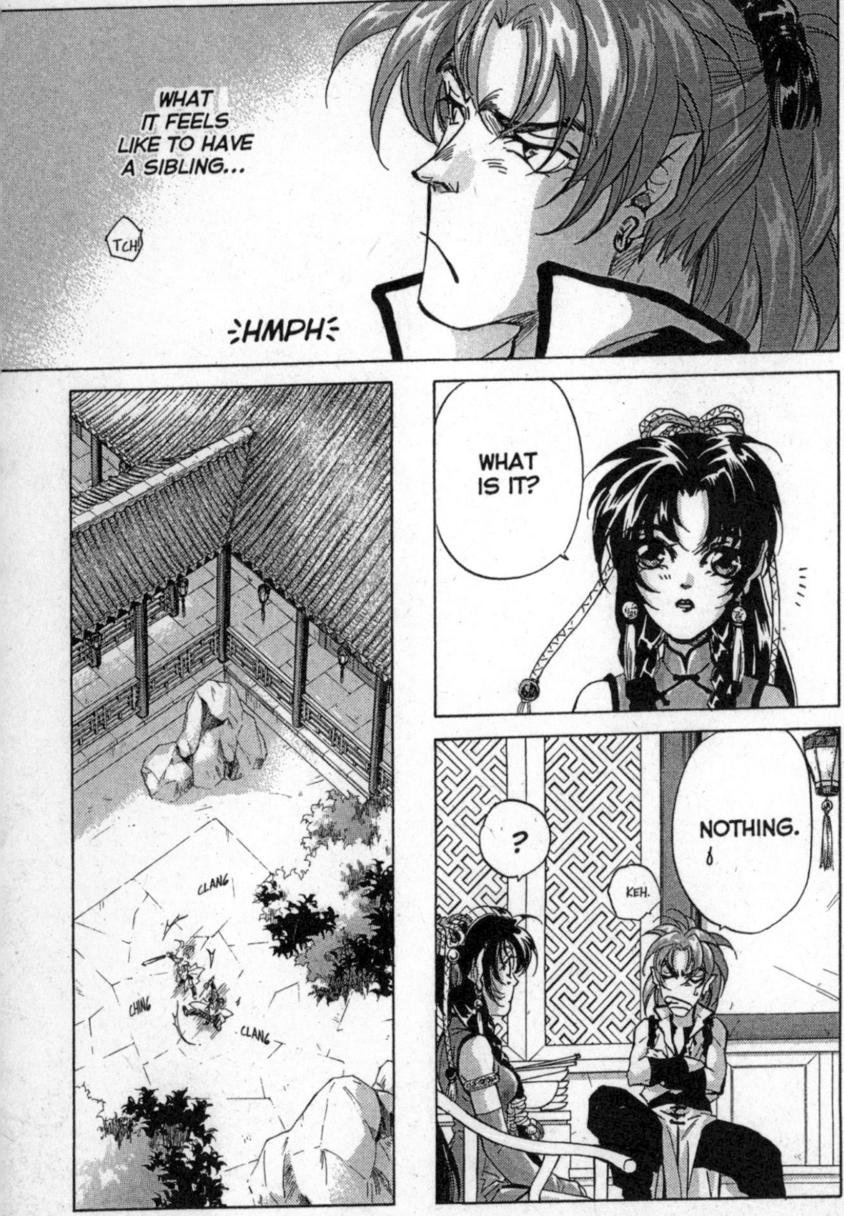
WHAT IT FEELS LIKE TO HAVE A SIBLING...
TCH!
HMPH
WHAT IS IT?
NOTHING.
?
KEH.
CLANG
CHING
CLANG

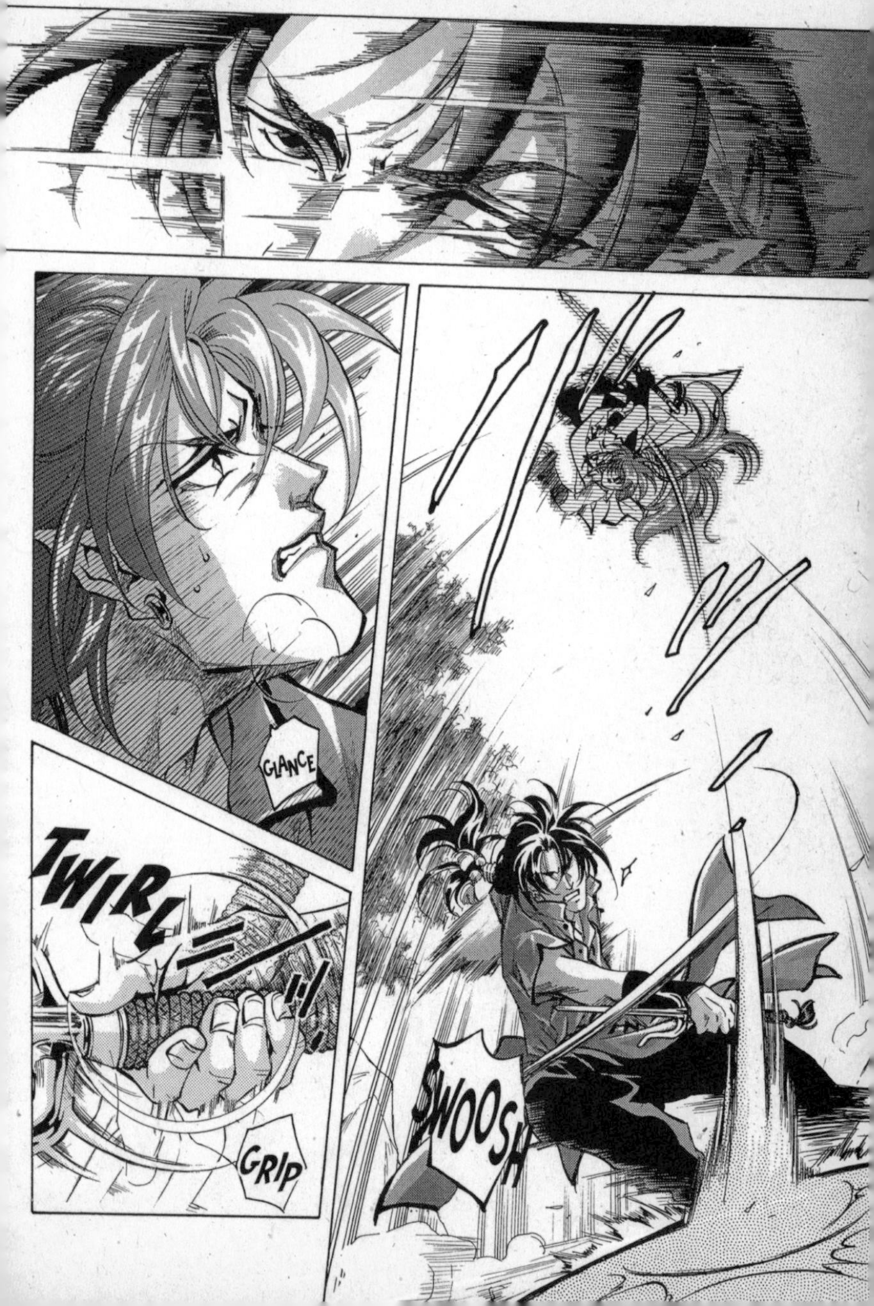
SWOOSH
GLANCE
TWIRL
GRIP

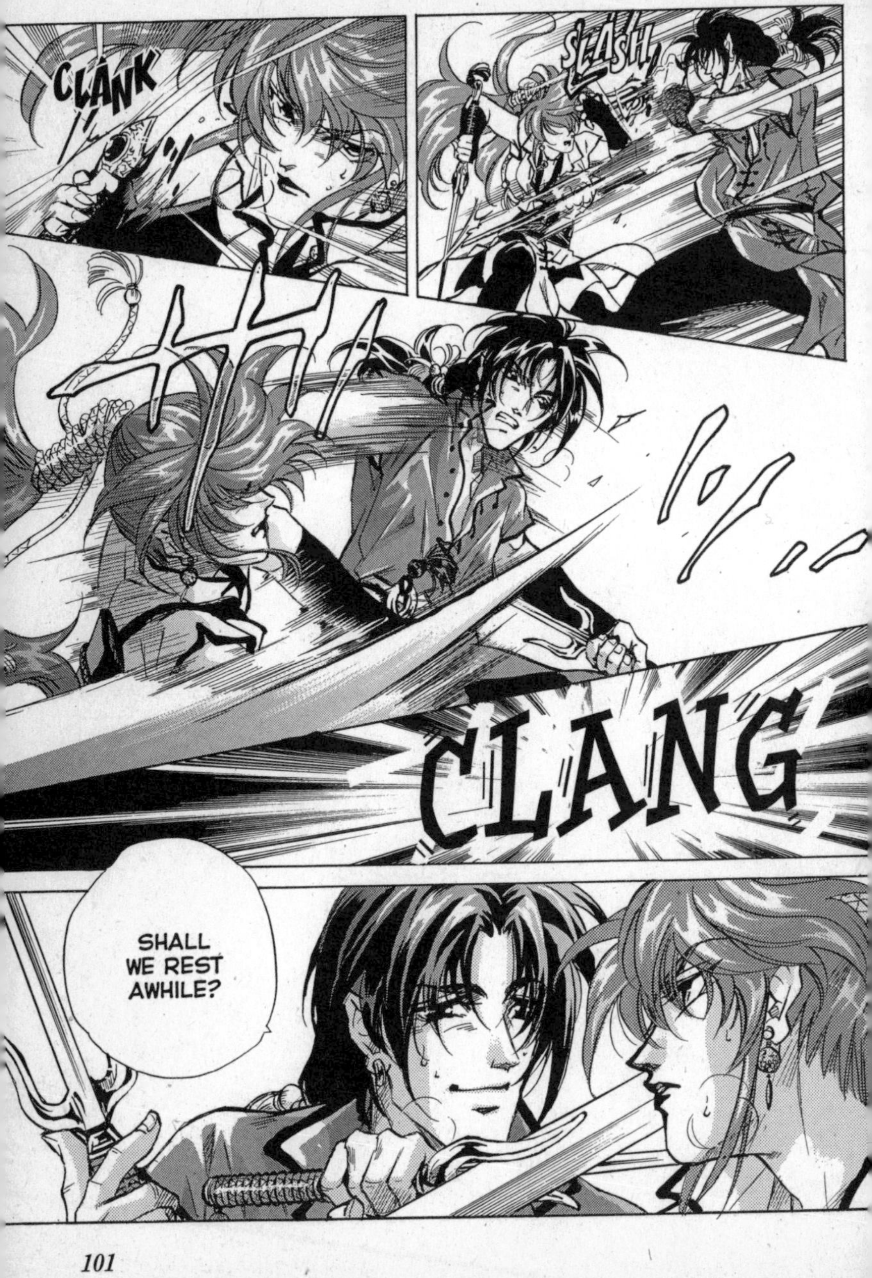
SLASH
CLANK
CLANG
SHALL WE REST AWHILE?

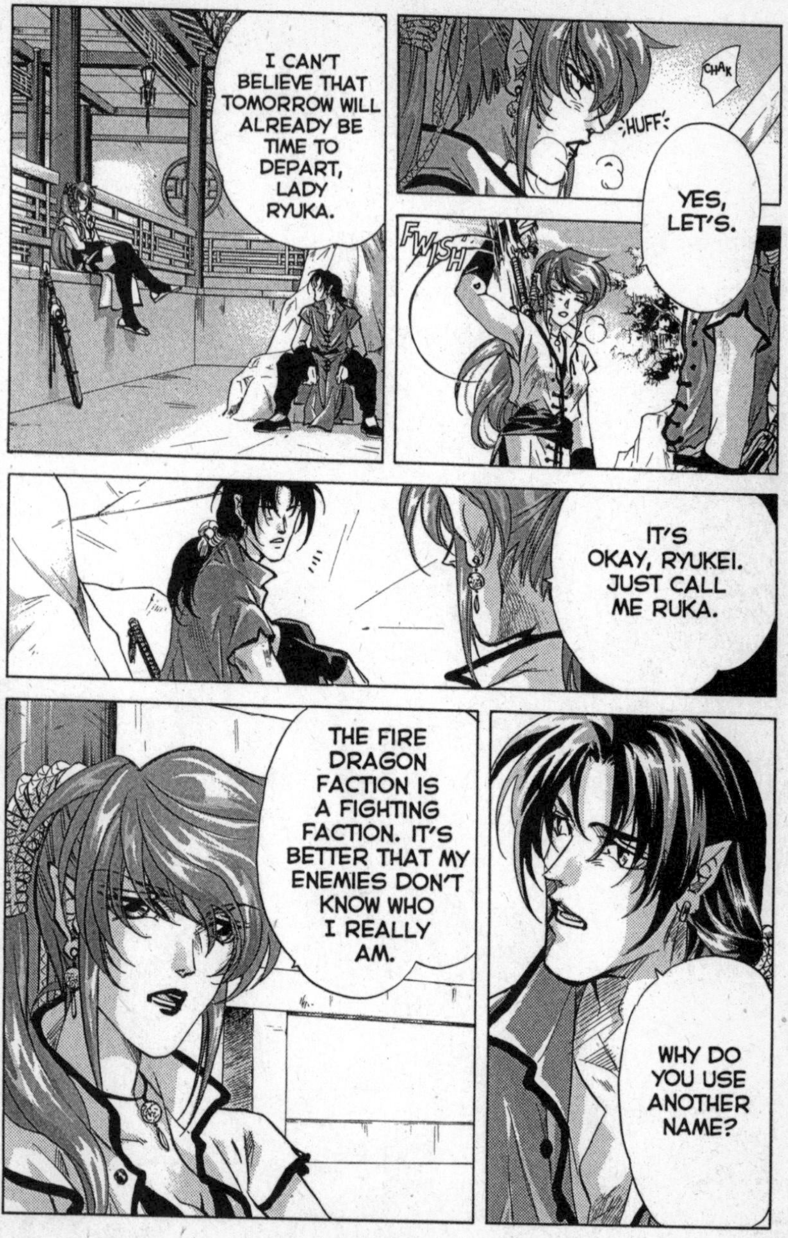
CHAK
HUFF
FWISH
YES, LET'S.
I CAN'T BELIEVE THAT TOMORROW WILL ALREADY BE TIME TO DEPART, LADY RYUKA.
IT'S OKAY, RYUKEI. JUST CALL ME RUKA.
WHY DO YOU USE ANOTHER NAME?
THE FIRE DRAGON FACTION IS A FIGHTING FACTION. IT'S BETTER THAT MY ENEMIES DON'T KNOW WHO I REALLY AM.

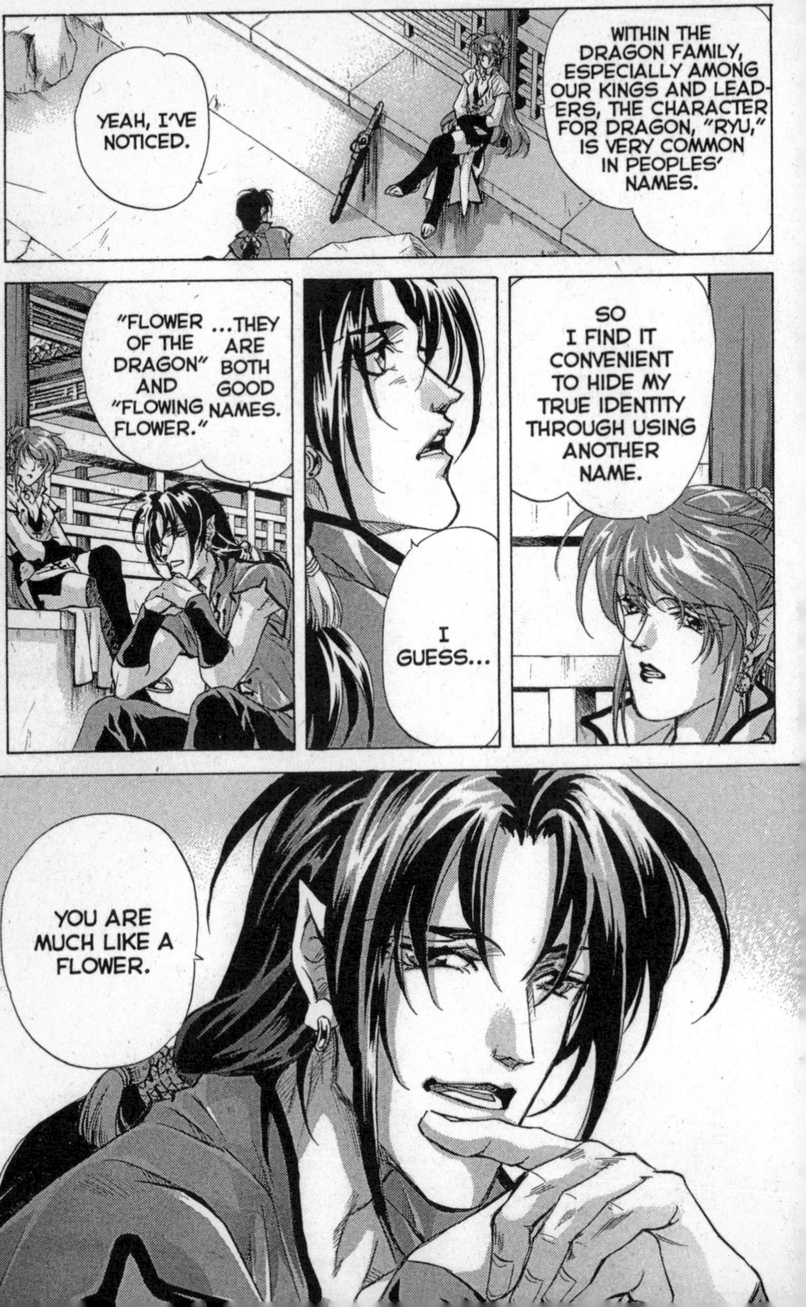
WITHIN THE DRAGON FAMILY, ESPECIALLY AMONG OUR KINGS AND LEADERS, THE CHARACTER FOR DRAGON, "RYU," IS VERY COMMON IN PEOPLES' NAMES.
YEAH, I'VE NOTICED.
SO I FIND IT CONVENIENT TO HIDE MY TRUE IDENTITY THROUGH USING ANOTHER NAME.
I GUESS...
"FLOWER OF THE DRAGON" AND "FLOWING FLOWER."
...THEY ARE BOTH GOOD NAMES.
YOU ARE MUCH LIKE A FLOWER.

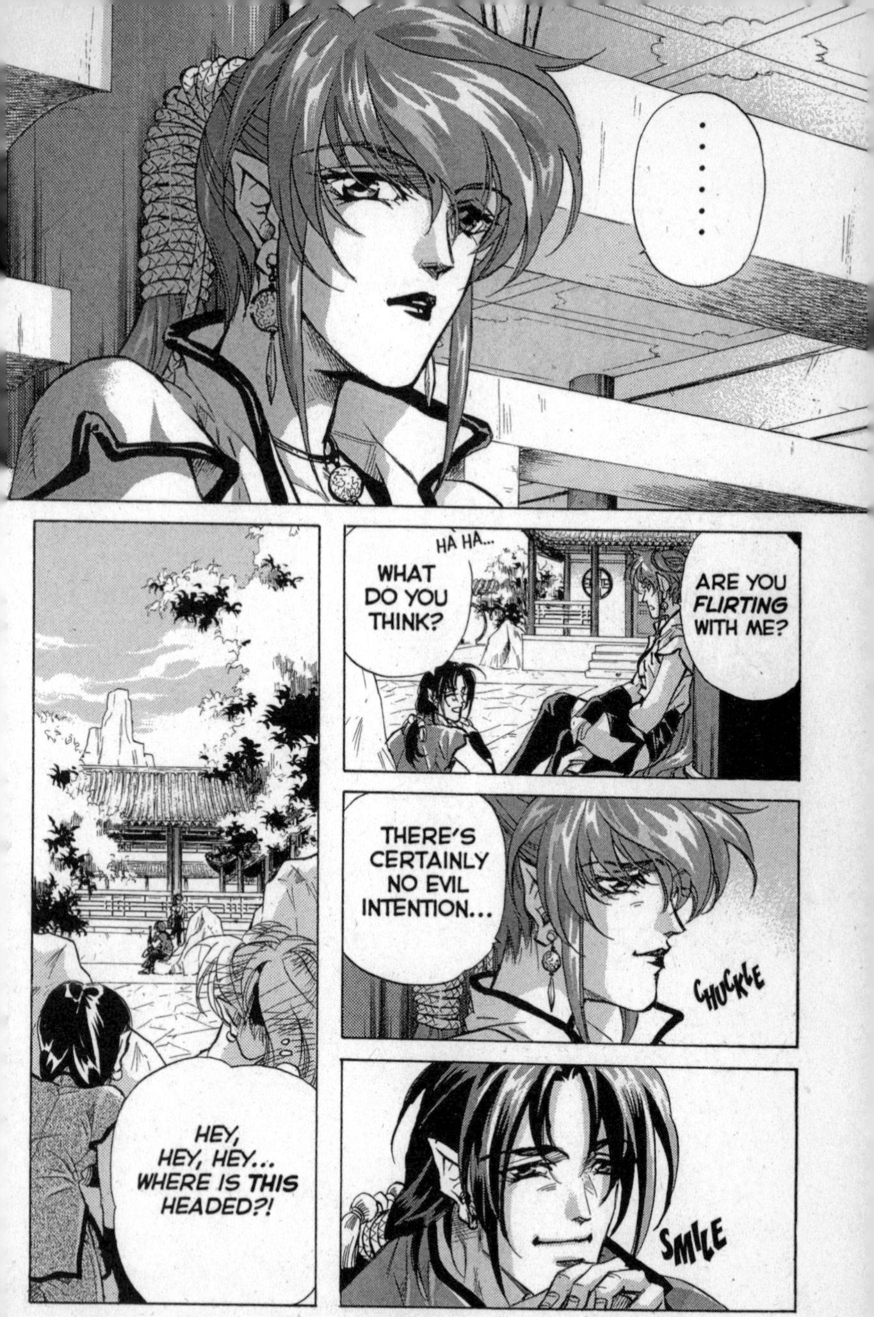
......
ARE YOU FLIRTING WITH ME?
HA HA...
WHAT DO YOU THINK?
THERE'S CERTAINLY NO EVIL INTENTION...
CHUCKLE
SMILE
HEY, HEY, HEY... WHERE IS THIS HEADED?!

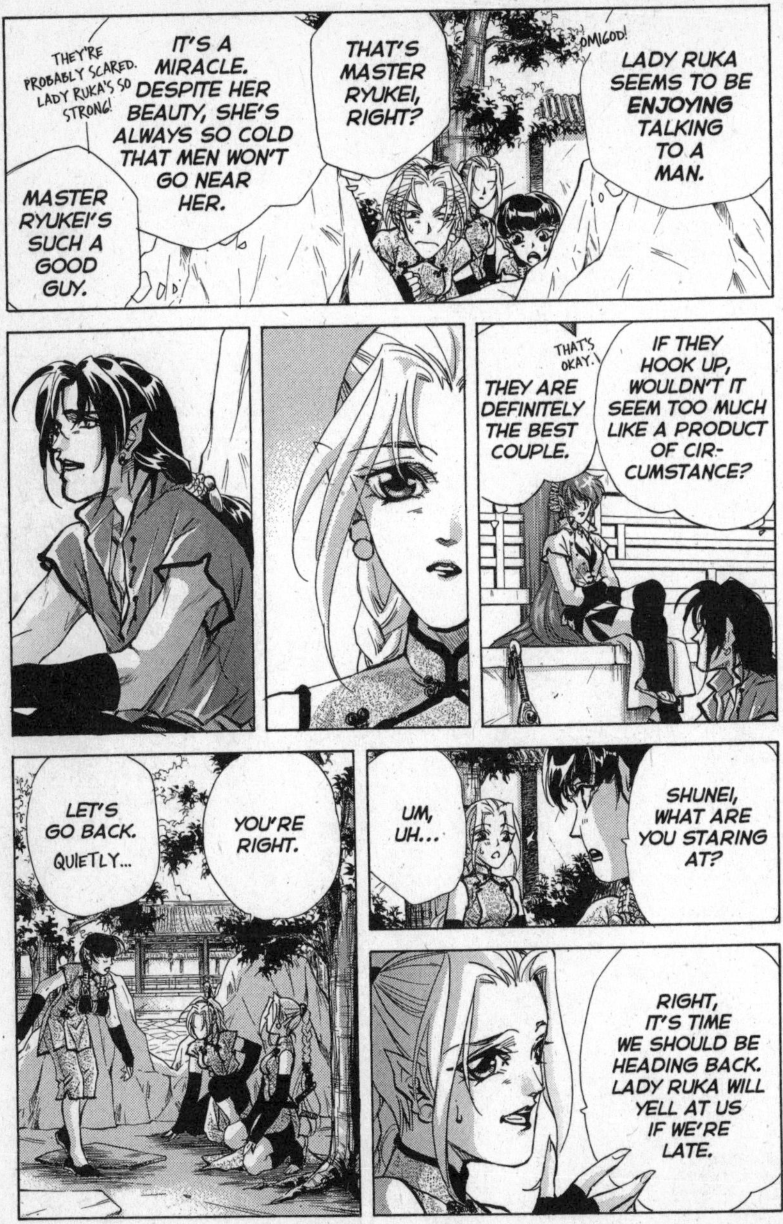
OMIGOD!
LADY RUKA SEEMS TO BE ENJOYING TALKING TO A MAN.
THAT'S MASTER RYUKEI, RIGHT?
IT'S A MIRACLE. DESPITE HER BEAUTY, SHE'S ALWAYS SO COLD THAT MEN WON'T GO NEAR HER.
THEY'RE PROBABLY SCARED. LADY RUKA'S SO STRONG!
MASTER RYUKEI'S SUCH A GOOD GUY.
IF THEY HOOK UP, WOULDN'T IT SEEM TOO MUCH LIKE A PRODUCT OF CIR-CUMSTANCE?
THAT'S OKAY.
THEY ARE DEFINITELY THE BEST COUPLE.
SHUNEI, WHAT ARE YOU STARING AT?
UM, UH...
RIGHT, IT'S TIME WE SHOULD BE HEADING BACK. LADY RUKA WILL YELL AT US IF WE'RE LATE.
YOU'RE RIGHT.
LET'S GO BACK.
QUIETLY...

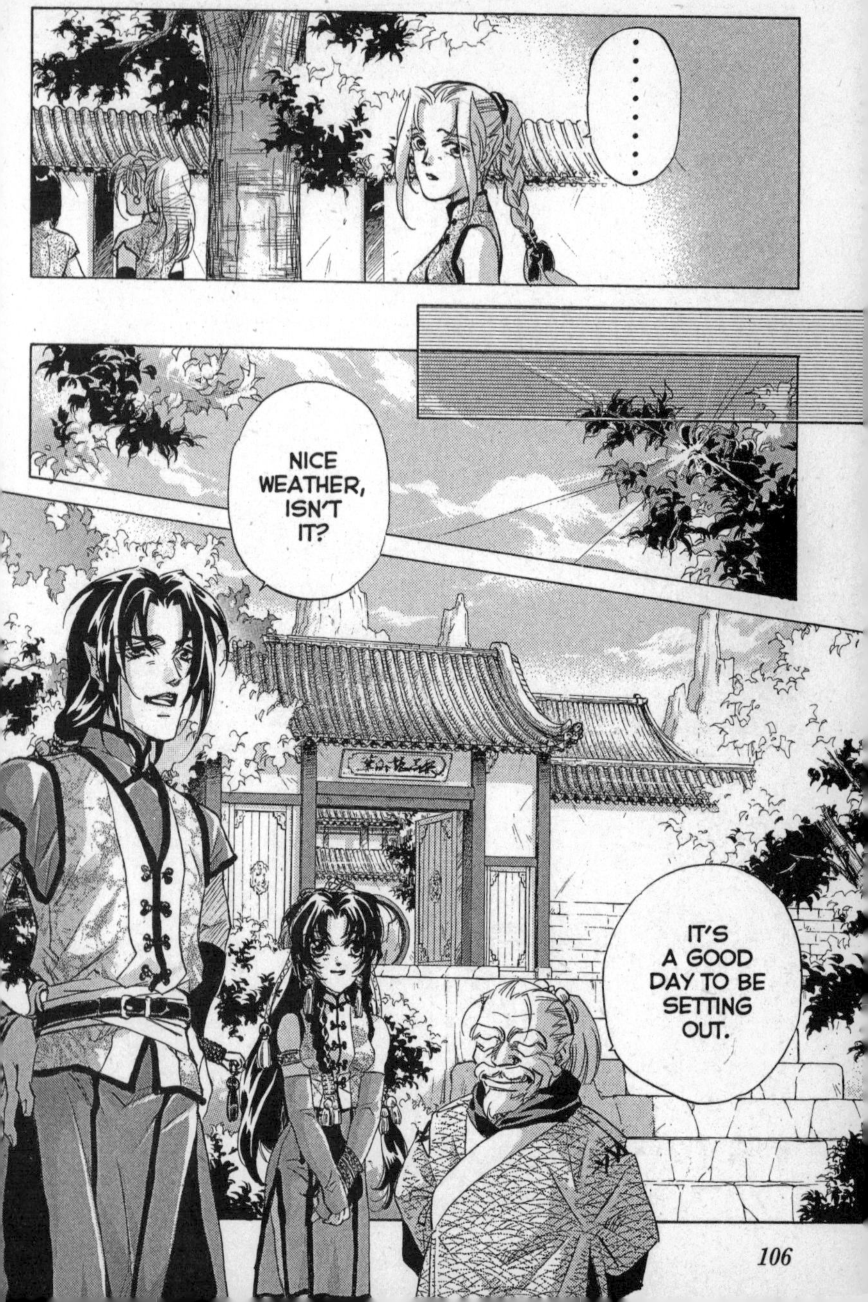
......
NICE WEATHER, ISN'T IT?
IT'S A GOOD DAY TO BE SETTING OUT.

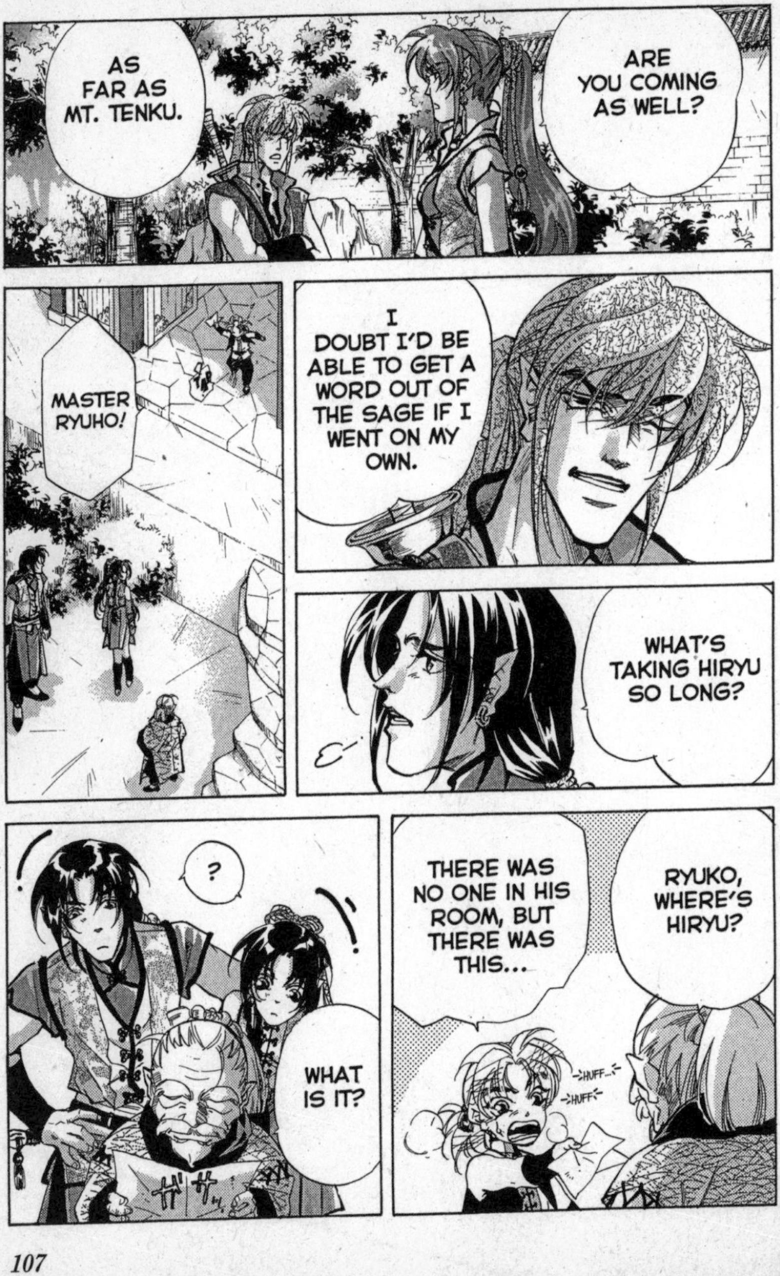
ARE YOU COMING AS WELL?
AS FAR AS MT. TENKU.
I DOUBT I'D BE ABLE TO GET A WORD OUT OF THE SAGE IF I WENT ON MY OWN.
WHAT'S TAKING HIRYU SO LONG?
MASTER RYUHO!
RYUKO, WHERE'S HIRYU?
THERE WAS NO ONE IN HIS ROOM, BUT THERE WAS THIS...
HUFF
HUFF
WHAT IS IT?
?

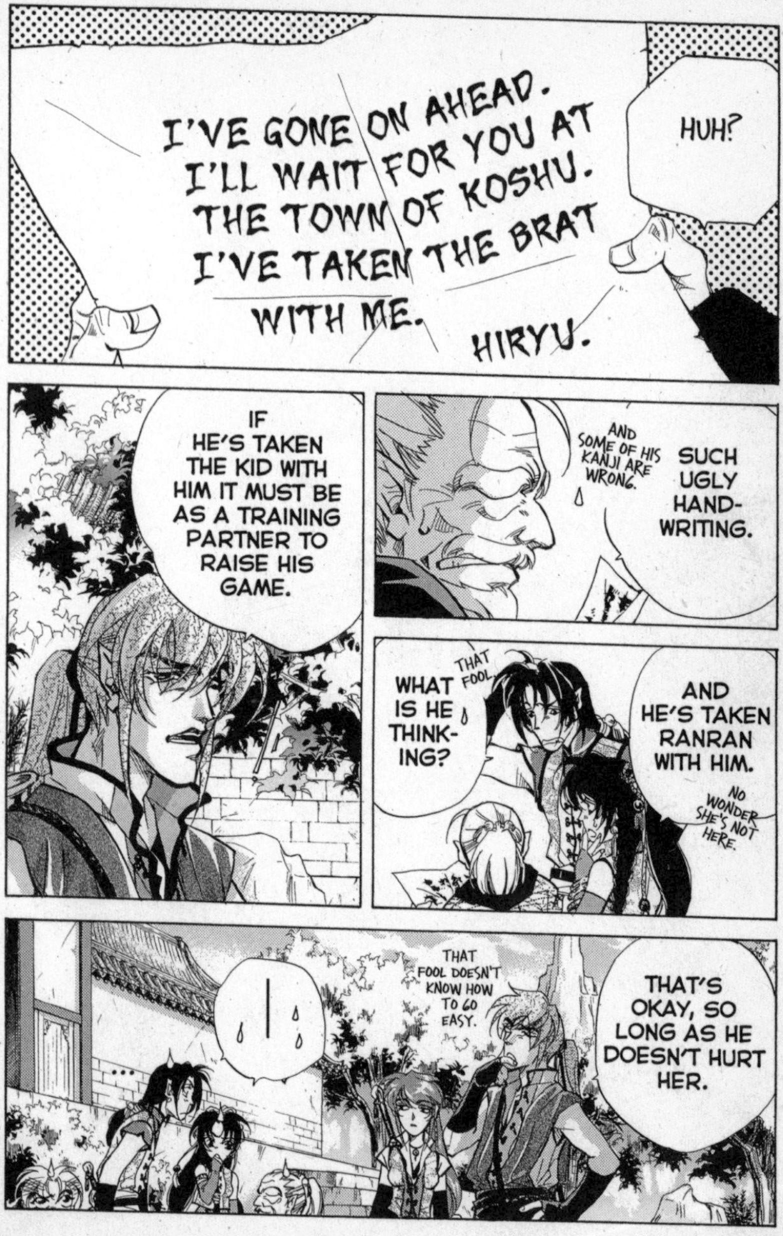
HUH?
I'VE GONE ON AHEAD. I'LL WAIT FOR YOU AT THE TOWN OF KOSHU. I'VE TAKEN THE BRAT WITH ME.
HIRYU.
SUCH UGLY HAND-WRITING.
AND SOME OF HIS KANJI ARE WRONG.
AND HE'S TAKEN RANRAN WITH HIM.
NO WONDER SHE'S NOT HERE.
THAT FOOL.
WHAT IS HE THINKING?
IF HE'S TAKEN THE KID WITH HIM IT MUST BE AS A TRAINING PARTNER TO RAISE HIS GAME.
THAT'S OKAY, SO LONG AS HE DOESN'T HURT HER.
THAT FOOL DOESN'T KNOW HOW TO GO EASY.
!
...

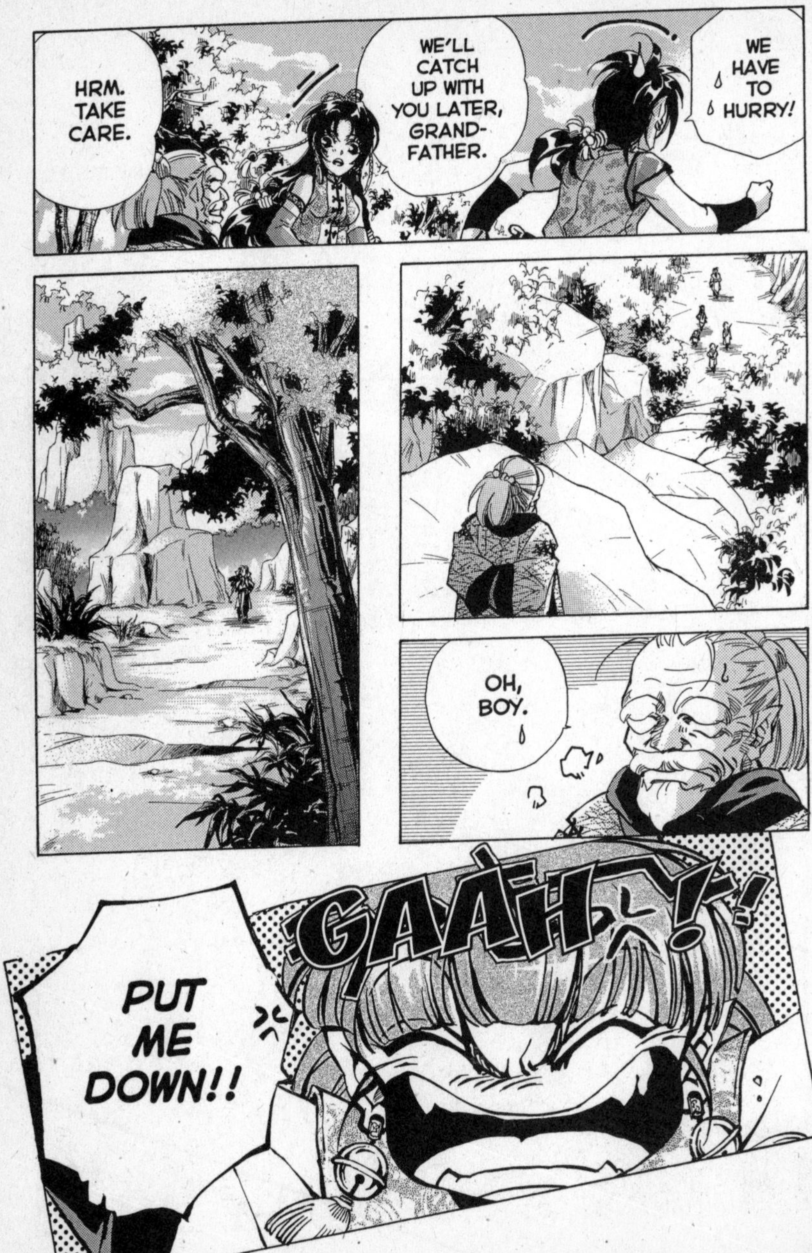
WE HAVE TO HURRY!
WE'LL CATCH UP WITH YOU LATER, GRAND-FATHER.
HRM. TAKE CARE.
OH, BOY.
GAAH!
PUT ME DOWN!!

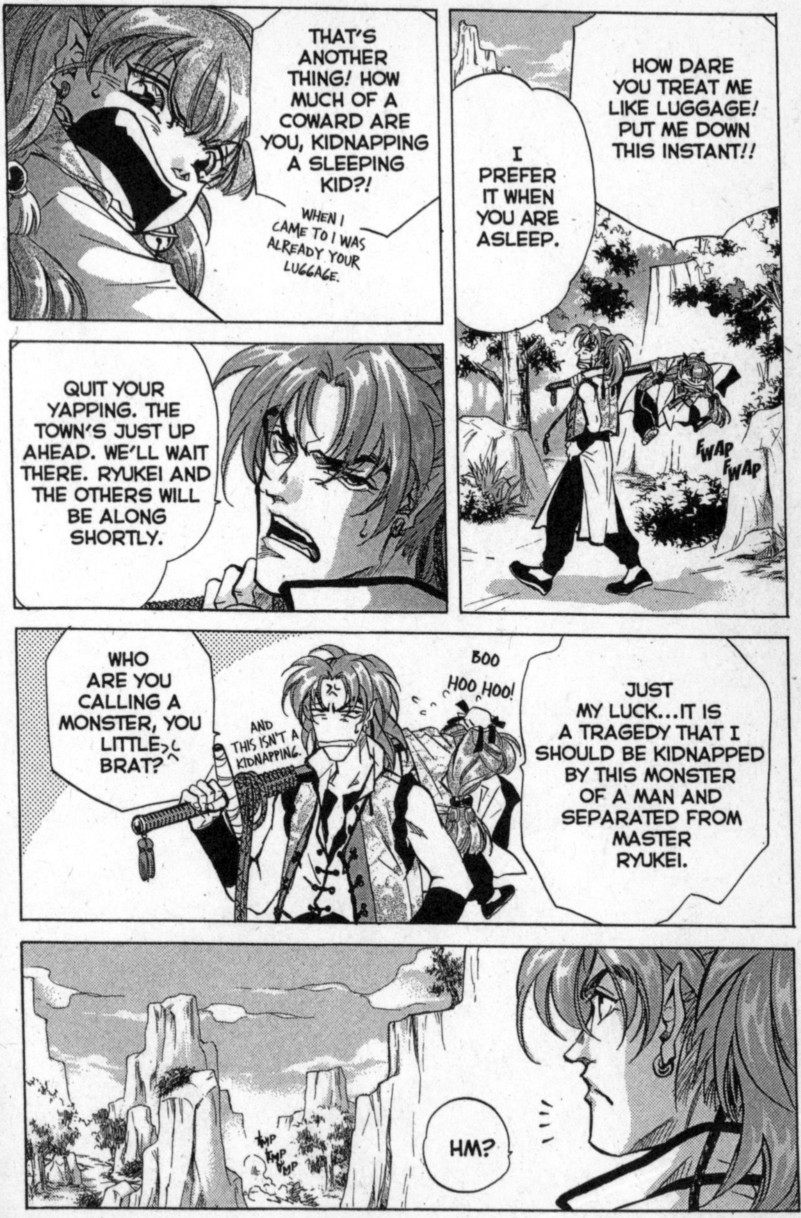
HOW DARE YOU TREAT ME LIKE LUGGAGE! PUT ME DOWN THIS INSTANT!!
I PREFER IT WHEN YOU ARE ASLEEP.
FWAP FWAP
THAT'S ANOTHER THING! HOW MUCH OF A COWARD ARE YOU, KIDNAPPING A SLEEPING KID?!
WHEN I CAME TO I WAS ALREADY YOUR LUGGAGE.
QUIT YOUR YAPPING. THE TOWN'S JUST UP AHEAD. WE'LL WAIT THERE. RYUKEI AND THE OTHERS WILL BE ALONG SHORTLY.
JUST MY LUCK...IT IS A TRAGEDY THAT I SHOULD BE KIDNAPPED BY THIS MONSTER OF A MAN AND SEPARATED FROM MASTER RYUKEI.
BOO HOO HOO!
WHO ARE YOU CALLING A MONSTER, YOU LITTLE BRAT?
AND THIS ISN'T A KIDNAPPING.
HM?
TMP TMP TMP

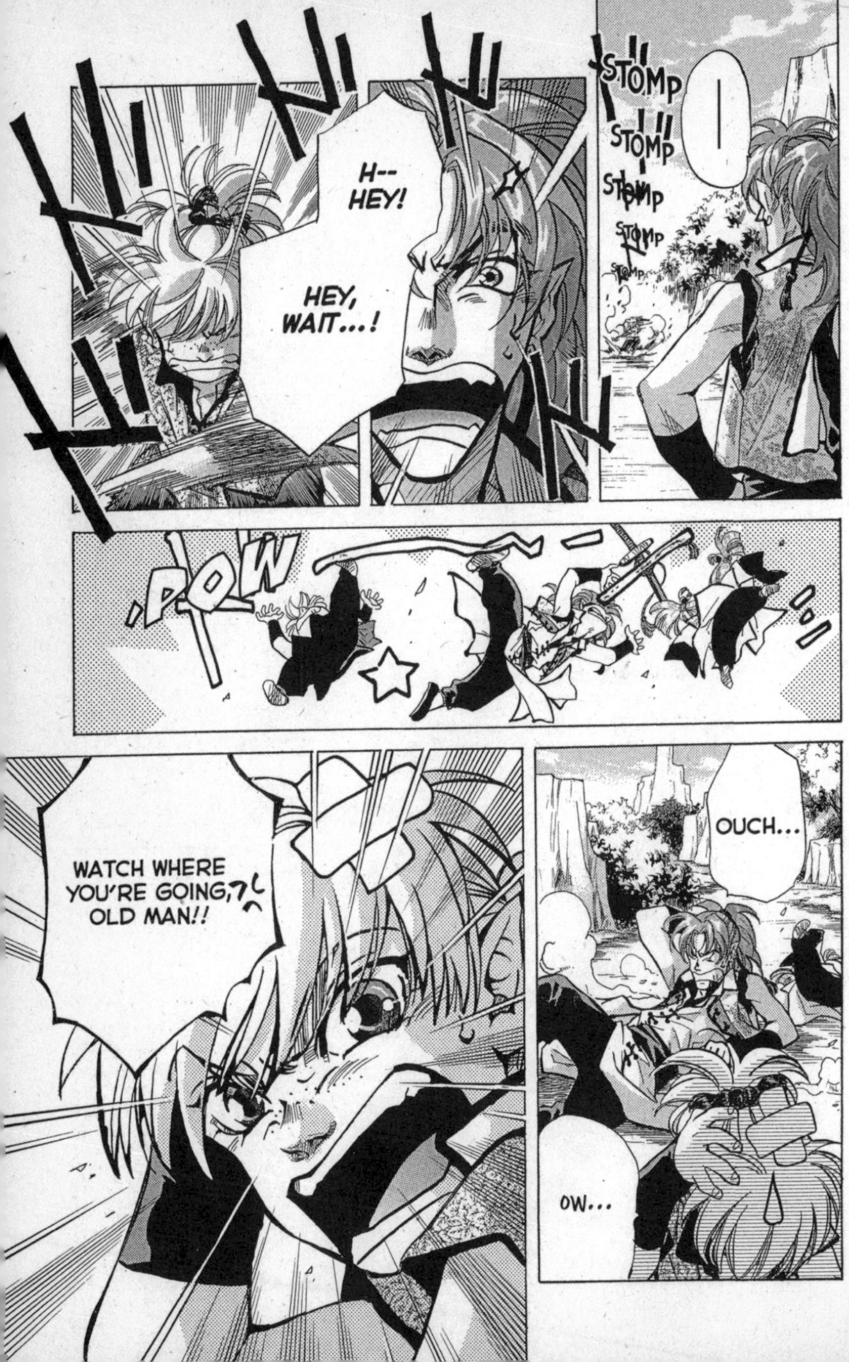
STOMP
STOMP
STOMP
STOMP
STOMP
H--
HEY!
HEY,
WAIT...!
POW
OUCH...
OW...
WATCH WHERE YOU'RE GOING, OLD MAN!!

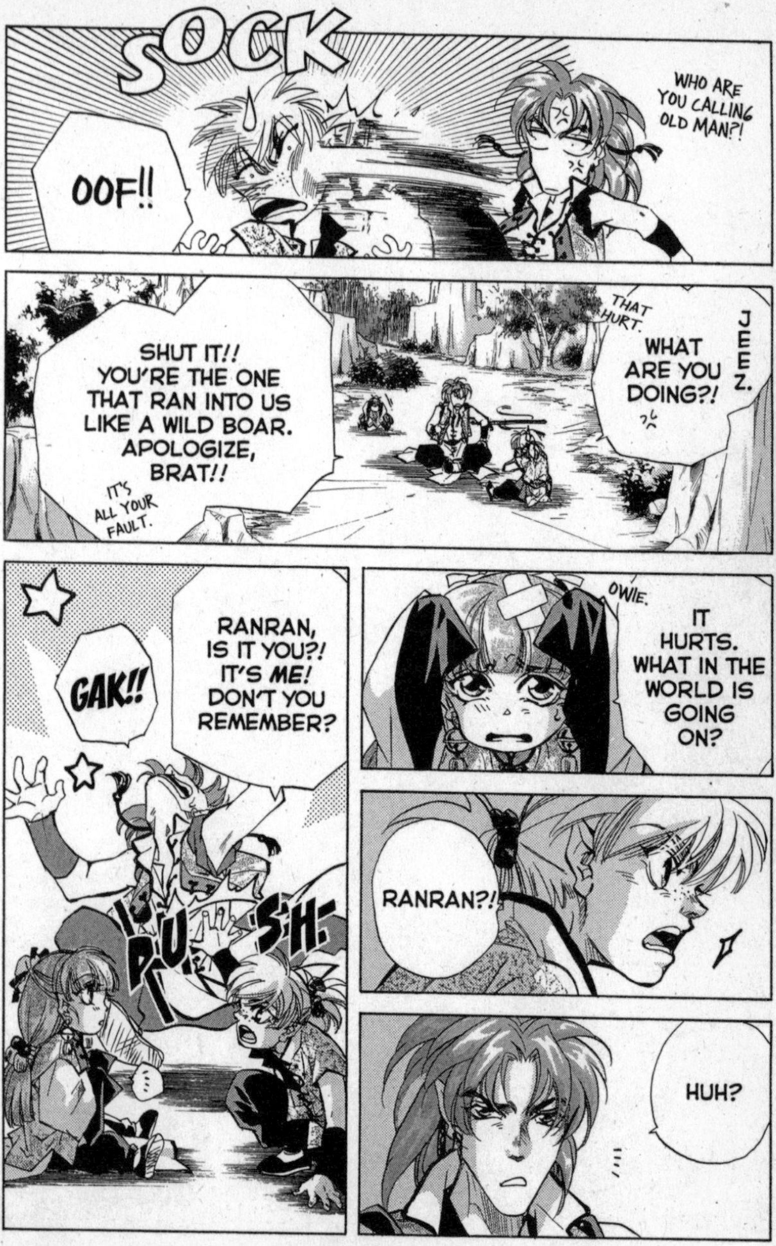
SOCK
WHO ARE YOU CALLING OLD MAN?!
OOF!!
JEEZ.
THAT HURT.
WHAT ARE YOU DOING?!
SHUT IT!! YOU'RE THE ONE THAT RAN INTO US LIKE A WILD BOAR. APOLOGIZE, BRAT!!
IT'S ALL YOUR FAULT.
OWIE.
IT HURTS. WHAT IN THE WORLD IS GOING ON?
RANRAN?!
HUH?
RANRAN, IS IT YOU?! IT'S *ME*! DON'T YOU REMEMBER?
GAK!!
PUSH
...

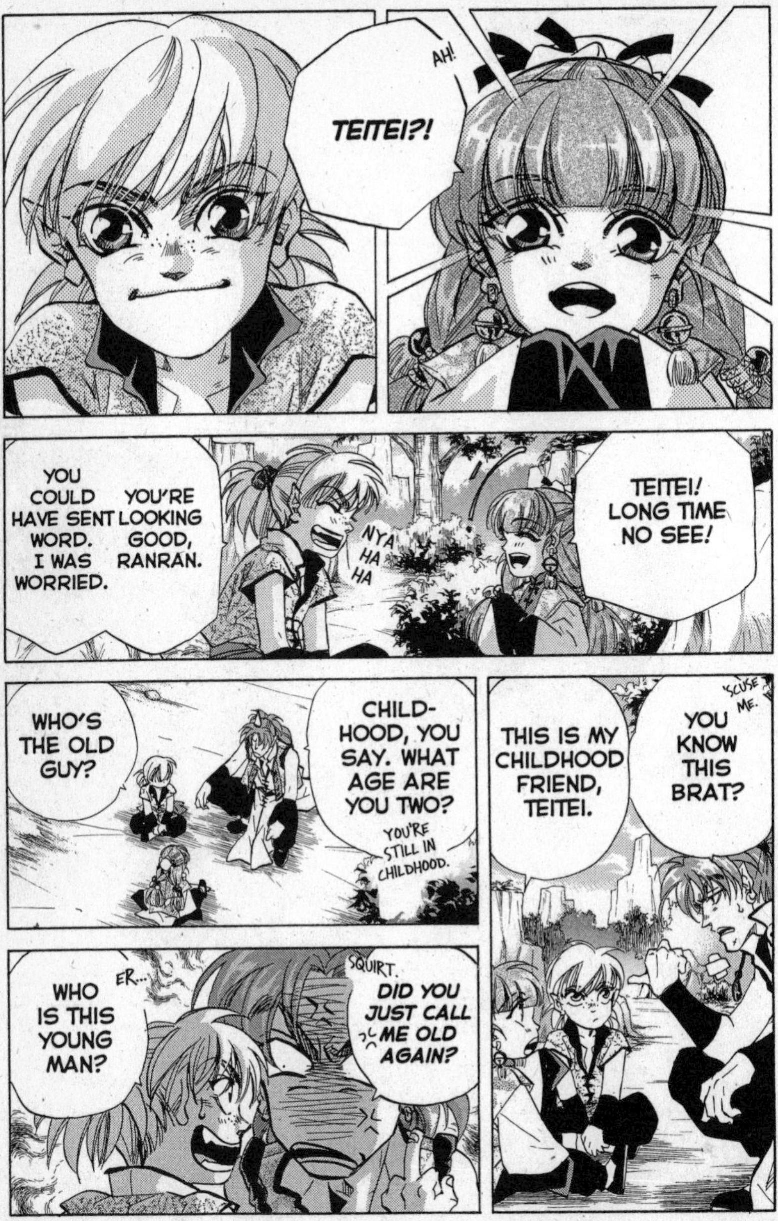
AH!
TEITEI?!
TEITEI! LONG TIME NO SEE!
NYA HA HA
YOU'RE LOOKING GOOD, RANRAN.
YOU COULD HAVE SENT WORD. I WAS WORRIED.
'SCUSE ME.
YOU KNOW THIS BRAT?
THIS IS MY CHILDHOOD FRIEND, TEITEI.
CHILDHOOD, YOU SAY. WHAT AGE ARE YOU TWO?
YOU'RE STILL IN CHILDHOOD.
WHO'S THE OLD GUY?
SQUIRT.
DID YOU JUST CALL ME OLD AGAIN?
ER...
WHO IS THIS YOUNG MAN?

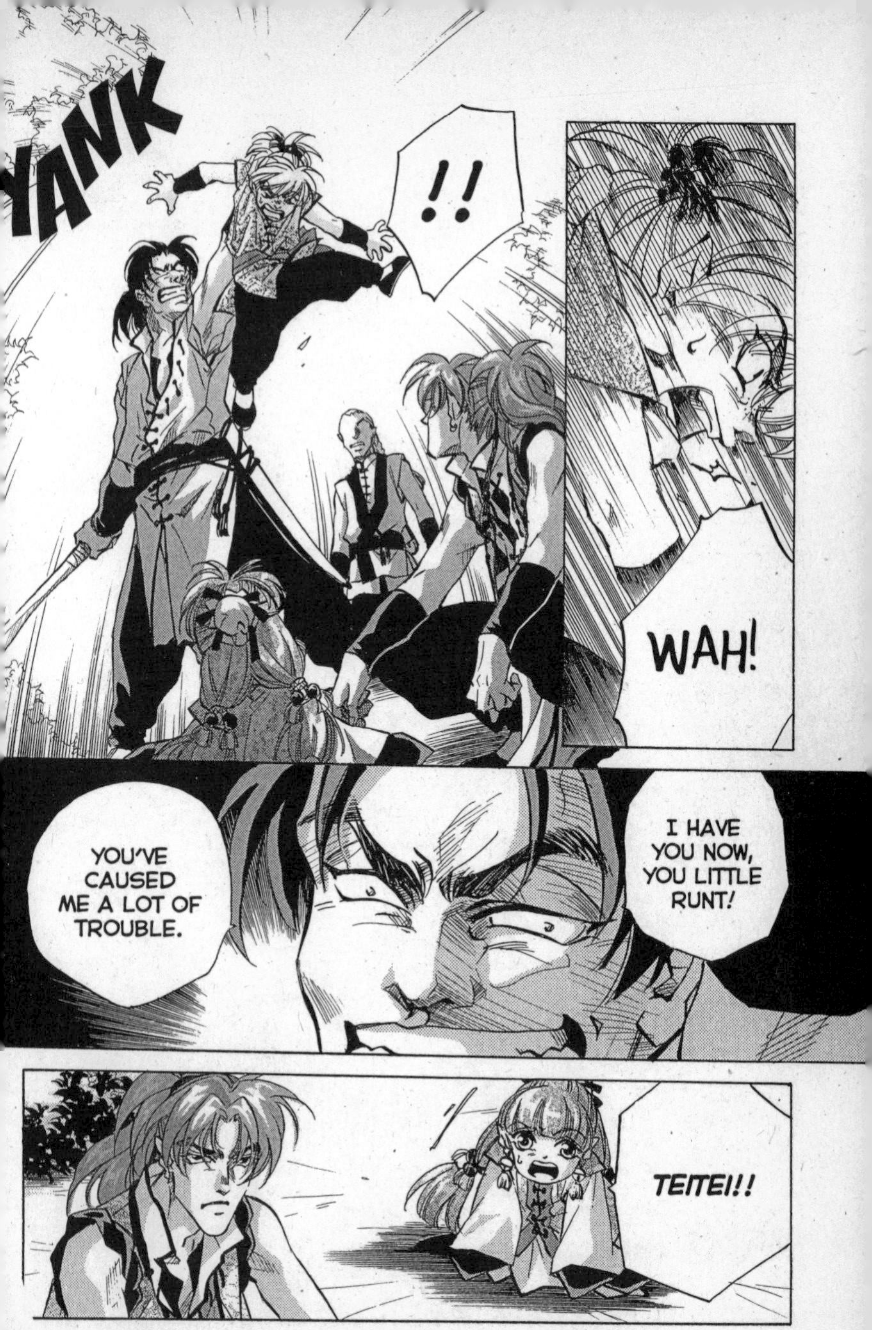
WAH!
!!
YANK
I HAVE YOU NOW, YOU LITTLE RUNT!
YOU'VE CAUSED ME A LOT OF TROUBLE.
TEITEI!!

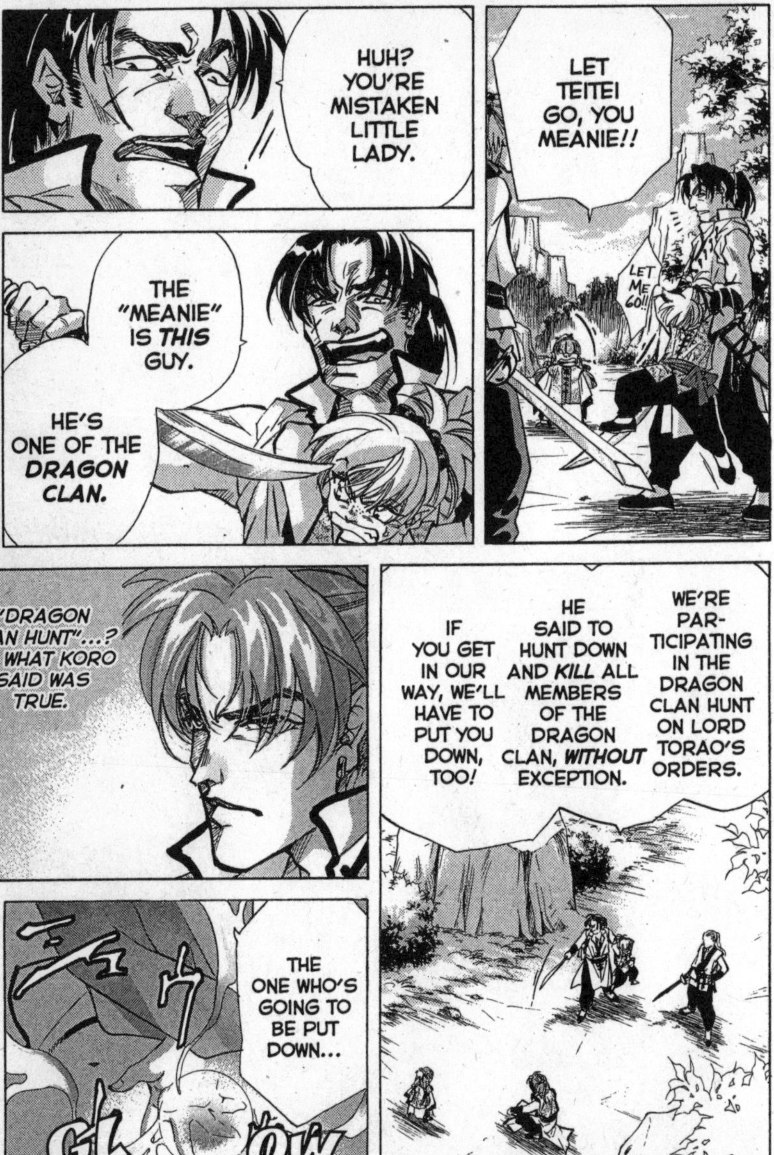
LET TEITEI GO, YOU MEANIE!!
LET ME GO!!
HUH? YOU'RE MISTAKEN LITTLE LADY.
THE "MEANIE" IS *THIS* GUY.
HE'S ONE OF THE *DRAGON CLAN.*
WE'RE PARTICIPATING IN THE DRAGON CLAN HUNT ON LORD TORAO'S ORDERS.
HE SAID TO HUNT DOWN AND *KILL* ALL MEMBERS OF THE DRAGON CLAN, *WITHOUT* EXCEPTION.
IF YOU GET IN OUR WAY, WE'LL HAVE TO PUT YOU DOWN, TOO!
"DRAGON CLAN HUNT"...? SO WHAT KORO SAID WAS TRUE.
THE ONE WHO'S GOING TO BE PUT DOWN...
GLOW

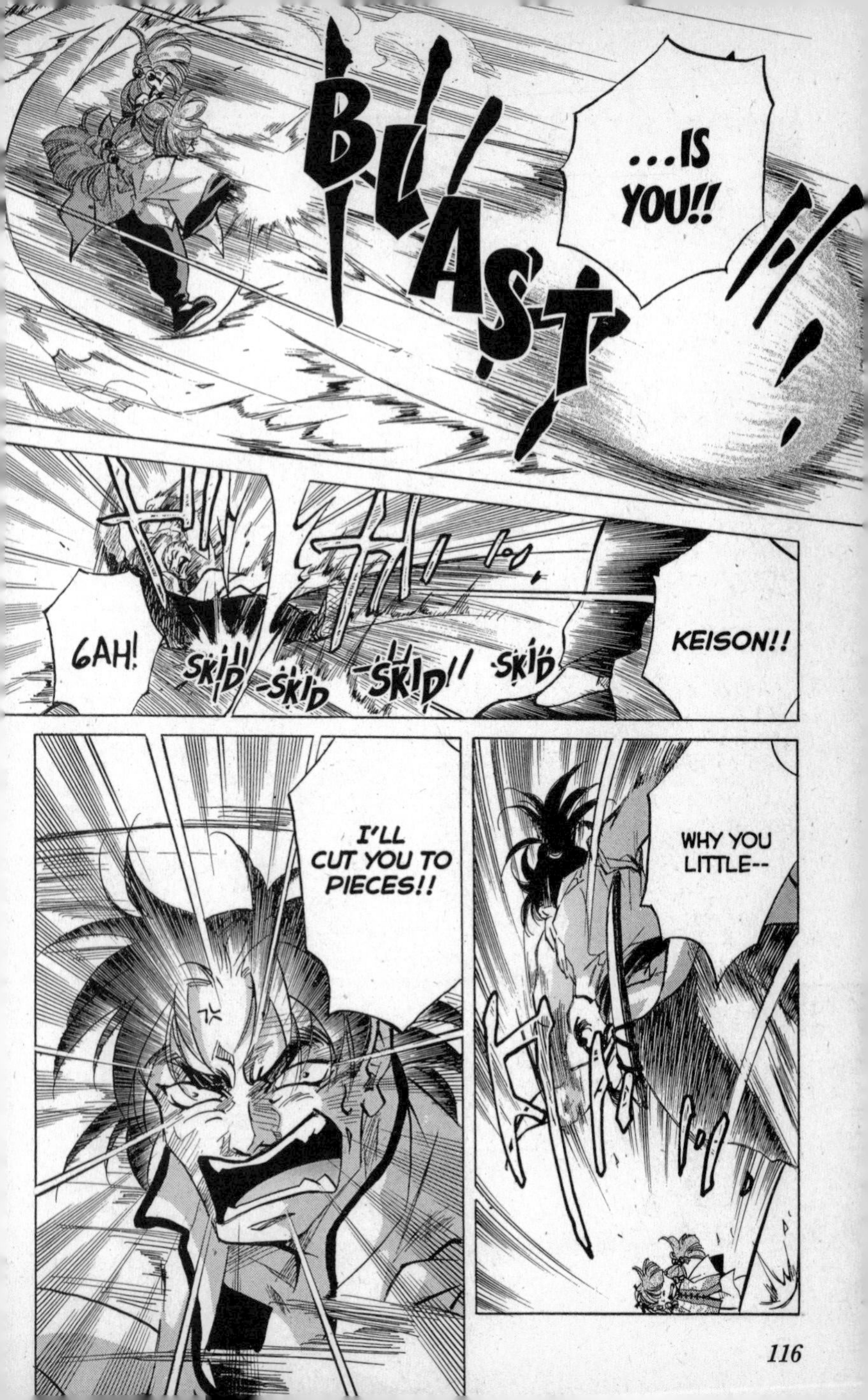
...IS YOU!!
BLAST
KEISON!!
SKID
SKID
SKID
SKID
GAH!
WHY YOU LITTLE--
I'LL CUT YOU TO PIECES!!

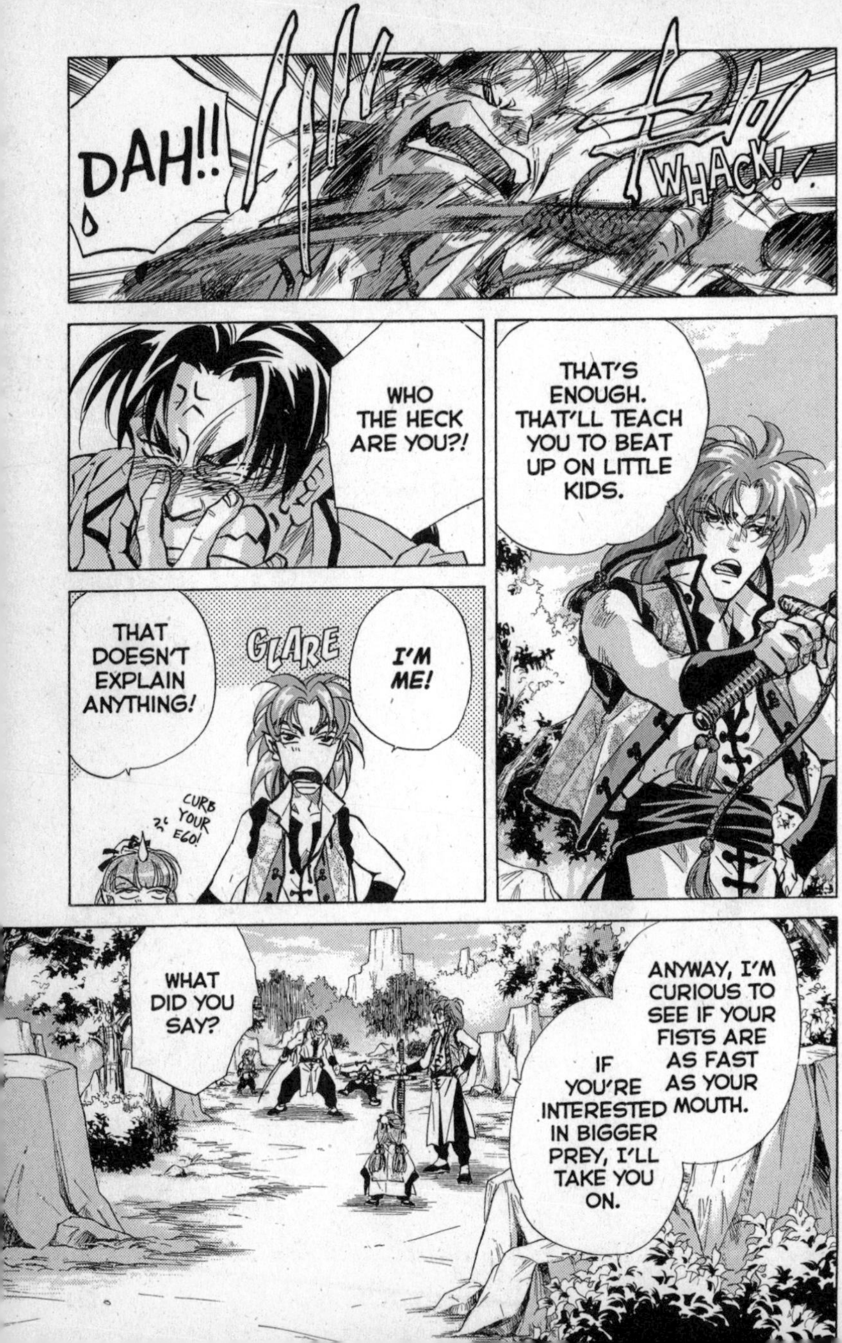
WHACK!!
DAH!!
THAT'S ENOUGH. THAT'LL TEACH YOU TO BEAT UP ON LITTLE KIDS.
WHO THE HECK ARE YOU?!
I'M ME!
GLARE
THAT DOESN'T EXPLAIN ANYTHING!
CURB YOUR EGO!
ANYWAY, I'M CURIOUS TO SEE IF YOUR FISTS ARE AS FAST AS YOUR MOUTH.
WHAT DID YOU SAY?
IF YOU'RE INTERESTED IN BIGGER PREY, I'LL TAKE YOU ON.

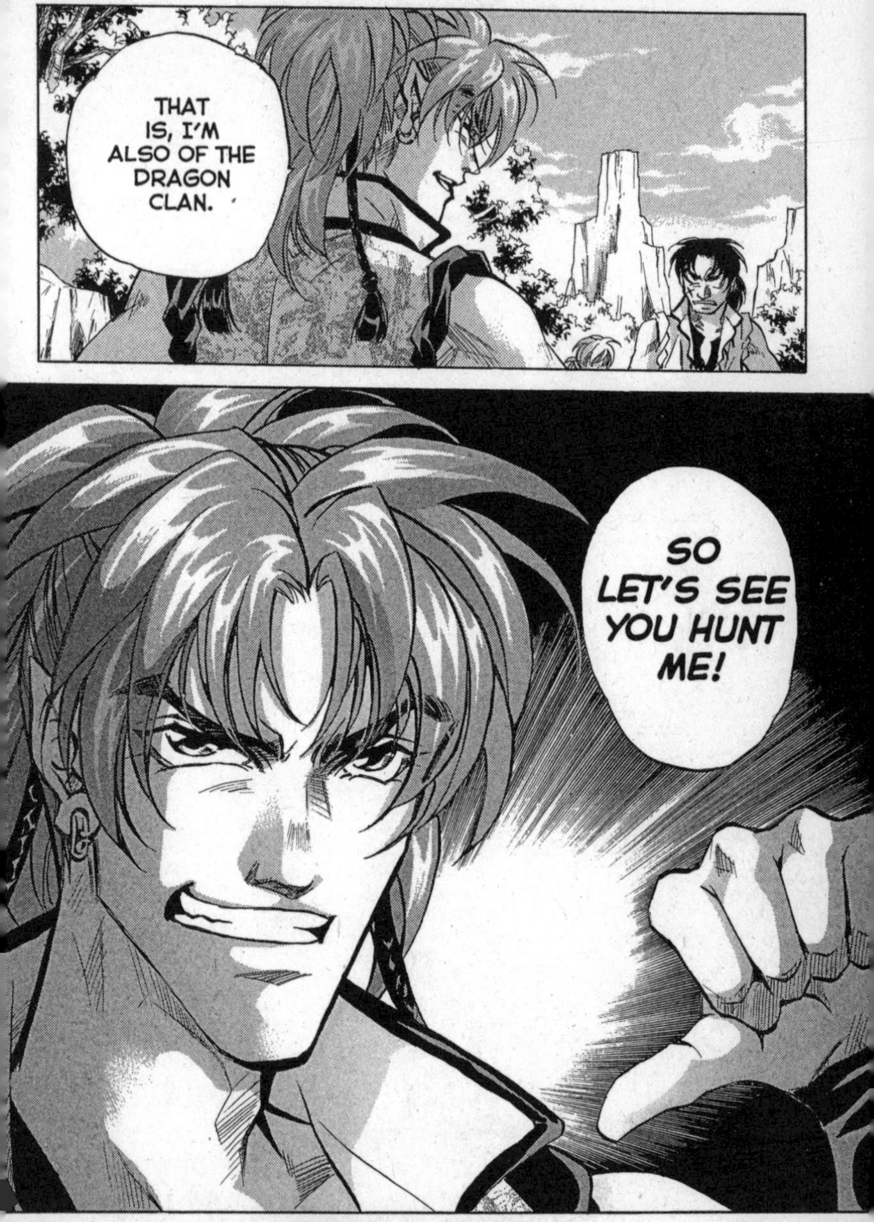
THAT IS, I'M ALSO OF THE DRAGON CLAN.
SO LET'S SEE YOU HUNT ME!

CHAPTER 10: END

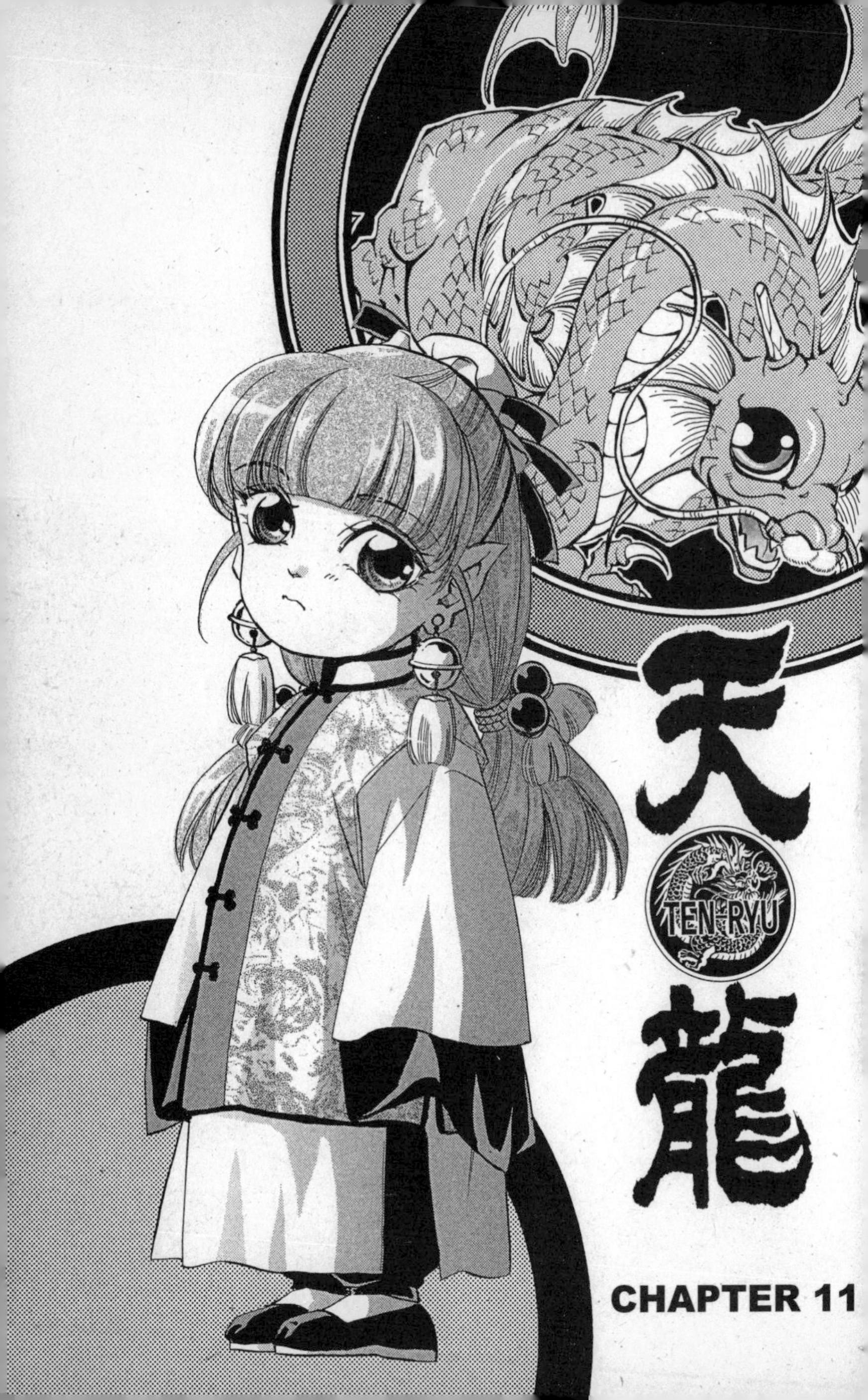
天龍
TEN-RYU
CHAPTER 11

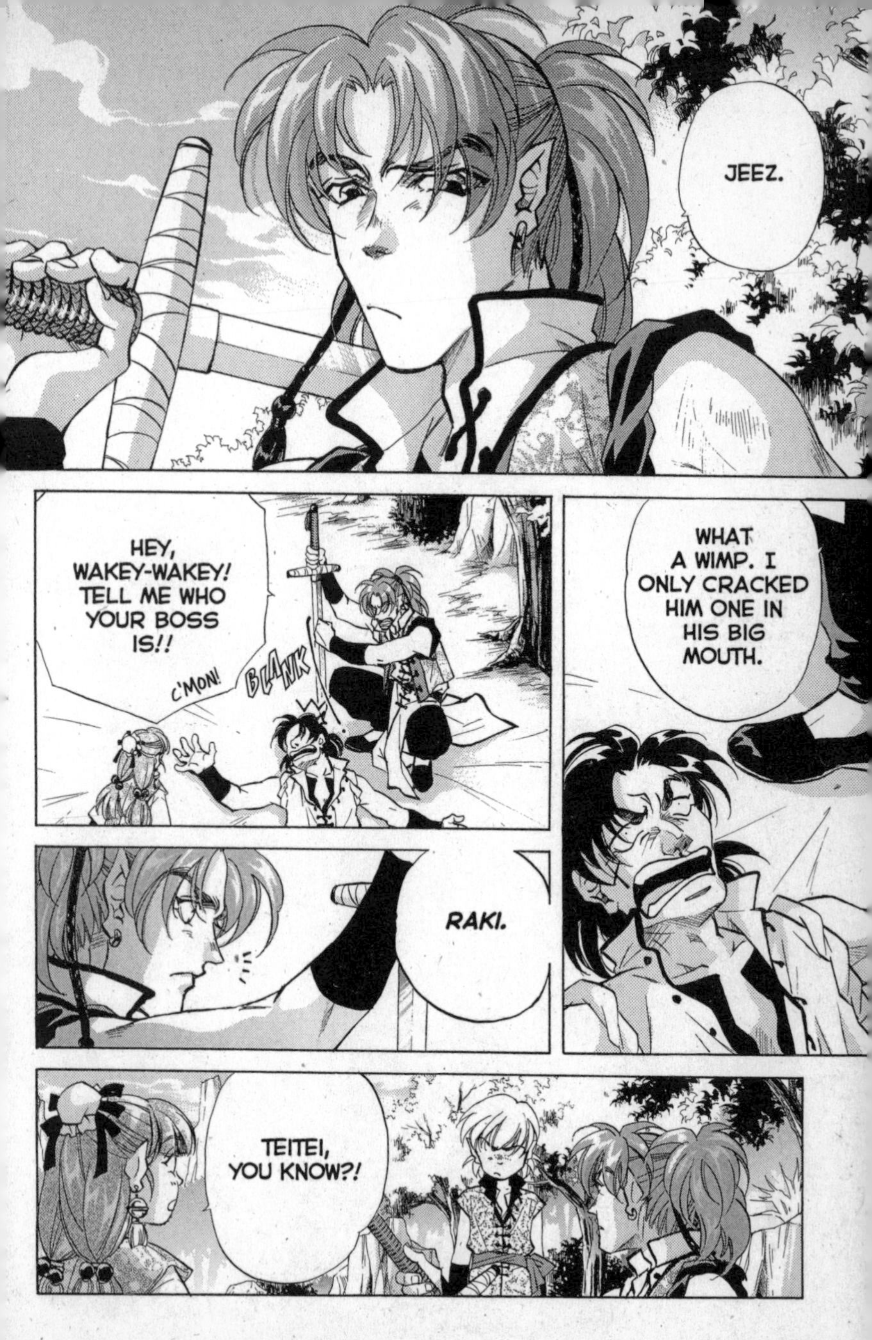
JEEZ.
WHAT A WIMP. I ONLY CRACKED HIM ONE IN HIS BIG MOUTH.
HEY, WAKEY-WAKEY! TELL ME WHO YOUR BOSS IS!!
C'MON!
BLANK
RAKI.
TEITEI, YOU KNOW?!

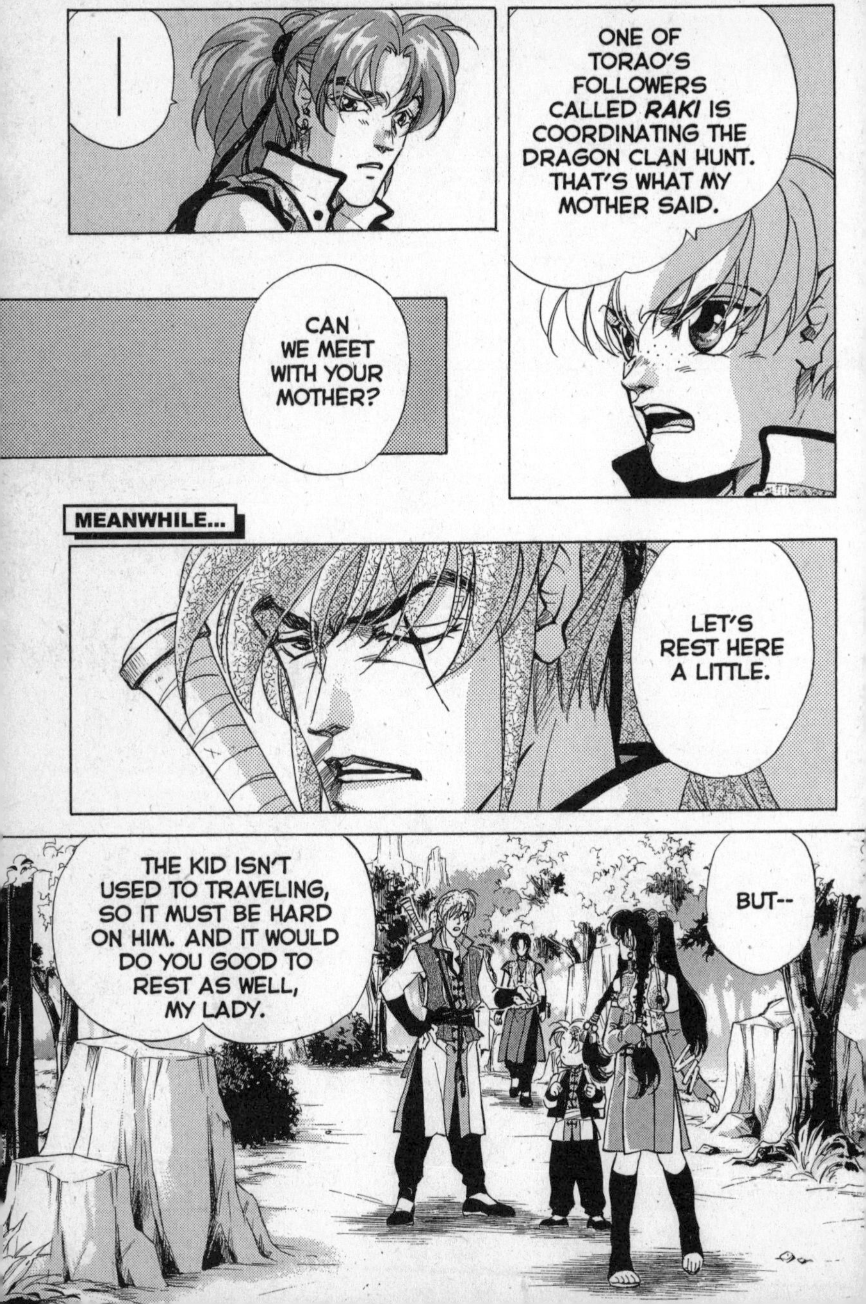
ONE OF TORAO'S FOLLOWERS CALLED *RAKI* IS COORDINATING THE DRAGON CLAN HUNT. THAT'S WHAT MY MOTHER SAID.
CAN WE MEET WITH YOUR MOTHER?
MEANWHILE...
LET'S REST HERE A LITTLE.
BUT--
THE KID ISN'T USED TO TRAVELING, SO IT MUST BE HARD ON HIM. AND IT WOULD DO YOU GOOD TO REST AS WELL, MY LADY.

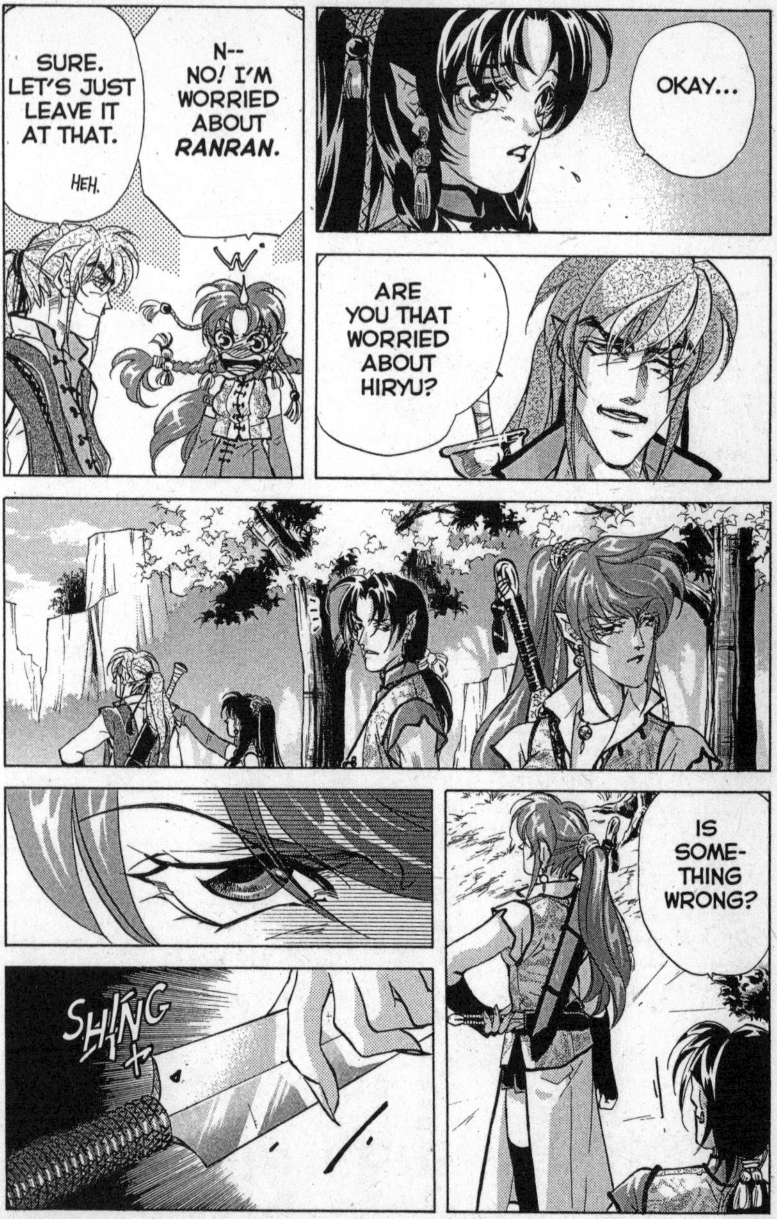
OKAY...
ARE YOU THAT WORRIED ABOUT HIRYU?
N-- NO! I'M WORRIED ABOUT *RANRAN*.
SURE. LET'S JUST LEAVE IT AT THAT.
HEH.
IS SOME-THING WRONG?
SHING

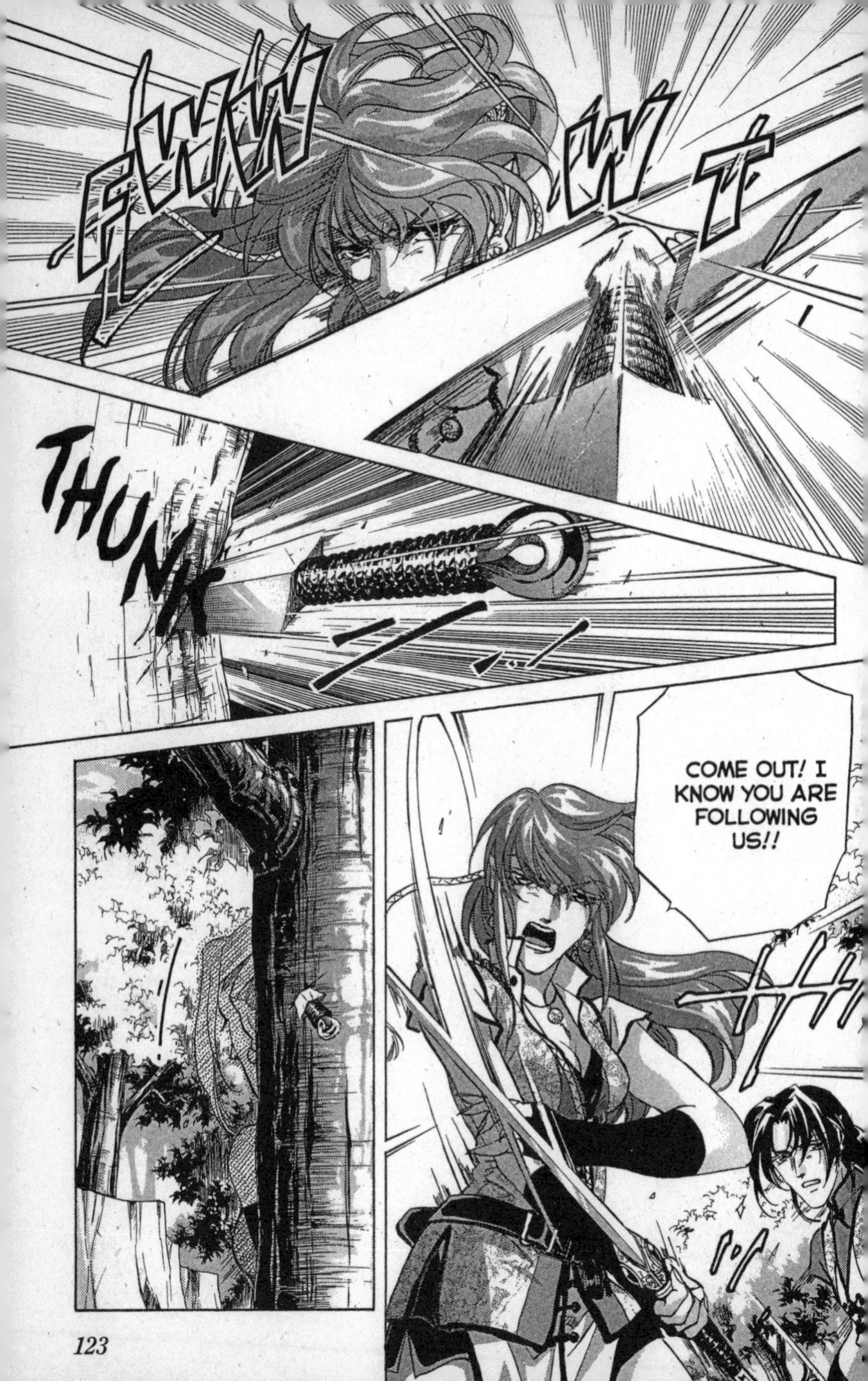

FWAN
FWT
THUNK
COME OUT! I KNOW YOU ARE FOLLOWING US!!

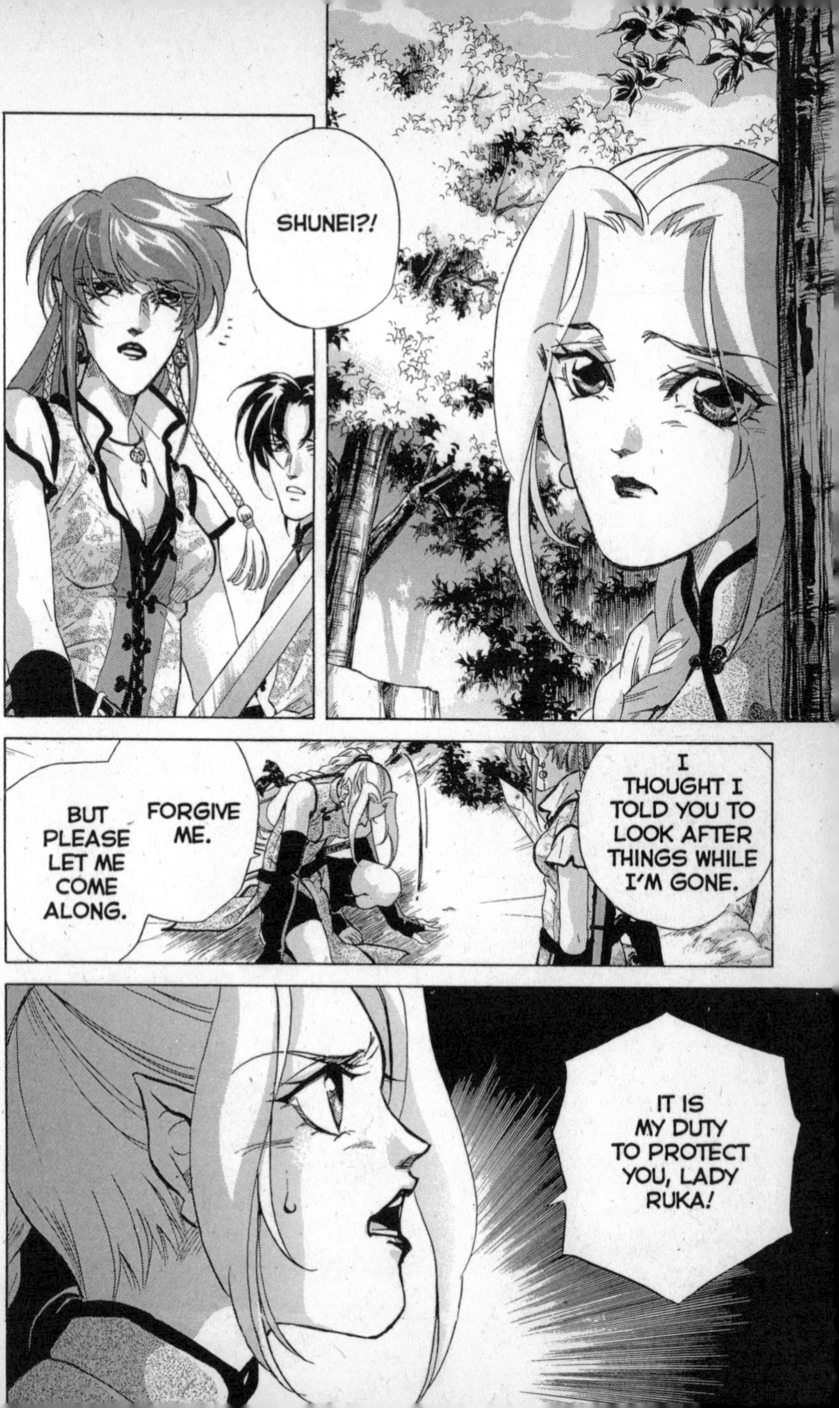
SHUNEI?!
I THOUGHT I TOLD YOU TO LOOK AFTER THINGS WHILE I'M GONE.
FORGIVE ME.
BUT PLEASE LET ME COME ALONG.
IT IS MY DUTY TO PROTECT YOU, LADY RUKA!

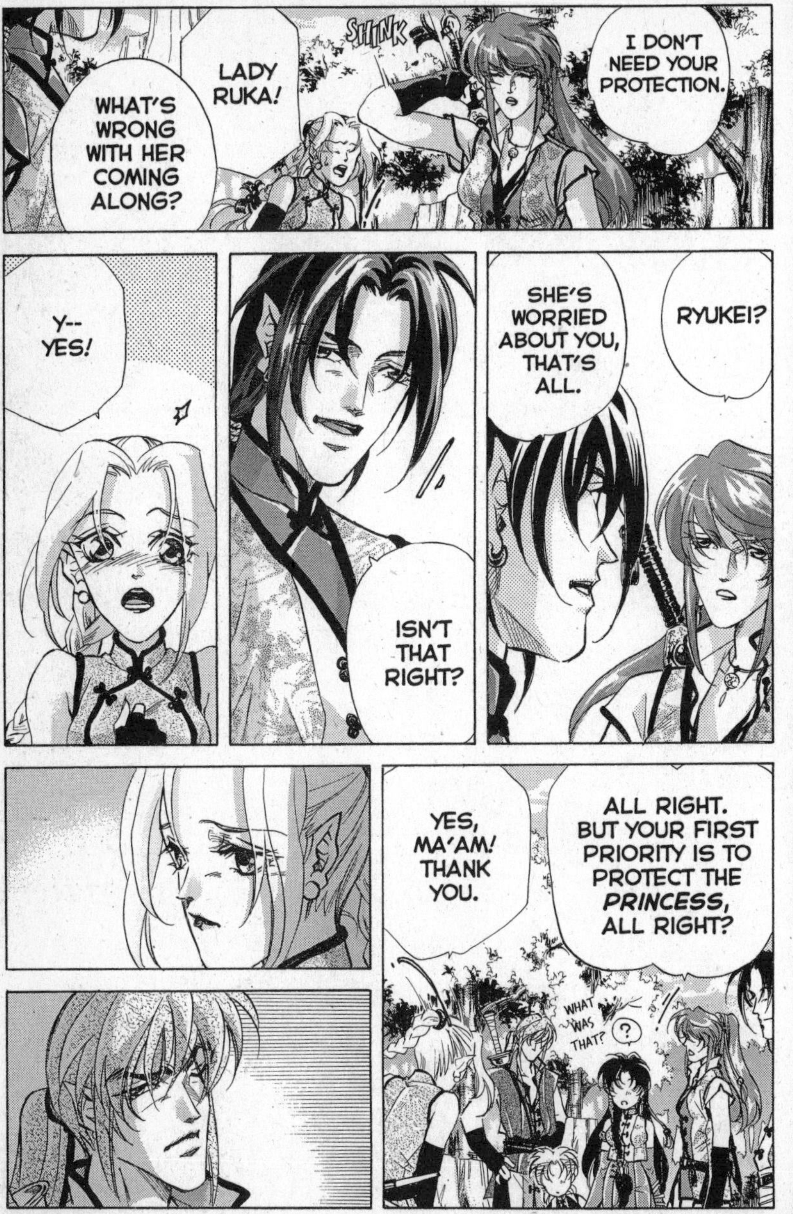
I DON'T NEED YOUR PROTECTION.
SHINK
LADY RUKA!
WHAT'S WRONG WITH HER COMING ALONG?
RYUKEI?
SHE'S WORRIED ABOUT YOU, THAT'S ALL.
ISN'T THAT RIGHT?
Y-- YES!
ALL RIGHT. BUT YOUR FIRST PRIORITY IS TO PROTECT THE *PRINCESS*, ALL RIGHT?
YES, MA'AM! THANK YOU.
WHAT WAS THAT?
?

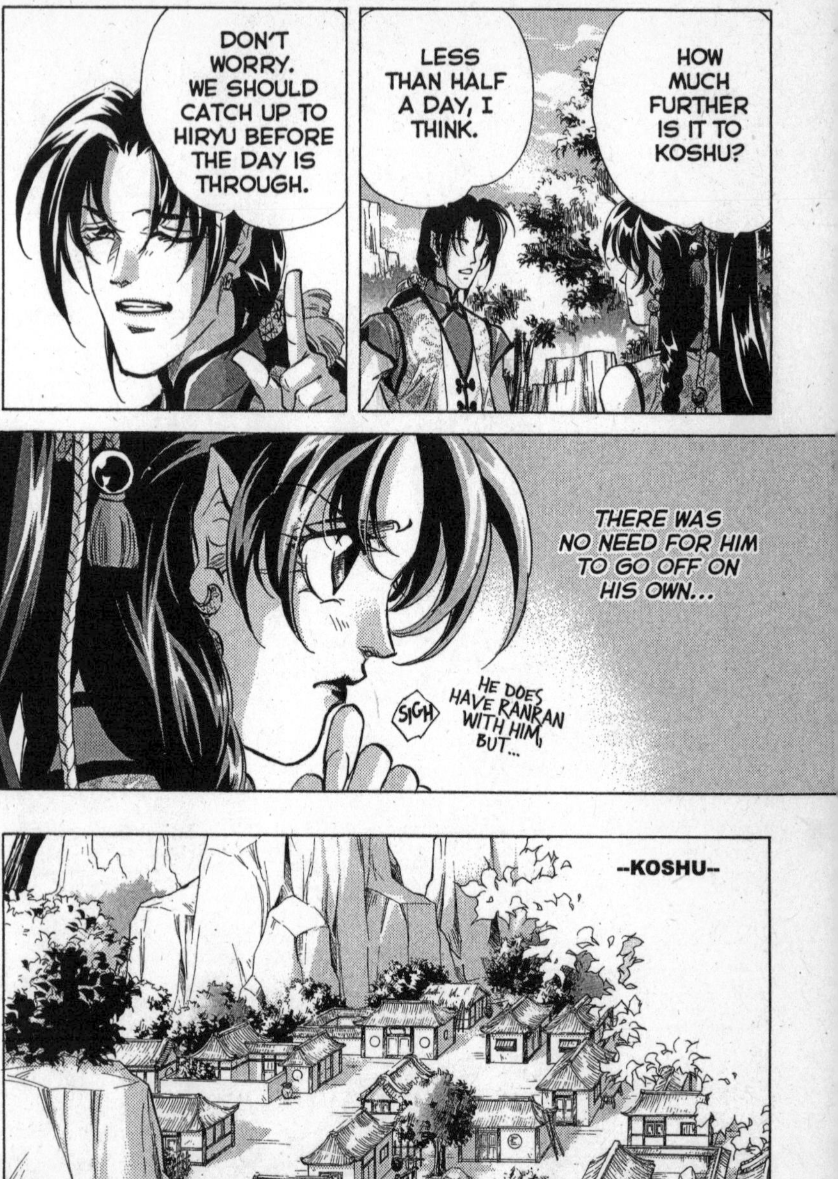
HOW MUCH FURTHER IS IT TO KOSHU?
LESS THAN HALF A DAY, I THINK.
DON'T WORRY. WE SHOULD CATCH UP TO HIRYU BEFORE THE DAY IS THROUGH.
THERE WAS NO NEED FOR HIM TO GO OFF ON HIS OWN...
SIGH
HE DOES HAVE RANRAN WITH HIM, BUT...
--KOSHU--

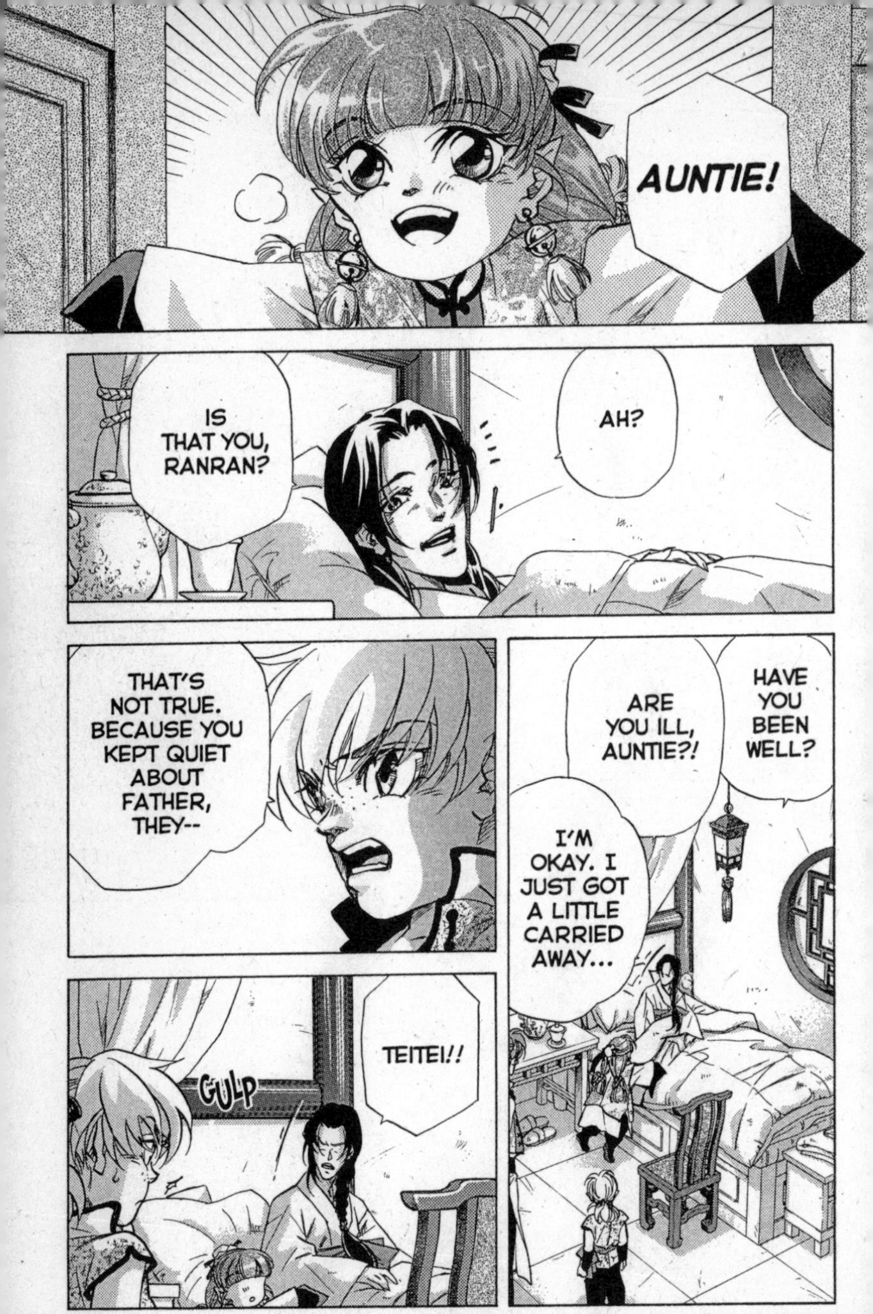
AUNTIE!
AH?
IS THAT YOU, RANRAN?
HAVE YOU BEEN WELL?
ARE YOU ILL, AUNTIE?!
I'M OKAY. I JUST GOT A LITTLE CARRIED AWAY...
THAT'S NOT TRUE. BECAUSE YOU KEPT QUIET ABOUT FATHER, THEY--
TEITEI!!
GULP

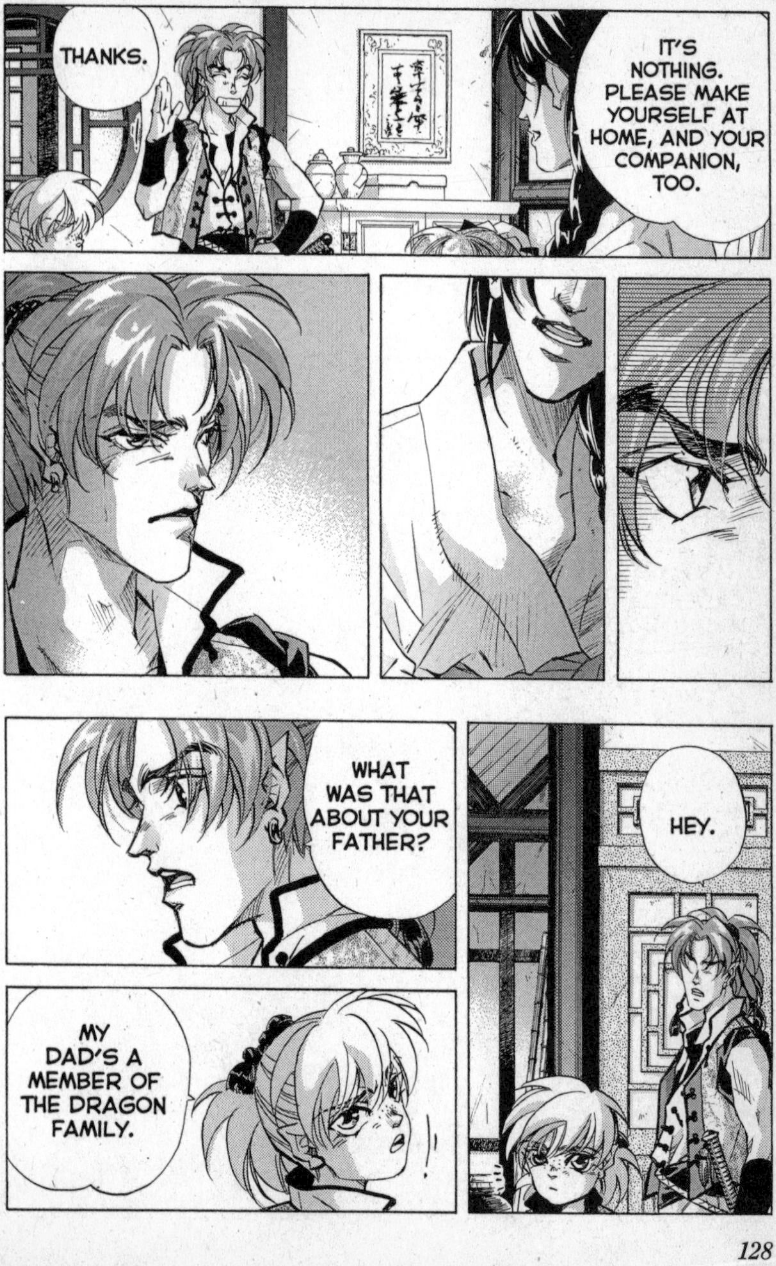
IT'S NOTHING. PLEASE MAKE YOURSELF AT HOME, AND YOUR COMPANION, TOO.
THANKS.
HEY.
WHAT WAS THAT ABOUT YOUR FATHER?
MY DAD'S A MEMBER OF THE DRAGON FAMILY.

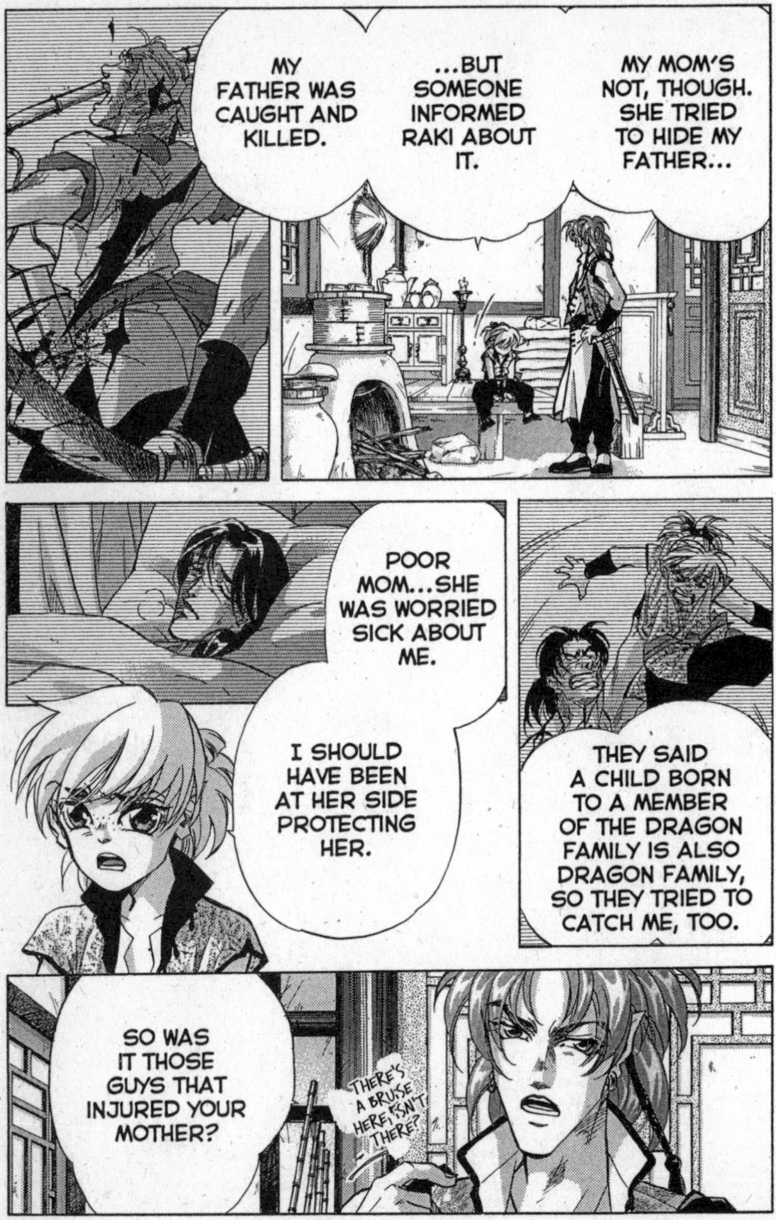
MY MOM'S NOT, THOUGH. SHE TRIED TO HIDE MY FATHER...
...BUT SOMEONE INFORMED RAKI ABOUT IT.
MY FATHER WAS CAUGHT AND KILLED.
THEY SAID A CHILD BORN TO A MEMBER OF THE DRAGON FAMILY IS ALSO DRAGON FAMILY, SO THEY TRIED TO CATCH ME, TOO.
POOR MOM...SHE WAS WORRIED SICK ABOUT ME.
I SHOULD HAVE BEEN AT HER SIDE PROTECTING HER.
SO WAS IT THOSE GUYS THAT INJURED YOUR MOTHER?
THERE'S A BRUISE HERE, ISN'T THERE?

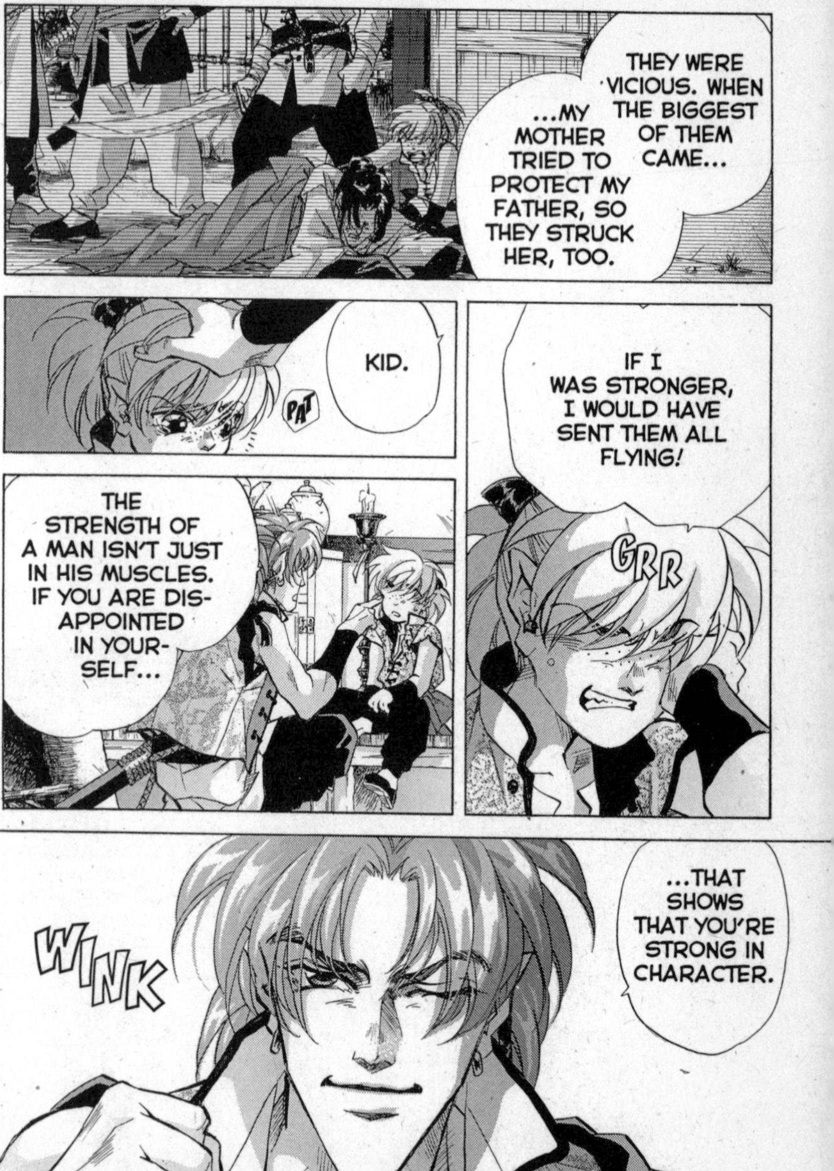
THEY WERE VICIOUS. WHEN THE BIGGEST OF THEM CAME...
...MY MOTHER TRIED TO PROTECT MY FATHER, SO THEY STRUCK HER, TOO.
IF I WAS STRONGER, I WOULD HAVE SENT THEM ALL FLYING!
GRR
KID.
PAT
THE STRENGTH OF A MAN ISN'T JUST IN HIS MUSCLES. IF YOU ARE DIS-APPOINTED IN YOUR-SELF...
...THAT SHOWS THAT YOU'RE STRONG IN CHARACTER.
WINK

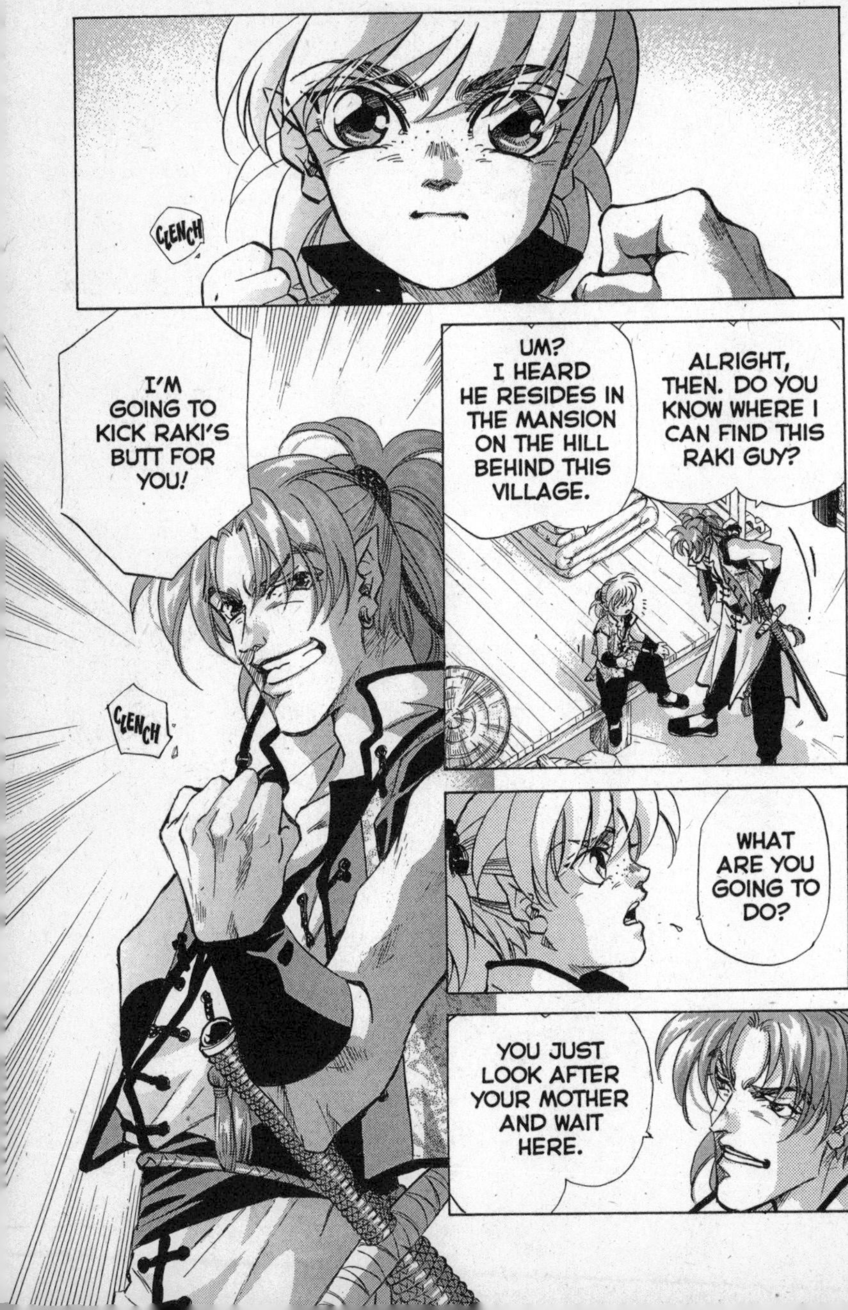
CLENCH
ALRIGHT, THEN. DO YOU KNOW WHERE I CAN FIND THIS RAKI GUY?
UM? I HEARD HE RESIDES IN THE MANSION ON THE HILL BEHIND THIS VILLAGE.
WHAT ARE YOU GOING TO DO?
YOU JUST LOOK AFTER YOUR MOTHER AND WAIT HERE.
I'M GOING TO KICK RAKI'S BUTT FOR YOU!
CLENCH

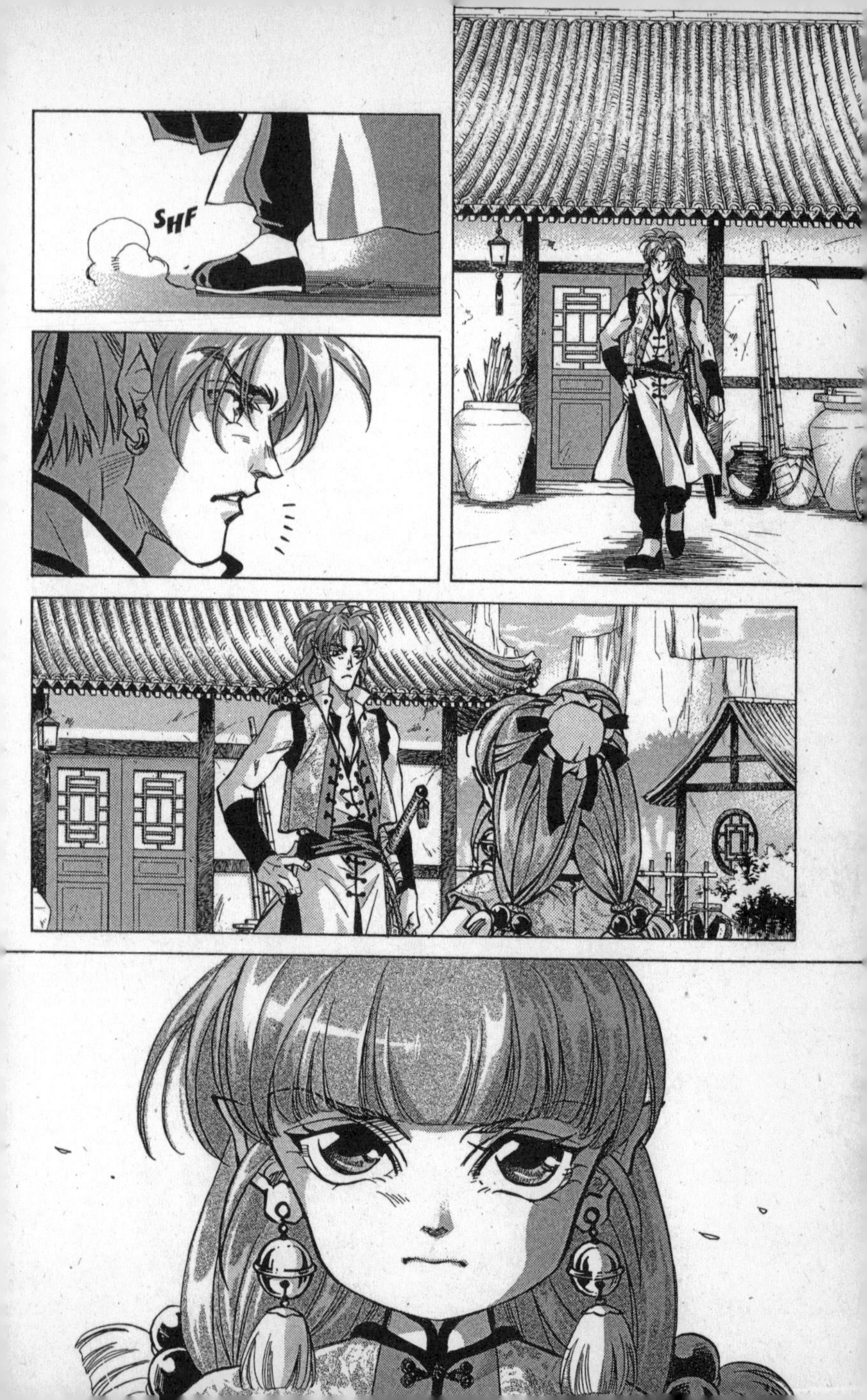
SHF

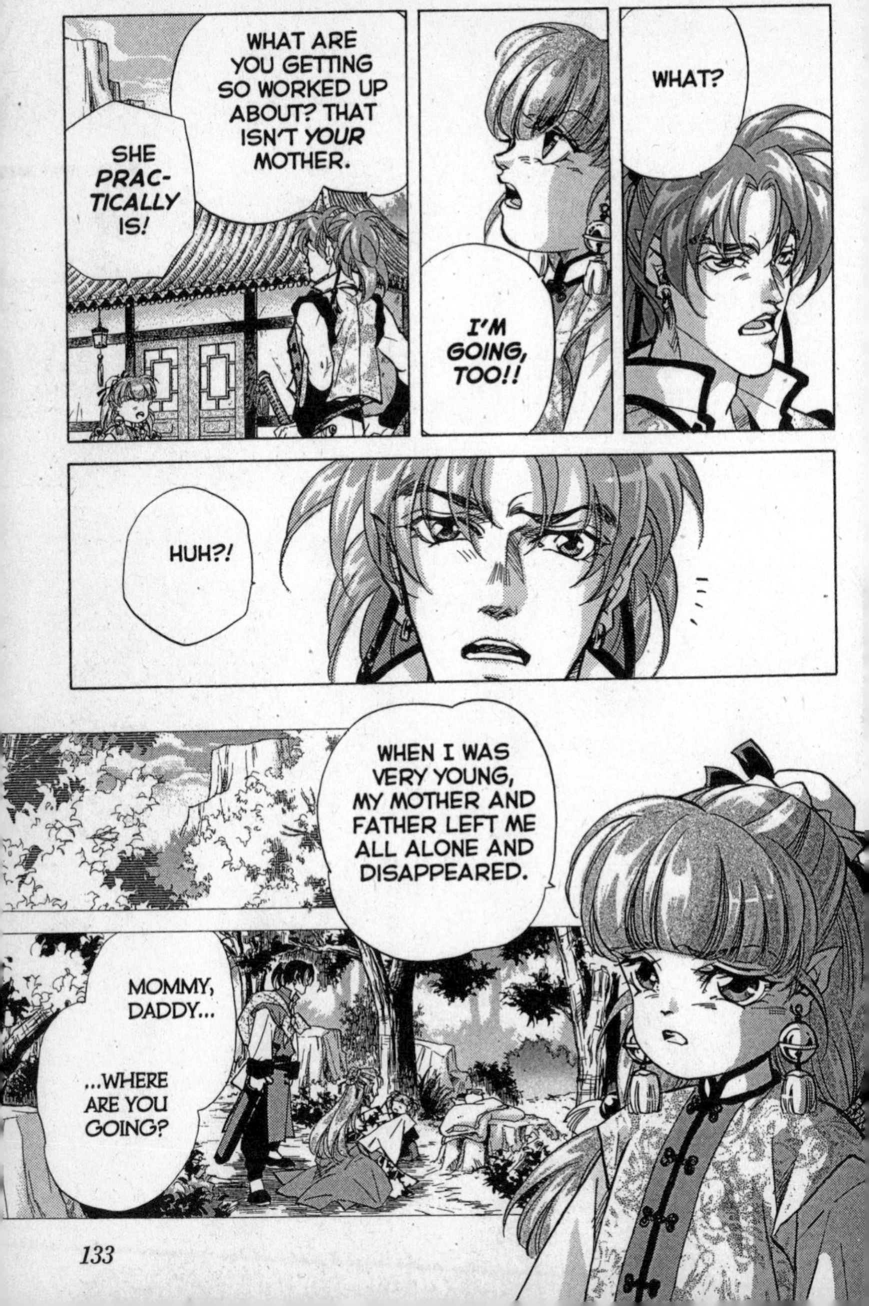
WHAT?
I'M GOING, TOO!!
WHAT ARE YOU GETTING SO WORKED UP ABOUT? THAT ISN'T *YOUR* MOTHER.
SHE *PRACTICALLY* IS!
HUH?!
WHEN I WAS VERY YOUNG, MY MOTHER AND FATHER LEFT ME ALL ALONE AND DISAPPEARED.
MOMMY, DADDY...
...WHERE ARE YOU GOING?

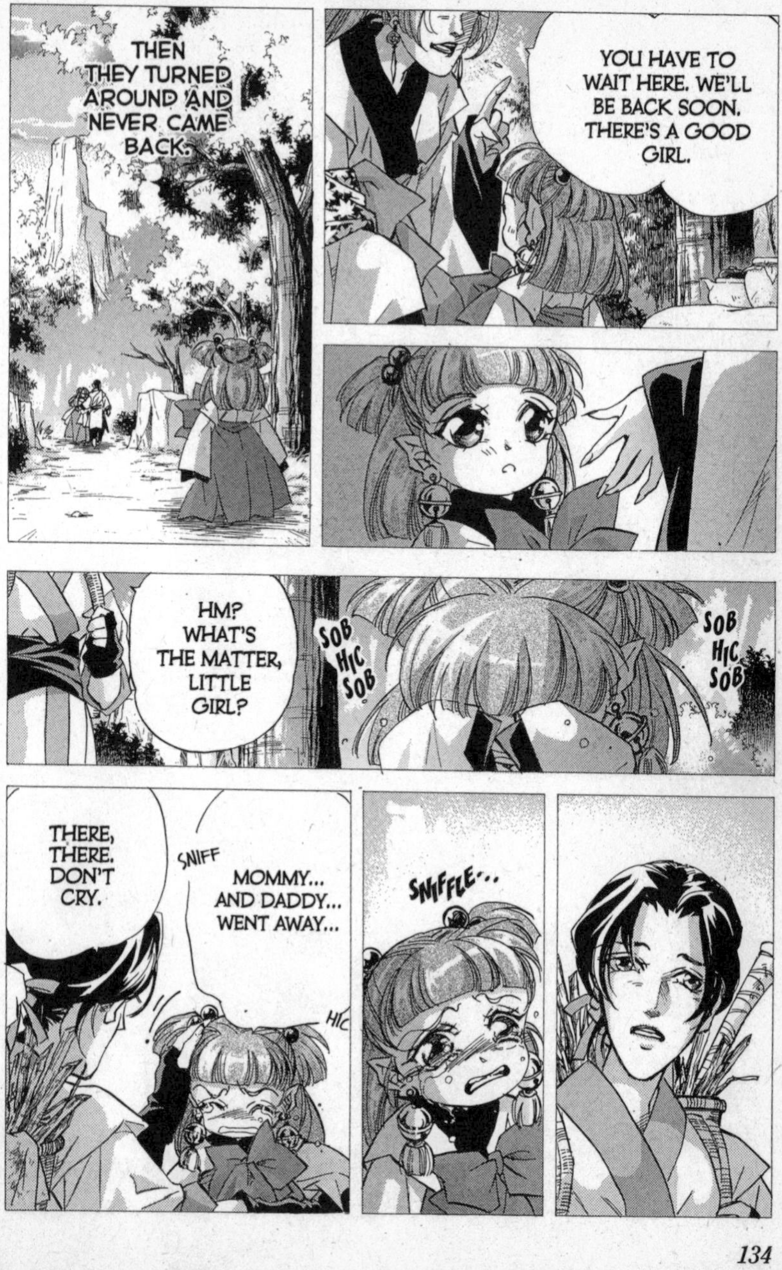
YOU HAVE TO WAIT HERE. WE'LL BE BACK SOON. THERE'S A GOOD GIRL.
THEN THEY TURNED AROUND AND NEVER CAME BACK.
SOB HIC SOB
SOB HIC SOB
HM? WHAT'S THE MATTER, LITTLE GIRL?
SNIFFLE...
SNIFF
MOMMY... AND DADDY... WENT AWAY...
THERE, THERE. DON'T CRY.
HIC

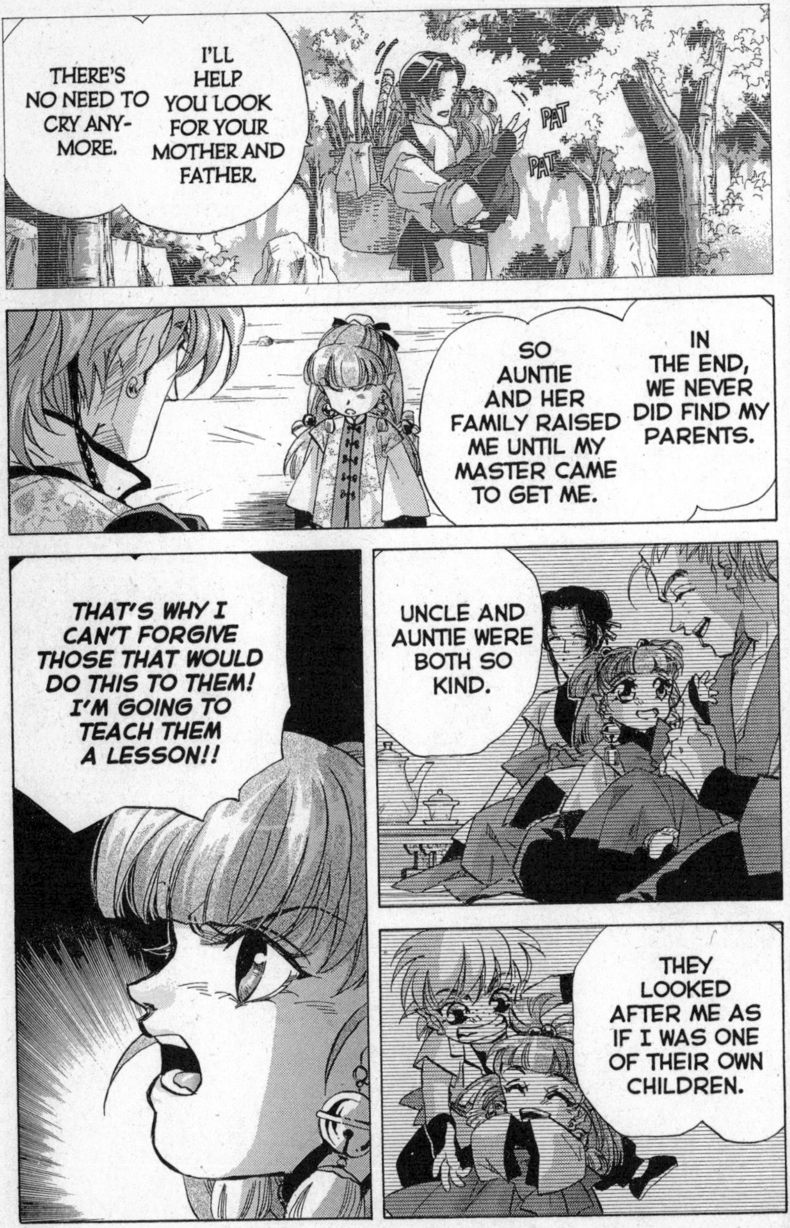
PAT
PAT
I'LL HELP YOU LOOK FOR YOUR MOTHER AND FATHER.
THERE'S NO NEED TO CRY ANY-MORE.
IN THE END, WE NEVER DID FIND MY PARENTS.
SO AUNTIE AND HER FAMILY RAISED ME UNTIL MY MASTER CAME TO GET ME.
UNCLE AND AUNTIE WERE BOTH SO KIND.
THEY LOOKED AFTER ME AS IF I WAS ONE OF THEIR OWN CHILDREN.
THAT'S WHY I CAN'T FORGIVE THOSE THAT WOULD DO THIS TO THEM! I'M GOING TO TEACH THEM A LESSON!!

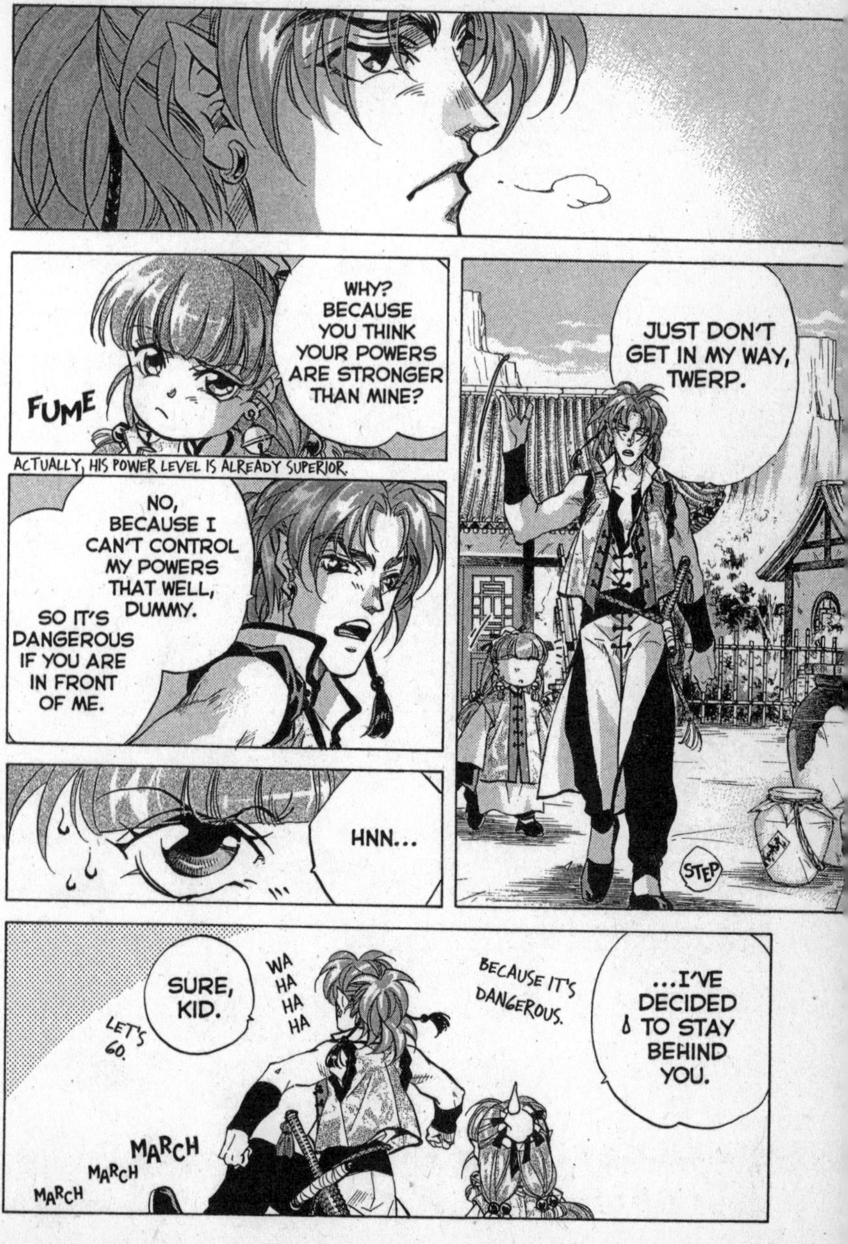
JUST DON'T GET IN MY WAY, TWERP.
STEP
FUME
WHY? BECAUSE YOU THINK YOUR POWERS ARE STRONGER THAN MINE?
ACTUALLY, HIS POWER LEVEL IS ALREADY SUPERIOR.
NO, BECAUSE I CAN'T CONTROL MY POWERS THAT WELL, DUMMY.
SO IT'S DANGEROUS IF YOU ARE IN FRONT OF ME.
HNN...
...I'VE DECIDED TO STAY BEHIND YOU.
BECAUSE IT'S DANGEROUS.
WA HA HA HA
SURE, KID.
LET'S GO.
MARCH MARCH MARCH

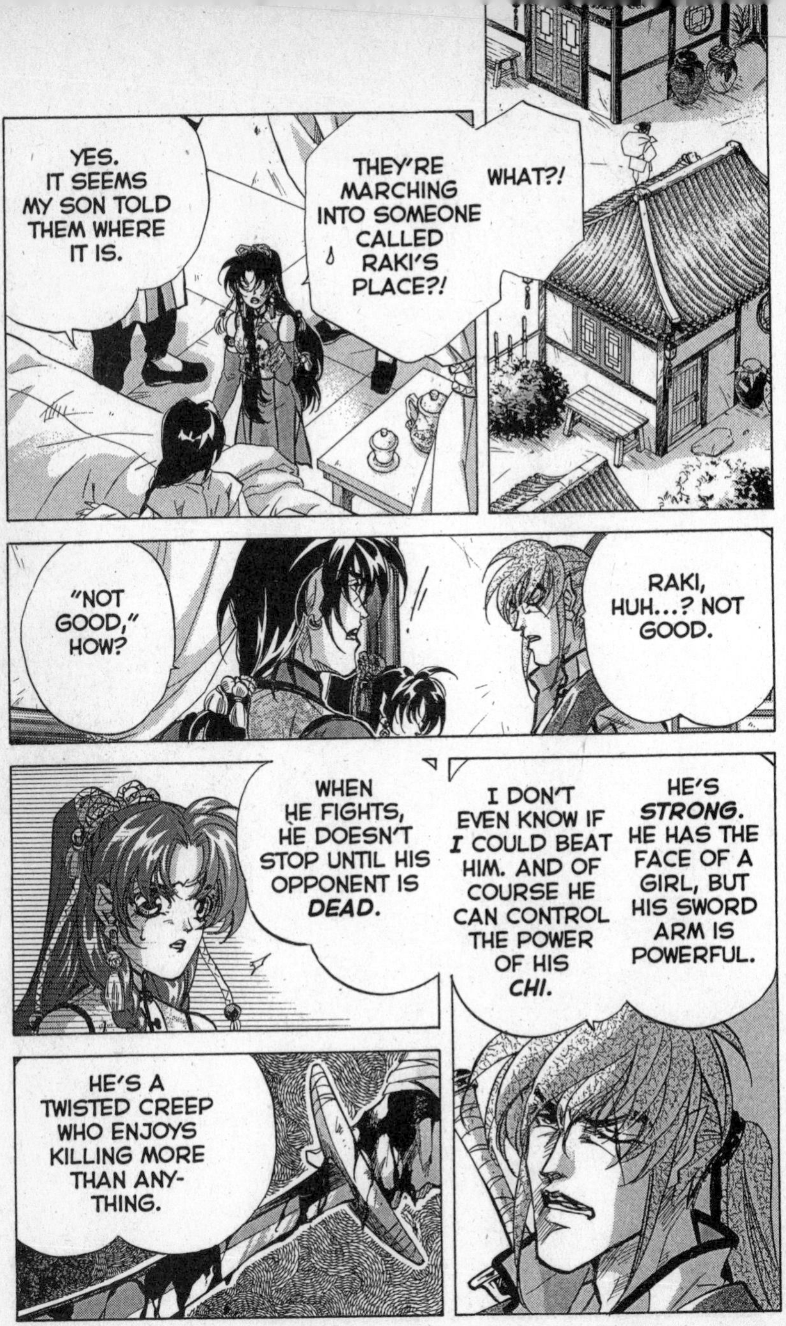
WHAT?!
THEY'RE MARCHING INTO SOMEONE CALLED RAKI'S PLACE?!
YES. IT SEEMS MY SON TOLD THEM WHERE IT IS.
RAKI, HUH...? NOT GOOD.
"NOT GOOD," HOW?
HE'S *STRONG*. HE HAS THE FACE OF A GIRL, BUT HIS SWORD ARM IS POWERFUL.
I DON'T EVEN KNOW IF *I* COULD BEAT HIM. AND OF COURSE HE CAN CONTROL THE POWER OF HIS *CHI*.
WHEN HE FIGHTS, HE DOESN'T STOP UNTIL HIS OPPONENT IS *DEAD*.
HE'S A TWISTED CREEP WHO ENJOYS KILLING MORE THAN ANY-THING.

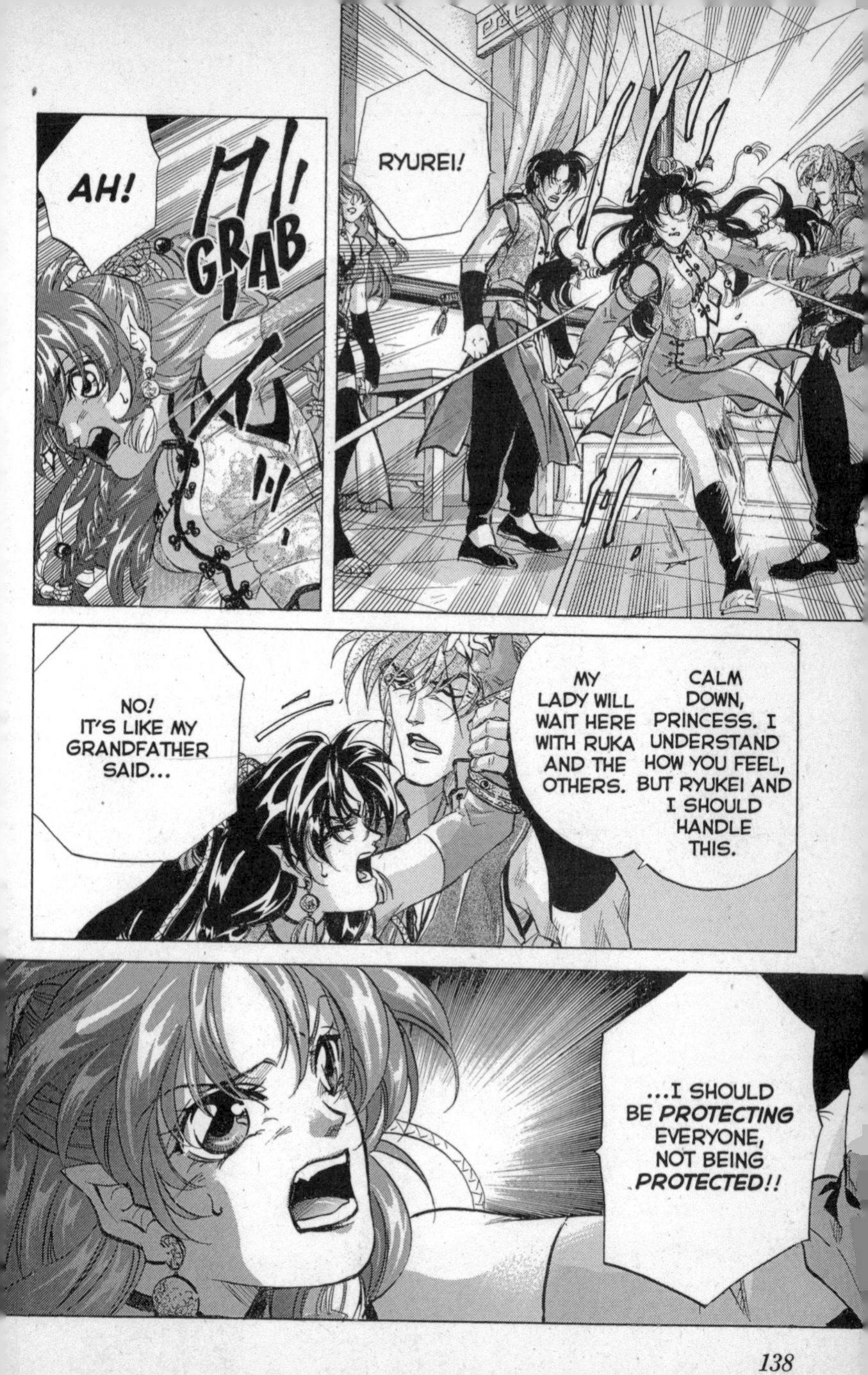
RYUREI!
AH!
GRAB
CALM DOWN, PRINCESS. I UNDERSTAND HOW YOU FEEL, BUT RYUKEI AND I SHOULD HANDLE THIS.
MY LADY WILL WAIT HERE WITH RUKA AND THE OTHERS.
NO! IT'S LIKE MY GRANDFATHER SAID...
...I SHOULD BE *PROTECTING* EVERYONE, NOT BEING *PROTECTED*!!

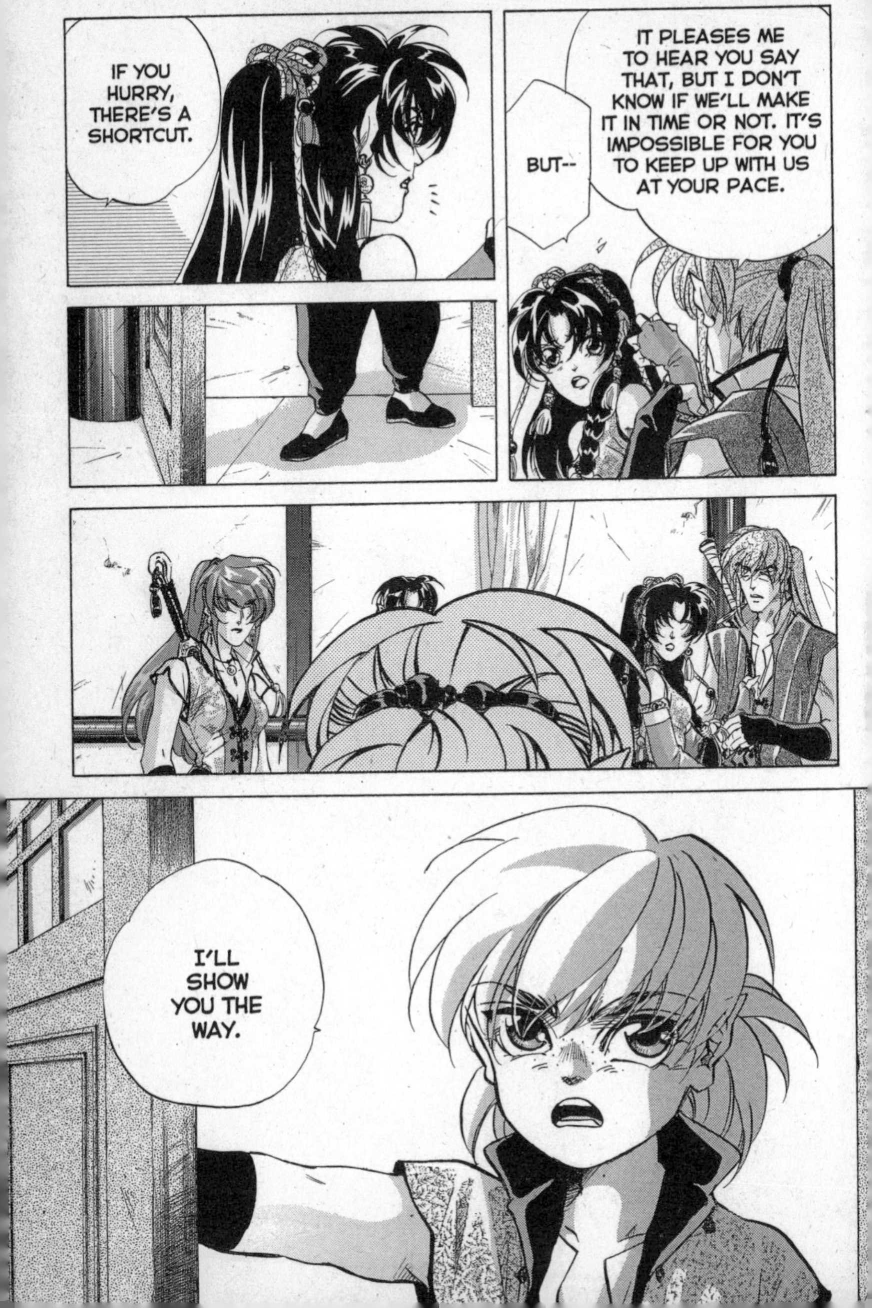
IT PLEASES ME TO HEAR YOU SAY THAT, BUT I DON'T KNOW IF WE'LL MAKE IT IN TIME OR NOT. IT'S IMPOSSIBLE FOR YOU TO KEEP UP WITH US AT YOUR PACE.
BUT--
IF YOU HURRY, THERE'S A SHORTCUT.
I'LL SHOW YOU THE WAY.

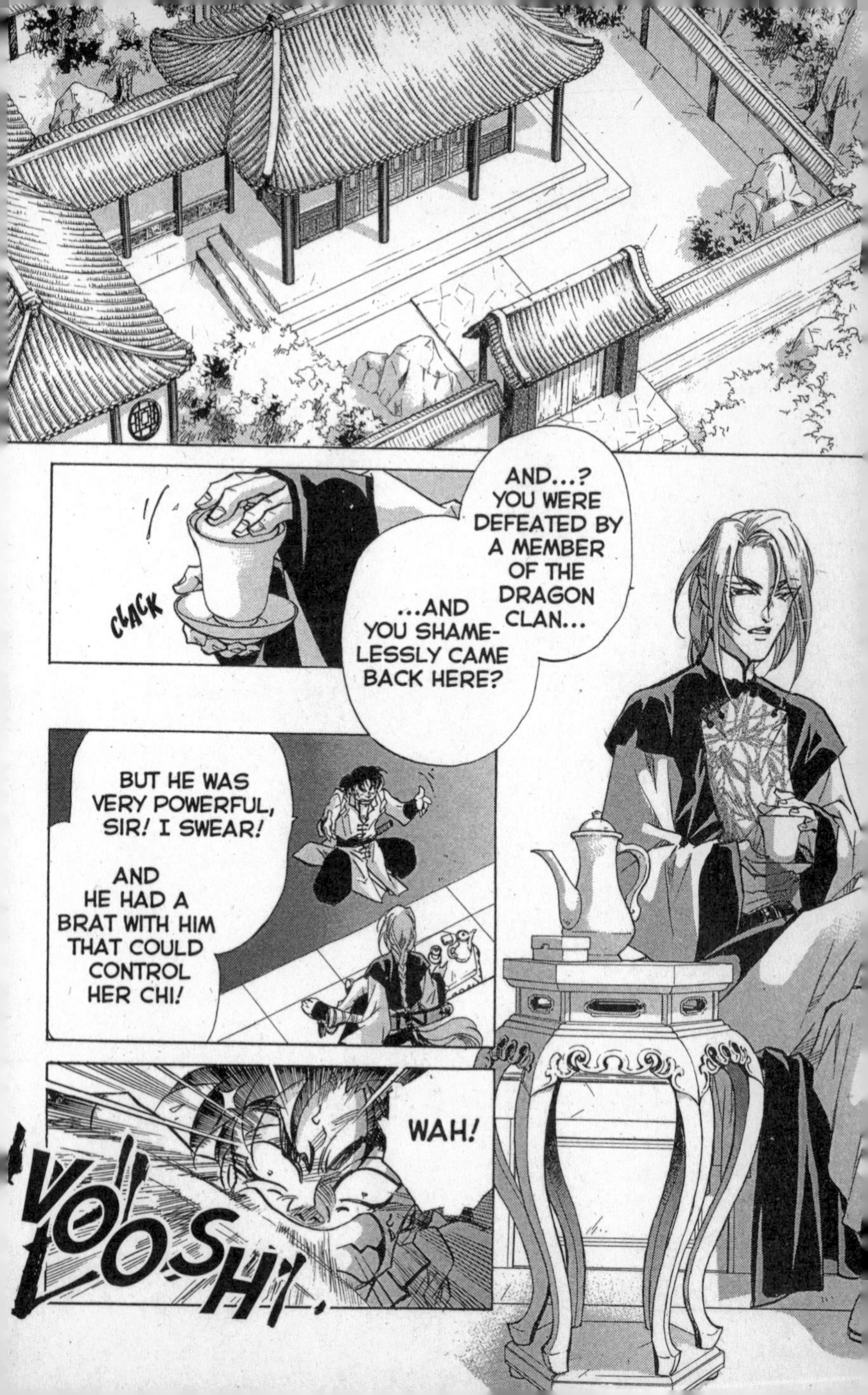
AND...? YOU WERE DEFEATED BY A MEMBER OF THE DRAGON CLAN...
...AND YOU SHAMELESSLY CAME BACK HERE?
CLACK
BUT HE WAS VERY POWERFUL, SIR! I SWEAR!
AND HE HAD A BRAT WITH HIM THAT COULD CONTROL HER CHI!
WAH!
VOOSH!

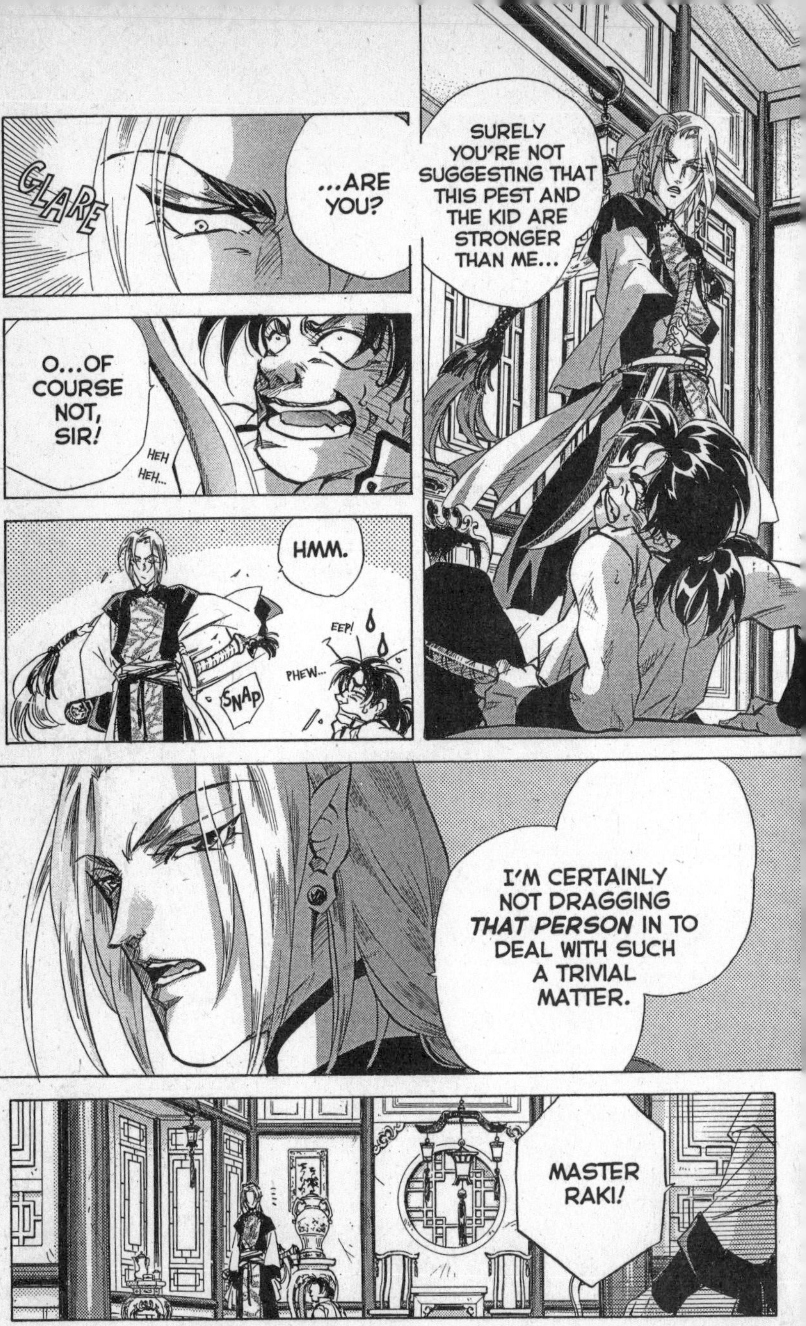
SURELY YOU'RE NOT SUGGESTING THAT THIS PEST AND THE KID ARE STRONGER THAN ME...
...ARE YOU?
GLARE
O...OF COURSE NOT, SIR!
HEH HEH...
HMM.
EEP!
PHEW...
SNAP
I'M CERTAINLY NOT DRAGGING *THAT PERSON* IN TO DEAL WITH SUCH A TRIVIAL MATTER.
MASTER RAKI!

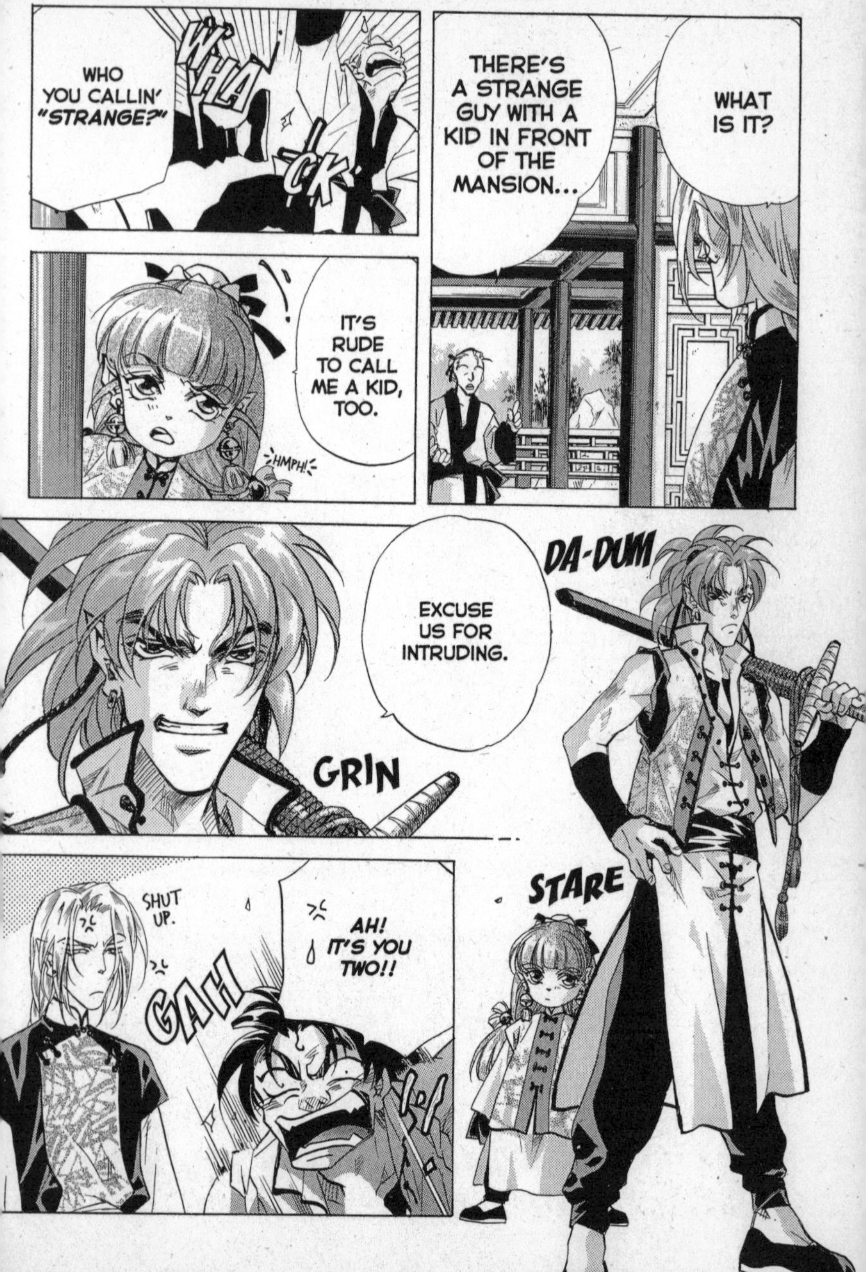
WHAT IS IT?
THERE'S A STRANGE GUY WITH A KID IN FRONT OF THE MANSION...
WHACK
WHO YOU CALLIN' "STRANGE?"
IT'S RUDE TO CALL ME A KID, TOO.
HMPH!
DA-DUM
EXCUSE US FOR INTRUDING.
GRIN
STARE
AH! IT'S YOU TWO!!
SHUT UP.
GAH

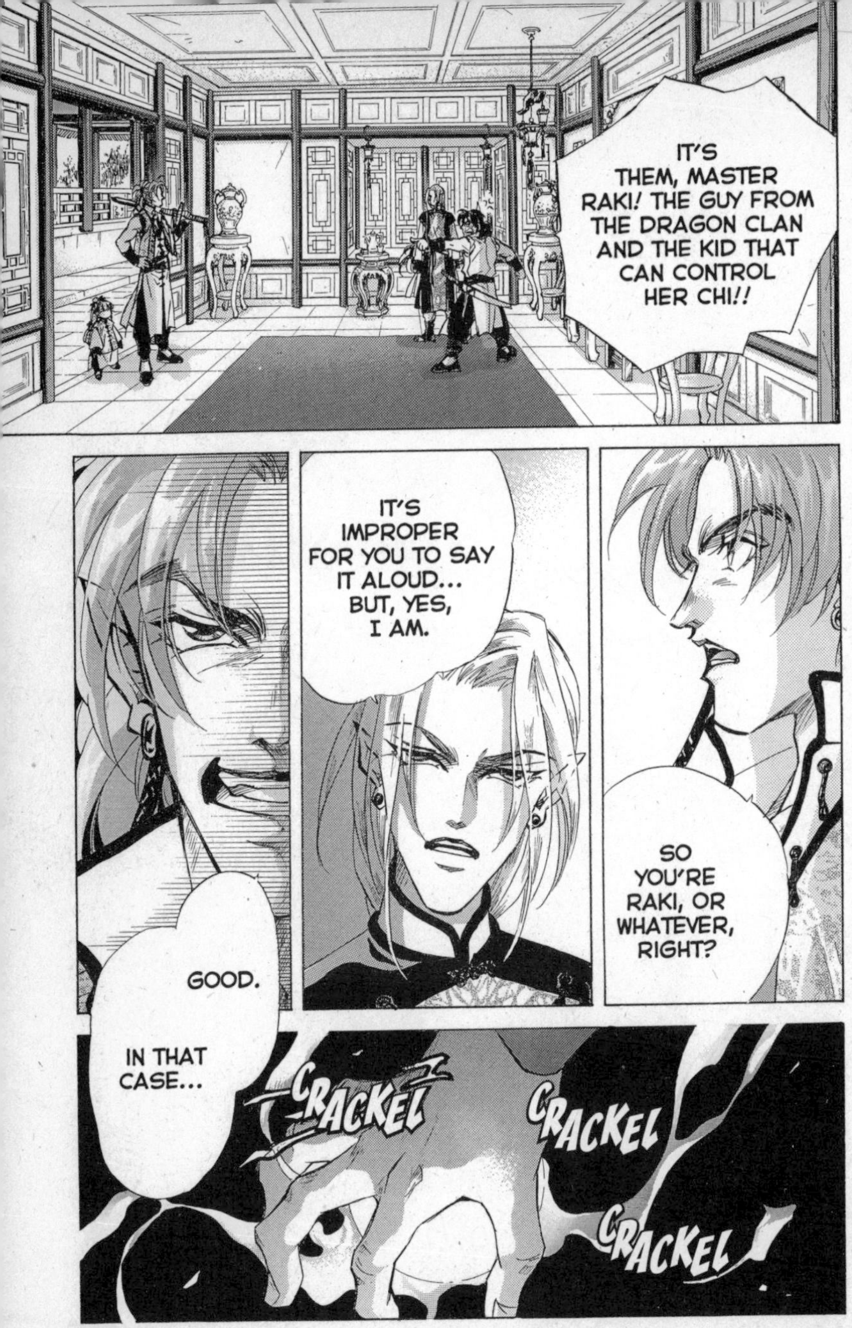
IT'S THEM, MASTER RAKI! THE GUY FROM THE DRAGON CLAN AND THE KID THAT CAN CONTROL HER CHI!!
SO YOU'RE RAKI, OR WHATEVER, RIGHT?
IT'S IMPROPER FOR YOU TO SAY IT ALOUD... BUT, YES, I AM.
GOOD.
IN THAT CASE...
CRACKEL
CRACKEL
CRACKEL

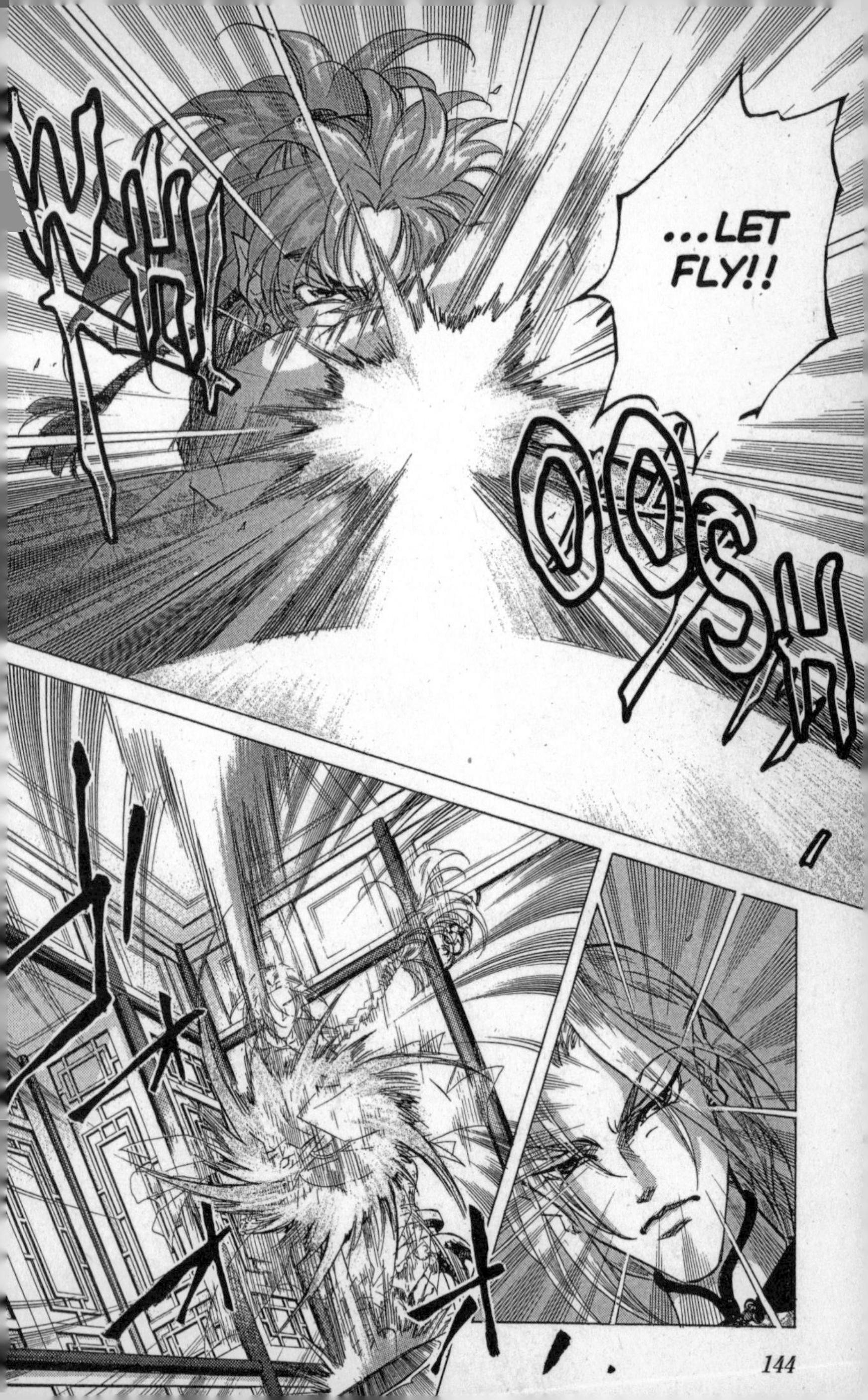
...LET FLY!!
WH
OOOSH

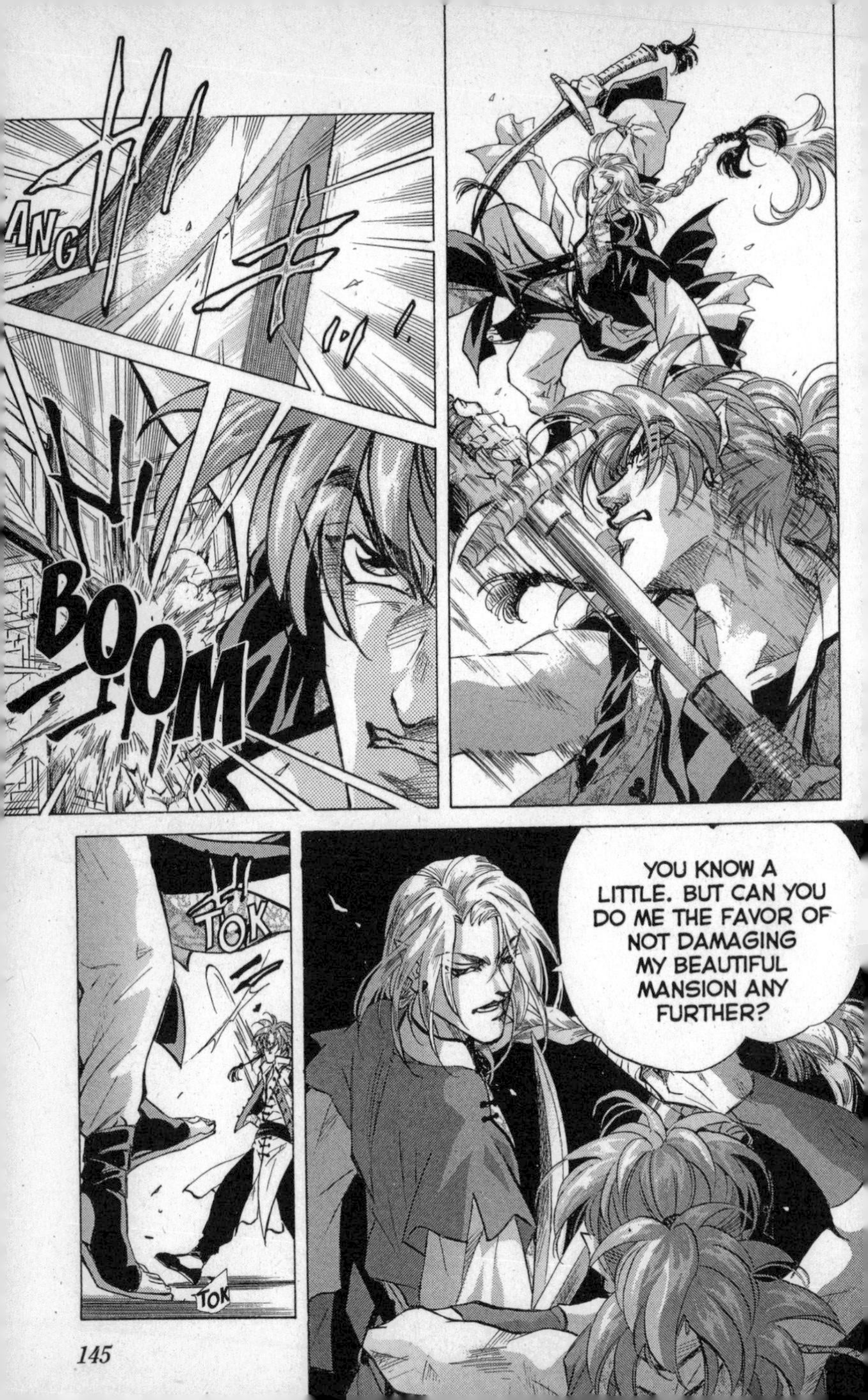
ANG
BOOM
YOU KNOW A LITTLE. BUT CAN YOU DO ME THE FAVOR OF NOT DAMAGING MY BEAUTIFUL MANSION ANY FURTHER?
TOK
TOK

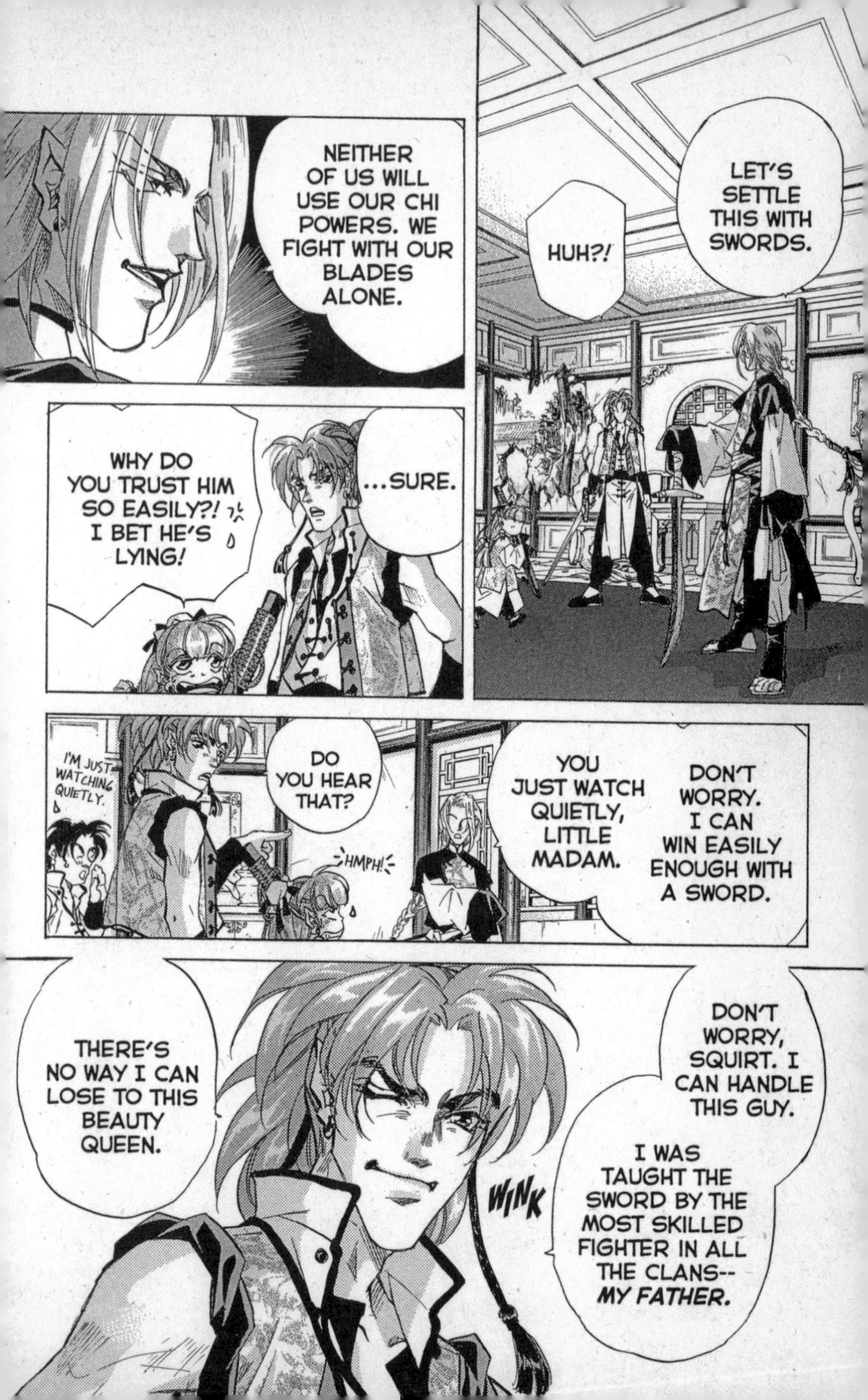
LET'S SETTLE THIS WITH SWORDS.
HUH?!
NEITHER OF US WILL USE OUR CHI POWERS. WE FIGHT WITH OUR BLADES ALONE.
...SURE.
WHY DO YOU TRUST HIM SO EASILY?! I BET HE'S LYING!
DON'T WORRY. I CAN WIN EASILY ENOUGH WITH A SWORD.
YOU JUST WATCH QUIETLY, LITTLE MADAM.
HMPH!
DO YOU HEAR THAT?
I'M JUST WATCHING QUIETLY.
DON'T WORRY, SQUIRT. I CAN HANDLE THIS GUY.
I WAS TAUGHT THE SWORD BY THE MOST SKILLED FIGHTER IN ALL THE CLANS-- *MY FATHER.*
WINK
THERE'S NO WAY I CAN LOSE TO THIS BEAUTY QUEEN.

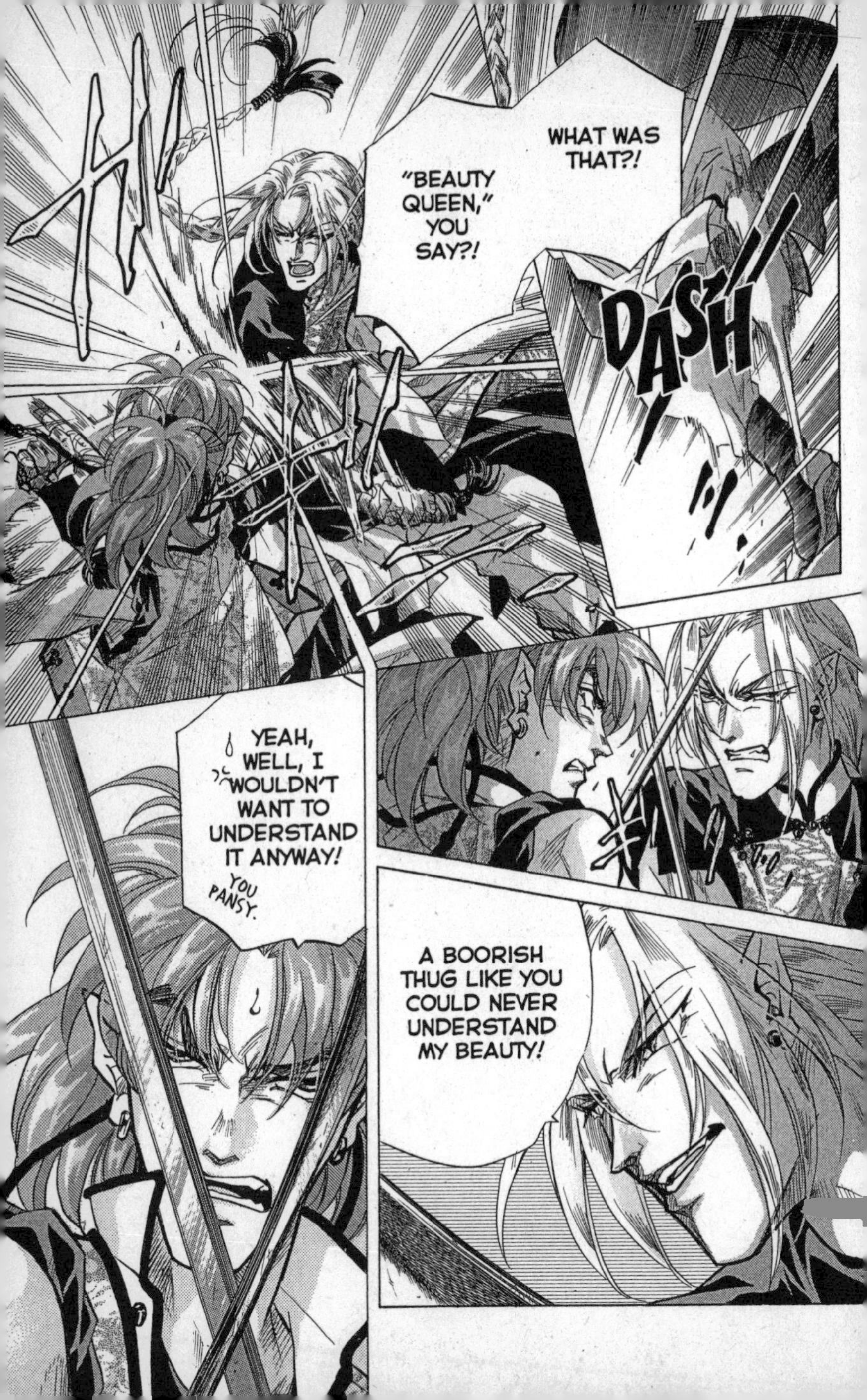
WHAT WAS THAT?!
"BEAUTY QUEEN," YOU SAY?!
DASH
A BOORISH THUG LIKE YOU COULD NEVER UNDERSTAND MY BEAUTY!
YEAH, WELL, I WOULDN'T WANT TO UNDERSTAND IT ANYWAY!
YOU PANSY.

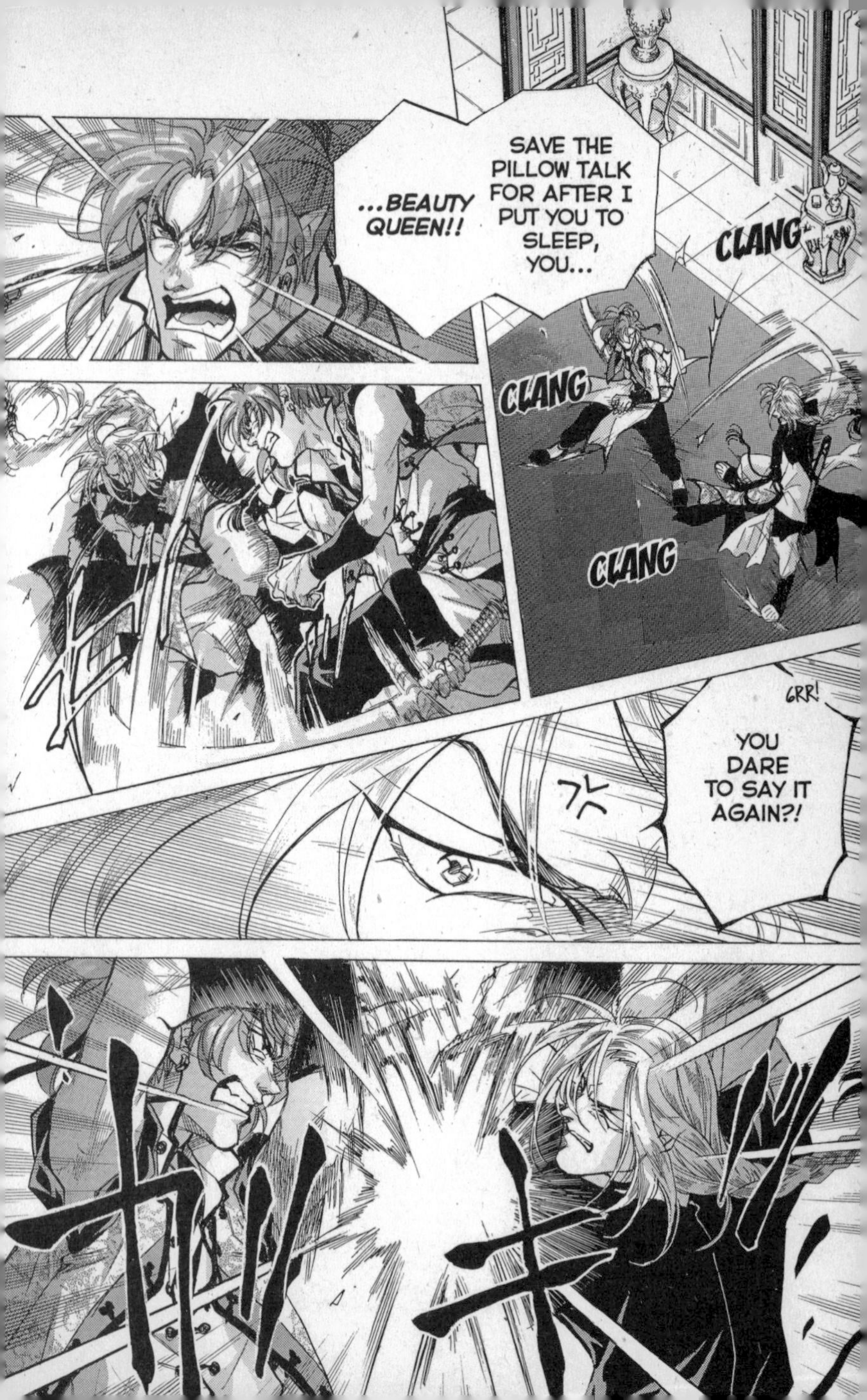
SAVE THE PILLOW TALK FOR AFTER I PUT YOU TO SLEEP, YOU...
...BEAUTY QUEEN!!
CLANG
CLANG
CLANG
GRR!
YOU DARE TO SAY IT AGAIN?!

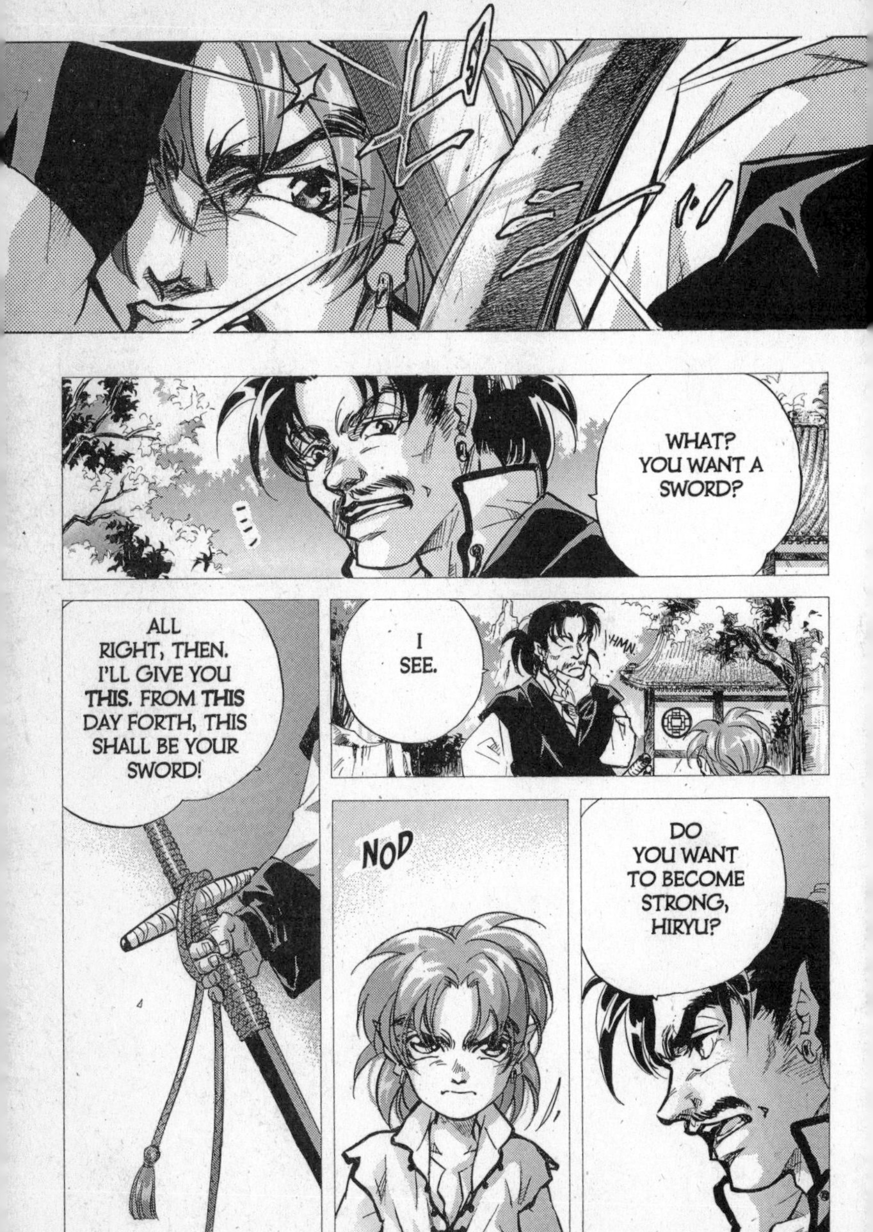
WHAT? YOU WANT A SWORD?
HMN
I SEE.
DO YOU WANT TO BECOME STRONG, HIRYU?
NOD
ALL RIGHT, THEN. I'LL GIVE YOU THIS. FROM THIS DAY FORTH, THIS SHALL BE YOUR SWORD!

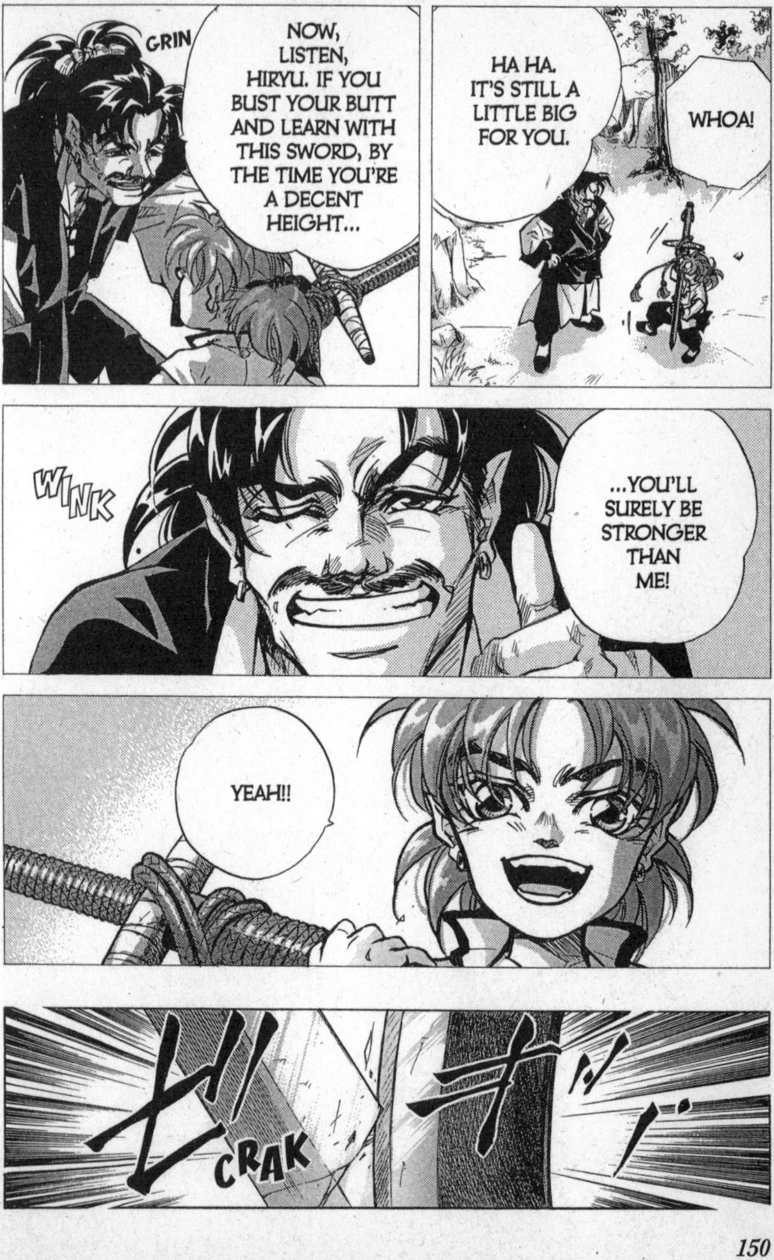
WHOA!
HA HA. IT'S STILL A LITTLE BIG FOR YOU.
NOW, LISTEN, HIRYU. IF YOU BUST YOUR BUTT AND LEARN WITH THIS SWORD, BY THE TIME YOU'RE A DECENT HEIGHT...
GRIN
...YOU'LL SURELY BE STRONGER THAN ME!
WINK
YEAH!!
CRAK

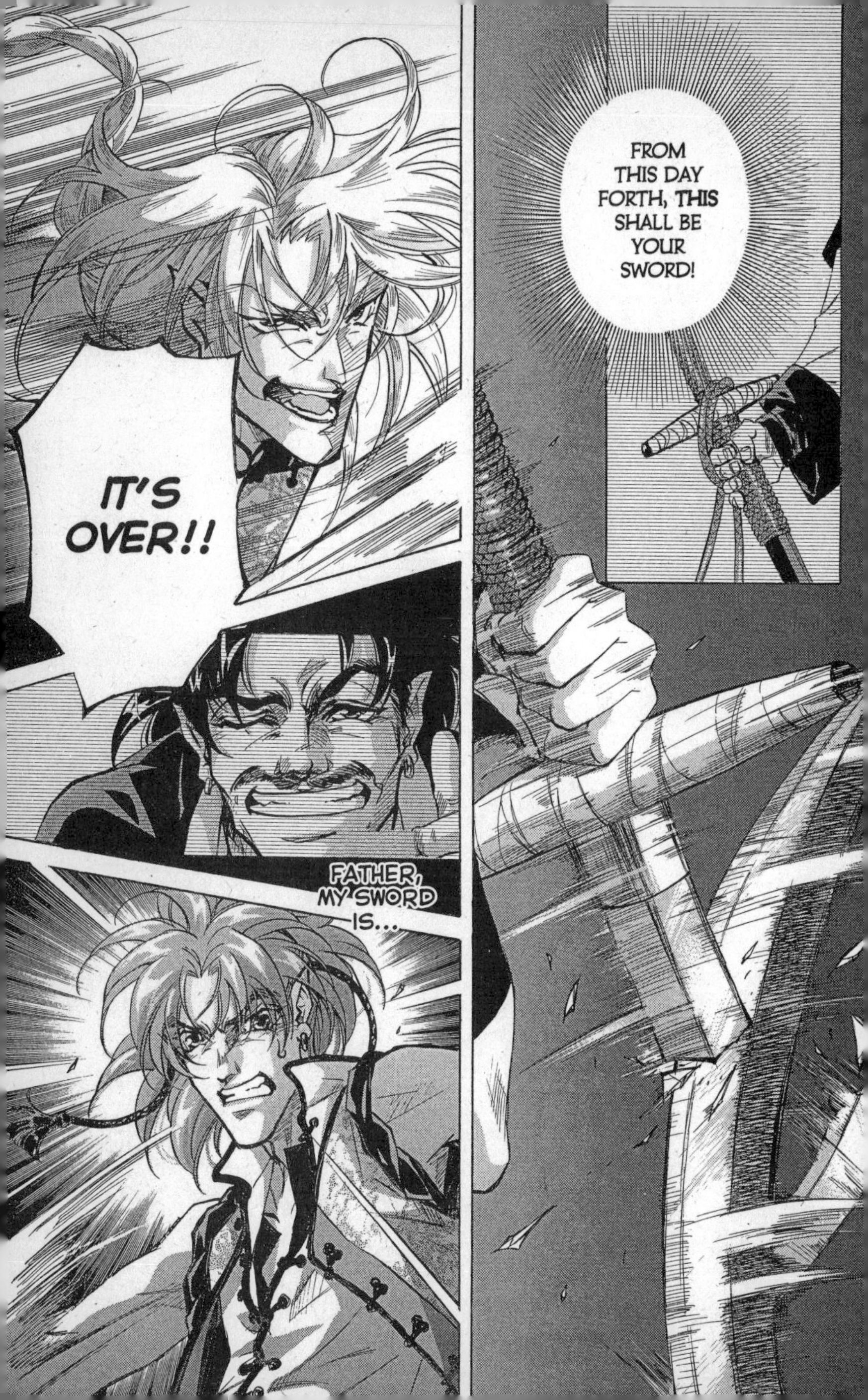
FROM THIS DAY FORTH, THIS SHALL BE YOUR SWORD!
IT'S OVER!!
FATHER, MY SWORD IS...

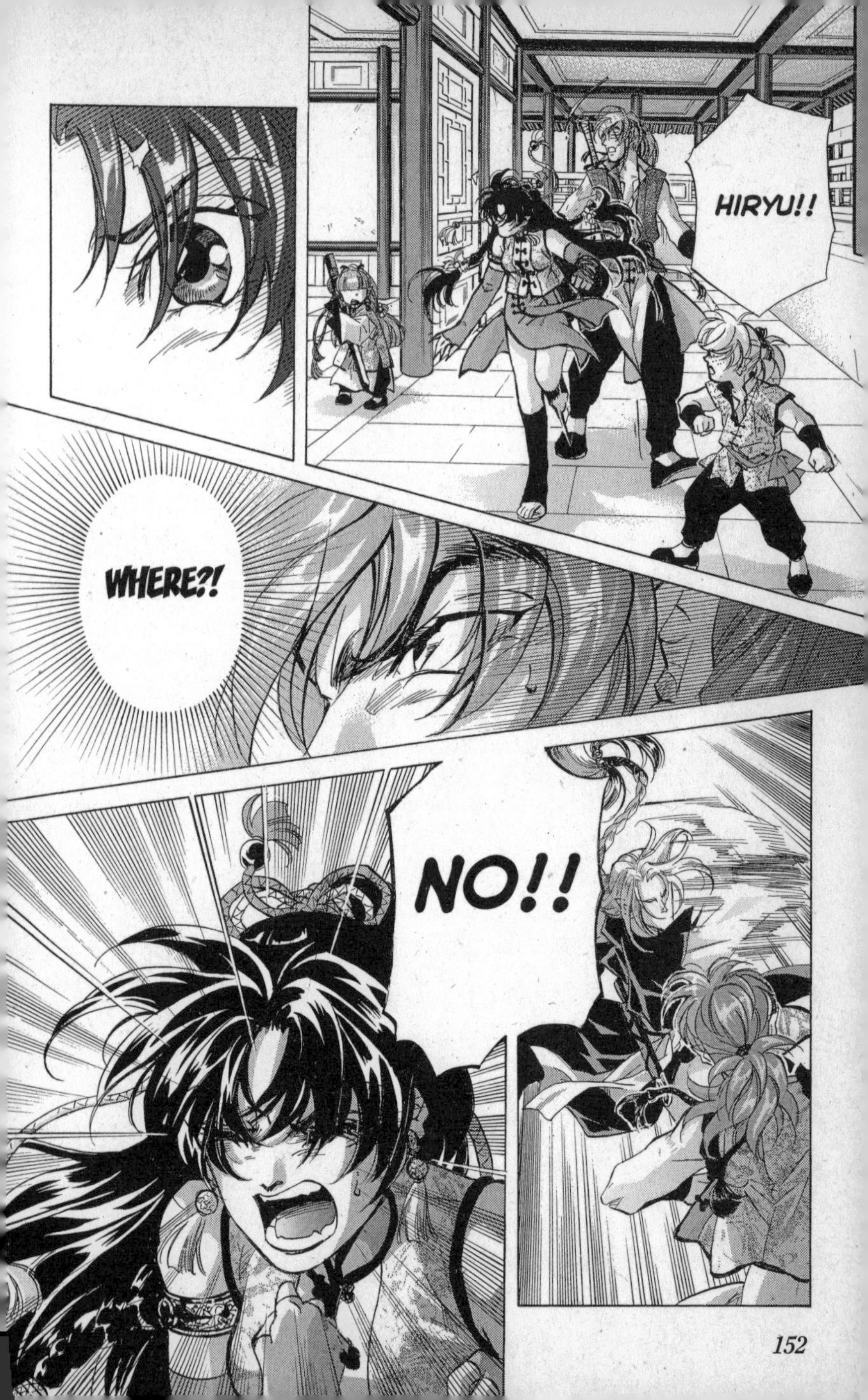
HIRYU!!
WHERE?!
NO!!

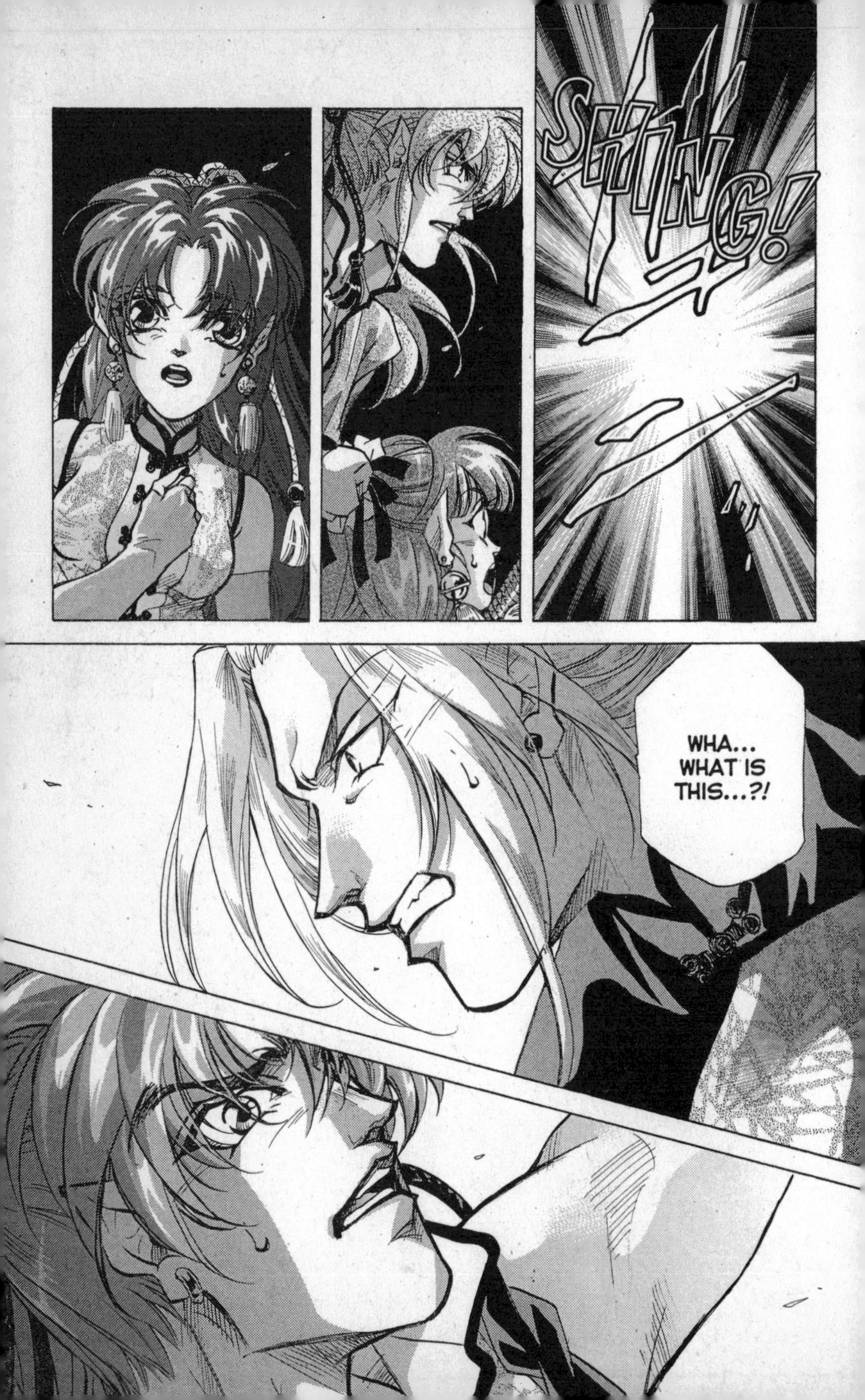
SHIING!
WHA...
WHAT IS
THIS...?!

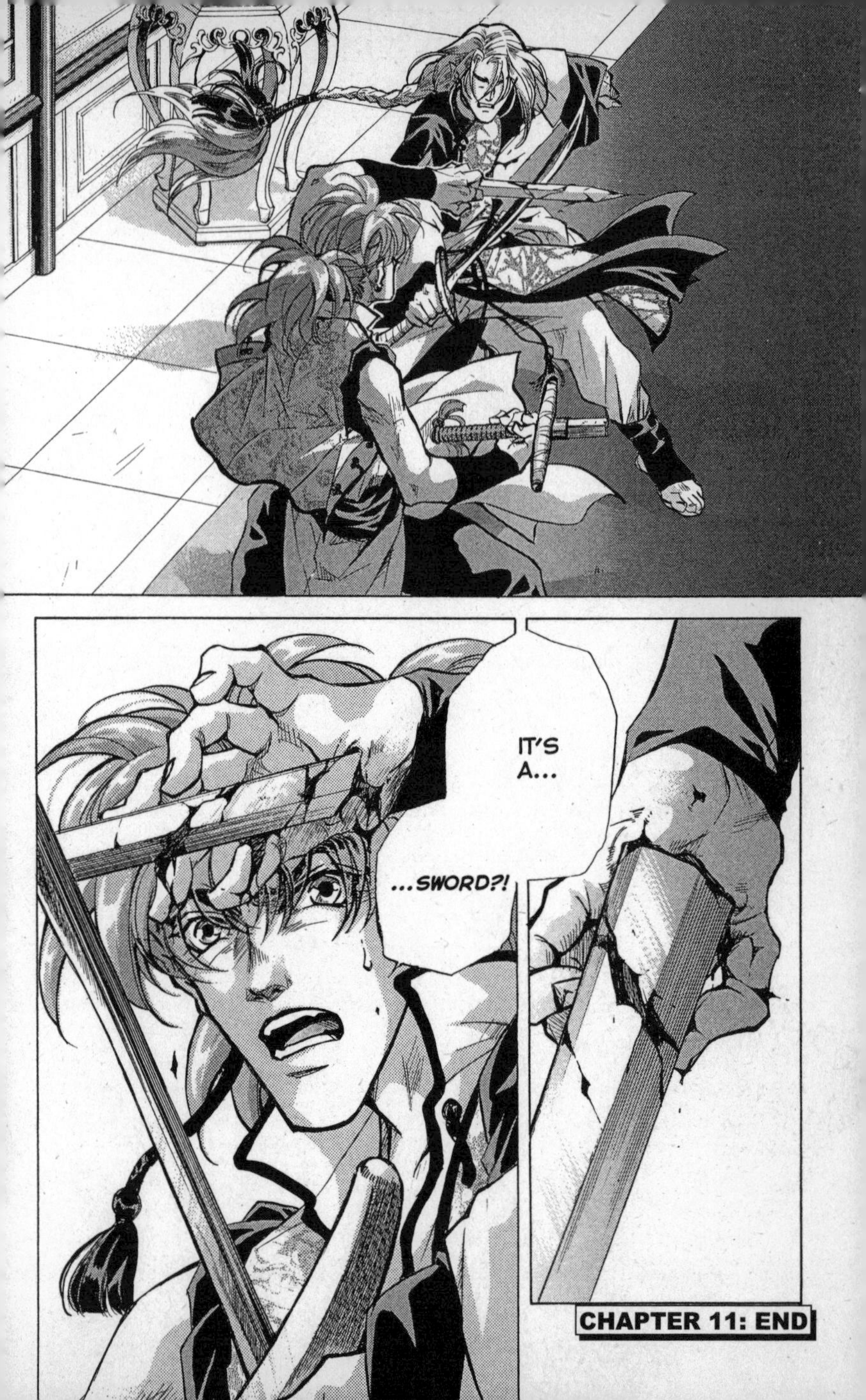
IT'S A...
...SWORD?!
CHAPTER 11: END

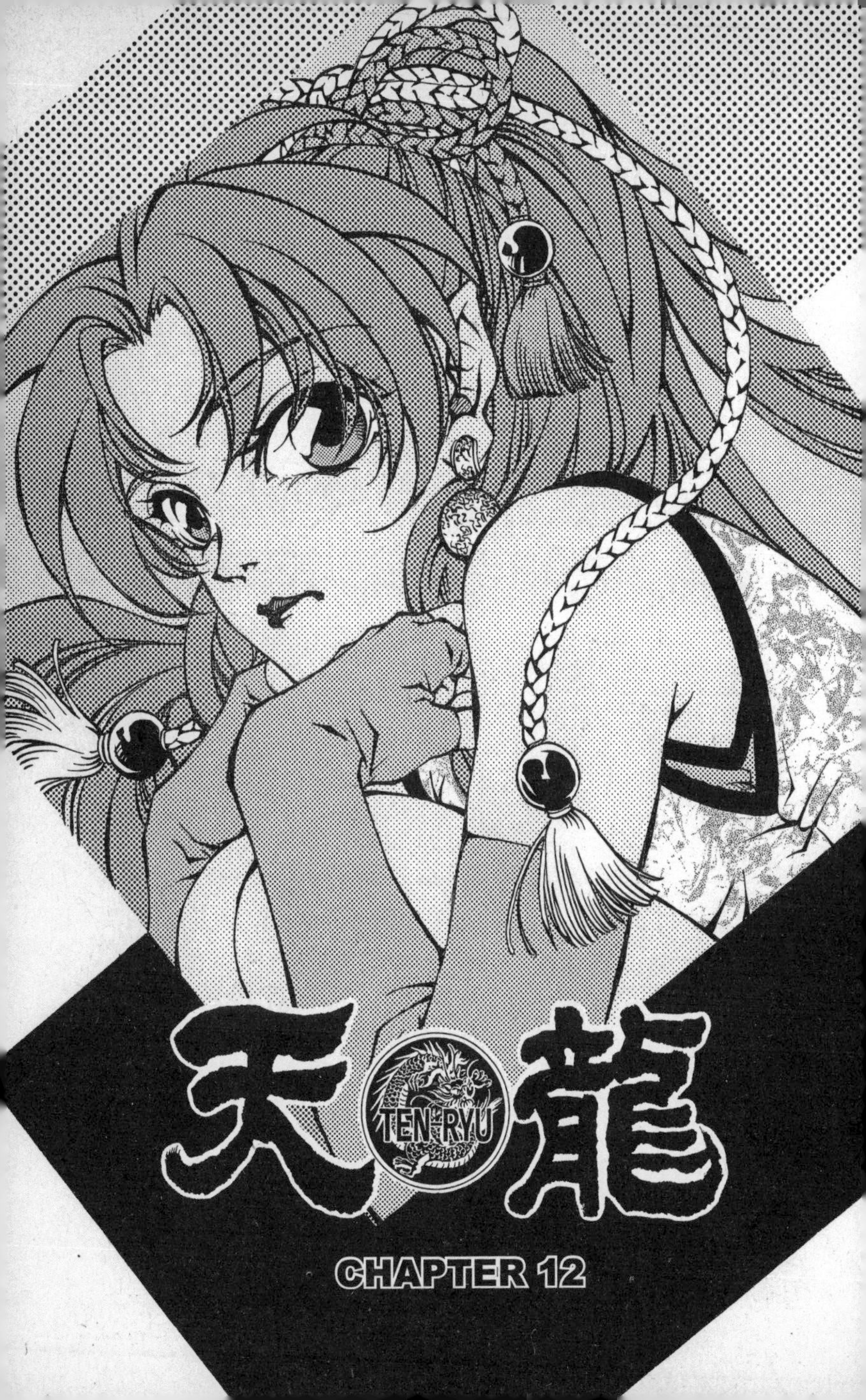

天龍
TEN-RYU
CHAPTER 12

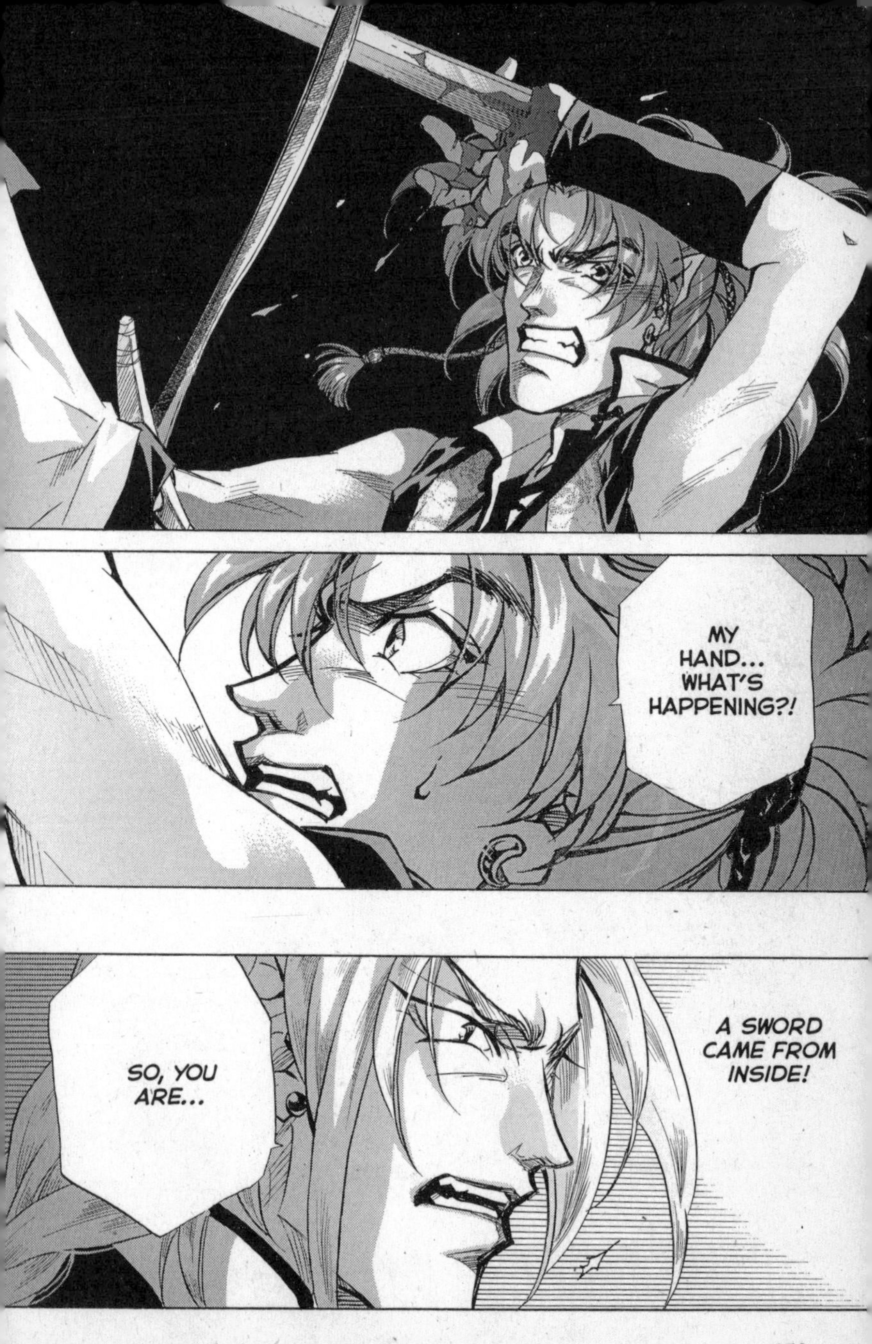
MY HAND... WHAT'S HAPPENING?!
A SWORD CAME FROM INSIDE!
SO, YOU ARE...

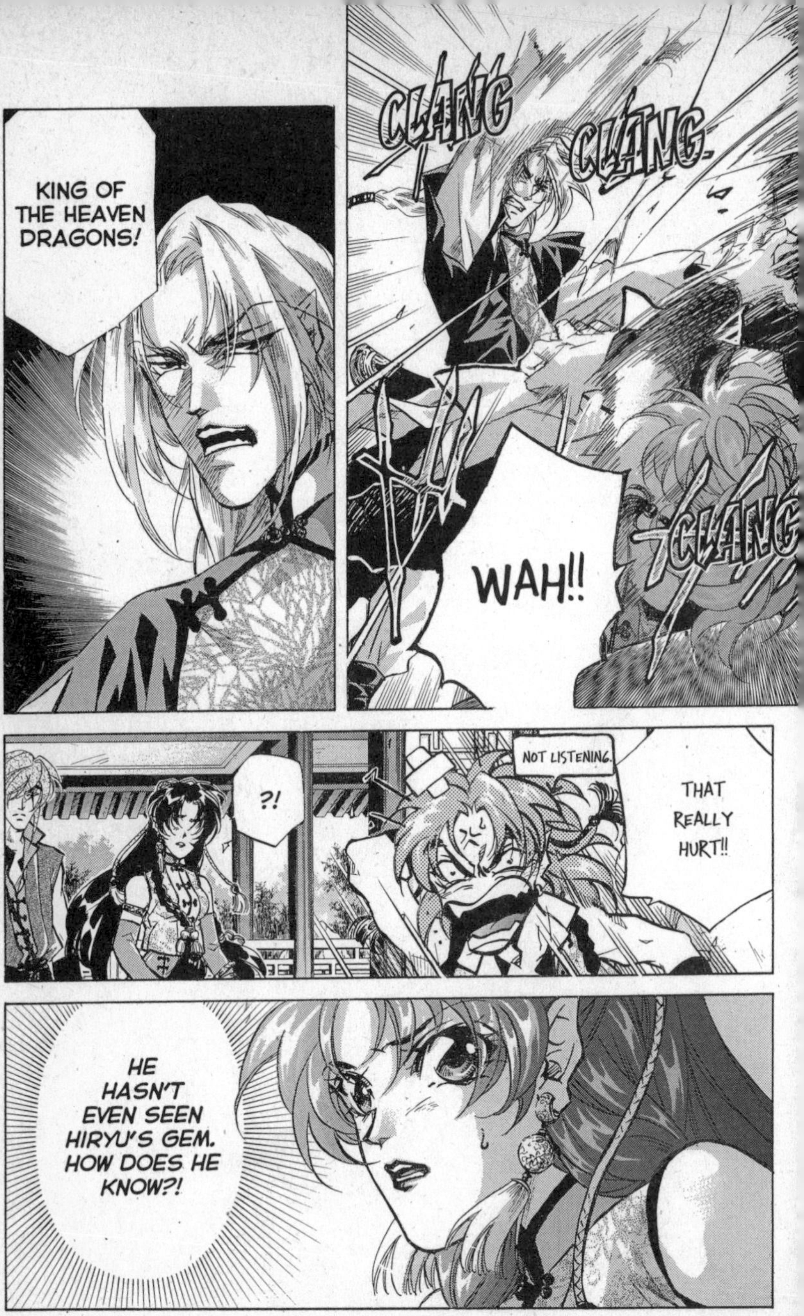
CLANG
CLING
CLANG
WAH!!
KING OF THE HEAVEN DRAGONS!
NOT LISTENING.
THAT REALLY HURT!!
?!
HE HASN'T EVEN SEEN HIRYU'S GEM. HOW DOES HE KNOW?!

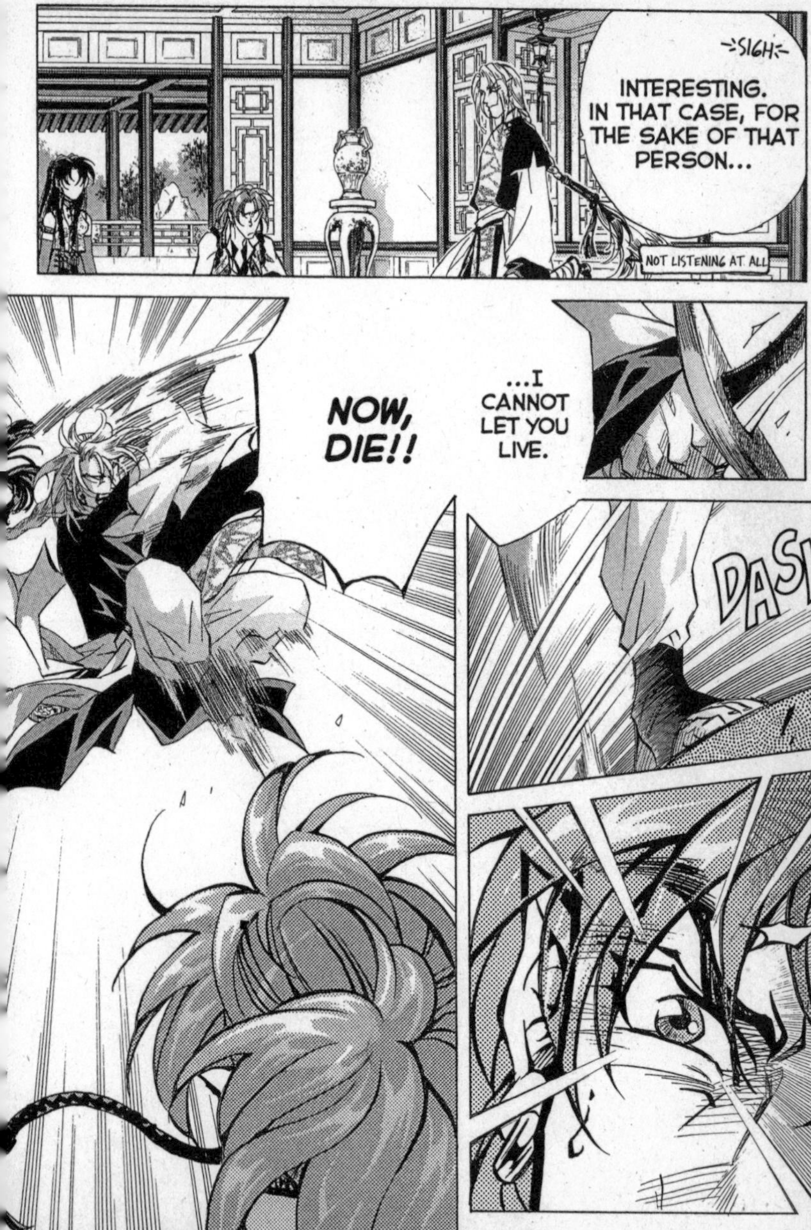
SIGH
INTERESTING. IN THAT CASE, FOR THE SAKE OF THAT PERSON...
NOT LISTENING AT ALL
...I CANNOT LET YOU LIVE.
NOW, DIE!!
DASH

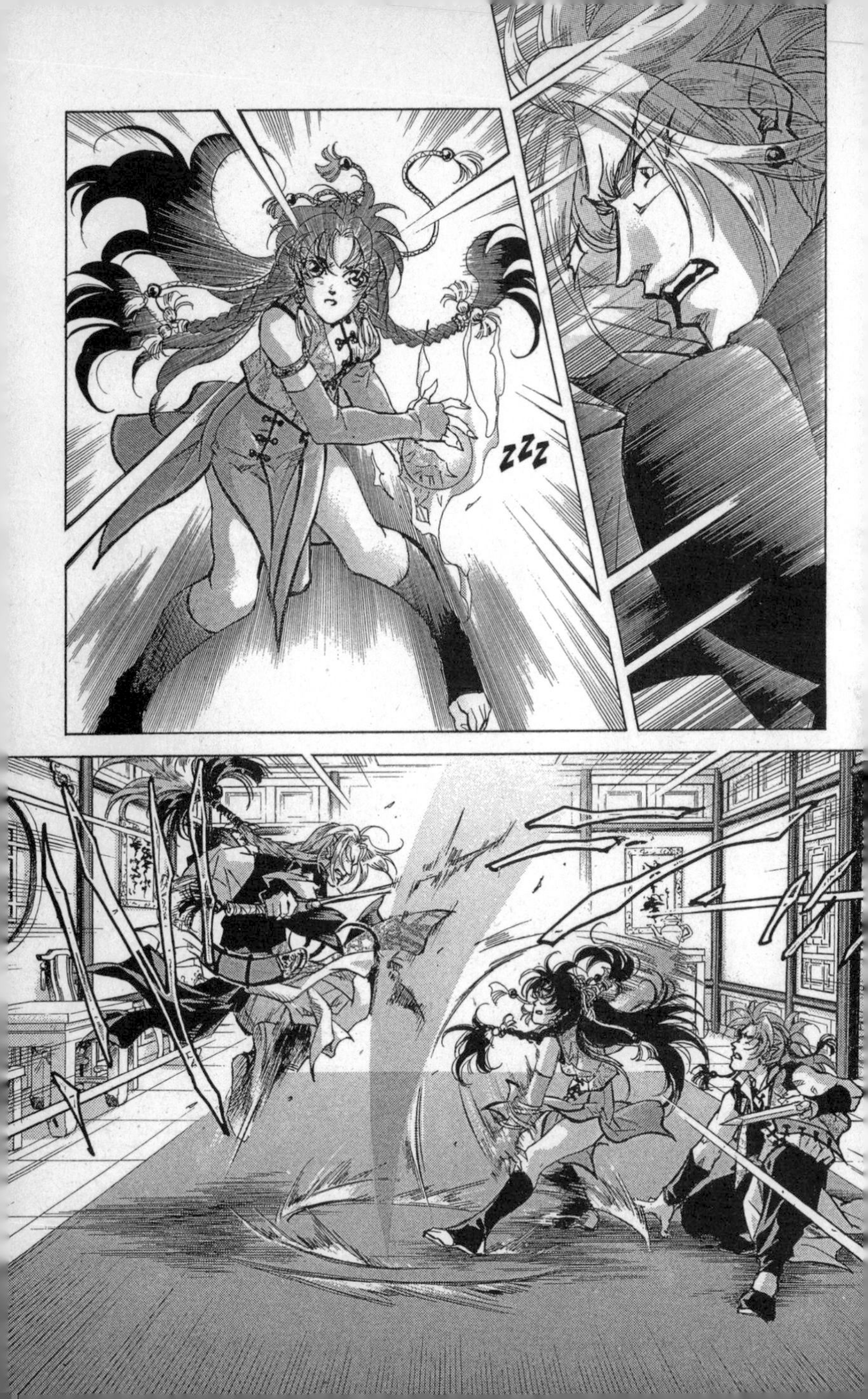
ZZZ

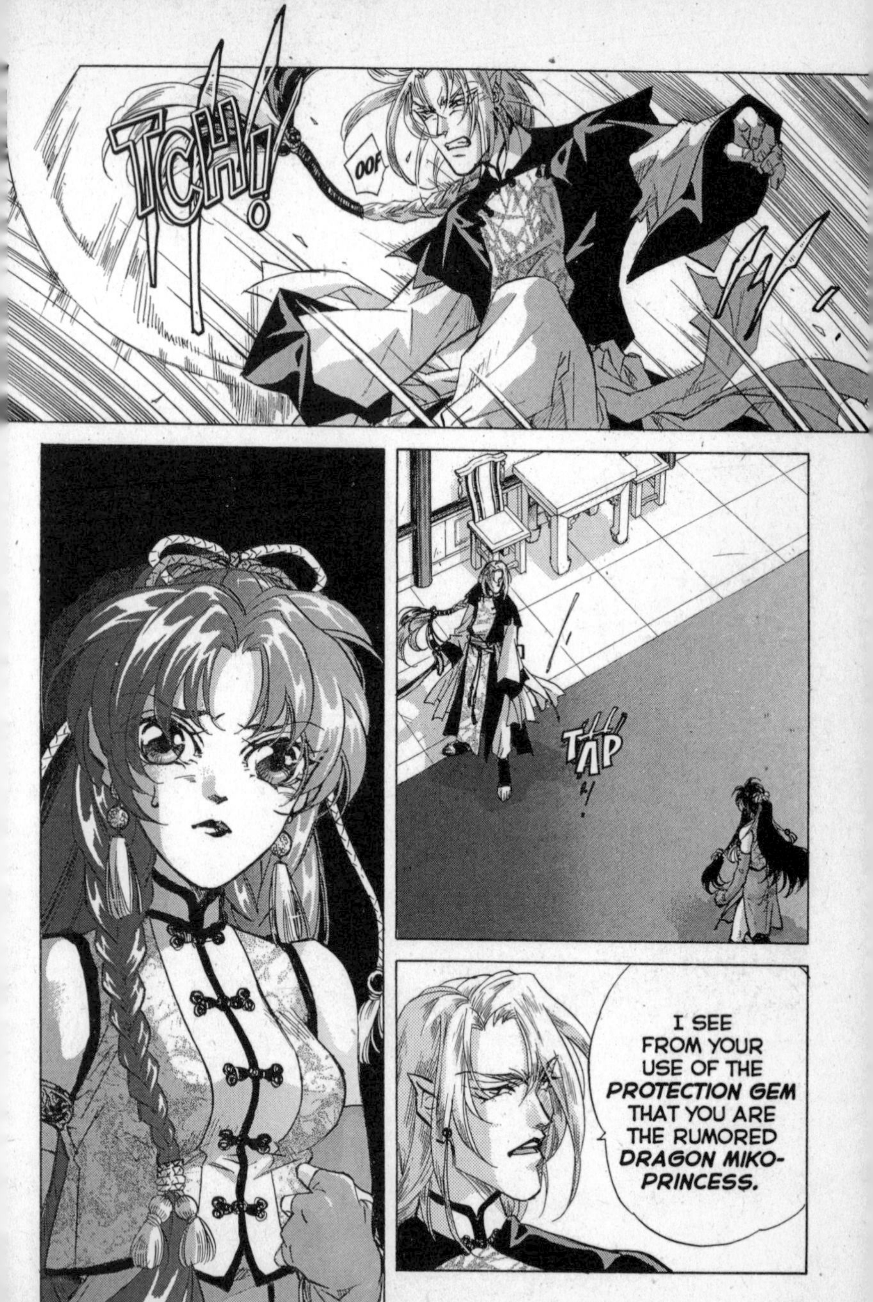
TCH!
OOF
TAP
I SEE FROM YOUR USE OF THE *PROTECTION GEM* THAT YOU ARE THE RUMORED *DRAGON MIKO-PRINCESS.*

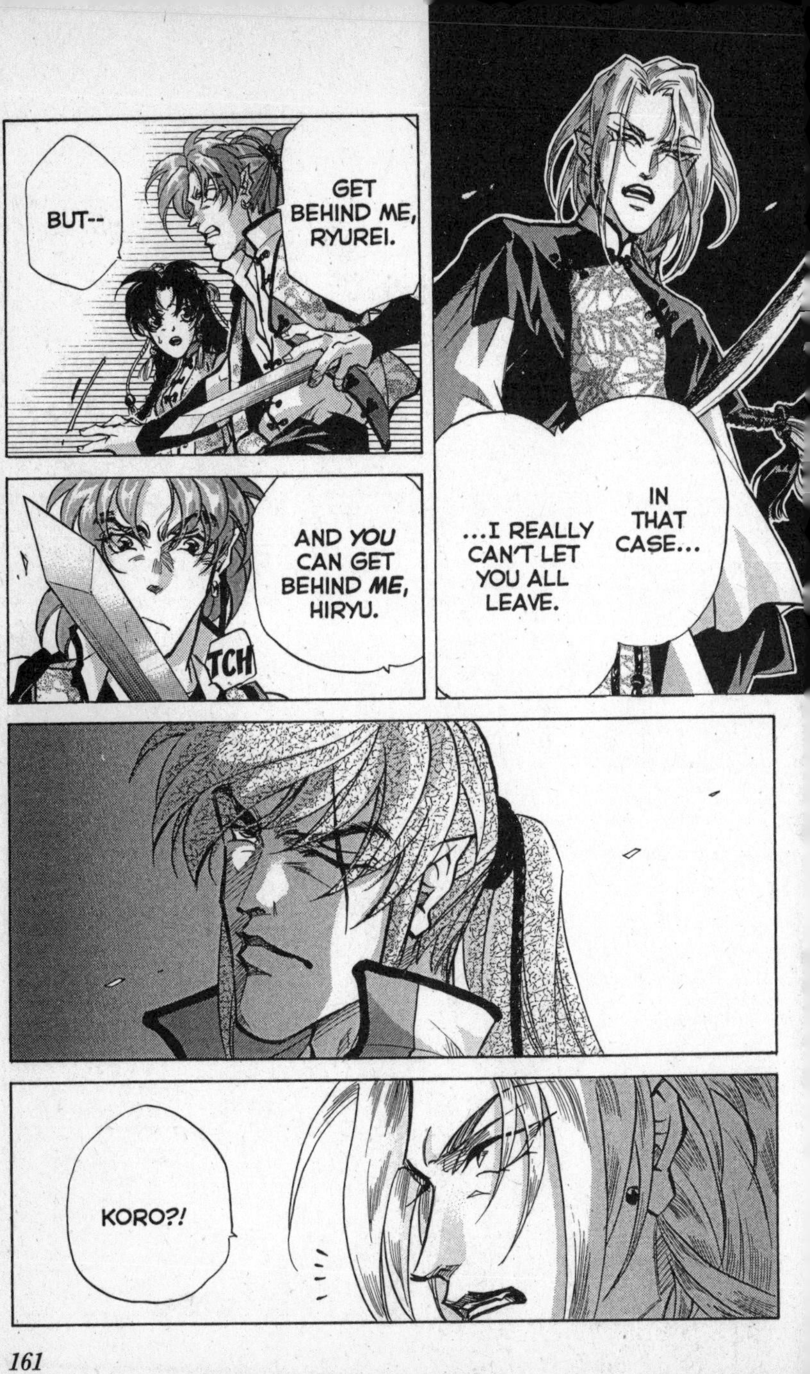
IN THAT CASE...
...I REALLY CAN'T LET YOU ALL LEAVE.
GET BEHIND ME, RYUREI.
BUT--
AND YOU CAN GET BEHIND ME, HIRYU.
TCH
KORO?!

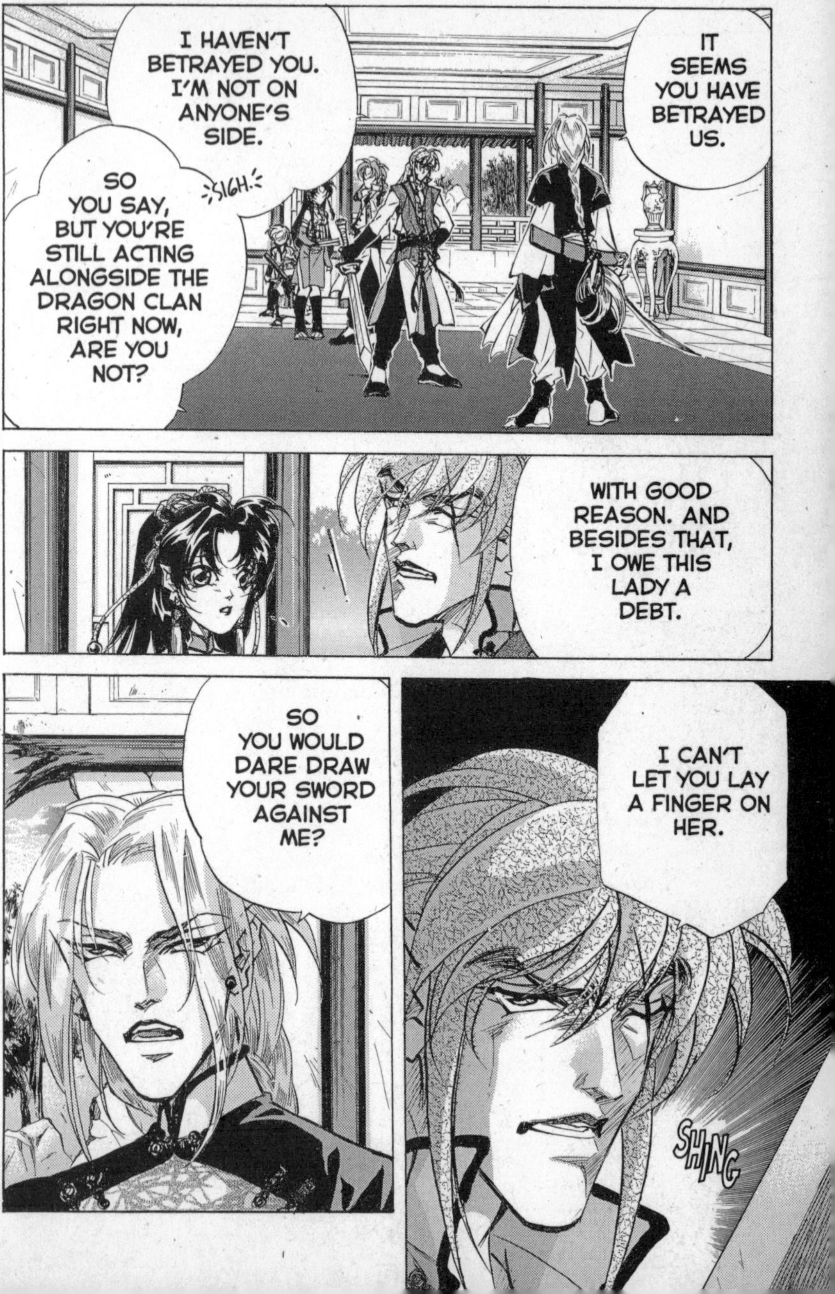
IT SEEMS YOU HAVE BETRAYED US.
I HAVEN'T BETRAYED YOU. I'M NOT ON ANYONE'S SIDE.
SIGH
SO YOU SAY, BUT YOU'RE STILL ACTING ALONGSIDE THE DRAGON CLAN RIGHT NOW, ARE YOU NOT?
WITH GOOD REASON. AND BESIDES THAT, I OWE THIS LADY A DEBT.
I CAN'T LET YOU LAY A FINGER ON HER.
SHING
SO YOU WOULD DARE DRAW YOUR SWORD AGAINST ME?

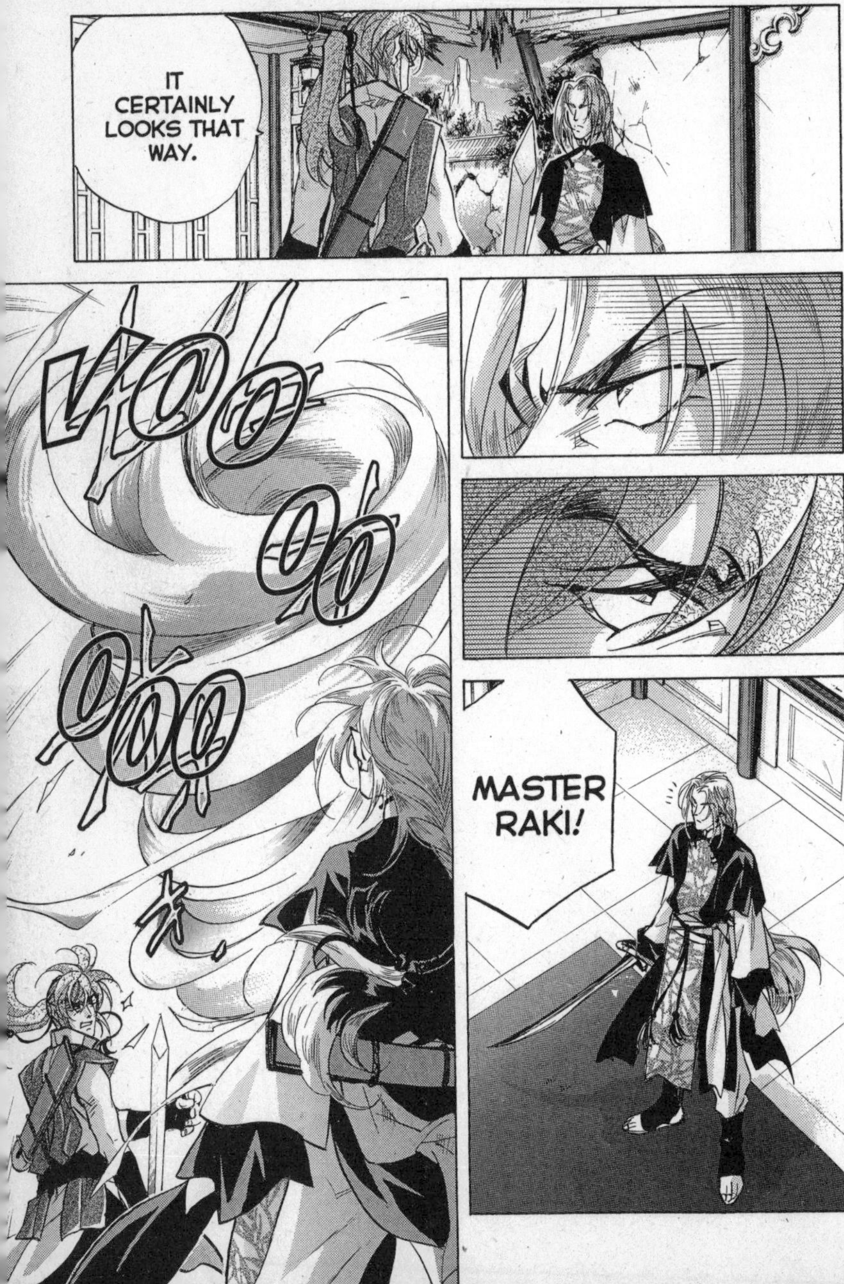
IT CERTAINLY LOOKS THAT WAY.
MASTER RAKI!
VOOOOOOOOOOO

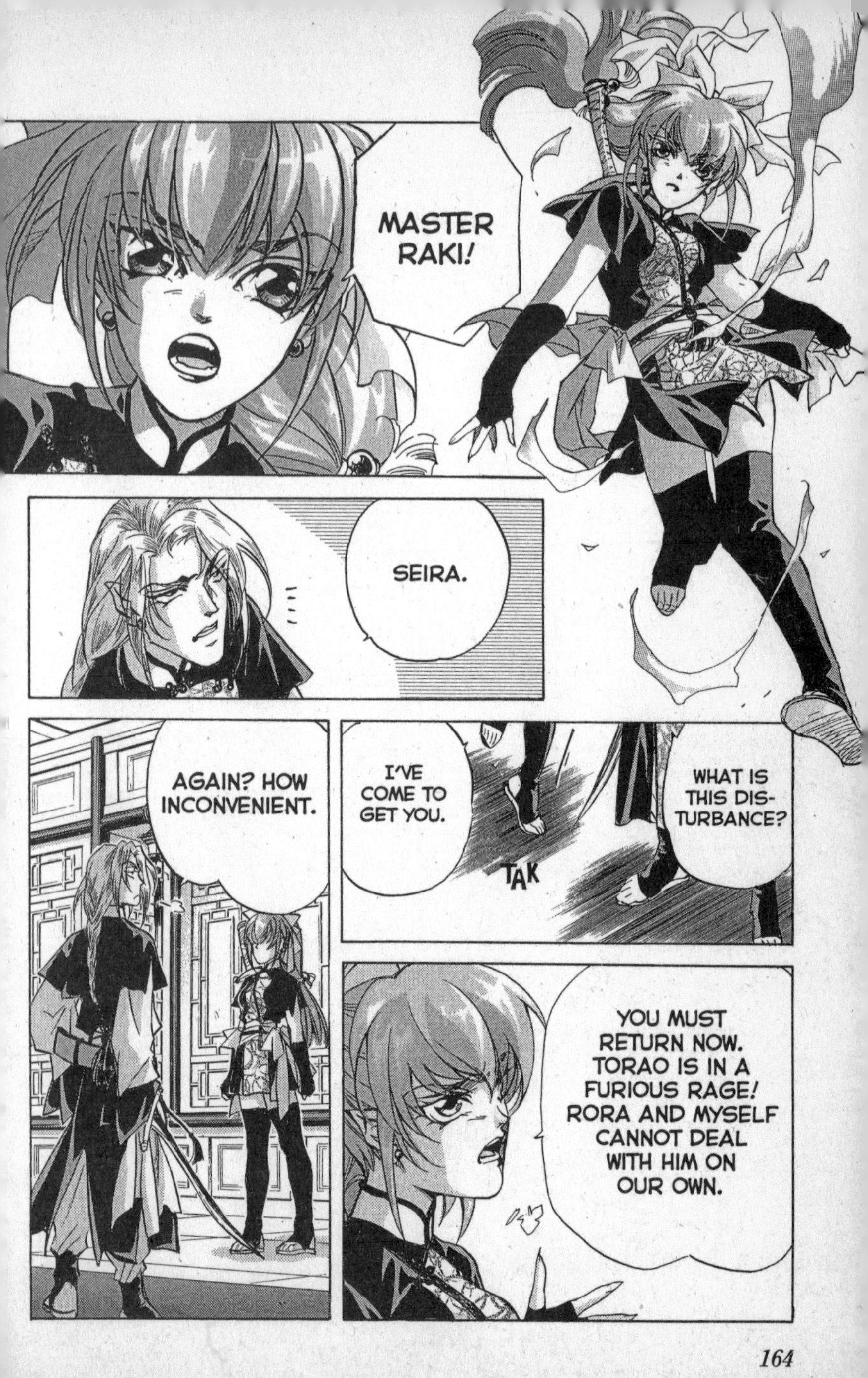
MASTER RAKI!
SEIRA.
WHAT IS THIS DIS-TURBANCE?
I'VE COME TO GET YOU.
TAK
YOU MUST RETURN NOW. TORAO IS IN A FURIOUS RAGE! RORA AND MYSELF CANNOT DEAL WITH HIM ON OUR OWN.
AGAIN? HOW INCONVENIENT.

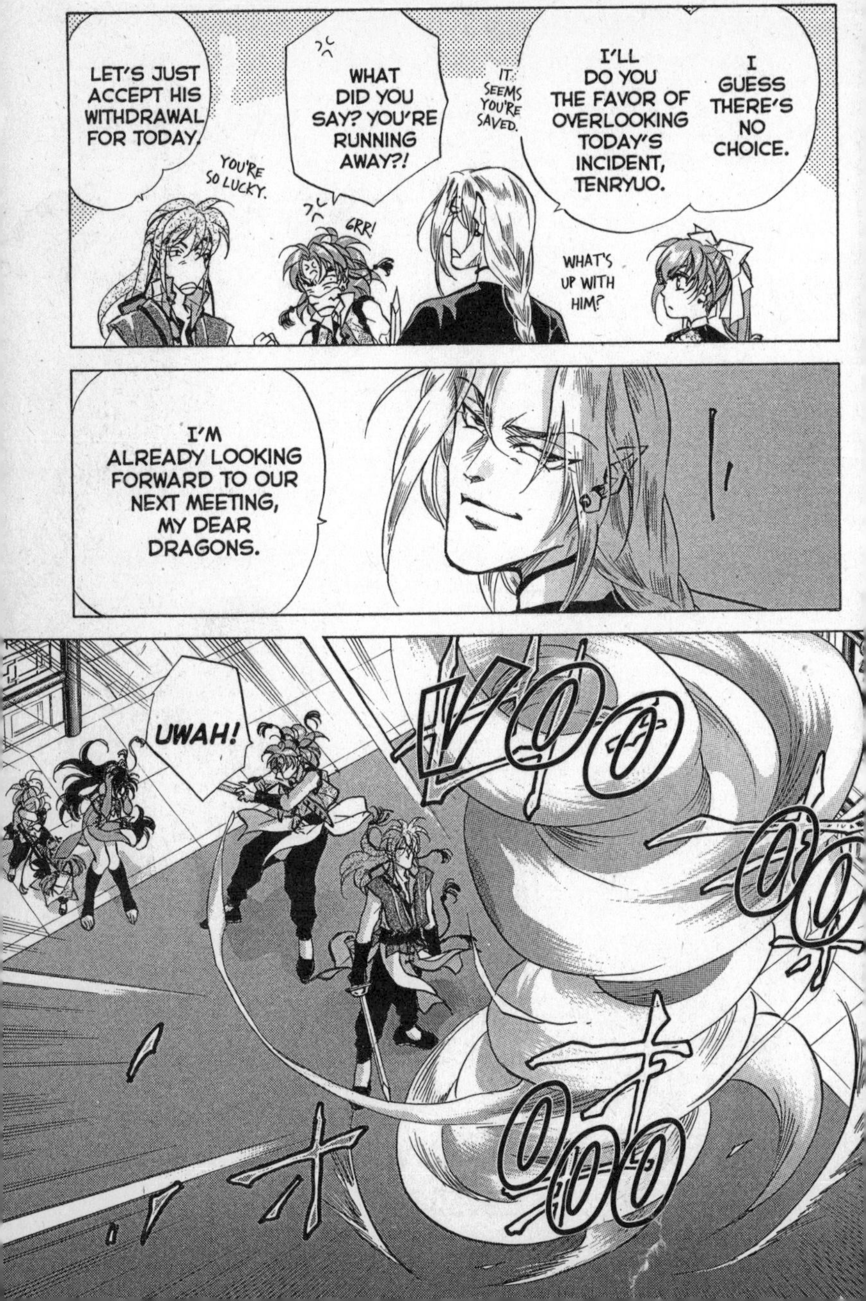
I GUESS THERE'S NO CHOICE.
I'LL DO YOU THE FAVOR OF OVERLOOKING TODAY'S INCIDENT, TENRYUO.
WHAT'S UP WITH HIM?
IT SEEMS YOU'RE SAVED.
WHAT DID YOU SAY? YOU'RE RUNNING AWAY?!
GRR!
YOU'RE SO LUCKY.
LET'S JUST ACCEPT HIS WITHDRAWAL FOR TODAY.
I'M ALREADY LOOKING FORWARD TO OUR NEXT MEETING, MY DEAR DRAGONS.
VOOOOOO
UWAH!

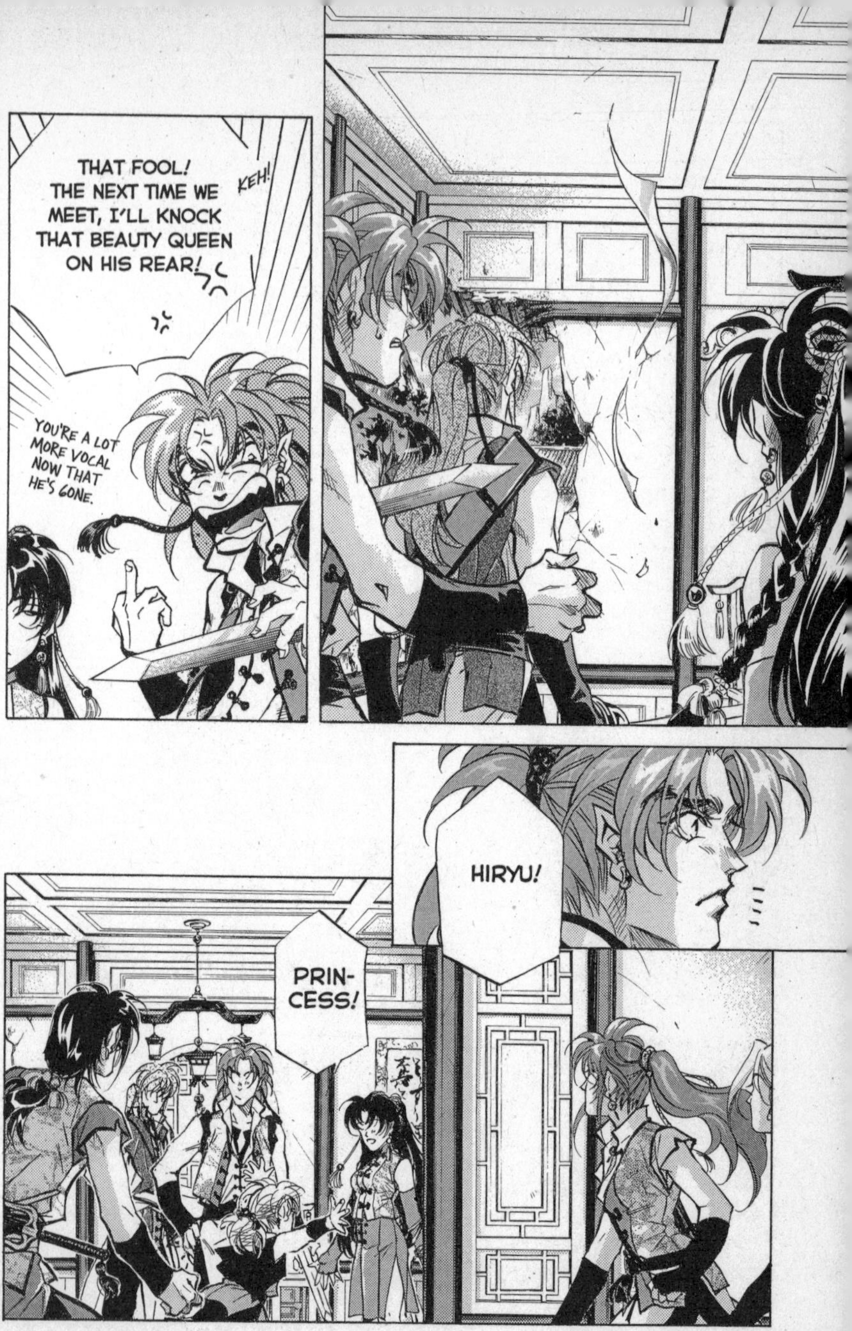
THAT FOOL! THE NEXT TIME WE MEET, I'LL KNOCK THAT BEAUTY QUEEN ON HIS REAR!
KEH!
YOU'RE A LOT MORE VOCAL NOW THAT HE'S GONE.
HIRYU!
PRIN-CESS!

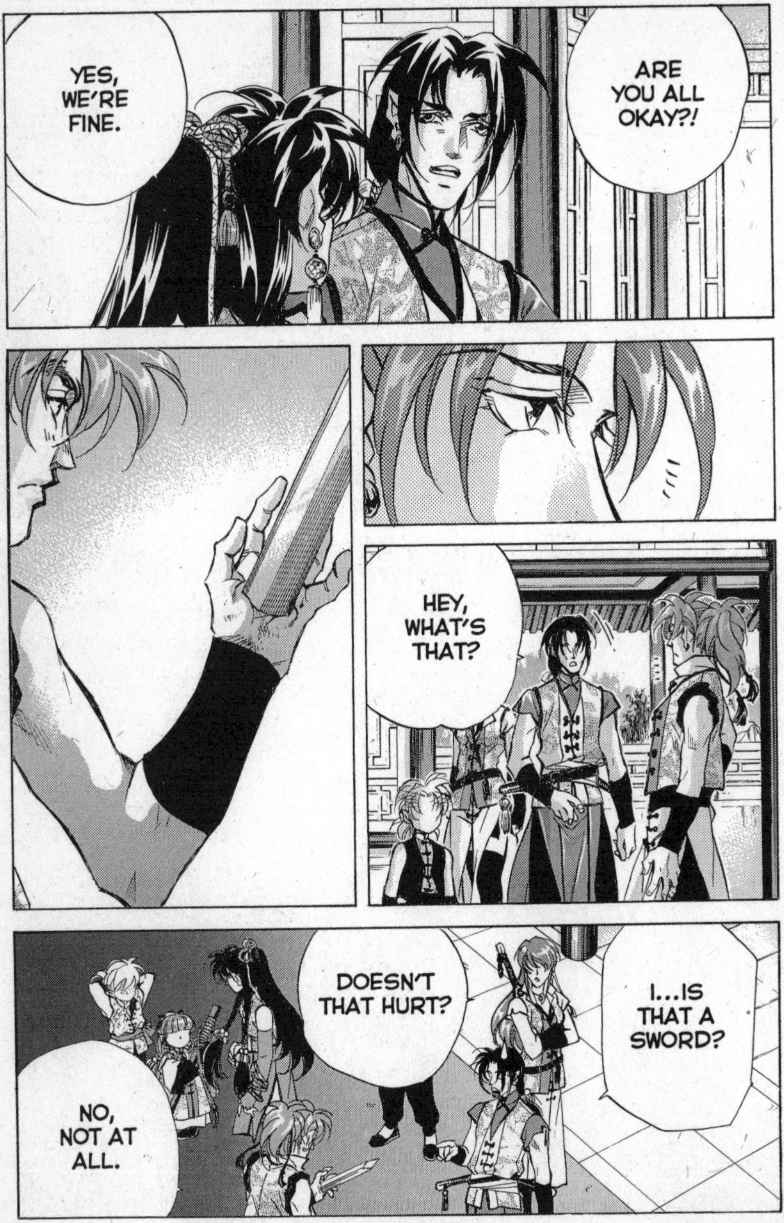
ARE YOU ALL OKAY?!
YES, WE'RE FINE.
HEY, WHAT'S THAT?
I...IS THAT A SWORD?
DOESN'T THAT HURT?
NO, NOT AT ALL.

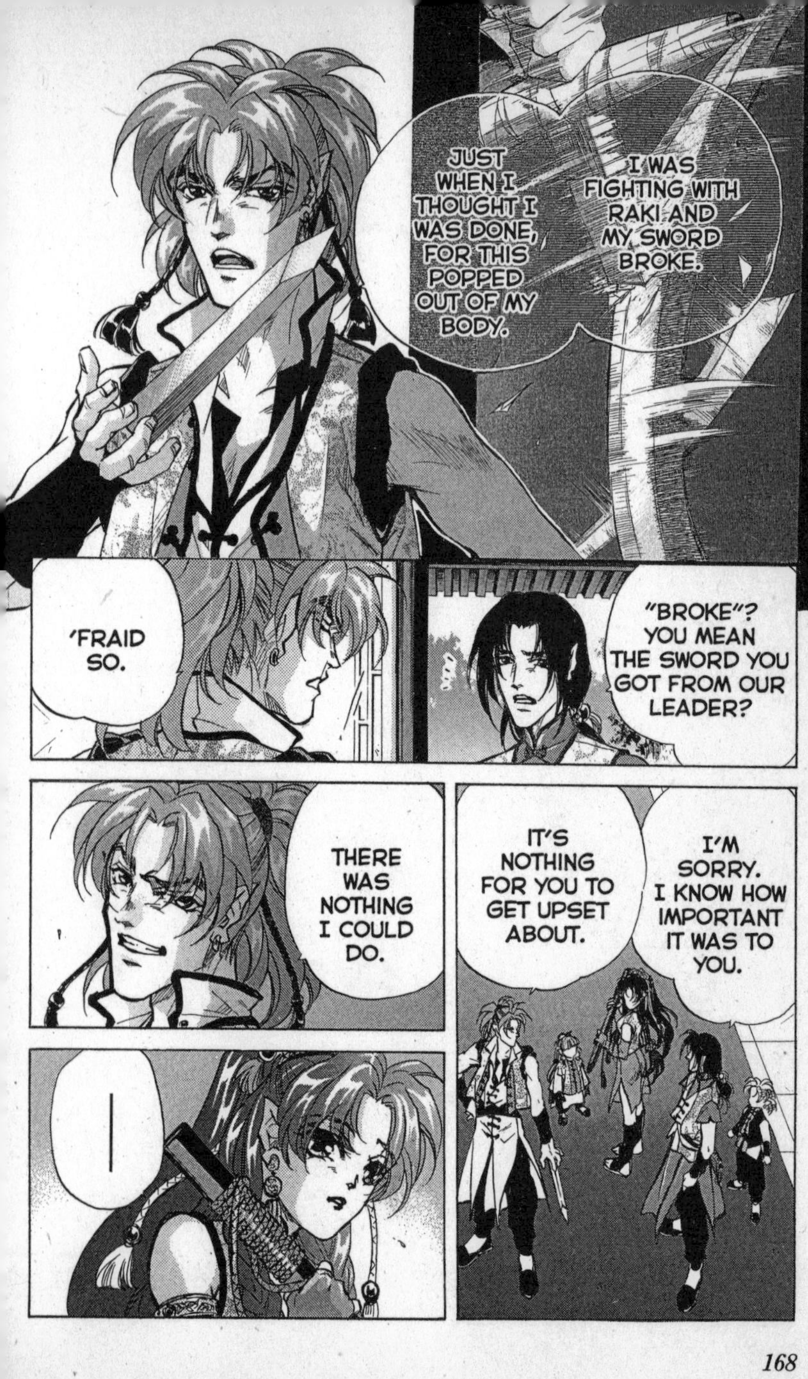
I WAS FIGHTING WITH RAKI AND MY SWORD BROKE.
JUST WHEN I THOUGHT I WAS DONE, FOR THIS POPPED OUT OF MY BODY.
"BROKE"? YOU MEAN THE SWORD YOU GOT FROM OUR LEADER?
'FRAID SO.
I'M SORRY. I KNOW HOW IMPORTANT IT WAS TO YOU.
IT'S NOTHING FOR YOU TO GET UPSET ABOUT.
THERE WAS NOTHING I COULD DO.

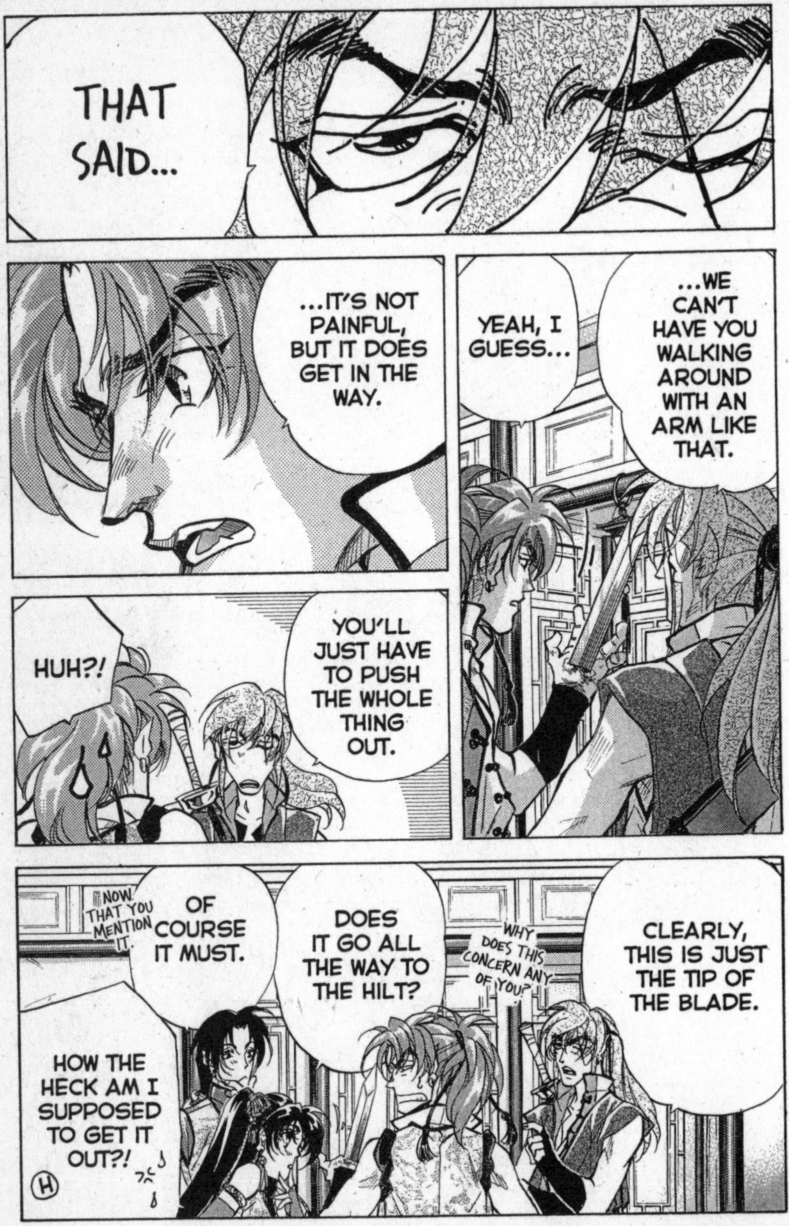
THAT SAID...
...WE CAN'T HAVE YOU WALKING AROUND WITH AN ARM LIKE THAT.
YEAH, I GUESS...
...IT'S NOT PAINFUL, BUT IT DOES GET IN THE WAY.
YOU'LL JUST HAVE TO PUSH THE WHOLE THING OUT.
HUH?!
CLEARLY, THIS IS JUST THE TIP OF THE BLADE.
WHY DOES THIS CONCERN ANY OF YOU?
DOES IT GO ALL THE WAY TO THE HILT?
OF COURSE IT MUST.
NOW THAT YOU MENTION IT.
HOW THE HECK AM I SUPPOSED TO GET IT OUT?!

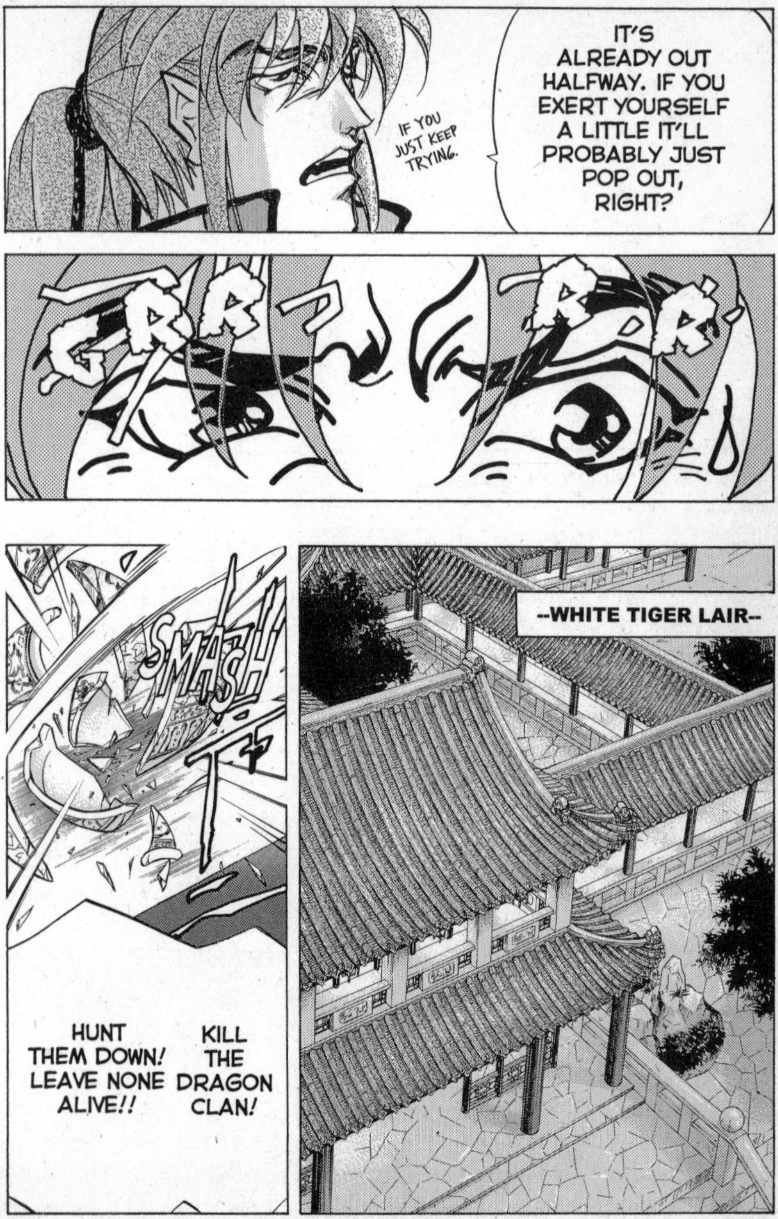
IT'S ALREADY OUT HALFWAY. IF YOU EXERT YOURSELF A LITTLE IT'LL PROBABLY JUST POP OUT, RIGHT?
IF YOU JUST KEEP TRYING.
GRR
RR
--WHITE TIGER LAIR--
SMASH
KILL THE DRAGON CLAN!
HUNT THEM DOWN! LEAVE NONE ALIVE!!

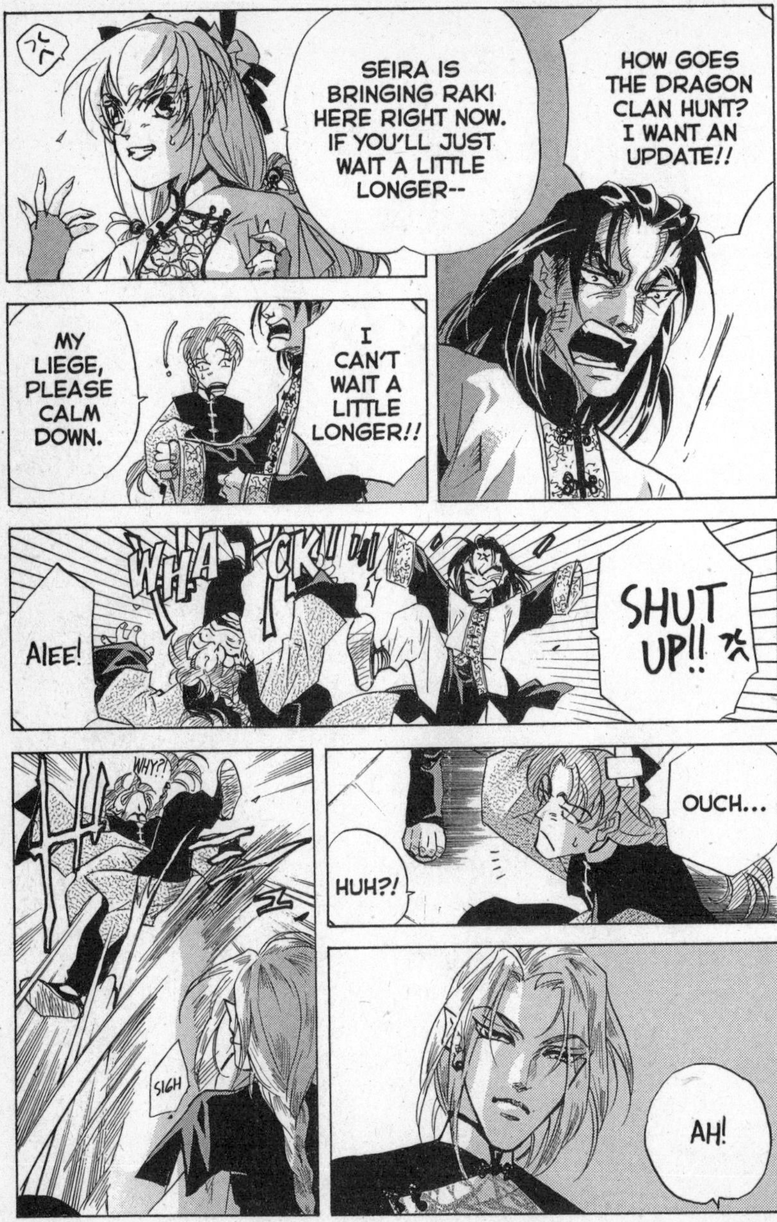
HOW GOES THE DRAGON CLAN HUNT? I WANT AN UPDATE!!
SEIRA IS BRINGING RAKI HERE RIGHT NOW. IF YOU'LL JUST WAIT A LITTLE LONGER--
I CAN'T WAIT A LITTLE LONGER!!
MY LIEGE, PLEASE CALM DOWN.
SHUT UP!!
WHA-CK!!
AIEE!
OUCH...
HUH?!
AH!
WHY?!
SIGH

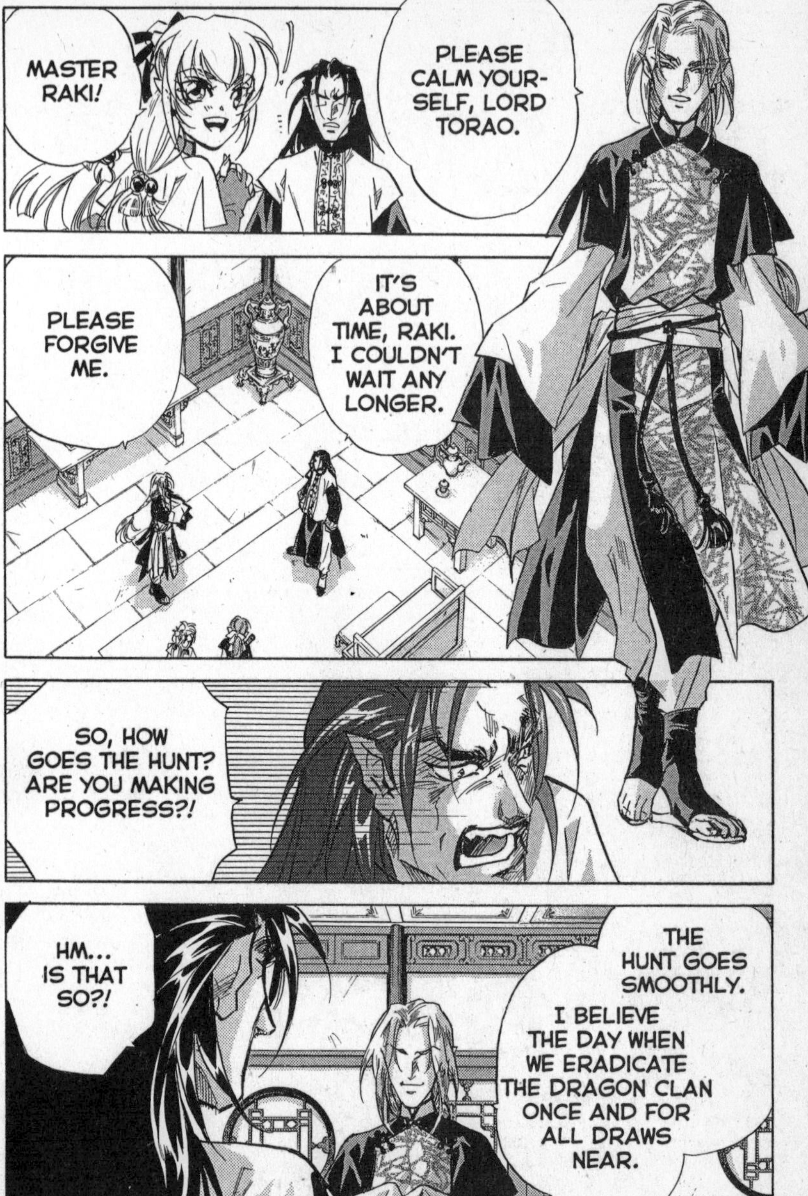
PLEASE CALM YOURSELF, LORD TORAO.
MASTER RAKI!
IT'S ABOUT TIME, RAKI. I COULDN'T WAIT ANY LONGER.
PLEASE FORGIVE ME.
SO, HOW GOES THE HUNT? ARE YOU MAKING PROGRESS?!
THE HUNT GOES SMOOTHLY.
I BELIEVE THE DAY WHEN WE ERADICATE THE DRAGON CLAN ONCE AND FOR ALL DRAWS NEAR.
HM... IS THAT SO?!

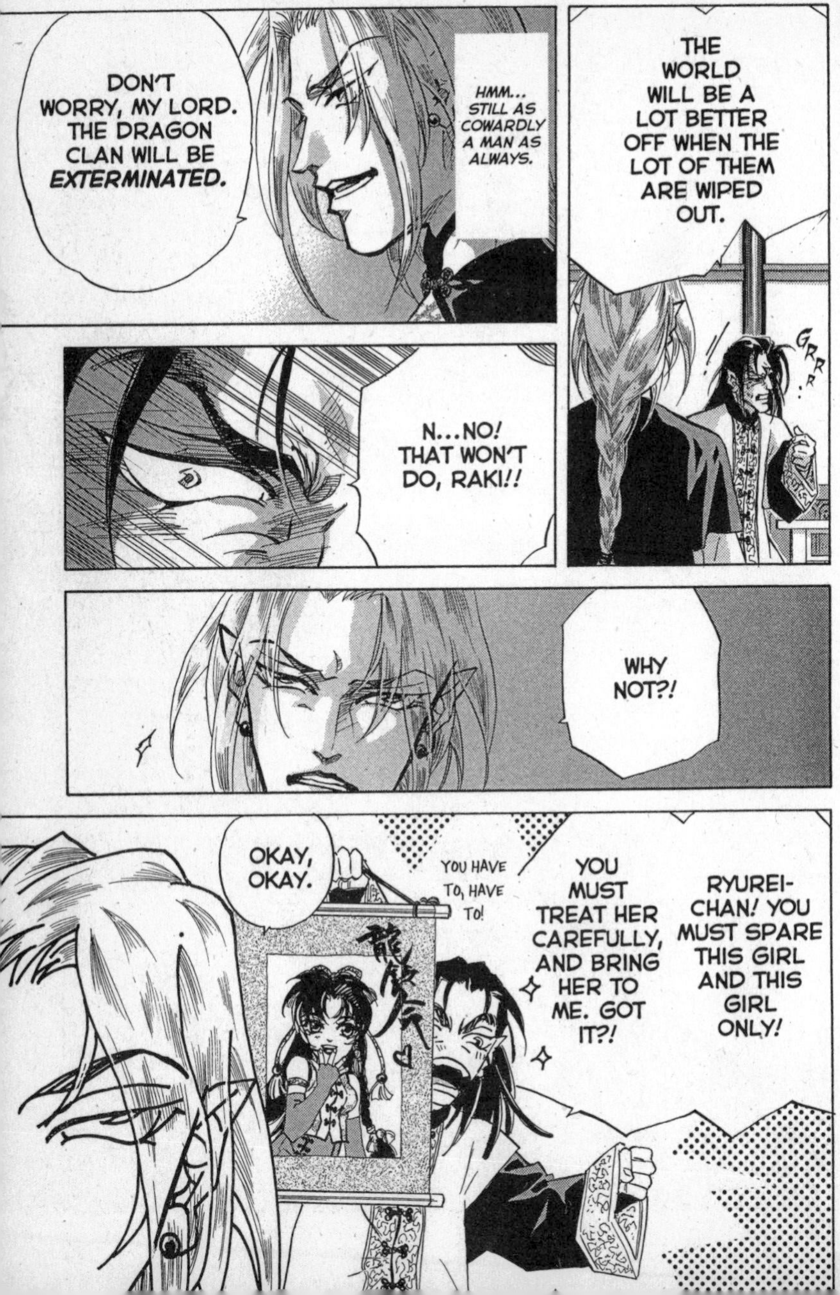
THE WORLD WILL BE A LOT BETTER OFF WHEN THE LOT OF THEM ARE WIPED OUT.
GRRR
DON'T WORRY, MY LORD. THE DRAGON CLAN WILL BE *EXTERMINATED.*
HMM... STILL AS COWARDLY A MAN AS ALWAYS.
N...NO! THAT WON'T DO, RAKI!!
WHY NOT?!
RYUREI-CHAN! YOU MUST SPARE THIS GIRL AND THIS GIRL ONLY!
YOU MUST TREAT HER CAREFULLY, AND BRING HER TO ME. GOT IT?!
YOU HAVE TO, HAVE TO!
OKAY, OKAY.

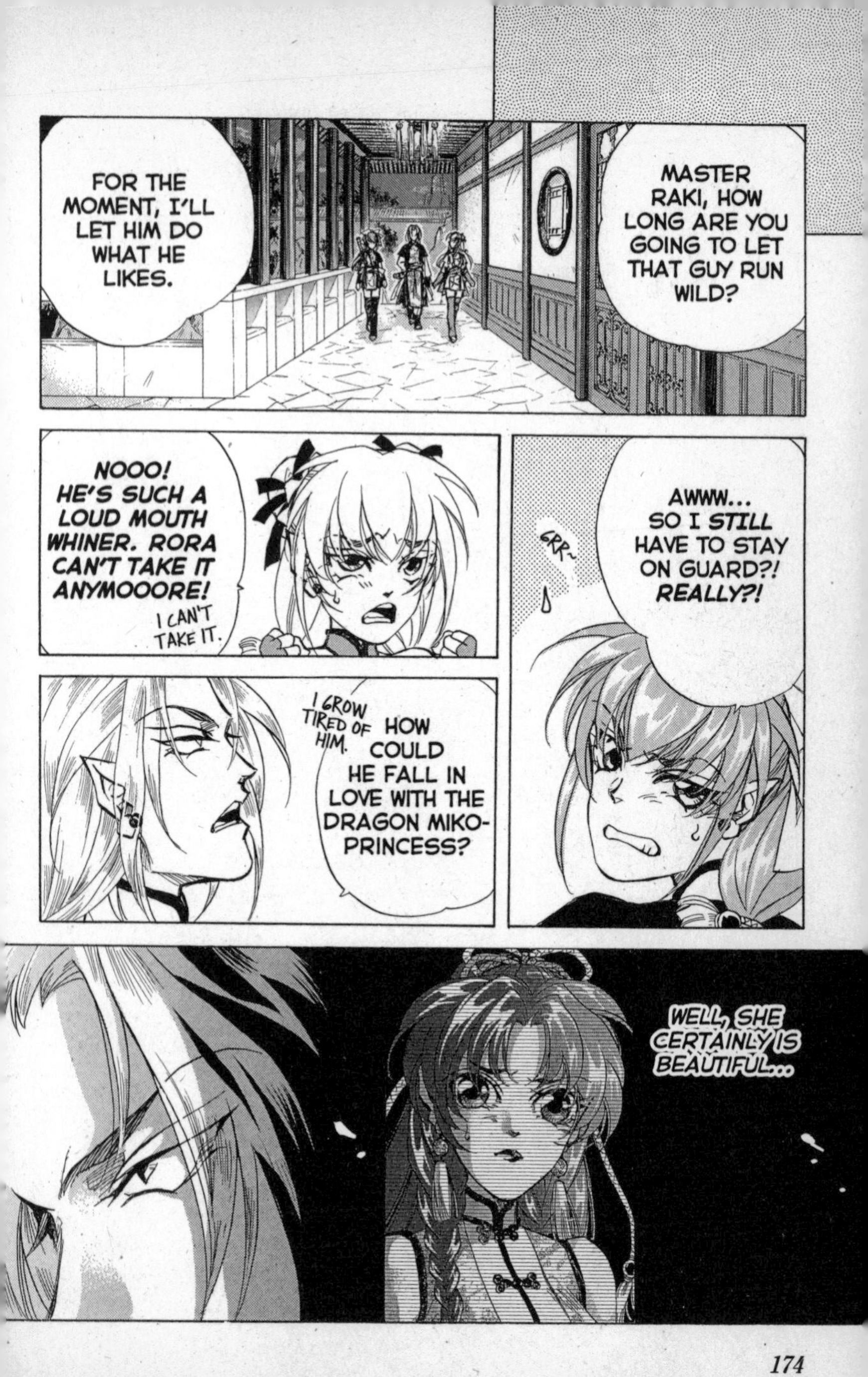
MASTER RAKI, HOW LONG ARE YOU GOING TO LET THAT GUY RUN WILD?
FOR THE MOMENT, I'LL LET HIM DO WHAT HE LIKES.
AWWW... SO I STILL HAVE TO STAY ON GUARD?! REALLY?!
GRR~
NOOO! HE'S SUCH A LOUD MOUTH WHINER. RORA CAN'T TAKE IT ANYMOOORE!
I CAN'T TAKE IT.
HOW COULD HE FALL IN LOVE WITH THE DRAGON MIKO-PRINCESS?
I GROW TIRED OF HIM.
WELL, SHE CERTAINLY IS BEAUTIFUL...

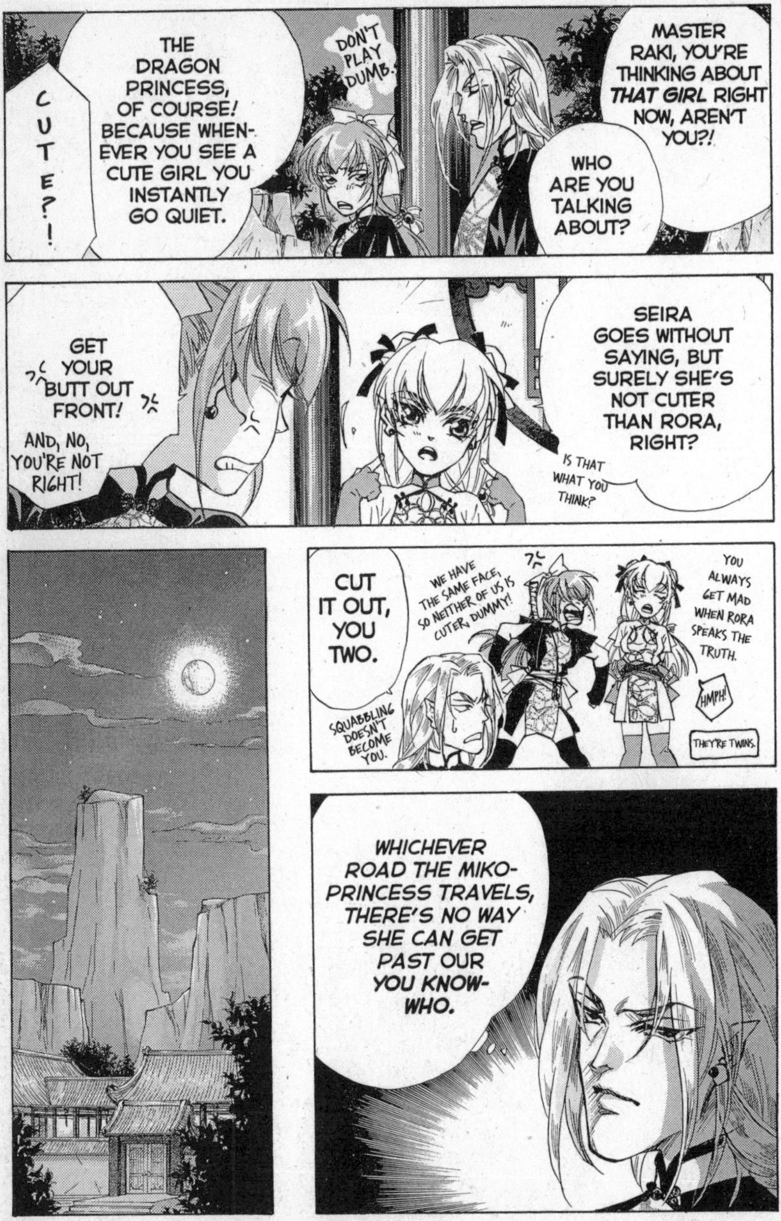
MASTER RAKI, YOU'RE THINKING ABOUT *THAT GIRL* RIGHT NOW, AREN'T YOU?!
WHO ARE YOU TALKING ABOUT?
DON'T PLAY DUMB.
THE DRAGON PRINCESS, OF COURSE! BECAUSE WHENEVER YOU SEE A CUTE GIRL YOU INSTANTLY GO QUIET.
CUTE?!
SEIRA GOES WITHOUT SAYING, BUT SURELY SHE'S NOT CUTER THAN RORA, RIGHT?
IS THAT WHAT YOU THINK?
GET YOUR BUTT OUT FRONT!
AND, NO, YOU'RE NOT RIGHT!
YOU ALWAYS GET MAD WHEN RORA SPEAKS THE TRUTH.
HMPH!
THEY'RE TWINS.
WE HAVE THE SAME FACE, SO NEITHER OF US IS CUTER, DUMMY!
CUT IT OUT, YOU TWO.
SQUABBLING DOESN'T BECOME YOU.
WHICHEVER ROAD THE MIKO-PRINCESS TRAVELS, THERE'S NO WAY SHE CAN GET PAST OUR **YOU KNOW-WHO.**

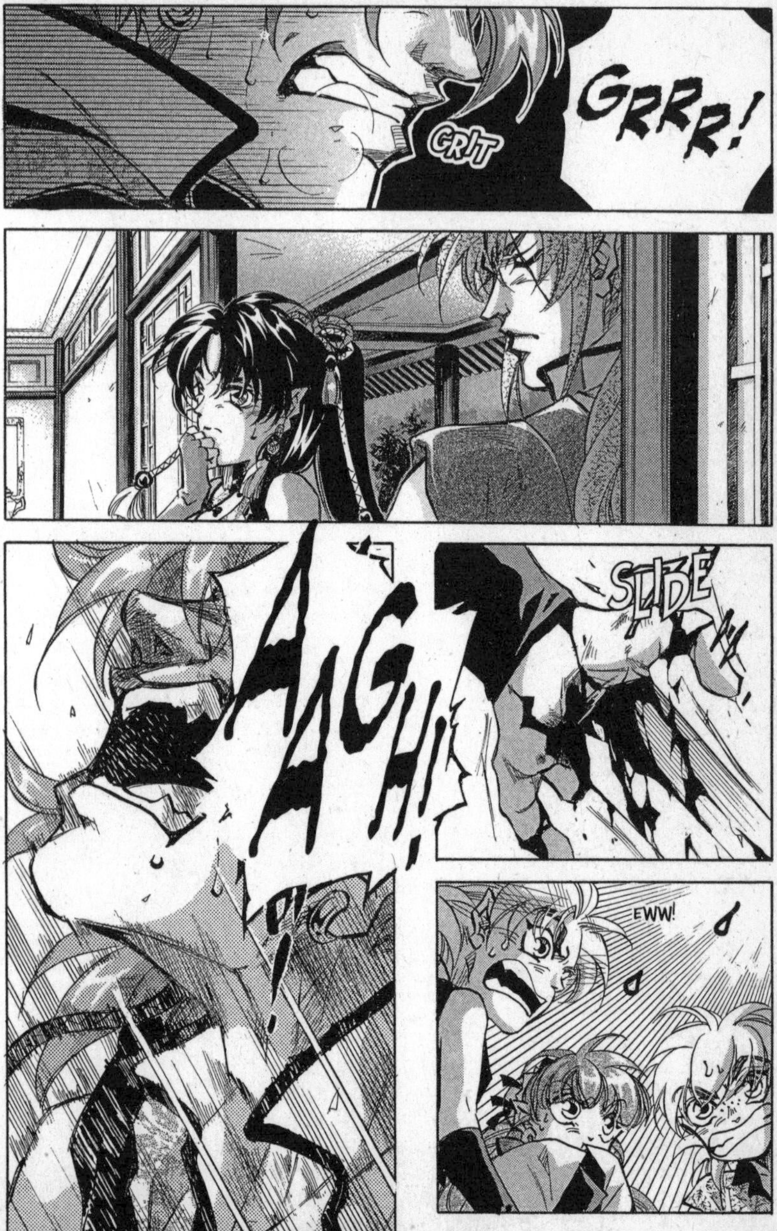
GRRRR!
GRIT
SLIDE
AAGH! AH!
EWW!

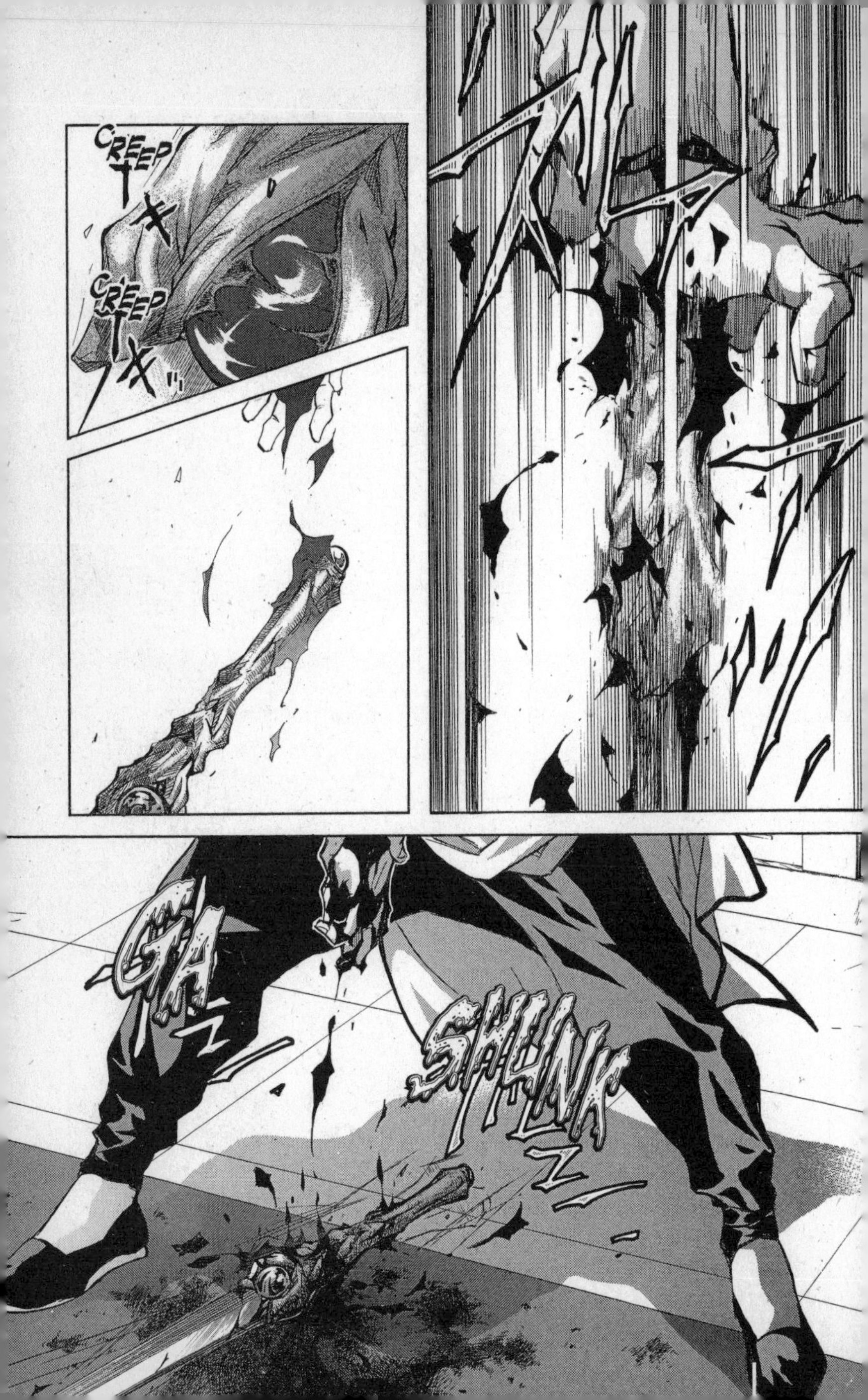
CREEP
CREEP
SHUNK
GA

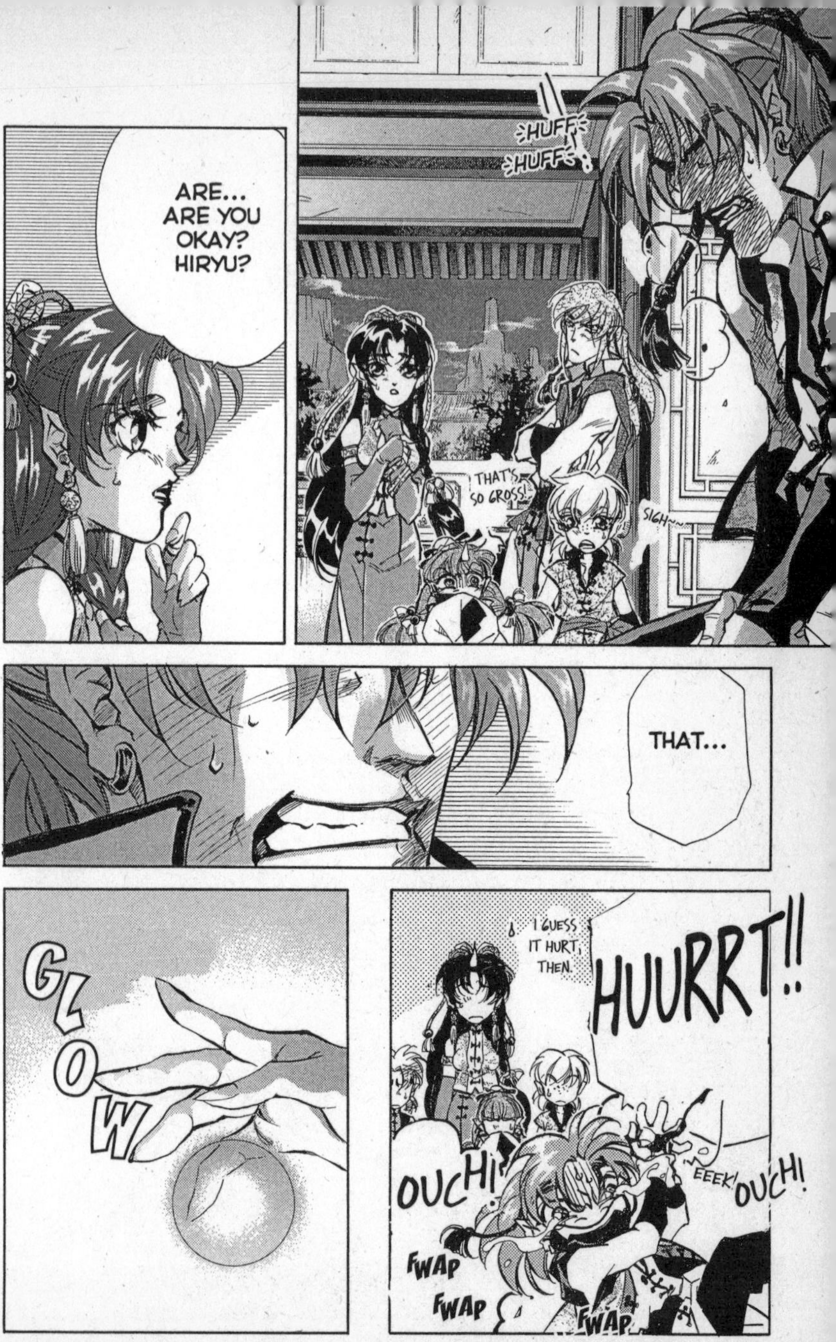
HUFF
HUFF
SIGH~~
THAT'S SO GROSS!
ARE... ARE YOU OKAY? HIRYU?
THAT...
HUURRT!!
I GUESS IT HURT, THEN.
OUCH!
EEEK!
OUCH!
FWAP
FWAP
FWAP
FWAP
GLOW

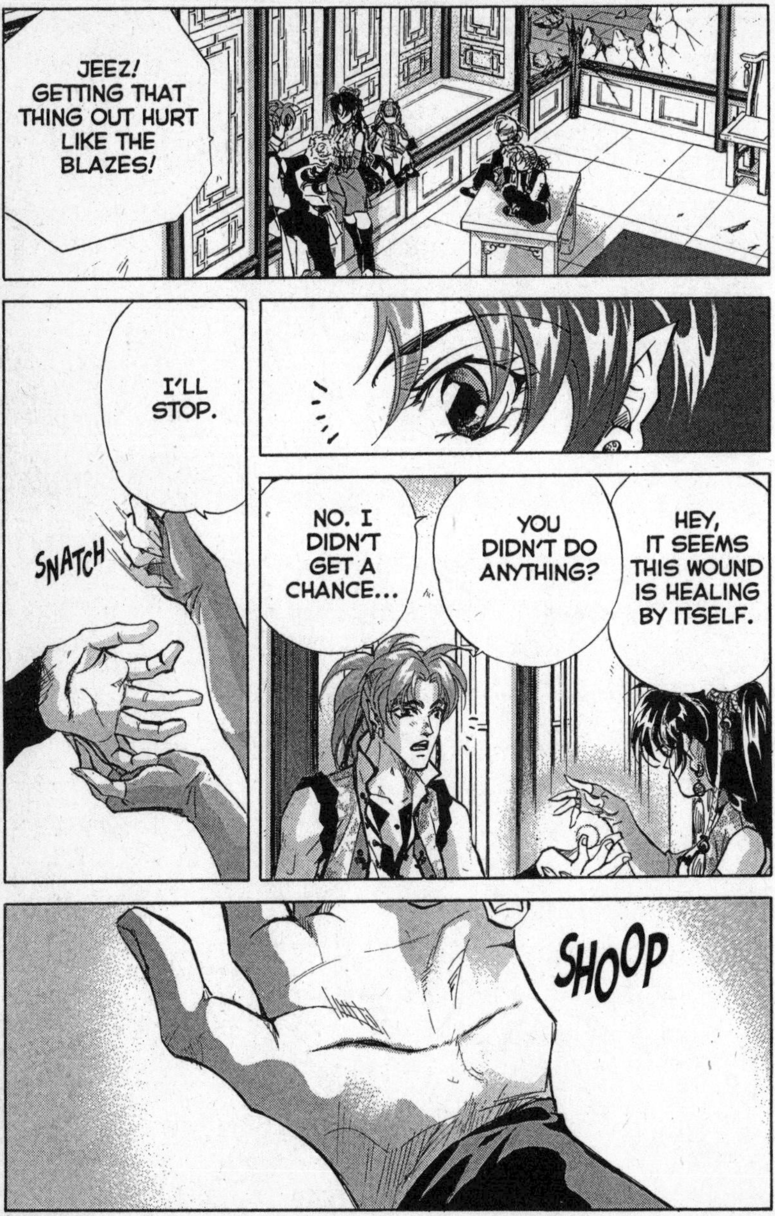
JEEZ! GETTING THAT THING OUT HURT LIKE THE BLAZES!
HEY, IT SEEMS THIS WOUND IS HEALING BY ITSELF.
YOU DIDN'T DO ANYTHING?
NO. I DIDN'T GET A CHANCE...
I'LL STOP.
SNATCH
SHOOP

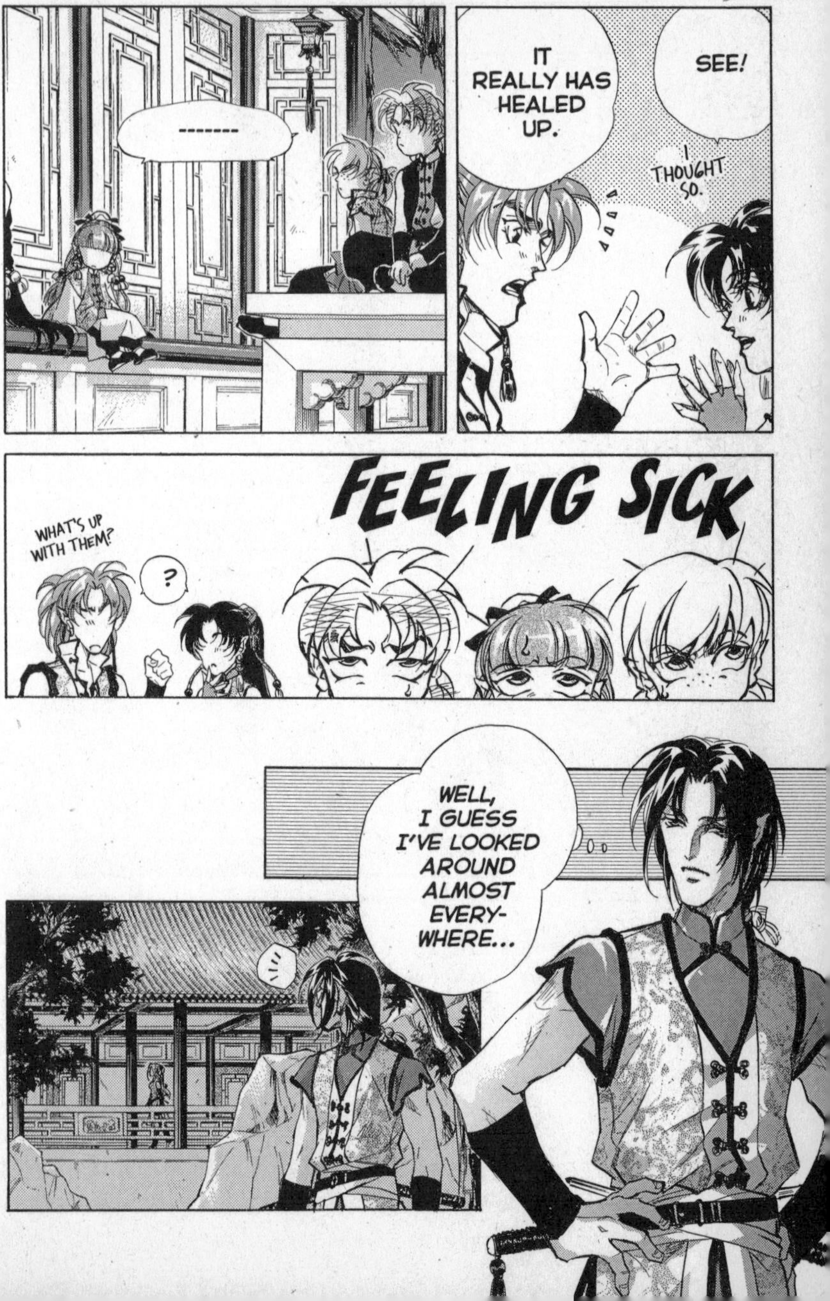
SEE!
I THOUGHT SO.
IT REALLY HAS HEALED UP.

FEELING SICK
?
WHAT'S UP WITH THEM?
WELL, I GUESS I'VE LOOKED AROUND ALMOST EVERY-WHERE...

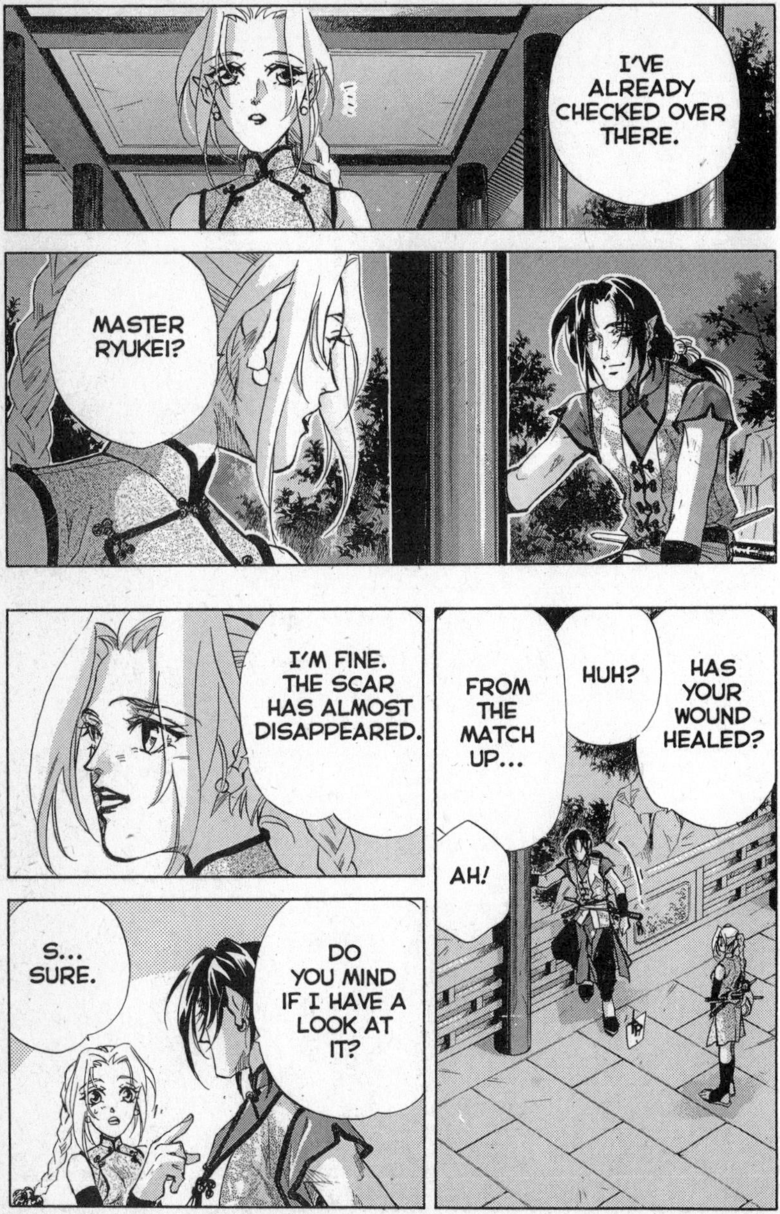
I'VE ALREADY CHECKED OVER THERE.
MASTER RYUKEI?
HAS YOUR WOUND HEALED?
HUH?
FROM THE MATCH UP...
AH!
I'M FINE. THE SCAR HAS ALMOST DISAPPEARED.
DO YOU MIND IF I HAVE A LOOK AT IT?
S... SURE.

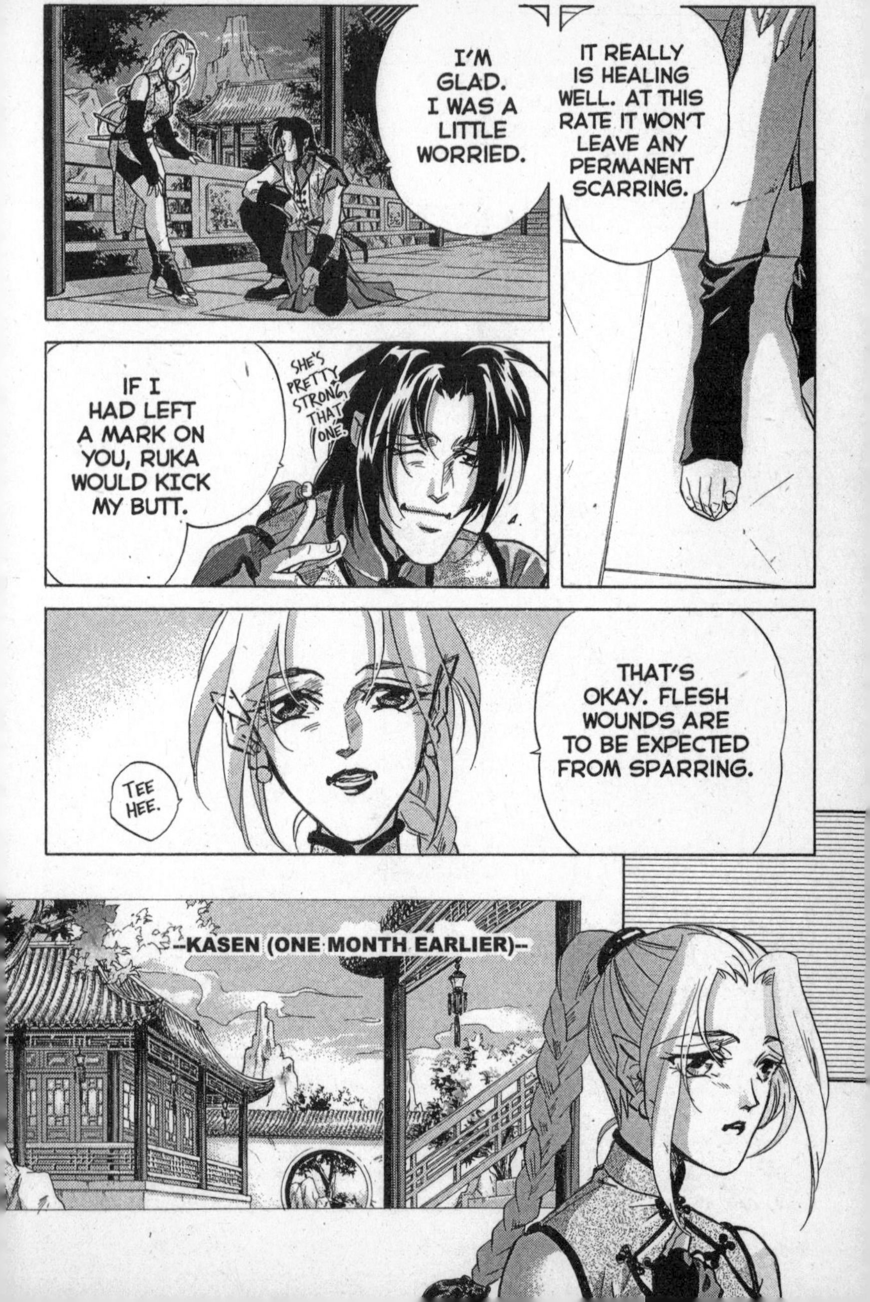

IT REALLY IS HEALING WELL. AT THIS RATE IT WON'T LEAVE ANY PERMANENT SCARRING.
I'M GLAD. I WAS A LITTLE WORRIED.
IF I HAD LEFT A MARK ON YOU, RUKA WOULD KICK MY BUTT.
SHE'S PRETTY STRONG, THAT ONE.
THAT'S OKAY. FLESH WOUNDS ARE TO BE EXPECTED FROM SPARRING.
TEE HEE.
--KASEN (ONE MONTH EARLIER)--

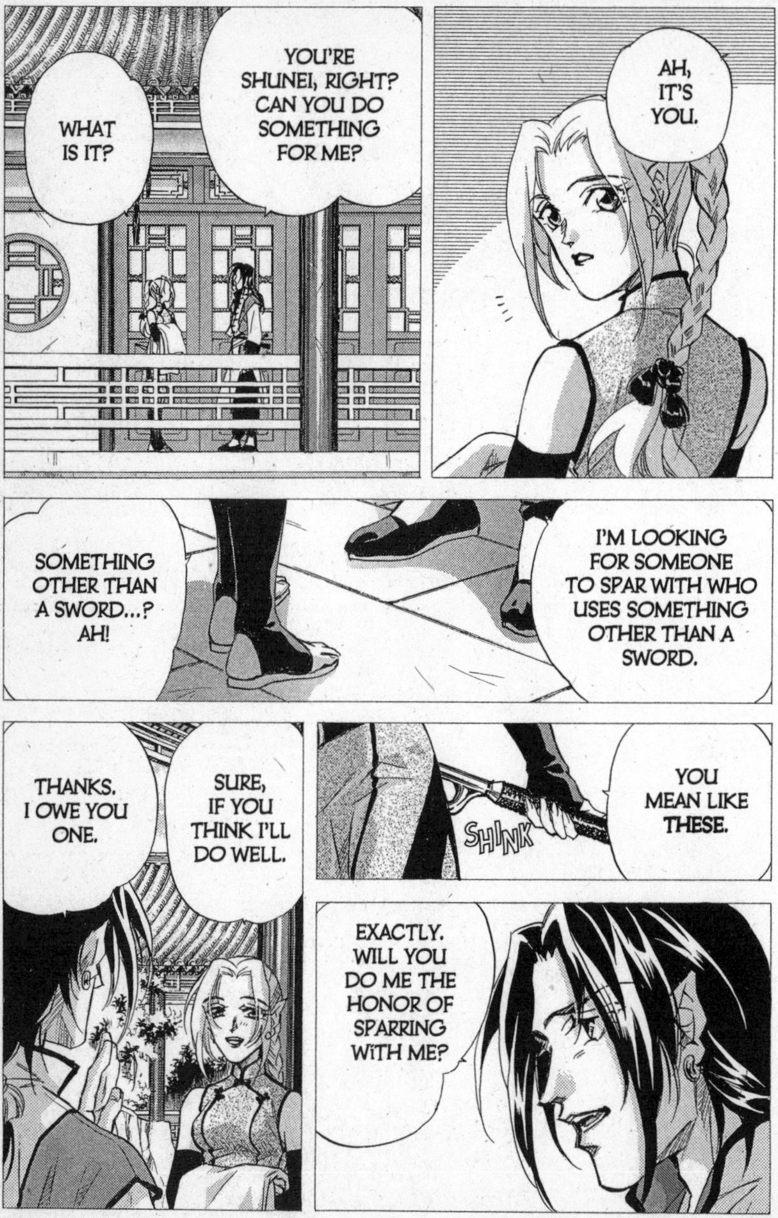
AH, IT'S YOU.
YOU'RE SHUNEI, RIGHT? CAN YOU DO SOMETHING FOR ME?
WHAT IS IT?
I'M LOOKING FOR SOMEONE TO SPAR WITH WHO USES SOMETHING OTHER THAN A SWORD.
SOMETHING OTHER THAN A SWORD...? AH!
YOU MEAN LIKE THESE.
SHINK
EXACTLY. WILL YOU DO ME THE HONOR OF SPARRING WITH ME?
SURE, IF YOU THINK I'LL DO WELL.
THANKS. I OWE YOU ONE.

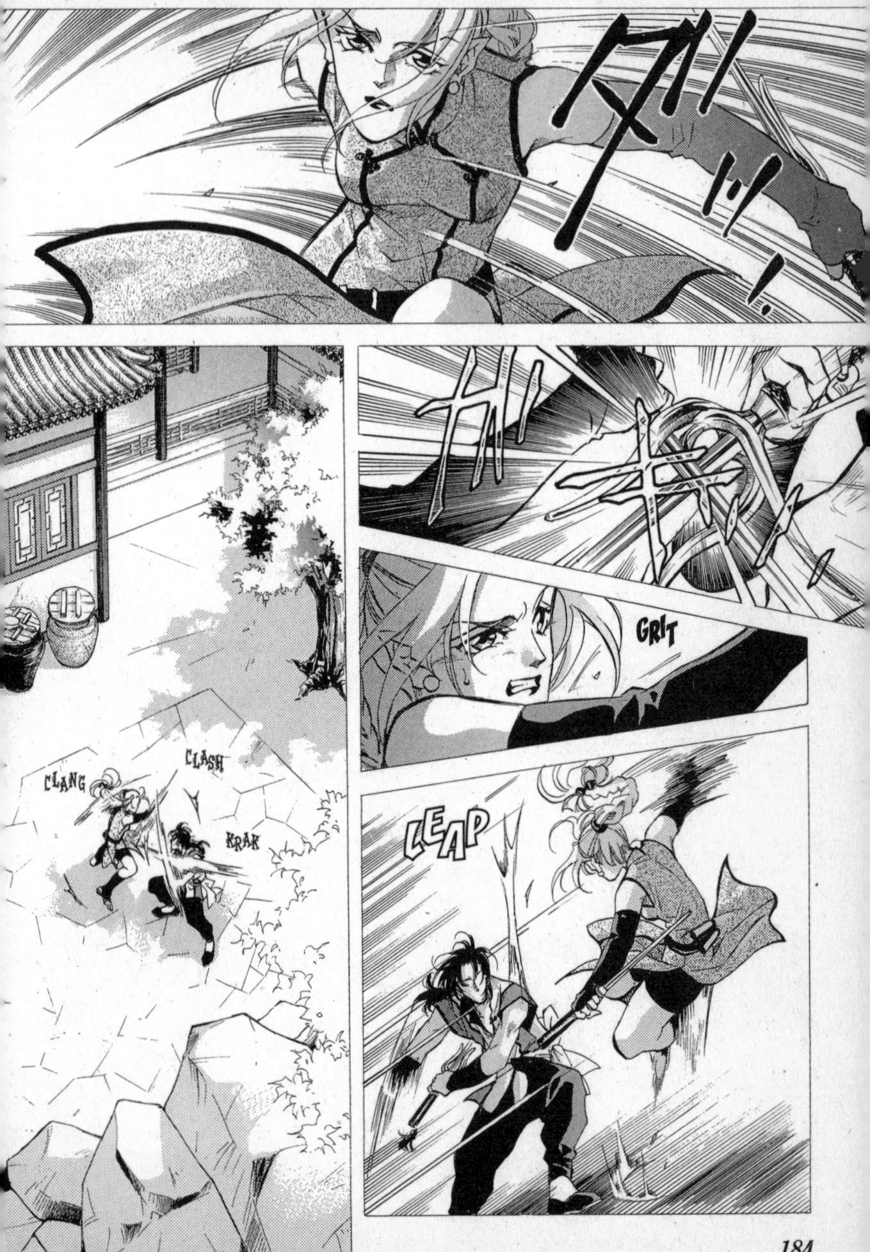
GRIT
LEAP
KRAK
CLASH
CLANG

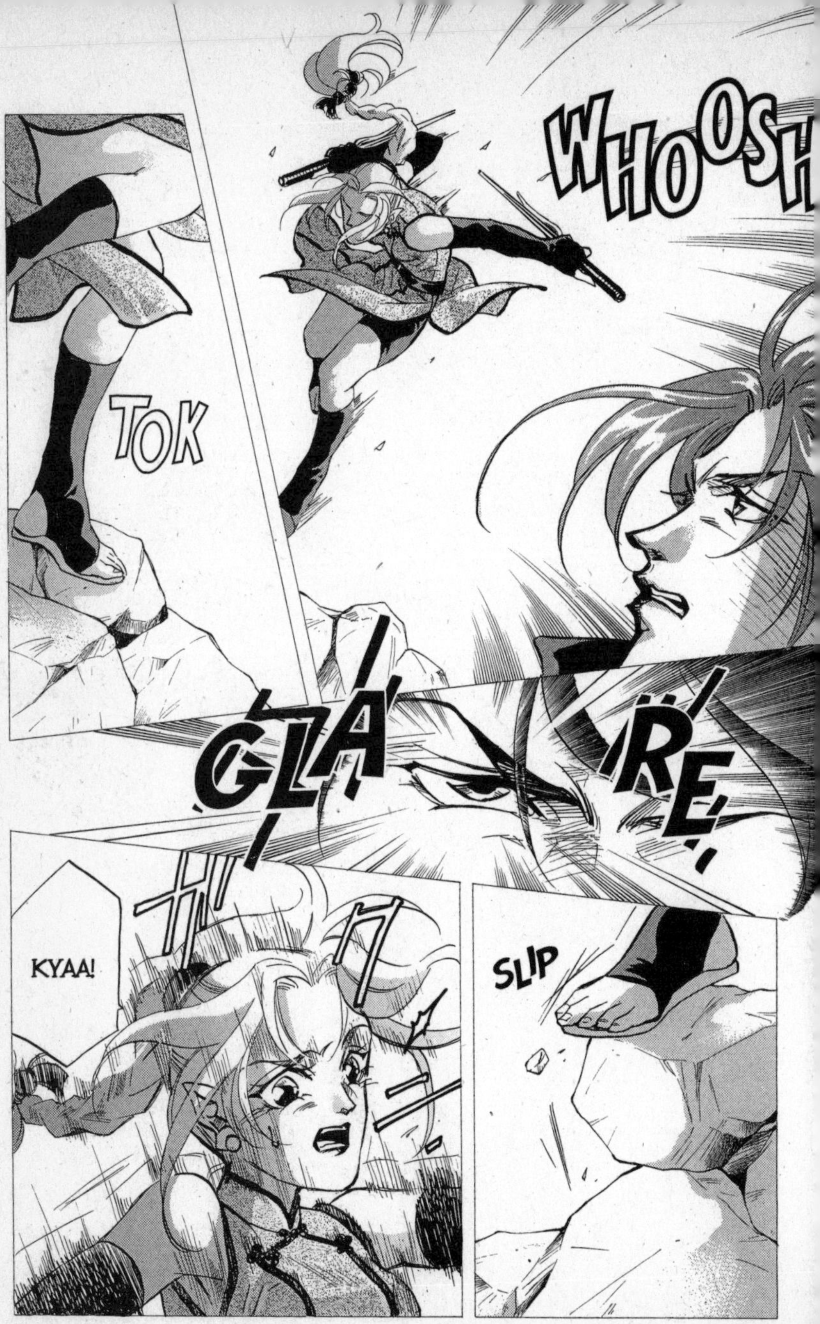
WHOOSH
TOK
GLARE
SLIP
KYAA!

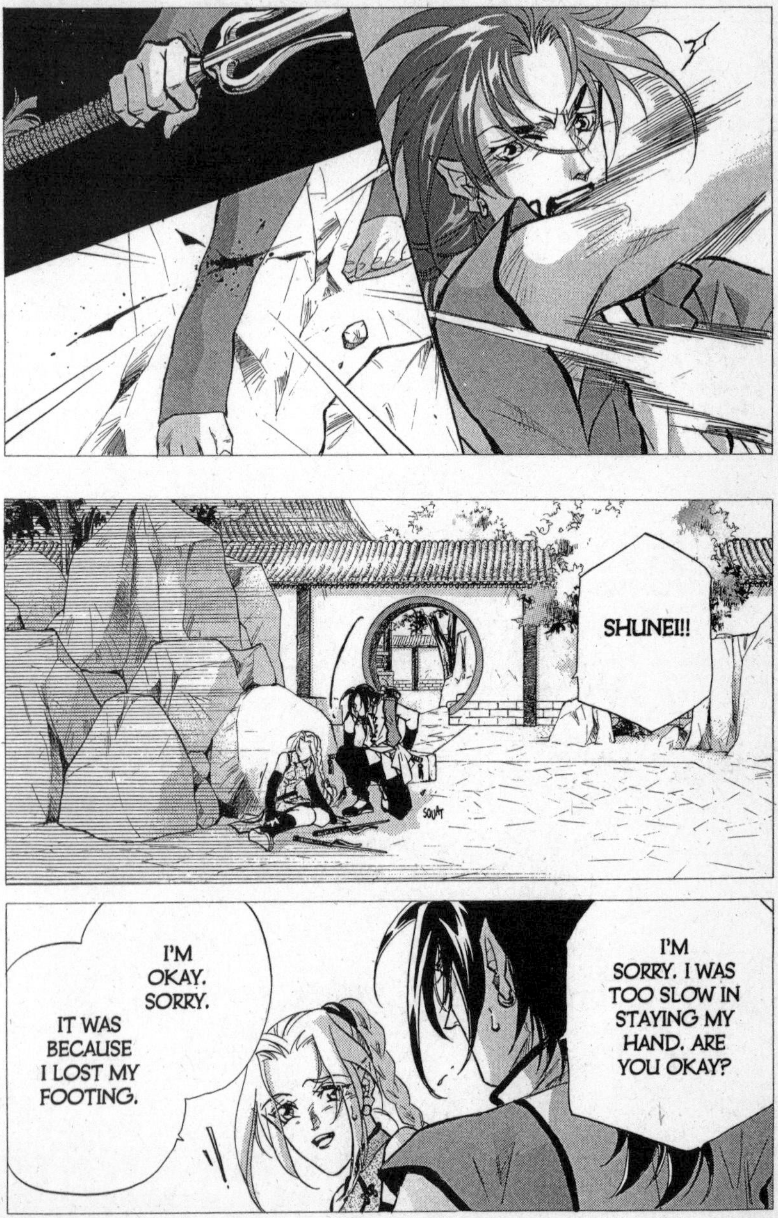
SHUNEI!!
SQUAT
I'M SORRY. I WAS TOO SLOW IN STAYING MY HAND. ARE YOU OKAY?
I'M OKAY. SORRY.
IT WAS BECAUSE I LOST MY FOOTING.

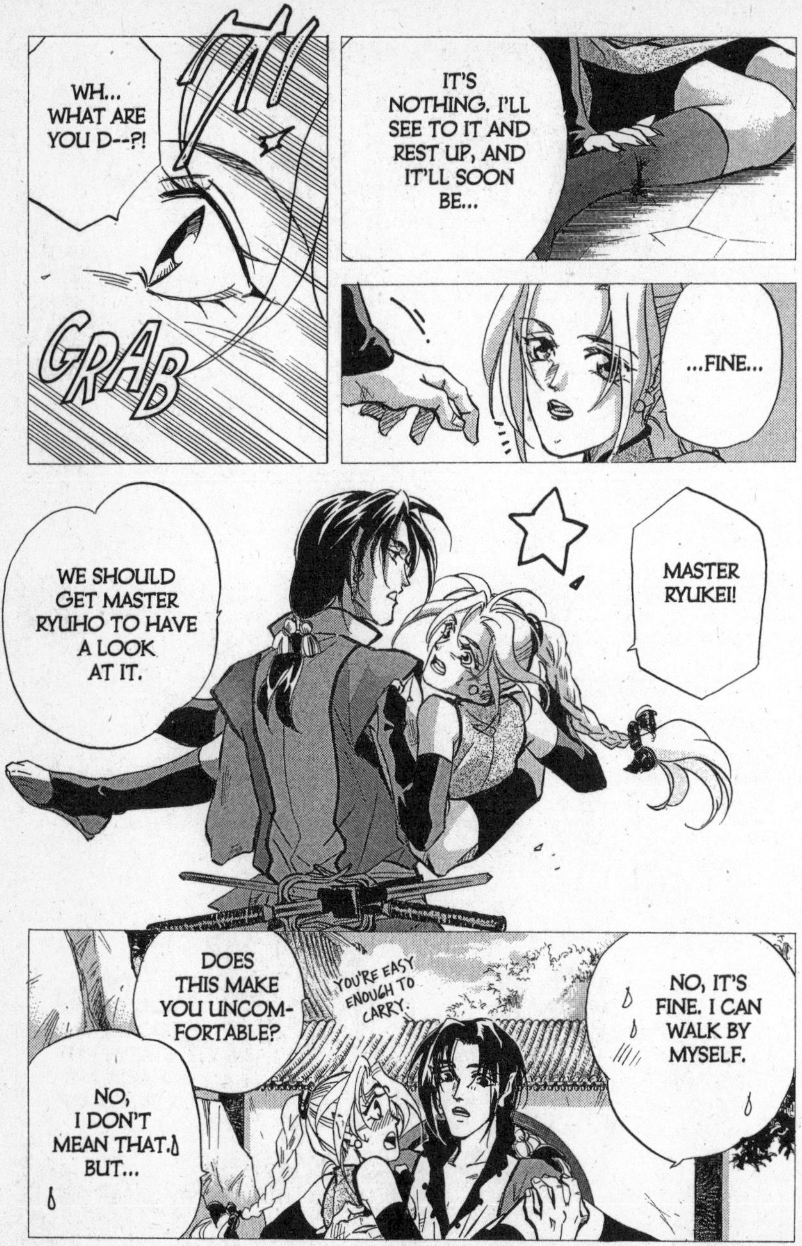
IT'S NOTHING. I'LL SEE TO IT AND REST UP, AND IT'LL SOON BE...
...FINE...
WH... WHAT ARE YOU D--?!
GRAB
MASTER RYUKEI!
WE SHOULD GET MASTER RYUHO TO HAVE A LOOK AT IT.
NO, IT'S FINE. I CAN WALK BY MYSELF.
YOU'RE EASY ENOUGH TO CARRY.
DOES THIS MAKE YOU UNCOMFORTABLE?
NO, I DON'T MEAN THAT. BUT...

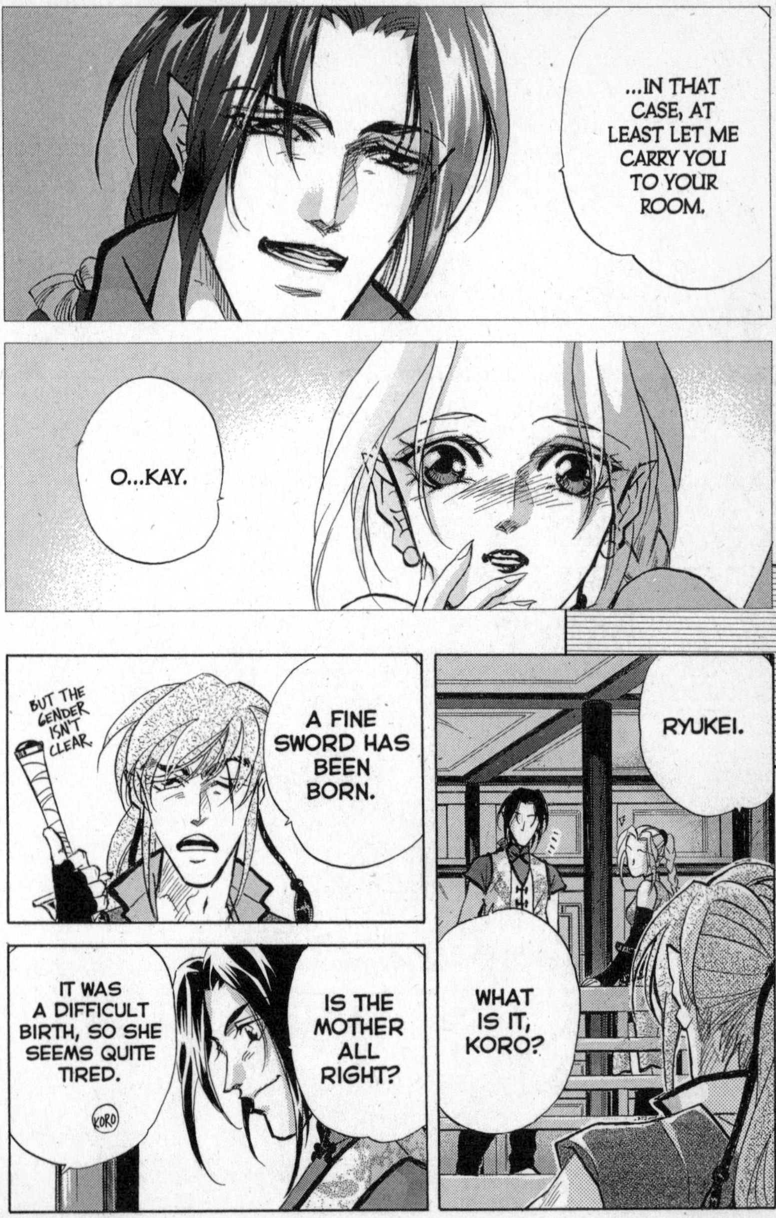
...IN THAT CASE, AT LEAST LET ME CARRY YOU TO YOUR ROOM.
O...KAY.
RYUKEI.
WHAT IS IT, KORO?
A FINE SWORD HAS BEEN BORN.
BUT THE GENDER ISN'T CLEAR.
IS THE MOTHER ALL RIGHT?
IT WAS A DIFFICULT BIRTH, SO SHE SEEMS QUITE TIRED.
KORO

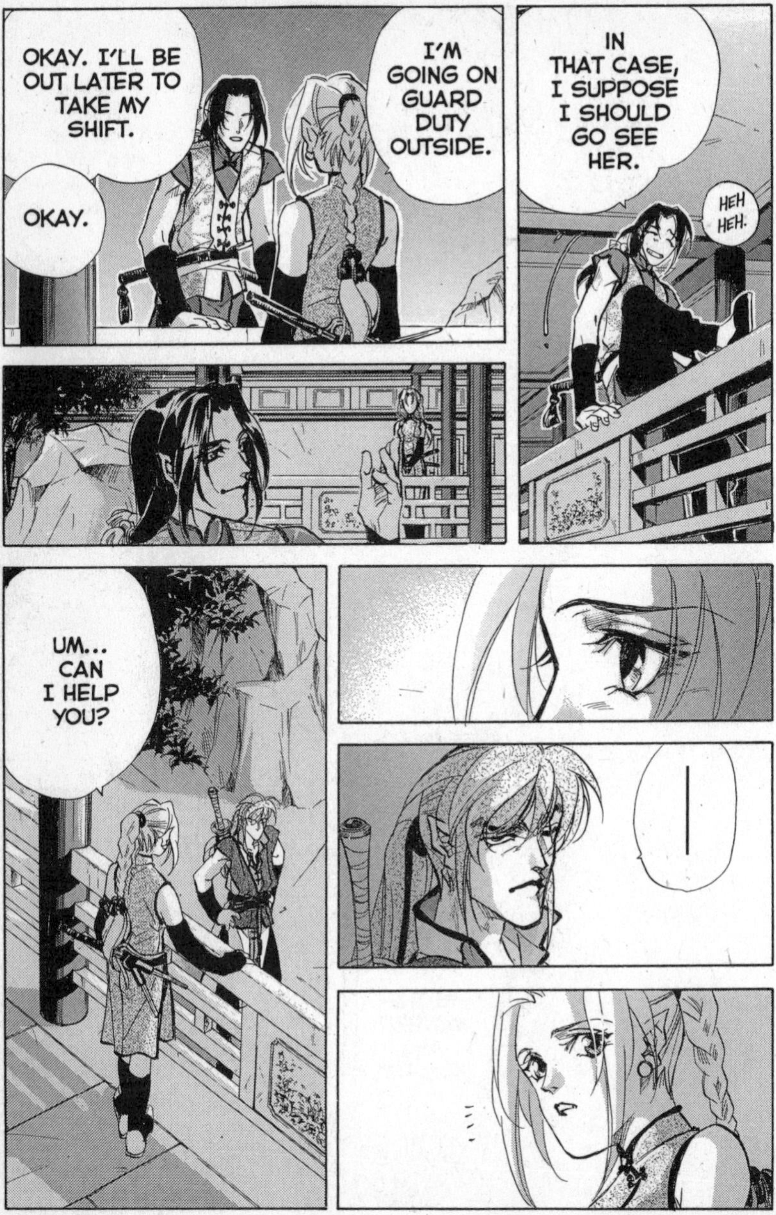
IN THAT CASE, I SUPPOSE I SHOULD GO SEE HER.
HEH HEH.
I'M GOING ON GUARD DUTY OUTSIDE.
OKAY. I'LL BE OUT LATER TO TAKE MY SHIFT.
OKAY.
—
...
UM... CAN I HELP YOU?

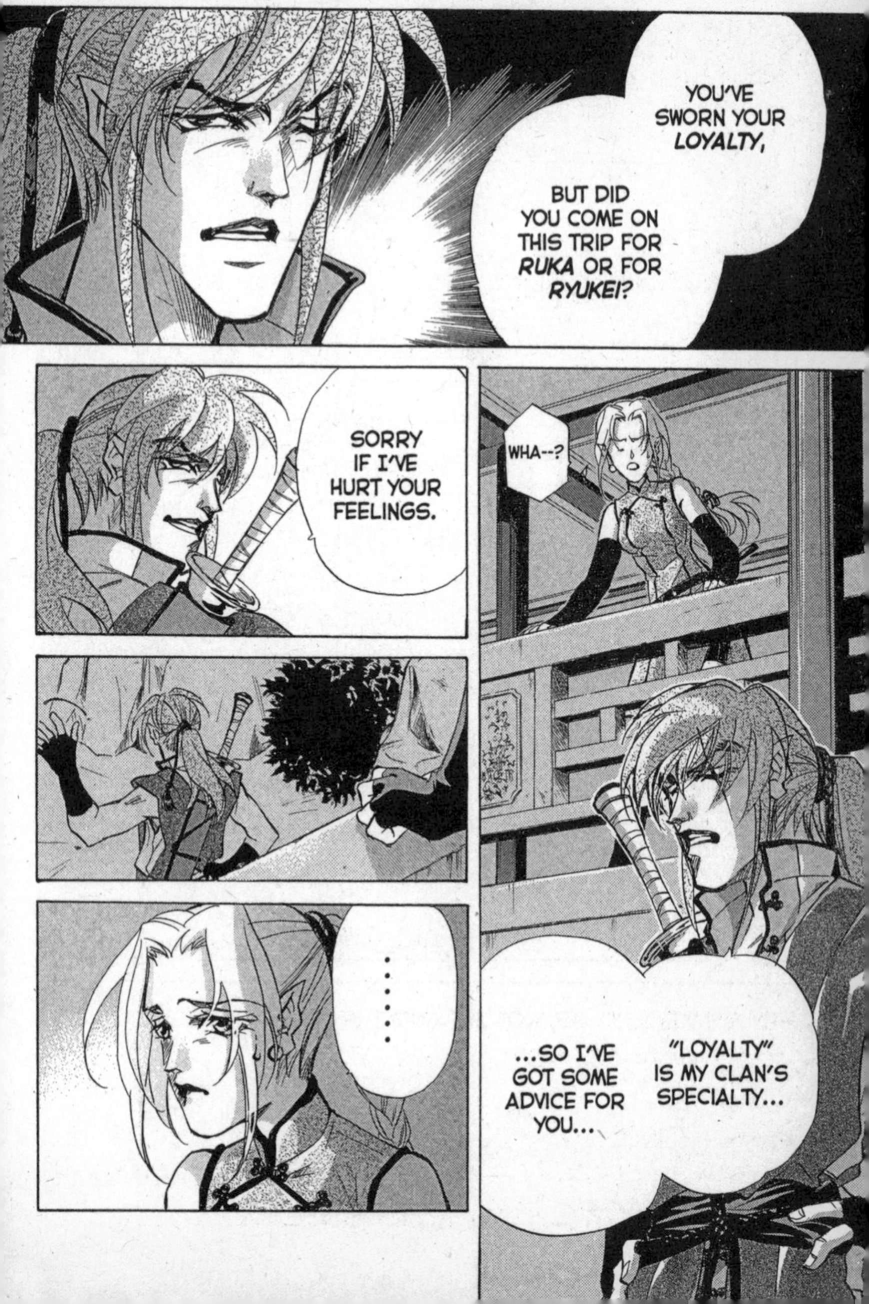
YOU'VE SWORN YOUR *LOYALTY*,
BUT DID YOU COME ON THIS TRIP FOR *RUKA* OR FOR *RYUKEI*?
WHA--?
"LOYALTY" IS MY CLAN'S SPECIALTY...
...SO I'VE GOT SOME ADVICE FOR YOU...
SORRY IF I'VE HURT YOUR FEELINGS.
......

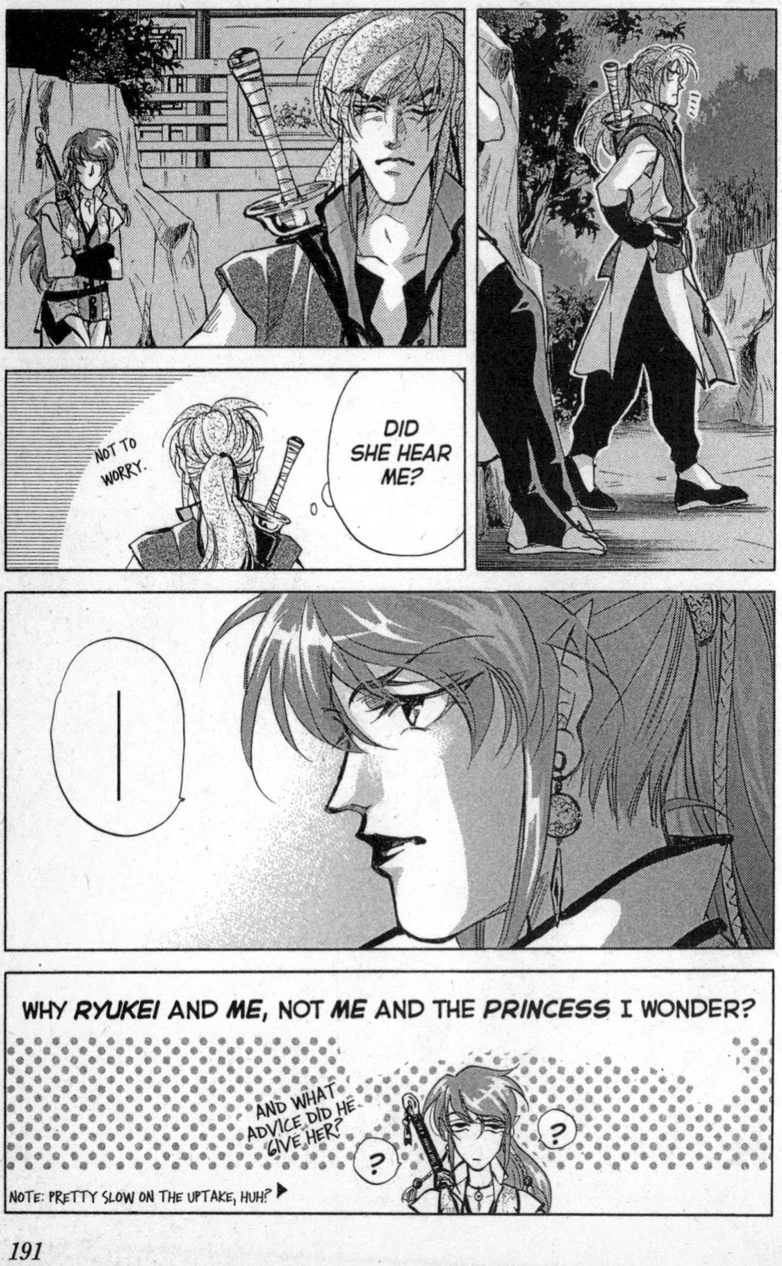
DID SHE HEAR ME?
NOT TO WORRY.
WHY RYUKEI AND ME, NOT ME AND THE PRINCESS I WONDER?
AND WHAT ADVICE DID HE GIVE HER?
?
?
NOTE: PRETTY SLOW ON THE UPTAKE, HUH?

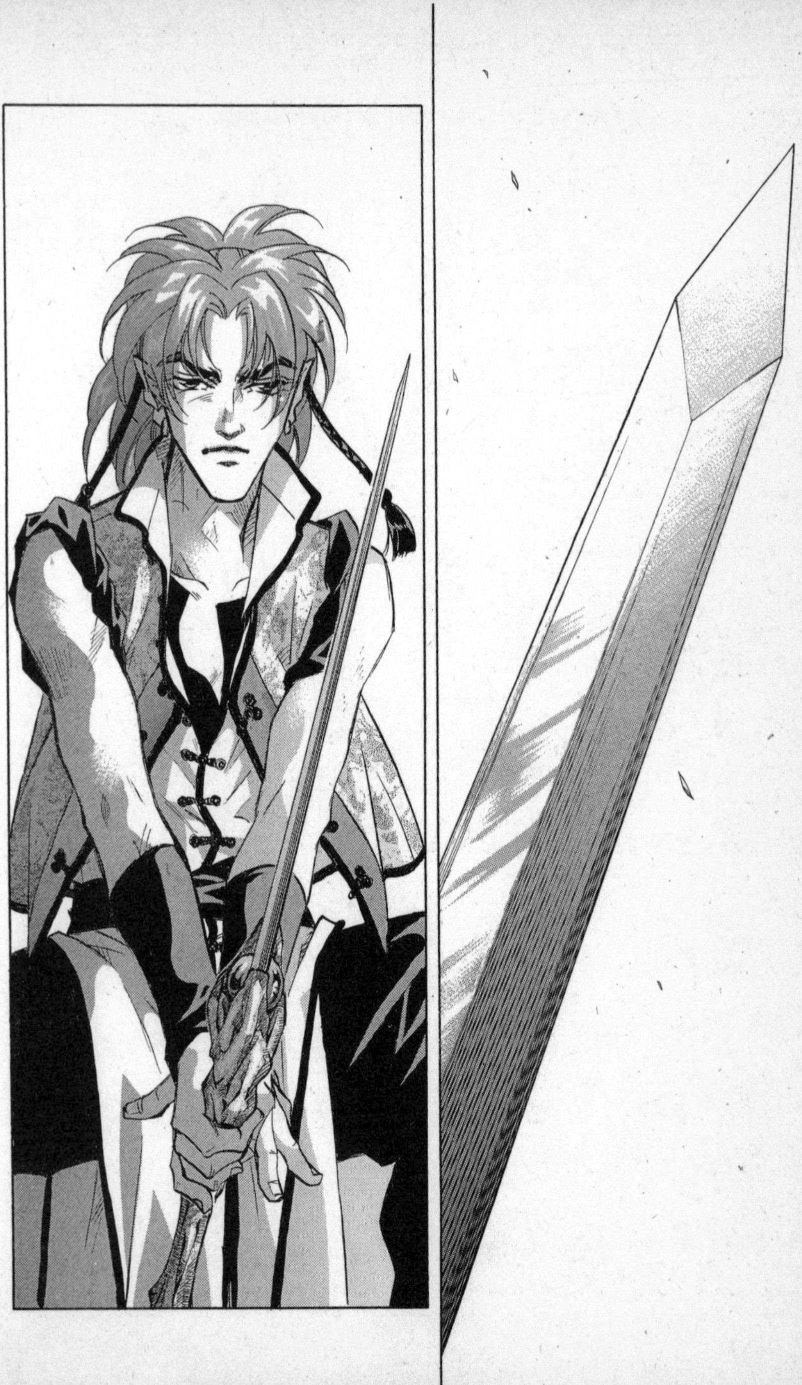

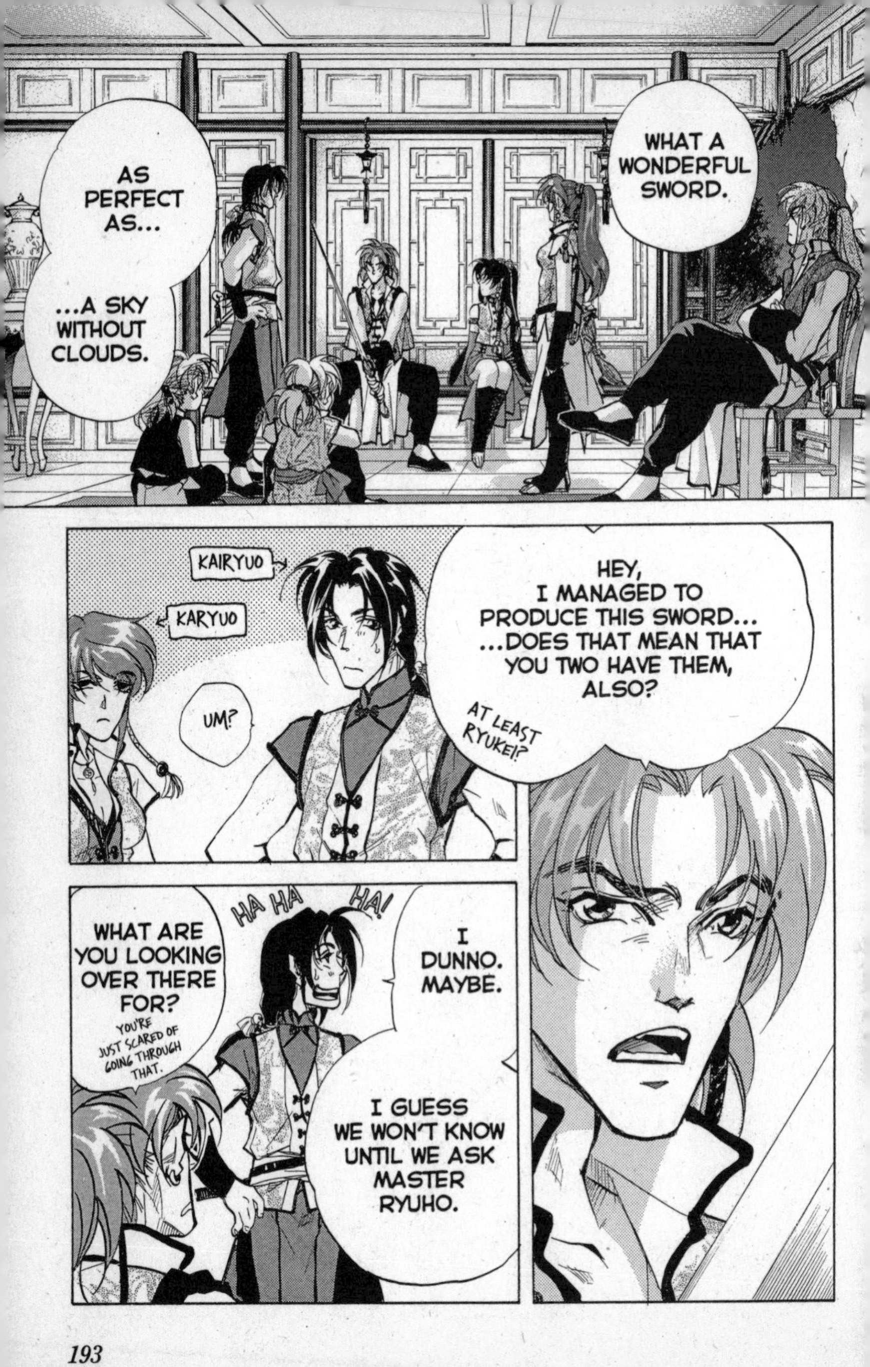
WHAT A WONDERFUL SWORD.
AS PERFECT AS...
...A SKY WITHOUT CLOUDS.
HEY, I MANAGED TO PRODUCE THIS SWORD... ...DOES THAT MEAN THAT YOU TWO HAVE THEM, ALSO?
AT LEAST RYUKEI?
KAIRYUO
KARYUO
UM?
HA HA HA!
I DUNNO. MAYBE.
WHAT ARE YOU LOOKING OVER THERE FOR?
YOU'RE JUST SCARED OF GOING THROUGH THAT.
I GUESS WE WON'T KNOW UNTIL WE ASK MASTER RYUHO.

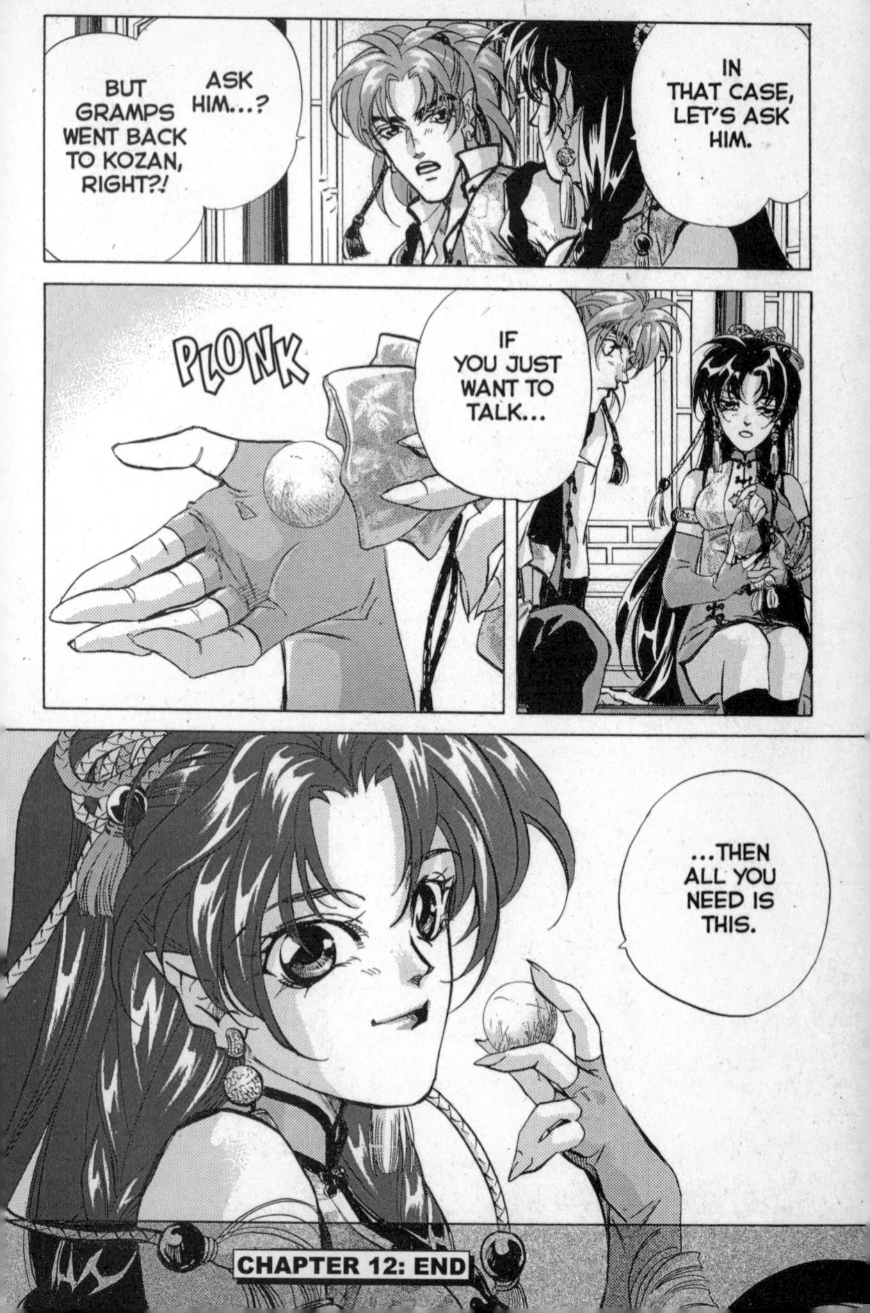
IN THAT CASE, LET'S ASK HIM.
ASK HIM...?
BUT GRAMPS WENT BACK TO KOZAN, RIGHT?!
IF YOU JUST WANT TO TALK...
PLONK
...THEN ALL YOU NEED IS THIS.
CHAPTER 12: END

Omake Information Manga

HIGH SCHOOL TEN-RYU!

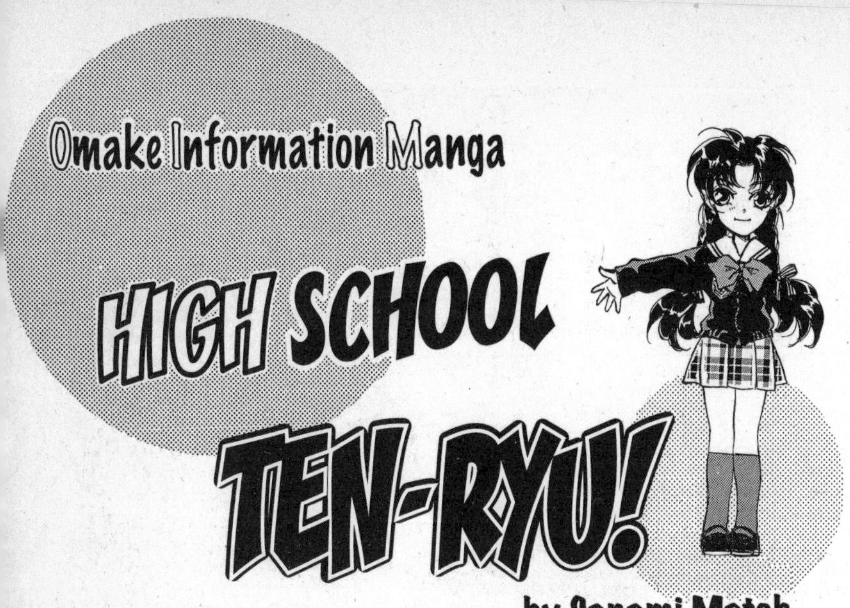

by Sanami Matoh

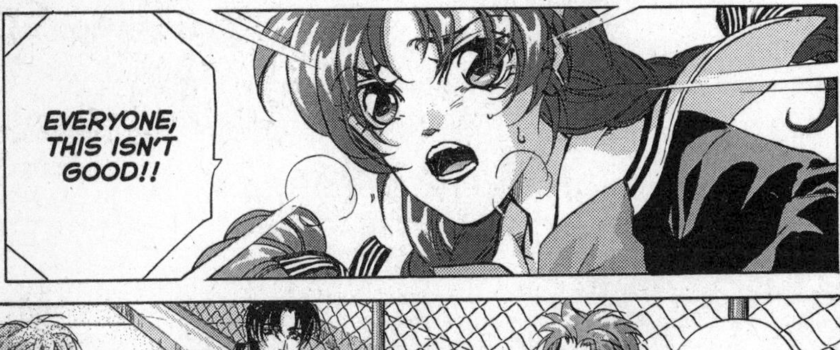
EVERYONE, THIS ISN'T GOOD!!

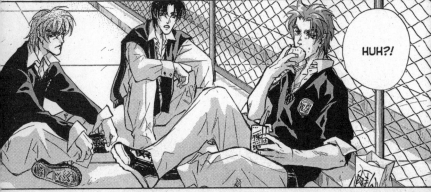

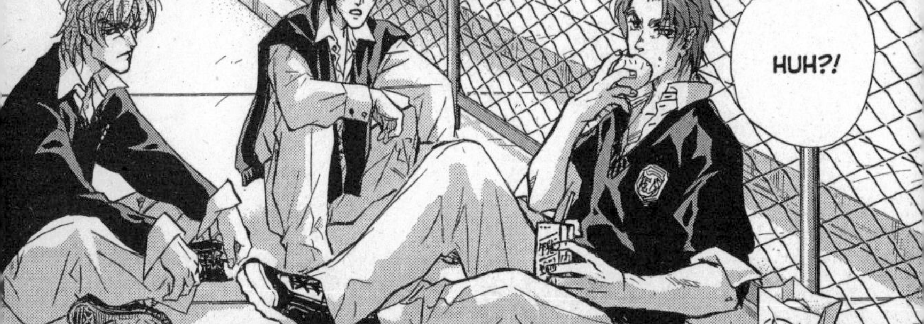
HUH?!

THEY LOOK LIKE THEY'VE BEEN HELD BACK A FEW YEARS. THEY'RE TOO OLD

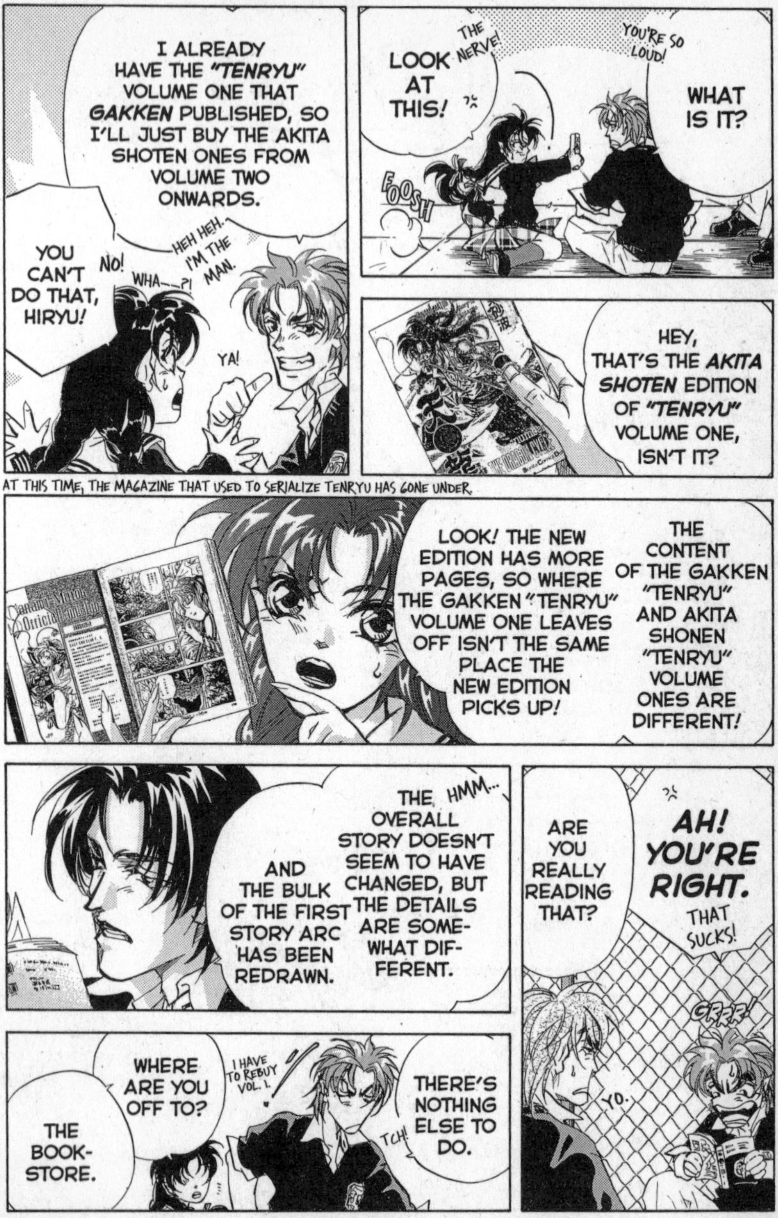
YOU'RE SO LOUD!
WHAT IS IT?
THE NERVE!
LOOK AT THIS!
FOOSH
HEY, THAT'S THE AKITA SHOTEN EDITION OF "TENRYU" VOLUME ONE, ISN'T IT?
I ALREADY HAVE THE "TENRYU" VOLUME ONE THAT GAKKEN PUBLISHED, SO I'LL JUST BUY THE AKITA SHOTEN ONES FROM VOLUME TWO ONWARDS.
HEH HEH. I'M THE MAN.
WHA--?!
NO!
YOU CAN'T DO THAT, HIRYU!
YA!
AT THIS TIME, THE MAGAZINE THAT USED TO SERIALIZE TENRYU HAS GONE UNDER.
THE CONTENT OF THE GAKKEN "TENRYU" AND AKITA SHONEN "TENRYU" VOLUME ONES ARE DIFFERENT!
LOOK! THE NEW EDITION HAS MORE PAGES, SO WHERE THE GAKKEN "TENRYU" VOLUME ONE LEAVES OFF ISN'T THE SAME PLACE THE NEW EDITION PICKS UP!
AH! YOU'RE RIGHT.
THAT SUCKS!
ARE YOU REALLY READING THAT?
GRRR!
YO.
HMM...
THE OVERALL STORY DOESN'T SEEM TO HAVE CHANGED, BUT THE DETAILS ARE SOMEWHAT DIFFERENT.
AND THE BULK OF THE FIRST STORY ARC HAS BEEN REDRAWN.
THERE'S NOTHING ELSE TO DO.
TCH!
I HAVE TO REBUY VOL. 1
WHERE ARE YOU OFF TO?
THE BOOKSTORE.

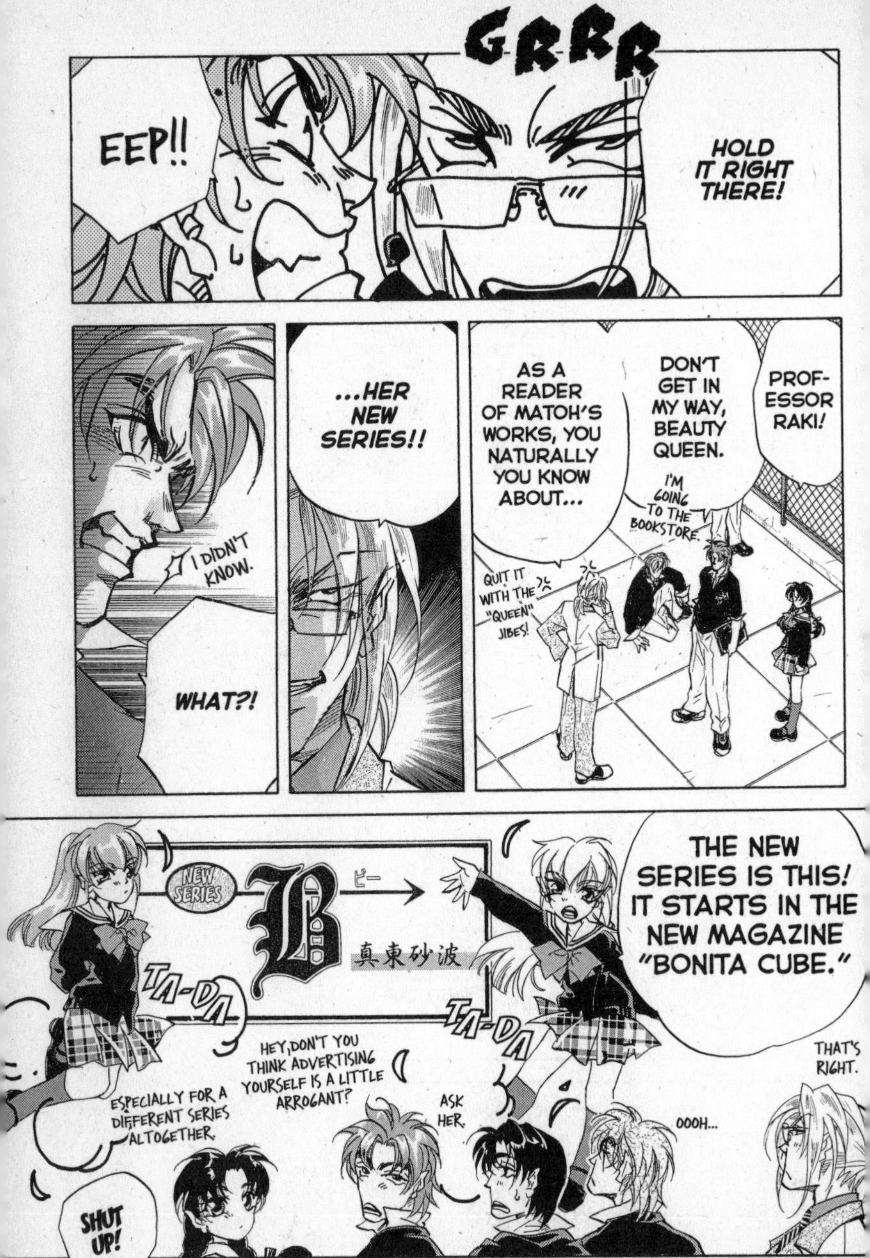
GRRR
HOLD IT RIGHT THERE!
EEP!!
PROF-ESSOR RAKI!
DON'T GET IN MY WAY, BEAUTY QUEEN.
I'M GOING TO THE BOOKSTORE.
AS A READER OF MATOH'S WORKS, YOU NATURALLY YOU KNOW ABOUT...
QUIT IT WITH THE "QUEEN" JIBES!
...HER NEW SERIES!!
I DIDN'T KNOW.
WHAT?!
THE NEW SERIES IS THIS! IT STARTS IN THE NEW MAGAZINE "BONITA CUBE."
THAT'S RIGHT.
OOOH...
ASK HER.
HEY, DON'T YOU THINK ADVERTISING YOURSELF IS A LITTLE ARROGANT?
TA-DA
TA-DA
NEW SERIES
B
ビー
真東砂波
ESPECIALLY FOR A DIFFERENT SERIES ALTOGETHER.
SHUT UP!

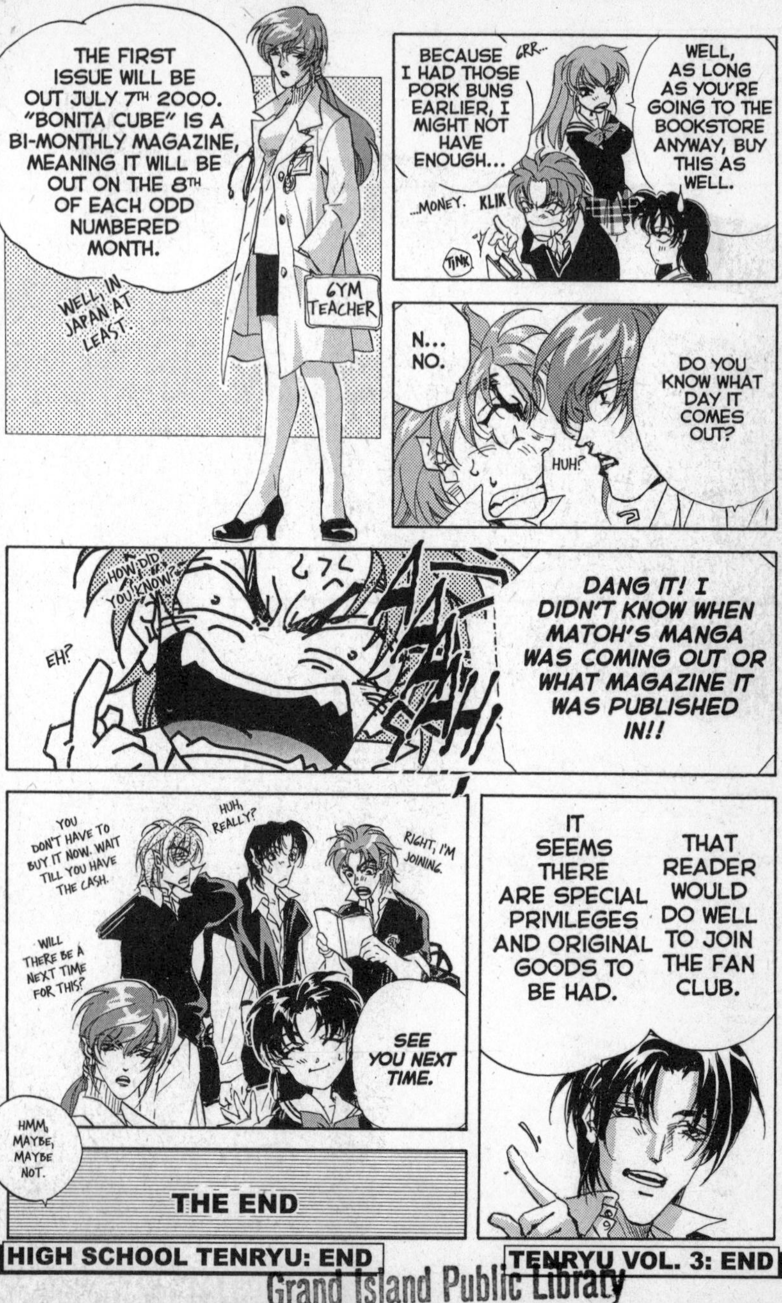
WELL, AS LONG AS YOU'RE GOING TO THE BOOKSTORE ANYWAY, BUY THIS AS WELL.
GRR...
BECAUSE I HAD THOSE PORK BUNS EARLIER, I MIGHT NOT HAVE ENOUGH...
...MONEY.
KLIK
TINK
DO YOU KNOW WHAT DAY IT COMES OUT?
HUH?
N... NO.
THE FIRST ISSUE WILL BE OUT JULY 7TH 2000. "BONITA CUBE" IS A BI-MONTHLY MAGAZINE, MEANING IT WILL BE OUT ON THE 8TH OF EACH ODD NUMBERED MONTH.
WELL, IN JAPAN AT LEAST.
GYM TEACHER
DANG IT! I DIDN'T KNOW WHEN MATOH'S MANGA WAS COMING OUT OR WHAT MAGAZINE IT WAS PUBLISHED IN!!
HOW DID YOU KNOW?
EH?
THAT READER WOULD DO WELL TO JOIN THE FAN CLUB.
IT SEEMS THERE ARE SPECIAL PRIVILEGES AND ORIGINAL GOODS TO BE HAD.
RIGHT, I'M JOINING.
HUH, REALLY?
YOU DON'T HAVE TO BUY IT NOW. WAIT TILL YOU HAVE THE CASH.
SEE YOU NEXT TIME.
WILL THERE BE A NEXT TIME FOR THIS?
HMM, MAYBE, MAYBE NOT.
THE END
TENRYU VOL. 3: END
HIGH SCHOOL TENRYU: END

THE DRAGON CYCLE (TENRYU) Volume 3 © 2000 by
Sanami Matoh. All Rights Reserved. First published in
Japan in 2000 by Akita Publishing Co., Ltd., Tokyo.

TENRYU Volume 3, published by WildStorm
Productions, an imprint of DC Comics, 888 Prospect St.
#240, La Jolla, CA 92037. English Translation © 2005.
All Rights Reserved. English translation rights in U.S.A.
and Canada arranged by Akita Publishing Co., Ltd.,
Tokyo, through Tuttle-Mori Agency, Inc., Tokyo. The
stories, characters, and incidents mentioned in this
magazine are entirely fictional. Printed on recyclable
paper. WildStorm does not read or accept unsolicited
submissions of ideas, stories or artwork. Printed in
Canada.

DC Comics, a Warner Bros.
Entertainment Company.

Neil Rae —Translation
Jake Forbes — Adaptation
Wilson Ramos — Lettering
John J. Hill — CMX Logo & Publication Design
Larry Berry — Additional Design
Ben Abernathy — Editor

ISBN: 1-4012-0671-9

FLIP IT!!

All the pages in this book were created—and are printed here—in Japanese RIGHT-to-LEFT format. No artwork has been reversed, so you can read the stories the way the creators meant for them to be read.

JAPANESE NAMES

Authentic Japanese name order is family name first, given name second. With previous volumes, CMX has honored authentic Japanese order. By popular request, we have converted to Western format (given name first, family name second) moving forward with this volume.

RIGHT TO LEFT?!

Traditional Japanese manga starts at the upper right-hand corner, and moves right-to-left as it goes down the page. Follow this guide for an easy understanding.

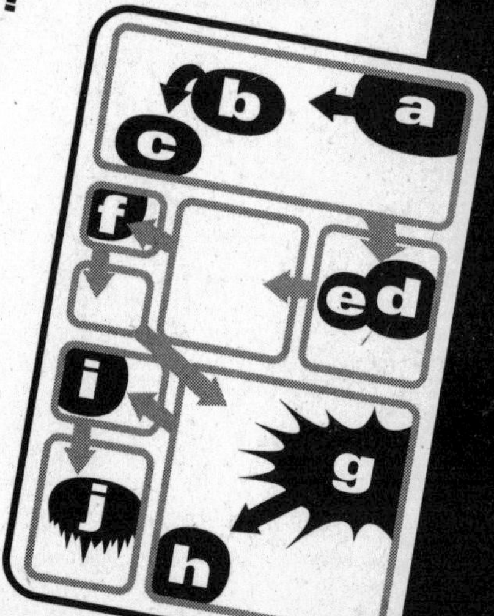

a
b
c
d
e
f
g
h
i
j

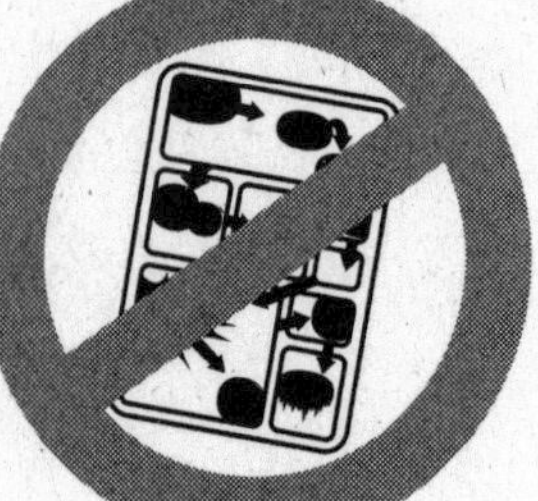

Catch the latest at cmxmanga.com!